CRM

This book introduces students to customer relationship management (CRM). With in-depth coverage of business and consumer markets in various vertical markets, the impact of new technology, and more, it helps readers to understand how an enhanced customer relationship environment can differentiate an organization in a highly competitive marketplace. Featuring the latest developments in the discipline, a cohesive approach, and pedagogical materials (including chapter exercises that connect theory with action), this book is the one-stop source for a comprehensive CRM course.

Roger J. Baran is an associate professor of Marketing at DePaul University. He received his Ph.D. and MBA degrees from the University of Chicago Graduate School of Business and his BBA from the University of Notre Dame. He is a fellow of the National Opinion Research Center, has served on the U.S. Department of Commerce Census Advisory Committee of the American Marketing Association, and was Chair of the Bank Marketing Association National Research and Planning Council. Dr. Baran serves as a consultant in the area of marketing strategy and marketing research for many well-known companies in the United States, Europe, Asia, and Middle-East. He is currently Vice-President of the Asian Forum on Business Education based in Bangkok, Thailand. His teaching and publishing specialties are marketing research, global marketing management, marketing of services, marketing management, customer relationship management, and social networking. He has served as visiting associate professor of marketing at the University of Chicago Graduate School of Business; Helsinki School of Economics and Business Administration; University of Hamburg; University of the Thai Chamber of Commerce, Siam University; Mahidol University in Bangkok, Thailand; Kimep University in Kazakhstan, and Prague School of Economics.

Robert J. Galka is an Executive-In-Residence at DePaul University. He received his MBA from Northwestern University's J. L. Kellogg Graduate School of Management. His area of expertise lies in CRM, Marketing Strategy, and Technology. Robert brings his academic research and 25 years' of business experience into the classroom, Professional Certificate programs and to universities as a visiting faculty in Bahrain, Taiwan, and New Zealand, with special programs in Japan. He co-authored a prior CRM text and has published a variety of supplemental materials for several publishers. His career started in computer science and he taught as an adjunct faculty in Computer Science for 8 years. His design of marketing systems brought him into a career in marketing where he consulted across seven vertical markets, culminating as a GM leading an SBU focusing on CRM and marketing strategy.

CRM

The Foundation of Contemporary Marketing Strategy

Roger J. Baran & Robert J. Galka

Routledge
Taylor & Francis Group

NEW YORK AND LONDON

First published 2013
by Routledge
711 Third Avenue, New York, NY 10017

Simultaneously published in the UK
by Routledge
2 Park Square, Milton Park, Abingdon, Oxon OX14 4RN

Routledge is an imprint of the Taylor & Francis Group, an informa business

Library of Congress Cataloging-in-Publication Data

Baran, Roger J. (Roger Joseph), 1945—
CRM : the foundation of contemporary marketing strategy / Roger J. Baran & Robert Galka.
     p. cm.
   Includes bibliographical references and index.
   ISBN 978-0-415-89656-6 (hbk.) — ISBN 978-0-415-89657-3 (pbk.) —
ISBN 978-0-203-10757-7 (ebook) 1. Relationship marketing. 2. Customer relations —
Management. I. Galka, Robert J. II. Title.
   HF5415.55.B35   2013
   658.8'02—dc23   2012026802

ISBN: 978-0-415-89656-6
ISBN: 978-0-415-89657-3
ISBN: 978-0-203-10757-7

Typeset in ITC Galliard
by Apex CoVantage, LLC

www.routledge.com/9780415896573

SFI Certified Sourcing
www.sfiprogram.org
SFI-00453

Printed and bound in the United States of America by Edwards Brothers Malloy, Inc.

Contents

Preface

This is the most heavily researched customer relationship management textbook on the market, and it includes the most recent findings on how social media have impacted company CRM efforts; unexpected relationships between satisfaction, loyalty, retention, and profits; new acquisition and retention tactics; the impact of cloud computing on CRM and the complete array of metrics to assess CRM success in improving service quality, customer knowledge, customer value, and company efficiency. Students, CRM practitioners, service industry executives, and sales and marketing personnel will all benefit from reading this book given its comprehensive coverage. The history and development of CRM highlight past mistakes companies made in introducing this concept and operation to their firm and the key elements of success. Thorough coverage of relationship marketing provides students and practitioners with the new twenty-first-century marketing paradigm that underlies the rationale for CRM: building one-to-one relationships as opposed to merely handling transactions. CRM tactics are greatest in the area of retention (acquisition and win-back being the other two stages). This book covers thirteen explicit retention strategies (with examples).

This book not only has an entire chapter on company use of social media in CRM efforts, but it delves into the most recent findings regarding why social media works (through the creation of social capital). The authors not only discuss how and why it works in the United States, but they discuss the many differences in social media usage in Asia and how companies must localize their social media efforts accordingly. They provide explicit examples of CRM social media successes and failures. Further, they provide a typology and examples of twenty-one social media strategies. The book discusses the hot issues of how to deal with message detractors and message hijackers; how to develop a community of users providing peer-to-peer support; how to reach high "clout" scorers; how to keep customers from "failing"; and how to promote a point of view and predict "hits," among other topics. The book has an entire chapter on CRM metrics and organizes them into four areas:

- Service quality, customer satisfaction and loyalty, and retention
- The CRM customer cycle measures: acquisition, retention, and win-back
- Company 3-E measures: efficiency, effectiveness, and employee behavior
- Customer knowledge measures derived through eleven marketing research applications, such as customer–company interaction scores and critical incident scores

The book discusses data management, data platforms, and customer data development in a way that is understandable to business students and yet challenging enough for computer and information science students who are looking for a venue in which to apply their skills. Evolving technologies such as cloud computing and RFID, with their implications for CRM strategy inclusion, are discussed. Growing consumer concerns over privacy and data usage required an evaluation of new and pending regulatory instruments. The potential impact of pending and new privacy regulations on the organization's CRM strategy and what it can do to manage these forces are outlined, along with what consumers can do to protect their privacy. We attempt to hold students' interest with unusual and interesting CRM vignettes from a variety of industries, including small businesses. Throughout, we strive to show how CRM aligns business processes with customer strategies in an effort to build customer loyalty and increase profits.

The book is based on the following premises:

1. CRM makes it possible for companies to differentiate themselves from their competitors in an area that cannot be easily copied, since CRM has its roots in organizational culture.
2. Maintenance, enhancement, and retention of customers through CRM strategies and tactics is as important as, or even more important than, simply acquiring customers.
3. CRM can increase marketing productivity through the entire range of marketing functions: identifying prospects, acquiring customers, developing customers, increasing loyalty and commitment, retaining customers, and customer win-back.
4. CRM can provide marketing and sales managers with a new array of marketing strategies not possible before.
5. CRM strategies must include the flexibility to adapt to rapidly evolving technology with varying degrees of consumer and business adoption.
6. Improvements in data capture and analytical methods using new and abundant sources of customer data place more pressure on organizations for adherence to privacy regulations and customer expectations on how their data is managed.

We believe our CRM text is unique in that it investigates CRM and CRM technology in the context of value chains as opposed to stand-alone organizations, because in today's environments, organizations' strategies are interwoven within their value chain. The text integrates CRM processes and application of CRM technology for marketing strategy, marketing communications, and sales force use. The text also provides analytical tools to identify customer behavior patterns.

While we are both currently professors of marketing at DePaul University in Chicago, Illinois, our business backgrounds are in marketing research, marketing management, CRM, and sales. The book is, in part, based on a combined sixty-five years of business and consulting experience—forty of which were almost exclusively focused on CRM.

After nearly fifteen years of teaching numerous CRM modules in our marketing management, sales, and research classes, we had accumulated hundreds of slides and a substantial amount of original content for use in our courses. When DePaul asked us to develop a stand-alone CRM course, we spent almost a year gathering CRM research articles, theoretical academic articles, CRM articles appearing in the business press, and every book we could find on the topic. In organizing this material, we found a glaring omission that was confirmed by academic colleagues we met at CRM-related conferences: although almost 100 business- and technique-oriented CRM books (primarily authored by those in the business) were available, there was no CRM textbook! This glaring deficiency was confirmed during our discussions with three major business textbook publishers in the United States. So after developing our CRM course, we spent four years developing the *Principles of CRM* textbook, which was published in 2008. Thereafter, a plethora of CRM research findings and the introduction and growth of social media and cloud computing led us to write this new text, which initially was over 1,000 pages.

We reduced the size of the text through the development of a dynamic website, an instructors' manual, a case matrix, a test bank, and other approaches. Half of the content of this book is new material. It should prove valuable to practicing executives involved in CRM, and on the academic side, we feel we have provided text material that can be effectively covered in a quarter or semester course. Professors teaching CRM courses or CRM modules in business courses now have a CRM text with exhaustive ancillary materials around which to structure their course. The primary market for this text is academic, with usage at both the MBA and advanced business course undergraduate levels. Professors and students in the areas of marketing management, marketing strategy and planning, brand management, service marketing, marketing research, and sales will find the book invaluable, as will students in information sciences looking for business applications for their skills.

Highlights of this Book

- *Theory in Action* features in every chapter that provide real-world examples of the text material
- Extensive use of diagrams, charts, figures, and tables to highlight material
- Numerous within-text examples and vignettes of CRM applications
- Specifically defined tactics in the areas of acquisition, retention, win-back, and social media
- Chapter summaries
- Key terms at the end of each chapter
- End-of-chapter questions
- End-of-chapter CRM exercises
- A complete list of references at the end of every chapter
- A focus on the strategic application of CRM to marketing and sales

Section 1

CRM Theory and Development

Chapter 1

Introduction to Customer Relationship Management

TOPICS

1.1 Definition of CRM and CRM Applications

1.2 The Purpose and Benefits of CRM

1.3 The Tangible Components of CRM

1.4 Important Business Constructs Related to CRM

1.5 Who Uses CRM and Why?

CRM is often so broad that it lacks definition. If you can't define it, how can you assess it? No one knows what it is, but we know we have to have it.

—"CRM Starting to Live Up to Its Promise," *Wall Street & Technology* (January 4, 2004). Accessed at http://www.wallstreetandtech.com/articles/17200053.

1.1 Definition of CRM and CRM Applications

Customer relationship management (CRM) is everywhere. Let's take, for example, a family traveling to Florida over spring break. They fly on an airline from which their frequent flyer points provide free seats. They rent a car from a car rental company that gives them an upgrade based on their previous rentals. They stay in a hotel that awards them one free night for every three they pay for, based on the points accrued on their frequent-stay guest card. The amusement park they visit on the first day admits them one hour before general opening and allows them to stay an hour after general closing as a reward for the four-day ticket they purchased. In addition, they receive a 20 percent discount on all food, beverages, and souvenirs purchased during their four-day visit. As they are walking around that evening looking for a place in town to have dinner, a nearby restaurant texts them a promotional message, so they decide to eat there. And when they arrive home, the same establishments provide them with an array of thank-you messages and super-promotional offers they can use on their next visit—as long as it occurs during off-season. All of these are examples of programmatic benefits provided by CRM systems.

A few weeks later, the father calls his bank to inquire about his credit card bill. He is instructed to key in his card number, and, within seconds, a customer service representative (**CSR**) greets him by name and asks how he can help. The caller explains that he does not recall making a specific charge that appears on his bill. The CSR extracts the specifics of the charge, and the caller then recalls that the charge is legitimate. The CSR inquires whether the customer has any other questions and, it being the end of April, asks if the customer had an enjoyable spring break. A few weather-related anecdotes are also exchanged.

The CSR, after reviewing the customer's usage history, asks whether the customer is aware of the bank's new Travel and Entertainment Card. The customer is aware of the card but did not apply because of the application form and the annual fee. The CSR replies that, given the customer's good credit record, the card could be issued immediately without any application or annual fee. The customer agrees to the offer. The CSR extends his thank you, and the customer hangs up, completely satisfied with the service he has received.

The customer expected this to be just another transaction, but it was a friendly and satisfactory exchange. His question about the bill was answered, he acquired a card that would be useful in his business travels, and he shared a few laughs. Even more remarkable, the CSR was located in India and was empowered to make the Travel and Entertainment Card offer on the spot, based on the bank's experience with the customer. This is an example of a humanistic benefit provided by the financial institution's CRM system.

Both the customer and the CSR leave the exchange satisfied and more committed: the customer feels more committed to the bank, and the CSR feels more committed to his job. Over the years, the customer might recommend the bank to his friends and associates, further increasing the impact of this transaction. It is a win–win situation for both the customers and the institution, and it is made possible through a new and remarkable technique called **customer relationship management (CRM)**. While the example focuses on the impact of CRM on the end-user, CRM enables an organization to better manage relationships with suppliers, distributors, and dealers, among others.

Some view CRM as being so broad and multifaceted that it lacks definition. Even the letters "CRM" have been used as acronyms for numerous different terms, such as continuous relationship marketing, customer relationship marketing, as well as customer relationship management. Frederick Newell prefers the term CMR to stand for "customer management of relationships." CMR indicates a new balance of power that he advocates, "allowing the customer to tell us what she's interested in, what kind of information she wants, what level of service she wants to receive, and how she wants us to communicate with her—where, when, and how often."[1]

Customer relationship management is a difficult business practice to define because (1) it can apply to different levels of customers—for example, distributors, dealers, lateral partners, and consumers; (2) some of the key components of CRM shift when considering business-to-business (**B2B**) versus business-to-consumer (**B2C**) relationships—for example, sales force automation is more applicable to the former than the latter; and (3) the composition of CRM systems will be different in big versus small companies, even though their objectives will be the same.

Keeping in mind that CRM is a new and all-encompassing technique, it should not be surprising that numerous definitions for it exist. Payne and Frow provide a complete or holistic definition of CRM that identifies its purpose, strategic focus, data orientation, and organizational under-pinnings:

> CRM is a strategic approach that is concerned with creating improved shareholder value through the development of appropriate relationships with key customers and customer segments. CRM unites the potential of relationship marketing strategies and IT to create profitable, long-term relationships with customers and other key stakeholders. CRM provides enhanced opportunities to use data and information to both understand customers and co-create value with them. This requires a cross-functional integration of processes, people, operations, and marketing capabilities that is enabled through information, technology, and applications.[2]

Through extensive research and discussions with CRM executives and practitioners, they identified five key processes that help define CRM:[3]

1. *Strategy development*: at both the business level and customer level, with the latter involving decisions regarding the appropriateness of various customer segmentation approaches: mass, segmented, and one-to-one.
2. *Value creation*: involves determining what product/service attributes customers value and which customers and customer segments are valuable to the company. CRM enables companies to identify and direct relationship efforts to those with high customer lifetime values (CLV).
3. *Multichannel integration*: involves efforts to provide the "perfect customer experience" through integrating sales personnel, outlets, customer contact centers (CCCs), direct marketing, e-commerce, and m-commerce (mobile phones, SMS, and 3G and 4G mobile services).
4. *Information management*: involves collecting, organizing, and using customer data and customer information from all touch points (including sales force automation [SFA] and CCCs) in order to learn more about each customer and generate the appropriate marketing response.
5. *Performance assessment*: includes measuring the success of CRM efforts through metrics on customer acquisition, retention, win-back, satisfaction, loyalty, and profits.

Based on the writers' orientations, definitions of CRM can be grouped as follows:

1. Those that equate CRM with a software package, process, system, or technology.
2. Those that equate CRM with a focus on data storage and analysis.
3. Those that equate CRM with a change in corporate culture from a transaction focus to a relationship or customer-centric focus. (The key focus here is on establishing a dialogue with each customer on a one-to-one basis as opposed to generating merely a corporate monologue with large segments of customers.)
4. Those that equate CRM with the important concept of "managing demand."
5. Those that equate CRM with new strategies focused on current customers (identification, selection, acquiring, developing, cross-selling and up-selling, managing migration, and win-back).

Refer to Table 1.1 for definitions of CRM that appear in each of these areas.

Table 1.1 How CRM Is Defined
As a Software Package, Process, System, or Technology: "CRM systems are parameter-adjustable software packages that are intended to integrate and manage all aspects of customer interactions within the organization, and so considerably improve the ability of the organization to handle customer service, sales, marketing, online transactions, and orders."[4]
"CRM is a process to compile information that increases understanding of how to manage an organization's relationship with its customers. . . . It is a business strategy that uses IT to provide an enterprise with a comprehensive, reliable, and integrated view of its customer base so that all processes and customer interactions help maintain and expand mutually beneficial relationships. CRM is thus a technique or a set of processes designed to collect data and provide information that helps the organization evaluate strategic options."[5]
As Data Storage and Analysis: "CRM is the process of storing and analyzing the vast amounts of data produced by sales calls, customer-service centers, and actual purchases, supposedly yielding greater insight into customer behavior. CRM also allows a business to treat different types of customers differently—in some cases, for instance, by responding more slowly to those who spend less or charging more to those who require more expensive handholding."[6]

(Continued)

Table 1.1 **(Continued)**

As a Culture Change within the Organization Itself: "CRM is first and foremost a corporate culture change—that is, a different way of doing business, enabled with powerful technology at every customer touch point."[7]

As a Management Practice that Focuses on Relationships as Opposed to Transactions: "A broader definition of CRM would include all activities that turn casual consumers into loyal customers by satisfying or exceeding their requirements to the extent that they will buy again."[8]

"CRM is an ongoing process that involves the development and leveraging of market intelligence for the purpose of building and maintaining a profit-maximizing portfolio of customer relationships."[9]

As a Practice that Manages Demand: "CRM is the dynamic process of managing a customer–company relationship such that customers elect to continue mutually beneficial commercial exchanges and are dissuaded from participating in exchanges that are unprofitable to the company."[10]

As a Strategy that Focuses on Current Customers: "CRM comprises the business processes an organization performs to identify, select, acquire, develop, retain, and better serve customers. These processes encompass an organization's end-to-end engagement with its customers and prospects over the lifetime of its relationship with them."[11]

CRM is a business strategy with the following outcomes: "Optimization of revenue, profits, and customer satisfaction by organizing around customer segments, fostering customer-satisfying behaviors, and implementing customer-centric processes. CRM technologies should enable greater customer insight, increased customer access, more effective customer interactions, and integration throughout all customer channels and back-office enterprise functions."[12]

Let us investigate each of these CRM visions to better understand the various domains of CRM.

When CRM is viewed in terms of systems, most agree that it must do three things well: (1) gather customer data from all touch points; (2) warehouse the data, providing easy access for all; and (3) deliver useable information based on the data. *Touch points* are any point of contact that a customer or prospect has with the company, including phone inquiries, Web applications, e-mail, or in-person transactions.

When viewed as a system, most agree that a comprehensive CRM system should contain four major technology components:

1. A data warehouse containing customer, contract, transaction, and channel data. The main purpose of data storage is to enable managers to develop strategies and close the loop that begins with the system that stores customer data. A data warehouse is the repository for all relevant customer and prospect information. Basically anything related to a marketing activity can be included in the data warehouse, including information from each customer touch point, sales force input, and even survey data.
2. Analytical tools to identify customer behavior patterns
3. Campaign management tools to develop and evaluate the results of marketing communications, such as advertising and sales promotion campaigns
4. Interfaces to maintain the database

Peel provided perhaps the most specific, complete, and technologically oriented definition of CRM:

CRM is the automation of horizontally integrated business processes involving "front-office" customer touch points—sales (contact management, product configuration), marketing (campaign management, marketing), and customer service (call data center, field service)—via multiple, interconnected delivery channels (telephone, e-mail, Web, direct interaction). The CRM application architecture must combine both operational (transaction-oriented business process management) technologies as well as analytical (data mart–centered business performance management) technologies.[13]

As Peel pointed out later, however, CRM is not only about technology but is also about developing appropriate relationships with customers through communications to create long-term profit. It is not about call centers but about communication; therefore, CRM provides a transition from a transaction-based to a relationship-based business model that concentrates on the acquisition, development, and retention of profitable customer relationships. With this in mind, Meyer and Kolbe's definition of CRM is instructive:

> Generally, CRM is a technologically driven, or at least technologically supported, customer-focused concept that enables organizations to tailor specific products and services to individual customers. CRM is about building long-term and profitable one-to-one relationships with customers.[14]

Many consultants and business practitioners agree that when CRM systems fail, it is usually due to cultural as opposed to technological issues. Many companies focus on the opposite of "relationship" (i.e., on the "transaction" itself). This is a short-term view that merely focuses on the exchange of a company's product or service, broadly defined, for money. Transactions are one-shot exchanges without any concern for the future. Transaction marketing views the sale as the end of the relationship, whereas relationship marketing views the sale as the beginning. In today's business world, relationships are actually possible, given advances in information and telecommunications systems. Relationships require two-way communications between customers and the organization. Further, information from these communications, when integrated, recorded, and managed, enables relationships to be developed and maintained. Ideally, the processing of this information leads to greater customer knowledge, which then results in greater customer satisfaction and loyalty.

For example, a customer contacts L. L. Bean to order a blue shirt that she has just seen in a recent catalog. The CSR reviewing the customer's purchase history notices that the last five shirts ordered have been blue. The CSR mentions this and suggests that perhaps she might be interested in ordering the shirt in another color. The customer may or may not do so, but she is likely to be impressed that in addition to simply selling her a shirt, L. L. Bean seems to have branched out into wardrobe planning.

What might have been simply a transaction was turned into something more than that. Relevant communication based on purchase history turned the buying situation into an opportunity for dialogue. The company exhibited concern for the consumer that, in turn, may lead to greater satisfaction, trust, and commitment to the company. With additional experiences such as this, the customer may develop a sense of company loyalty. Therefore, a company is practicing CRM when it has adopted a customer-centric focus and strengthens profitable customer relationships through the use of customer information.

Swift argued, "CRM's goal is to increase the opportunity (of customers buying again) by improving the process to communicate with the right customer, providing the right offer (product and price), through the right channel, at the right time."[15]

Contrary to the mechanics underlying the concept of market share (a company's product sales divided by total industry product sales), companies should not necessarily make it their goal to attract the greatest number of customers. After all, by giving your product away for free, a company can achieve 100 percent market share; however, it would not be in business long. Rather, a company should make its goal to attract the greatest number of profitable customers.

All customers are not created equal. With a limited number of tables near the band, a nightclub would maximize its revenue and profitability by making sure that those occupying the scarce tables drink Dom Perignon champagne rather than Heineken beer. The former customers are of greater value and will be treated differently than the latter. Prioritizing Dom drinkers, the beer drinkers may be told that they are sitting at a "reserved" table and must move after one drink order. It is certain that the manager will remember the best customers, provide them with better service, and, whenever possible, apprise them of "specials" on more expensive brands of champagne. Likewise, the purpose of CRM programs is to recognize the best customers, retain them, encourage greater usage of the company's product or service, and "trade them up" to more prestigious and expensive items over time.

Marketers are actually managers of demand. When demand is weak, marketers develop plans and programs to increase it. When the December 26, 2004, tsunami destroyed the most popular tourist resorts on the Andaman seacoast of Thailand, the entire resort industry suffered tremendous losses. Resort owners in conjunction with Thailand's government agencies had to develop marketing plans and programs to attract tourists back to the region to rebuild Thailand's second biggest industry. This is a demand-generating strategy and is most typically equated with marketers.

What many do not realize, however, is that situations exist in which marketers must attempt to lower demand for their product or service. This brings us to the concept of *de-marketing* (i.e., attempts to weaken or extinguish demand when they are unprofitable for the organization). Such strategies occur fairly frequently, with minimum order sizes or high admittance charges being common examples. In such ways, companies may reduce their ranks of unprofitable customers.

On a larger scale, financial institutions want to dissuade people from applying for their charge cards if they do not use them or if they pay off their balances before interest can accrue. One way to weed out unprofitable customers is to charge an annual fee for lack of profitable usage. The financial institutions hope the unprofitable customers will then open accounts with their competitors instead.

While the term "relationship" is important, the term "management" is also important when defining CRM as it pertains to the organization's ability to develop strategies that attract and retain customers. Management can be defined as the identification of prospects, selection and acquisition of relevant prospects, and development of the relationship (i.e., providing an increasing number of products and services that add value for the customer and are lucrative for the organization in the hopes of maximizing the profitable lifetime value of the relationship). Companies should recognize that customer relationships are the underlying tool for building customer value and realize that growing customer value is the key to increasing enterprise value.[16]

Managing strategies and tactics requires effective planning and effective and timely implementation. (Strategy formulation is discussed more thoroughly in Chapter 10.) Needless to say, the best plans and strategies are for naught if they break down during the implementation phase. Later in this chapter, we discuss the challenges of implementing CRM.

While there is significant debate about how an organization should manage CRM, there is agreement that the relationship among marketing, communication, and CRM is strong. This enables CRM to become the basis for branding strategy:

> CRM integrates marketing, sales, and service functions through business process automation, technology solutions, and information resources to maximize each customer contact. CRM facilitates relationships among enterprises, their customers, business suppliers, and employees.[17]

If the key to successful relationships is communication, successful CRM communication is founded on engaging customers in a dialogue that results in greater brand and/or organization satisfaction. CRM can enhance brand value by providing customers with the information they require, providing offers that add value to purchasing the brand, and transparently facilitating the acquisition of information to improve future CRM efforts.

The term "relationship marketing," introduced by Leonard L. Berry,[18] is concerned with how organizations manage and improve their relationships with customers for long-term profitability. CRM uses information technology to implement relationship marketing strategies. Thus, it is a link between information technology (IT) and strategies aimed at identifying, acquiring, developing, and retaining customers. CRM is information intensive, and the better the quality of information that an organization obtains from and about its customers, the better it is able to understand, develop, and implement its relationship strategies.

Kutner and Cripps[19] suggest that CRM is founded on four tenets: (1) customers should be managed as important assets; (2) not all customers are equally desirable; (3) customers vary in their needs, preferences, and buying behaviors; and (4) by better understanding their customers, companies can tailor their offerings to maximize overall value. Managing customers as important assets to the company is part of the resource-based view of customers. The more a company knows its customers, the greater the opportunity to increase market penetration and share of wallet. This leads to greater market share, the opportunity to trade customers up and increase the speed of new product acceptance, and, eventually, quickened cash flow with less volatility and risk.

By better understanding their customers, companies are able to market to them individually rather than as part of a mass-market segment, which is not as efficient or cost effective. CRM enables a company to invest the right amount in the right customer, to find more customers like the existing profitable ones, and to develop retention strategies that engender loyalty among those groups of customers.[20]

CRM is all about managing the customer experience. To do this effectively, organizations must understand their customers' needs and purchasing behaviors and effectively manage each interaction they have with each customer. These interactions can arise with personnel in the store, customer contact center, or elsewhere in the channel, but also through advertising, sales, and sales promotion. CRM "raises the bar" for customer service expectations as companies exhibit greater customer recognition and treat customers as individuals. Thus, CRM can provide organizations in many industries with a competitive advantage.

We offer a Gestalt view of CRM, taking into consideration technology, corporate culture, relationships with both customers and partners, and management strategy. CRM is the initiation, enhancement, and maintenance of mutually beneficial customer and partner long-term relationships through business intelligence-generated strategies based on the capture, storing, and analysis of information gathered from all customer and partner touch points and transaction processing systems.

1.2 The Purpose and Benefits of CRM

As the acronym indicates, the focus of CRM is the customer, particularly existing ones. Acquiring new customers and bringing them into the "pipeline" or "funnel," however, is necessary for long-term business success. The knowledge base contained in a CRM system will, in fact, aid in the acquisition of new customers. As companies gather information about their current customers, view their purchase history and interactions with the organization, compute customer lifetime value (discussed later in this chapter), and understand what motivates them to increase their purchases or trade up to higher-priced items, the company has a knowledge base that will help them attract more customers like these.

Likewise, as companies gather information about current customers who buy infrequently, buy only when products or services are on sale, frequently return merchandise, and complain often, the company can avoid attracting similar customers. It is anathema for some marketers to consider avoiding certain types of customers; after all, once in the company fold, would it not be possible to market some products and services to them at a profit? Perhaps not. There is the eye-opening but true story of a long-distance telephone company that spent millions of dollars each year sending out zero-balance statements to 20 million subscribers who never used the service.

Many nonusers are long-time customers, so the purpose of CRM systems is not simply to retain customers, nor is the purpose simply to please customers (any company can do this by giving the product or service away for free). The purpose is to identify, retain, and please the right kind of customer and to foster their repeat usage. Relationship building should be contingent on value. Some customers are transactional and do not value a relationship with the firm. Research shows that these customers can be profitable as long as relationship building resources directed to these customers remain modest. Likewise, many long-term (loyal) customers may be unprofitable. A good CRM system identifies potentially profitable and unprofitable customers early on. While many think CRM systems primarily focus on customer retention, to create value, CRM systems sometimes point toward de-marketing to certain groups. For example, it may behoove a company to add or raise fees to certain customers in order to either make them profitable or drive them away.

While weeding out unprofitable customers is an important function of CRM systems, companies such as L. L. Bean, Lands' End, and Amazon.com use their CRM systems to make their customers feel they are important assets to the company. These companies use CRM systems to establish relationships with their customer base that cultivate loyalty and trust and enable the company to offer products and services that are price inelastic. While this may not be very difficult when a company's base of customers is small, it is far more difficult for companies whose customer base is in the millions. The problem becomes one of scale—how to provide good, personalized customer service to millions of your best customers.

Like the moat and castle fortifications that protected the residents of medieval towns, CRM systems help protect companies' customers. As such, CRM systems become the major bulwark used in what M. D. Johnson and F. Seines call "defensive marketing"[21]:

> "Offensive marketing" typically refers to activities aimed at increasing the size of a firm's customer base, and "defensive marketing" refers to activities aimed at existing customers, such as customer retention and service recovery efforts. Current thought in marketing theory and practice is that defensive marketing has become more profitable, and the implication is that companies should allocate resources to build more cooperative and long-lasting relationships with their customers.

In other words, mass marketing, with its emphasis on sending out the same message to millions of prospects, is being deemphasized in favor of one-to-one marketing's ability to customize communication with individuals—primarily a company's own customers. Technology has certainly been a force in this transformation, but there are many other forces at work as well. These will be discussed later in the chapter.

As we already know, the focus of CRM is on relationships; however, as M. D. Johnson and F. Seines point out, after progressing from being a stranger, there are actually three types of relationships: relationships that exist among acquaintances, among friends, and among partners. Acquaintance relationships are based on satisfaction, and companies have to provide only parity value to achieve this (i.e., produce products and services equal to the competition). Friendly relationships are based on trust, and companies have to provide differential value to achieve this (i.e., produce products and services that are somehow different from the competition's). Partner relationships are based on commitment, and companies have to provide customized value to their customers in order to achieve partner status. Often, partner relationships are developed and maintained by a shared structural component (e.g., shared systems and software) that enables them to operate more efficiently and effectively.

Through transactions, the supplier provides the customer with differential advantages and value. The supplier's image improves because the customer's perceived risk in dealing with the supplier decreases. Over time, trust develops and the relationship transforms from acquaintanceship to friendship to partnership. Using CRM systems, suppliers are able to recognize the individuality of their consumer or business customers and offer customized products and services. For this, many are willing to pay a price premium or commit themselves to the supplier for an extended period. Customers do not have to find better alternatives, and the commitment between customer and supplier leads to loyalty. It has been argued (although there are some recent articles to refute this) that customers who are closer to the firm tend to buy more (because they are better acquainted with the firm's offerings), cost less to serve (because the firm knows them better), and be less price sensitive (because they have higher switching costs).[22]

Thus, the goal of CRM systems is not merely to establish and maintain a relationship with customers but rather to increase the strength of the relationship from acquaintanceship to friendship to partnership. One must not overlook that there must be some mechanism in place to feed potential customers into the system (i.e., to convert strangers to acquaintances). Some feel that mass-marketing efforts will therefore always have a role because they focus on bringing strangers into the "funnel." In marriage, as in business, having a partner is very useful in fighting off other suitors because a partner, by definition, implies one's customer is impervious to a competitor's offerings.

As companies shift from mass-marketing to one-to-one marketing, they shift from broadcast (sending the same message to many different people) to dialogue (real-time communication with their customer). As Regis McKenna pointed out, when you have dialogue, you can maintain continuous connections with customers and provide them with customized products and services.[23] Ultimately, marketing should involve the customer as a partner in development and production. End users' comments should become part of a company's development process. When customers are involved in the development of a product or service, they are less likely to become dissatisfied, and one of the important reasons CRM is in such wide use today is to avoid dissatisfied customers. For example, Yahoo! brings product-development personnel into their focus groups so the qualitative findings can be interpreted, when possible, as product-specific as opposed to general recommendations.

Dissatisfied customers drain company resources in many ways. They make more calls to customer service, are more likely to "churn" (i.e., defect), and are more likely to "bad-rap" the company to their family, friends, and coworkers. Numerous studies support the finding that satisfied customers tell 4 to 8 people about their experiences, while dissatisfied customers tell as many as 20 people. In the age of social media, however, dissatisfied customers can reach hundreds and even thousands of people. One customer whose guitar was broken by United Airlines baggage handlers reached over 10 million people with YouTube videos, and the viewership is still growing.

A straightforward answer to why CRM systems are being used is that they can enhance productivity across the range of key marketing functions:

1. Identifying prospects
2. Acquiring customers
3. Developing customers

4. Cross-selling
5. Up-selling
6. Managing migration
7. Servicing
8. Retaining
9. Increasing loyalty
10. Winning back defectors

The ultimate success of CRM rests on a company's ability to create a competitive advantage via their CRM activities.

A recent McKinsey & Company report shows that CRM systems can be highly effective in reducing acquisition costs and in developing customers by increasing usage of company products and services.[24] In addition, CRM is extremely effective in increasing upward migration (convincing customers of the value of "trading up") and increasing cross-sell (getting customers to buy other company products and services). CRM has also proven effective in increasing client retention (CRM databases provide an early warning as to which customers are ready to leave the relationship), reducing silent attrition (customers stop buying or reduce their buying significantly) through migration management, and reducing downward migration (customers "trading down"). CRM systems can also dramatically increase the quality of service a company provides its customers by improving cueing, matching callers with the most appropriate CSP (i.e., customer service personnel), and directing customers to use the most profitable channels in communicating with the company.

As Peppers et al. point out in their seminal article regarding one-to-one marketing, there are really four basic steps in CRM:

1. Identify your customers in as much detail as possible, including demographics, psychographics, habits, and preferences.
2. Differentiate among them (e.g. most and least profitable).
3. Interact with your customers (make this interaction more cost effective through automation whenever possible).
4. Customize your offerings to fit each customer's needs through mass customization or individual tailoring.[25]

Through these four stages, a company is better able to learn and understand its customers and provide more relevant and customized offerings. Thus, Peppers and Rogers suggested that the real purpose of relationship/one-to-one/CRM marketing is the establishment of a "learning relationship." Learning relationships are possible when there is dialogue resulting in increasingly more detailed feedback over time. B. J. Pine, D. Peppers, and M. Rogers said the following:

> A learning relationship is an ongoing connection between an organization and its customer that becomes smarter as the two interact with each other. In learning relationships, individual customers teach the company about their preferences and needs. The more customers teach the company, the better it becomes at providing exactly what they want and the more difficult it will be for a competitor to entice them away.[26]

Building learning relationships may be easier for companies in some industries than others. Travel agencies know their customers and their preferences. Most large retailers do not—unless they provide their customers with something of value in order to collect customer information, such as supermarket ID cards. In return for completing an application form and letting the supermarket record your purchases against your demographic data, the shopper gets sizable discounts on items. Once a company learns about its customers, it must be able to tailor its products, services, or promotions to cash in on the learning relationship. For example, hotels can record guests' preferences (view from their room, newspapers, restaurants, pillows, time of servicing the room, promotional specials) and deliver these customized preferences upon check-in or throughout the stay. Most retailers would have a harder time providing such customer customization.

Of course, the benefits of CRM do not just happen. How does a company develop customers, up-sell, cross-sell, service, retain, increase loyalty, and win back defectors? The answer is through well-thought-out, effective marketing strategies and specialized campaign management. The latter can be oriented toward customer niches (small market segments) or even individuals. Through effective strategies and campaign management, companies are able to achieve returns on their CRM investment by facilitating customer loyalty and engendering their migration toward upscale, new, and a greater variety of products and services. Generating customer referrals also ensures that new customers will be entering the pipeline. Wireless phone companies' campaigns providing discounts for customers' family and friends are an example of how customer referrals can be generated. Airlines' frequent flyer programs are examples of how repeat business (if not loyalty) can be generated. Hotels' campaigns to upgrade guests to mini-suites or reduced-price suites are examples of how companies can trade up their customer preferences.

THEORY IN ACTION

"Put the Gun in the Bird's Hands"

David Holvey, senior vice president of consumer banking, Wells Fargo & Company, said that Wells Fargo went through a number of stages before reaching the customer-initiated relationship stage.

Stage 1: Shooting at the Sky: Once a week, Wells Fargo had Pizza Calling Night, when employees stayed late to target all Wells Fargo customers.
Problem: They would often shoot the same multiple-account holder two or more times.

Stage 2: Shooting at the Flock: During Pizza Calling Night, they would target specific customer segments—for example, savings account customers.
Problem: They would often shoot the same savings account customer who had multiple accounts two or more times.

Stage 3: Shooting at the Bird: During Pizza Calling Night, they would target specific customers and then keep track of what accounts those customers opened.
Problem: Customers were still getting shot.

Stage 4: Putting the Gun in the Bird's Hands: Guided by the philosophy "Don't shoot the customers; they are your friends," Wells Fargo decided to let their customers contact Wells Fargo when they have a need.

End result: Wells Fargo expanded the number of customers getting personal attention.

Presentation by David Holvey, senior vice president of consumer banking, Wells Fargo & Company, at the MSI conference "Taking Stock of Customer Relationships" (March 2, 2006).

CRM systems can also lower the substantial costs of doing business, making the recruitment of customers more cost effective, reducing the costs of sales, and, by increasing customer retention and loyalty, reducing the need for frequent and expensive efforts to attract new customers. CRM systems also reduce costs involved in marketing to low-profit customers, since they can be identified. On the revenue side, CRM systems allow companies to identify and focus on their high-profit customers while enabling companies to transform low-value customers into higher-value ones. While some companies have seen very quick paybacks—two years or less—the payback for most CRM systems comes over time.

Some retail banks have realized the following benefits from CRM[27]:

- An increase in the average number of products sold per customer over one year—from 4.6 to 6.2
- A decrease in administrative costs of 3 to 5 percent over one year
- A 200 percent return on technology investment through cost reduction over one year
- A 96 percent reduction in the average time it takes for a call center agent to refer a customer to a branch loan office—from 45 minutes to 2 minutes
- An 83 percent decrease in average customer information retrieval time—from 12 minutes to 2 minutes per customer inquiry
- An 80 percent reduction in average time to escalate a service request that is not resolved during the initial conversation with a call center agent—from 5 minutes to 1 minute
- An 80 percent reduction in the average time elapsed before a telesales agent refers a customer to another business unit to complete a product purchase—from 15 minutes to 3 minutes
- An 80 percent decrease in average preparation time, including employee training and system setup, prior to the execution of a telesales campaign—from 40 hours to 8 hours
- A 15 percent increase in financial product revenue in one year

Kimberly-Clark spent huge quantities of marketing dollars, uncertain of which promotions were producing retailer loyalty, shelf space, and sales and which ones were going to waste. A CRM-based business planner rapidly proved a success. In its first year, the system was used to manage more than 2,300 promotional events involving all of the company's U.S. consumer product lines.[28] DHL once took 10 days to approve salespeople's quote prices. Now, using a CRM system, a salesperson's quote can be delivered and approved on the spot because of IT and data warehousing.[29]

While companies have made progress in their customer retention efforts, J. Griffin and M. W. Lowenstein published a defection rate table (Table 1.2) indicating that defection rates are still extremely high.[30]

Table 1.2 Annual Customer Defection Rates

Product	% Defection
Newspaper subscriptions	66
Residential tree and lawn care	32
U.S. long-distance telephone	30
German mobile telephone market	25
Clothing catalogs	25
Internet service providers	22

Having continuous relationships with customers provides a learning environment for the organization that may be far superior to quantitative surveys and focus groups. CSRs, if brought into the research loop, can provide marketers and engineers with what customers are really saying about the product. While the purpose of CRM may be to enhance customer service, customers with their feedback may help enhance the product or service, too.

The benefits of a customer focus are retention of loyal customers and a greater share of the customer's wallet through cross-selling and up-selling. The pioneering work of F. F. Reichheld and W. E. Sasser Jr.[31] found a strong relationship between customer retention and company profits. They found that just a 5 percent increase in customer retention yielded improved profitability in net present value from 20 to 85 percent across a wide range of businesses.

It is no longer just a question of whether or not an organization should create a CRM system. CRM systems are proving to be a necessity because of heightened customer expectations. Organizations cannot allow their competitors to have a differential advantage in this area. In many areas, consumers deal with multiple organizations (e.g., charge card–issuing banks). If one bank consistently provides better service and another cannot resolve billing disputes quickly, the consumer can easily discontinue using the latter's card.

CRM systems are also necessary to reduce waste in an organization's communication and marketing efforts. Following the introduction of CRM systems, companies are able to delineate the profitable customers and customer segments. They are then able to tailor their communication and marketing expenditures to these high-profit segments, while at the same time finding more customers like them. Concurrently, they can reduce or eliminate expenditures on nonprofitable individuals or segments. This money can then be spent on retention strategies directed toward the most profitable segments.

CRM systems have enabled organizations to move from less efficient and effective mass-marketing strategies to increasingly fine segmentation strategies, ultimately enabling them to focus on single individuals in one-to-one marketing. With a one-to-one orientation, organizations can focus on events that may trigger people's purchases, such as life-stage changes (marriage, birth of a child, retirement, etc.) or events (automobile accident, house fire, sale of a second home, etc.). Being able to target individuals can increase marketing efficiency because companies can send customers more relevant and appropriate offers.

To summarize, the objectives of CRM systems include the following:

- Identifying potential customers
- Understanding customer needs, both current and latent
- Differentiating profitable from unprofitable customers and segments
- Decreasing attrition by increasing value and satisfaction
- Increasing usage of current products and services
- Increasing usage of a greater number of a company's products and services
- Increasing usage of more prestigious items produced by a company (trading up)
- Increasing customer service and satisfaction
- Improving campaign management
- Increasing referrals
- Winning back lost customers
- Moving customers up the relationship hierarchy from strangers to acquaintances to friends to partners
- Integrating marketing and sales efforts throughout the various channels used by the company

One problem addressed by the CRM program is the recognition that not all customers are equally profitable—and some will never be profitable. Telecommunications industry studies have shown that as much as 80 percent of profits can come from as little as 3 percent of the buildings in a company's territory.

—K. Thompson, L. Ryals, S. Knox, and S. Maklan, "Developing Relationship Marketing through the Implementation of Customer Relationship Management Technology," *Proceedings of the 16th Annual IMP Group Conference* (2000).

1.3 The Tangible Components of CRM

As with most services, there is a tangible component to CRM. These include data warehouses, customer touch points, customer call centers, sales force automation, and the 360-degree view of customers. Perhaps by investigating the basic tangible components of a CRM system, we can address more completely the question "What is CRM?"

1.3a The Five Key Areas of Any CRM System

Figure 1.1 displays the basic architecture of a CRM system, which brings together the five key areas of any CRM system:

1. The integrated front office provides complete customer profiles to all customer-facing persons, including marketing, sales, and customer service personnel. The technologies include call centers, sales force automation, and the Internet.

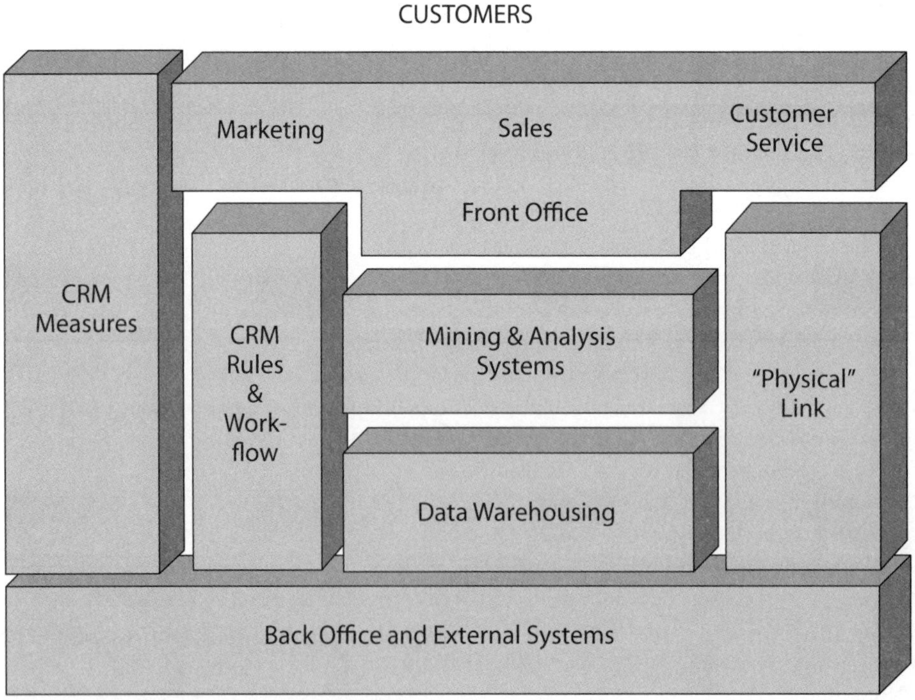

CUSTOMERS

Figure 1.1 Basic Architecture of a CRM System

2. The business intelligence (BI) system captures information from all customer touch points. BI systems consist of data warehouses, data marts, and data mining/analytic techniques. While the data warehouse and data mart merely store and update information, data mining and intelligence tools enable an organization to segment its customer base, attach value to each segment, and differentiate its service messages to each group.

3. Workflow and business rules transmit BI to front-office personnel, enabling them to understand the value they can give each customer when asked to satisfy their requests or as part of a retention strategy.

4. Physical links to back-office systems, such as inventory control, accounts receivable, and so on, enable front-office personnel to make fulfillment promises that the company can keep.

5. Performance metrics enable the company to determine the success of their CRM efforts and the value of each customer.

These areas form the CRM "ecosystem" in which the back office and front office are integrated with each other through the exchange of data, systems, and business processes. The CRM "ecosystem" produces knowledge about the customer. With more data being added all the time, the "ecosystem" continues to grow, adding to the company's knowledge of its customers.

1.3b Multichannel Marketing

Multichannel can be defined as the variety of channels (store, telephone, ATM/kiosk, catalog, social networks, and online) consumers use to interact and transact with an organization. A recent McKinsey & Company report predicted that multichannel marketing will be a necessity in B2C and B2B sectors in many industries. The report predicted that over 50 percent of customers (the percentage is already over 50 percent in apparel retailing and retail banking)—typically the highest-value customers—will be using multiple channels for shopping and purchasing. The challenge to companies today is to build systems that will integrate field, phone, and Internet sales and service, while avoiding the "3E" trap: everything to everyone, everywhere. McKinsey pointed out that on an individual basis, retail customers using multiple channels for purchasing have two to four times more to spend than those using one channel. In retail banking, multichannel customers are 25 to 50 percent more profitable than single-channel users.[32]

THEORY IN ACTION

Hilton Hotels Corporation

Hilton has found that:

A single-channel customer has 2 stays per year.

A two-channel customer has 6 stays per year.

A three-channel customer has 12 stays per year.

Presentation by Jim Von Derheide, vice president of CRM strategy, Hilton Hotels Corporation, at the MSI conference "Taking Stock of Customer Relationships" (March 1, 2006).

Customers are switching to multichannel shopping and purchasing because it provides greater convenience and the ability to obtain more targeted information and advice. In the area of brokerage and financial services, multichannel business propositions have become a necessity. Brick-and-click business propositions have led to the success of Charles Schwab. Customers can easily conduct transactions online, and when they need investment advice, they can visit a Charles Schwab office.

Companies are training their customers and prospects to use the most cost-effective channels for shopping and purchasing. For example, while many airlines charge $20 for a paper ticket, e-tickets are free. Many companies provide incentives for encouraging trial of new cross-channel offerings—for example, frequent flyer miles. McKinsey & Company reported decreases in customer acquisition costs of 10 to 30 percent and, in some cases, higher than 70 percent and a doubling of conversion rates through the use of online CRM.[33]

There is considerable evidence that the multichannel customer buys more (Figure 1.2). The key issue is why? Is it because they are receiving more types of marketing communications and messages? Is it because they increase their loyalty to companies serving them more effectively? Or is it possible that nothing has changed, and a company's multichannel users would have been their best, high-volume customers anyway? S. A. Neslin suggested that they buy more because of the increase in marketing communication and messages that multichannels provide. He also suggested that a company's Internet channel minimally cannibalizes other channels—although many companies say otherwise.[34]

Some feel that portal technology that connects customers with the best resources in the firm—whether it be a company's toll-free number, e-mail, or website—and puts all of the different types of contacts into a common cue will be the key to a successful CRM strategy. A customer relationship portal provides consistent information about all of a customer's interactions and enables an organization to measure the effectiveness of its contact personnel.

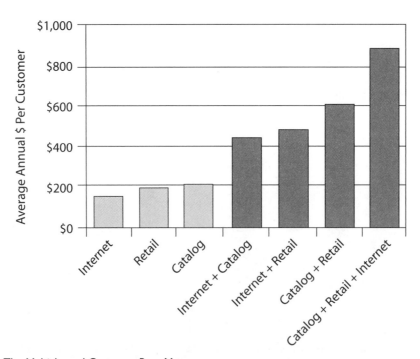

Figure 1.2 The Multichannel Customer Buys More

S.A. Neslin, Dartmouth College, as adapted from Double-Click (2004)

THEORY IN ACTION

Companies Try to Encourage Customer Use of Cost-Effective Channels

To encourage flyers to purchase e-tickets as opposed to purchasing tickets involving human transactions, many airlines charge $20 for nonelectronic transactions. Customers seem to have accepted this surcharge. However, when First National Bank of Chicago, in an effort to encourage e-banking as opposed to teller transactions, began imposing a $3 surcharge every time a retail banking customer saw a teller, customers revolted, and the media "crucified" the bank. The bank soon dropped the surcharge.

Some hotels offer discounts to guests who book over the Internet. Hilton Hotels, however, does not offer discounts; its rates remain constant across channels. It does use points, however, to encourage specific channel usage.

According to V. Kumar, interactive technologies are gaining momentum as a way that businesses and their customers can interact on a timely basis. Interactive technologies consist of devices (cellular phones, Web-browsing functions, GPS technologies, and social networking) and information infrastructures (search bookmarking and information organization technologies).[35] In fact, it has been said that social media as a source of shopping information will become more important than all other channels in the near future.

THEORY IN ACTION

Social Networking, Groupon, and Sprout Social

Groupon sends its followers coupon deals-of-the-day good at local businesses and encourages them to share the coupon offer with their social networks. Eric Lefkofsky and Andrew Mason formed Groupon, which is basically a social-coupon website. Eric believes that future marketing will revolve around each customer's social connections. In fact, he just invented a company called Sprout Social that creates a social media dashboard for businesses, enabling them to monitor their brand on the Web by monitoring tweets, reviews, blog posts, and news. It can target customers who have the most social connections—in effect using their best customers to sell to others just like them in their social networks.[36]

The "group coupon" is activated only after a minimum number of customers purchase the deal. Groupon sends out deals daily, as well as spur-of-the-moment deals that are available on the day of purchase only. In 2012, the company claimed to have 70 million plus subscribers in 45 countries and runs about 900 deals per day on its Groupon.com website. Groupon also posts its deals on Facebook and Twitter. Customers can earn $10 in Groupon Bucks through referring a friend to a deal.

Sprout Social emphasizes the four components of social media effectiveness: monitoring, engagement, measurement, and growth. With a single click, companies can publish and schedule updates across social channels. They can also monitor their brand's and competitors' brands performances across social channels and the Web.

1.3c Database/Data Warehouse/Data Mart/Data Mining/SaaS

A database is an aggregation of computer-based data that is arrayed in a format to facilitate retrieval. The **data warehouse** is the central element in the CRM system and requires that relevant customer data be entered, stored, and available for analysis and dissemination to people in the organization. The data that resides within the warehouse must be current, accurate, secure, and easily obtainable for all who need it. The data warehouse contains data from the customer, company, and outside sources and is used to extract patterns of customer behavior. It usually contains information from each customer touch point (electronic point of sale [POS], telephone, Internet, etc.), information input by the sales force, and perhaps survey data. A warehouse usually contains data applicable for an entire business unit, and it should provide a single view of the customer.

The data warehouse contains such a huge quantity of data that it may prove unwieldy for country managers who merely want to analyze their country subset or for product managers who merely want to analyze product-related customer behavior. **Data marts** contain a subset of the data in the data warehouse and allow for more efficient analysis of the relevant portion of the firm's transactions. For example, if a business unit focuses on selling herbicides to farmers and insecticides to pest control operators, separate data marts may exist for farmers on the one hand and pest control operators on the other.

All of the best data in the world is useless, however, if it cannot be reported and analyzed quickly and efficiently. To aid managers in their analysis of vast amounts of data, data visualization software provides them with data in table, chart, graph, and three-dimensional form. Because there is such a huge amount of data in a data warehouse or even a data mart, statistical techniques are available that can help managers find important relationships between variables or indicate trends. **Data mining** is the process of using statistical techniques to uncover patterns or relationships among variables in the data warehouse or data mart. In data mining, analytical tools search for relationships in the database that can lead to better acquisition, development, retention, win-back of lost customers, and forecasts of customer behavior.

THEORY IN ACTION

Capital One

Capital One, a major global credit card issuer, generates over 4,000 promotional campaigns annually and tests the effectiveness of each one by extracting key data from its data marts. This type of activity shows that CRM can be effective—perhaps most effective—in solving specific, well-defined problems. Further, the data contained in data warehouses and data marts can be valuable in determining when to make an offer. Timing is everything and is often based on changes in a customer's life stage or life cycle. This type of CRM-based promotion is based on a future-looking (predictive modeling) view of the consumer's profit potential as opposed to projections based on an historic view of past transactions.

L. Bielski, "CRM R.I.P.? Not Exactly," *ABA Banking Journal* (September 2004), 55–60.

Since 2000, software as a service (SaaS) has been a growing force in the area of CRM, especially as a sales force application. With SaaS, the software and associated data are hosted centrally on the Internet by a service provider and are typically accessed by users using a Web browser. This eliminates the huge fixed investment that companies previously had to make on computers, related technologies, and software. Unlike traditional software, conventionally sold as a perpetual license with an associated upfront fee, SaaS providers generally price their applications using a subscription fee, most commonly a monthly fee or an annual fee, based on some usage parameters, such as the number of users using the application. The concept of SaaS has been popularized by Salesforce.com. Other vendors include NetSuite, Microsoft, Google, and Rackspace.

According to a Gartner Group estimate, SaaS sales in 2010 reached $10 billion. Gartner Group estimates that SaaS revenue will be more than double its 2010 numbers by 2015 and reach a projected $21.3 billion. CRM continues to be the largest market for SaaS. SaaS revenue within the CRM market reached $3.2 billion in 2010 and is forecast to reach $3.8 billion by 2012.[37]

1.3d Touch Points

A **touch point** is any point of contact that a customer or prospect has with the company. It can be an inquiry over the phone, in person, or via e-mail, or a purchase transaction over the Internet, over the telephone, at an ATM or a kiosk, or at a trade show. Touch point possibilities are endless. (Refer to the Hilton Touch Point Landscape in Figure 1.3.)

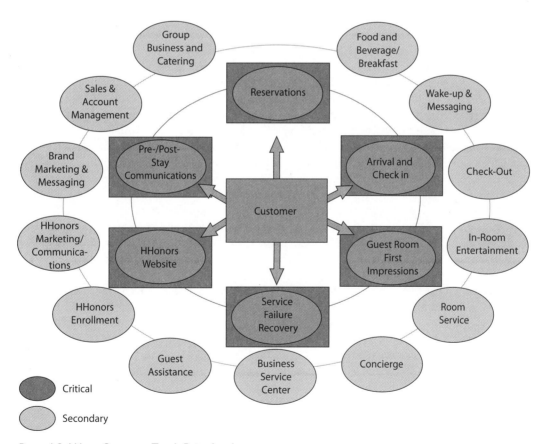

Figure 1.3 Hilton Customer Touch Point Landscape

Source: Jim Von Derheide, VP, CRM Strategy, Hilton Hotels Corporation Presentation at MSI Conference: Taking Stock of Customer Relationships, March 1, 2006. Used by permission of Jim VonDerheide.

POS terminals that scan product data from bar codes while correlating them with customer data available through their use of a store ID card are an example of a touch point. When customers make inquiries or purchases over the Internet, they are using another touch point. Banks can identify individual customers at ATMs and tailor advertisements to them based on the information contained in their CRM data bank. Banks can also identify noncustomers using their ATMs and tailor messages to acquire them.

Newer touch points are constantly being introduced. Social media channels and short message service (SMS) are two examples. Social media channels include many forms such as Internet forums, blogs and microblogs (e.g., Twitter), and social networking sites (e.g., Facebook). These channels enable consumers not only to establish social relationships with companies to learn about sales, new products and services, and events, but to air their dissatisfaction and complaints about the company and its products and brands as well. Therefore, companies must monitor these channels 24/7 in order to react accordingly.

Many companies are using SMS to interact with their customers. For as little as several dollars a day, local merchants can send messages to people in their market area using geo-locators and systems provided by a Web-based service provider. For example, SMS is being used by sports teams to increase ticket sales, by bakeries to sell baked goods, and by health clubs to sell memberships.

Local merchants are not the only ones using SMS to interact with customers. Following significant investment in e-mail marketing, airlines discovered that during the period less than 48 hours before a flight, e-mail was not a sufficient communication method for urgent disruption notifications. Thus, airlines needed an instantaneous communication channel for alerting passengers of last-minute flight update information. SMS proved to be the best solution. SMS proved its value when the Icelandic volcanic eruptions caused travel chaos around the world. The ash cloud spewed from Iceland's Eyjafjallajökull volcano caused worldwide air travel to come to a grinding halt, with more than 1.2 million individuals affected every day. While some travelers were left frustrated at the lack of information, others were kept up to date on developments and travel solutions via SMS by airlines. ConTgo's Mobile Travel Assistant (MTA) sent out information regarding flight cancellations, accommodations, and even meals. As a result of the global ubiquity of the mobile phone, with a penetration rate of close to 4 billion and a subscription rate of more than 4.6 billion, it makes sense to use SMS as a communications vehicle, especially where time-sensitive or urgent information is concerned. After all, a cell phone is always carried, it is always on, and it doesn't require an Internet connection or a static power supply.[38]

SMS is effectively ubiquitous: every handset is SMS enabled, and the vast majority of users understand and know how to use it. Moreover, the GSM network coverage that supports SMS is near ubiquitous on a global basis. SMS has been applied by airlines in many different ways:

- *Ticketing*: One of the clearest applications of SMS in the airline industry, and one that has already been adopted by a number of players, is mobile ticketing. SMS can be used to replace paper tickets in a variety of scenarios. By using industry-standard on-screen bar code technology, it is possible to text a ticket to a handset that can then be scanned and redeemed at check-in or departure gate.
- *Identify authentication*: Mobiles can serve as a powerful identity authentication channel. For example, a traveler buying a ticket on an airline website could be asked for her mobile number when registering on the site. Then, each time she makes a subsequent ticket purchase, a one-time password would be sent to her phone, which would be entered into the site to complete the purchase. This mechanic adds a simple and cost-effective second factor of authentication, ensuring enhanced security for airline and passenger alike.

- *Staff communications*: The nature of the airline industry is such that staff are, by definition, globally distributed. As such, any communications mechanism faces real challenges in reaching every team member. SMS, however, has the advantage of global coverage, a simple interface, and low cost. Using SMS, flight crews can, for example, log their flying hours or receive updated scheduling information reliably and cost effectively wherever they are in the world.
- *Alerting*: This can be as straightforward as a message confirming that a passenger's plane is leaving on time to travel information, such as interesting locations in the destination of their choice. SMS can enable the fast, cost-effective transmission of this information wherever the customer is located, making it an ideal medium for globally dispersed customer audiences.
- *Two-way SMS*: Two-way SMS has been driven by enhanced CRM systems. Whereas SMS has traditionally been viewed as a one-way push mechanism—for example, sending an offer to a customer—it can now be a two-way responsive mechanic. For example, if an airline sends a customer a text to confirm his booking, it would now be possible for the customer to reply to the airline's text with any additional booking details, such as seating or dietary requirements.[39]

Companies should attempt to obtain as much customer information as possible at each touch point, while not overburdening the customer or prospect. Remember that effective CRM systems make their owners a "learning" organization, and effectiveness is enhanced when the company learns something about their customers.

If one extends the notion of "customer" to include suppliers, distributors, dealers, employees, and so forth, then the notion of a touch point can be extended to **"transaction processing**

THEORY IN ACTION

Alberta Treasury Banks

Alberta Treasury Banks (ATB), a US$11 billion full-service bank based in Edmonton, Alberta, Canada, with 144 branches throughout the province, had a customer contact center (**CCC**) that lacked the functionality to service customers quickly. Customers trying to reach their local branch often had their calls redirected to a centralized CCC that had trouble viewing the various screens necessary to see the customers' transaction histories.

ATB selected a software package, eFinance, and first deployed it in their CCC. Customer interactions could be captured across all touch points—whether an ATM, interactive voice response unit, the Internet, or a branch office—and made available to the reps. Now when a call comes into the CCC, a profile of the customer will pop up, giving the rep customer information, including a description of the customer's last contact with the bank.

D. E. Sharp, *Customer Relationship Management Systems Handbook* (New York: Auerbach Publications, 2003): 152–153.

systems." These systems consist of inventory, order entry, billing, and accounts receivables and provide a wealth of information on the firm's stakeholders.

> This introduces the generic problem that most enterprises are starting to have with the proliferation of channels through which their customers want to be able to transact business. The same request could have been sent into the enterprise by:
>
> Web application
> Free-form e-mail
> Completion of a Web form
> Telephone, through a live call center agent
> Internet telephony Voip through a live call center agent
> Text chat with a live call center agent
> Telephony through the bank's interactive voice response system
> Internet telephony to an H.232-enabled interactive voice response system
> Fax
> A WAP phone application
> An ATM application
> A video kiosk application in a shopping center or airport
> The customer entering a branch office
>
> —J. Peel, *CRM: Redefining Customer Relationship Management*
> (Amsterdam: Digital Press, 2002).

1.3e Call Center/Customer Contact Center

For many companies, the call center is the hub of activity, for this is where customer communications occur. Currently, about 100,000 call centers exist in the United States, and this number does not include telemarketers.[40] Despite common perceptions, fewer than 10 percent of call centers are based outside the United States. Call centers for large corporations receive as many as 300,000 calls each day; therefore, technological advances can be very beneficial in the servicing of customers. Israel-based NICE Systems can check 26 parameters of a customer's voice, including pitch, tone, tempo, and cadence. Once a "baseline" recording of a voice is taken during the first few seconds, the system can detect customer anger or frustration levels. If high, a supervisor may be notified to handle the call.[41]

Call centers, however, focus on the telephone. Contact centers extend their coverage to include not only the telephone but also mail, fax, and e-mail. The concept of the contact center has been broadened to what many refer to as the customer interaction center (CIC), which has the ability to generate revenue for the organization. CICs extend contact center coverage across all channels and functions (marketing, R&D, sales, finance, manufacturing, field service, etc.). Today's CICs work with interactive technologies, such as the Internet and cell phones, to provide callers with quicker, more personal service. In some CICs, automated intelligence, such as bots and avatars, are being used to solve customer problems and deliver customized promotions based on the customer's individual characteristics and purchase history.

Lands' End in Dodgeville, Wisconsin, has a very well-developed CCC. It has every item of clothing it sells within reach in case its customers have questions about the "feel" of the clothing; thus, CCC personnel can answer any tactile-related questions. They can also answer if various clothing items match or are color coordinated.

1.3f Sales Force Automation

While the origins of CRM are many, some feel that today's CRM systems morphed from sales force automation (SFA). While SFA products were originally introduced to improve sales force productivity and provide better documentation for the organization, today they are increasingly oriented toward developing customer relationships and improving satisfaction. SFA systems are an important subset of CRM systems because they provide management of:

- The sequence of sales activities
- Sales territories
- Data across and within a company's client organization
- Leads and opportunities
- The building of items into a total package for customers
- Information

Salesforce.com is a leader in SFA, with more than 100,000 customers and 2 million subscribers worldwide. As an application service provider (ASP), it provides a hosted Web portal that allows users to outsource the operation and maintenance of all data and transaction information dealing with their sales force–customer interactions.

1.3g 360-Degree View

CRM systems should provide everyone in the organization a standardized, consistent, and complete view of the customer based on the customer's data array from all touch points collected across the business cycle. The second-generation **360-degree view** suggests that companies should treat customers throughout the business cycle based on their lifetime profitability. The focus is profitability and not revenue or value. Note that the business cycle consists of the following: analyze, market, sell, produce, fulfill, service, and administer. K. C. Cooper claimed that SFA systems provide a 30-degree view and that most CRM systems provide a 90-degree view. Therefore, a CRM system, in order to provide a 360-degree view, must address the end-to-end transaction relationship defined by the business cycle.[42] Most companies, however, might be wiser to start with systems providing a 90-degree view focusing on one or two customer touch points rather than attempting to start with a 360-degree view. This is because the transition to a 360-degree view may be easier than attempting to develop a perfect all-encompassing view of the customer at the onset.

THEORY IN ACTION

Lead Sources and Prioritization

The ability of Monster.com to effectively direct its large sales force depends on the quality of information and leads that can be fed into the CRM system. Historically, lead sources were relegated to lists of companies and/or consumers from list brokers. With the advent of the Internet, it is possible to create software programs that collect sales lead information from websites. For example, the software that Monster uses can identify companies that are currently looking to fill open positions in its organization. These leads can then be scored and fed into the CRM system for sales to call upon.

Jesse Harriott, former Vice President of Research, Monster Worldwide, Inc.

Organizations that do not implement CRM systems in support of relationship marketing strategies are at risk of being seriously disadvantaged. Customers are beginning to expect the added value delivered through tailoring products or services to individual customers or micro-segments and are demanding greater participation in CRM implementation.

—Dawes & Rowley, 1998

1.4 Important Business Constructs Related to CRM

As with any new business system, there are constructs so intimately related to CRM that it is necessary to know something about them to understand the system itself. This section reviews these constructs, most of which did not exist until CRM did.

1.4a Customer Lifetime Value and Second Lifetime Value

Caesars Entertainment, which owns or manages more than 40 casinos, gives gamblers a card that records their gambling transactions. Gamblers earn points and can move from gold to platinum to diamond status. At each higher level, they accrue increasing amounts of benefits, such as room upgrades, discounts, and so forth. Points accumulate across any of Caesars's casinos. Caesars found that if a customer has a very satisfying experience at its casinos, they will increase their spending on gambling at Caesars by 24 percent per year.[43]

Customer lifetime value (CLV), which is covered in-depth later in the text, is the net present value of the future profits to be received from a given number of newly acquired or existing customers during a specified period of years. It is not the customer's lifetime that is being estimated but rather the period of time that a company can reasonably expect them to be a customer. Sophisticated CLV calculations can also factor in potential profits from customer referrals. According to Gupta and Lehmann, nearly 80 percent of profit from a customer can be realized within the initial three years. Consequently, for many applications, CLV is computed over the first three years of the customer's relationship with the firm and not his or her lifetime.[44]

The estimated lifetime value of a customer with a family of four for a supermarket is approximately $25,000, which appears to be only half of the expenditures that the family will make on food-related purchases. P. Temporal and M. Trott reported that an example of CLV's usefulness is in the training that Mercedes salespeople receive. They are told to imagine that every customer who walks into the showroom has $1 million stuck to his or her forehead because that is what that person will be worth in sales over his or her lifetime.[45] In the Middle East and Southeast Asia, the imagined amount may be substantially higher.

While **lifetime value (LTV)** is typically defined as the net present value of the customer's profitability throughout the customer–firm relationship, when a company reacquires a lost customer, one can compute a **second lifetime value (SLTV)**. SLTV focuses only on the net present value (NPV) generated after a customer has been reacquired.[46]

1.4b Privacy

An emerging social issue that will impact CRM is consumer privacy. As organizations have increased their ability to capture and leverage growing amounts of consumer data, consumers have become very concerned about the need for privacy. Deighton suggests that issues of trust could significantly undermine CRM activities by leading consumers to keep their data private or distort the data.[47]

To prevent indiscriminate marketing, some companies have appointed **chief privacy officers**, and industry groups have been formed to try to prevent CRM abuse. There are now privacy and good practice associations. In addition, most organizations now ask their customers for permission to open communications (**opt-in agreements**) and provide their customers with the ability to terminate communications at any time (**opt-out agreements**). A majority of firms claim to use **"permission-based marketing"** in which a firm asks a current or prospective customer for permission to contact and make product offers (usually via e-mail).[48] From a practical point of view, those customers who "opt in" are typically better customers.

Most customers are willing to provide information and data to an organization as long as they have trust in the company they give it to. The biggest breach of trust occurs when an organization sells or shares a customer's information with a third party without the customer's approval.

THEORY IN ACTION

Monster.com Opt-In/Opt-Out Process

Monster.com maintains large databases for employers and job seekers and communicates with each group for many different reasons. For example, Monster may contact job seekers with career information that might help their job search, job listings that might be of interest, surveys about Monster products, or information about other career services. Monster goes to great lengths to manage an opt-out process so job seekers and employers dictate when and how they would like to receive information from Monster. This results in better-performing CRM campaigns for Monster and a better customer experience for job seekers and employers.

Jesse Harriott, former Vice President of Research, Monster Worldwide, Inc.

With regard to privacy, companies must make sure that their databases are secure, keep abreast of privacy regulations in all relevant markets, and ensure ownership of privacy by, for example, letting customers opt in and opt out. Some companies provide their customers with full access to their information. Customers can change their own profiles at any time. Privacy and ethics issues are covered in depth in Chapter 11.

1.4c Customization versus Personalization

"Customization" means a manufacturer designs a product to suit a customer's needs. **"Personalization"** means the customer is a creator or co-creator of the content. For example, a nursery in Connecticut has an online program that allows the customer to develop personalized landscape designs for his yard. The program then allows the customer to see what the landscaping will look like during the four seasons.

Mass customization is a technique companies use to service a particular customer's needs in a cost-effective way. Companies that are mass customizers have developed techniques to give each customer exactly what they want. Aston Martin automobiles are built to an individual's specifications. Customers can even visit the plant to watch their cars being built. Because Aston Martin deals with only a few thousand customers per year, however, it could hardly be called a mass customizer. Custom tailors also provide clothes sewn to fit an individual, but they also deal with a limited number of customers. The real magic behind mass customization efforts is when a company that sells to millions of customers each year is able to give each customer exactly what he or she wants. Clothing and shoe companies that use magnetic resonance–type equipment to measure each individual's size and width precisely, and custom make the clothing and shoes to fit each of their millions of customers, are using mass customization techniques.

THEORY IN ACTION

Examples of Companies Practicing Personalization Through Their Websites

Nike launched NIKEiD, a website through which consumers can order shoes tailored to their specifications and personalized with an eight-letter identity on the back.

Dell Computer allows customers to custom build a system on Dell's website.

The Scotts Miracle-Gro Company's home page enables visitors to conduct research on everything from lawn care chemicals' environmental impact to where to purchase products.

Ingersoll Rand uses Web technologies and involves its distributors in providing customer service. It has an online portal that lets its dealers place and track orders and check inventory at the company or at other distributors. The system gathers customer data and allows the manufacturer to interact with customers for the first time.

J. Nelson in J. G. Freeland, ed., *The Ultimate CRM Handbook: Strategies and Concepts for Building Enduring Customer Loyalty and Profitability* (New York: McGraw-Hill, 2003).

The terms *customization* and *personalization* also pertain to websites. With customization, the company modifies the website to suit the needs of the customer. With personalization, the customer modifies the website to suit his or her own purposes. Most feel that companies should co-create a website with their users rather than trying to create the perfect site on their own.

Adaptive personalization, also called collaborative filtering, is the sending of company communications and message content based on the company's learning of customer patterns and comparing them with similar customer patterns. Amazon.com's purchase circles suggest similar books based on the customer's past purchases and books that others in their location are reading.[49]

1.4d RFM

Recency, frequency, and monetary value (**RFM**) is covered in-depth in Chapter 7. Companies compute an RFM score for each customer to determine the likelihood that the customer will respond favorably to an offer, promotion, or catalog, for example. Many companies believe that customers who have bought most recently and most often and have spent the most within a specified period of time are most likely to respond favorably to a company's future offer. Such scores can determine, for instance, whether a customer is sent an expensive catalog or merely a postcard.

RFM measures have shortcomings, however, in that they ignore the "pacing" of a customer's purchases (i.e., the time between each purchase). This can result in overinvestment on lapsed customers.

THEORY IN ACTION

Using RFM and CLV Measures to Aid Decisions Regarding Marketing Expenditures

The Shipley family is going camping in the Smoky Mountains for three weeks. They have never taken this kind of vacation before and they need everything: tents, sleeping bags, canteens, gas stove, eating utensils, a canoe, fishing equipment, and outfits for the entire family. They order over $4,000 in merchandise from the L. L. Bean catalog. They have never bought anything from L. L. Bean before.

The Bell family orders from the L. L. Bean catalog every year—buying new fashion items they see, particularly in the summer and winter clothing catalogs. For eight years, they have ordered about $450 worth of items annually.

If you had $10 to invest in marketing efforts across these two families, how would you allocate your marketing expenditure over the next year? Which family is most likely to make the next purchase? If the families are the same age and stage in the family life cycle, which one is likely to be worth the most over their customer lifetime? RFM measures are developed to answer the first two questions, while CLV measures are developed to address the last question.

1.5 Who Uses CRM and Why?

Organizations without CRM capability will be at a serious competitive disadvantage. They will lose the competitive edge that knowledge of customers and a better understanding of customer needs can give them in anticipating and adapting to relationship marketing developments. For those that fail to implement CRM systems in time, customer service will be slow to improve, and service innovations that depend on investment in call centers, data warehousing, or e-commerce may not be implemented in time to recover from the situation.

—K. Thompson, L. Ryals, S. Knox, and S. Maklan, "Developing Relationship Marketing through the Implementation of Customer Relationship Management Technology," *Proceedings of the 16th Annual IMP Group Conference* (2000).

A July 2010 poll of 1,500 CIOs in 40 countries by the Gartner Group revealed that spending on CRM software was set to see the largest increase among all application software in 2010, with the global market for CRM solutions worth more than $16 billion. The Asia-Pacific region (excluding Japan) was the fastest-growing region with growth of over 28 percent from the previous year. Most CRM buyers focused on solutions that help retain customers and enhance their experience; solutions that encourage the development of customer communities and social networks; and SaaS as a delivery platform, with the latter expected to exceed $4 billion in software revenues by 2014. This represents one-third of the overall CRM market. Firms develop CRM systems for the following reasons:

1. To increase customer retention and customer loyalty
2. To stay even with their competition
3. To attempt to differentiate themselves from their competitors based on their ability to provide outstanding customer service
4. To encourage development of customer communities and social networks

There is a high correlation between a firm's size and the likelihood that it was using a CRM system. One study said only 20 percent of small businesses have implemented a CRM software solution, and these companies tend to be concentrated in the financial services, communications, and high-tech manufacturing industries.[50] Implementation of CRM has lagged among small and medium-sized enterprises (SMEs) because money, IT resources, and employees are often in short supply. One result is that SMEs tend to buy their CRM systems in modular increments.

The practice of CRM varies by industry. The greatest penetration of CRM is in telecommunications and credit companies, with financial services companies, pharmaceutical companies and transportation companies closely behind and retailers and utility companies following them.

For over ten years, Wells Fargo & Company of San Francisco has used one-to-one marketing through its ATM machines, which now number over 12,200.[51] While selling products is one of its program's goals, according to Jonathan Velline, senior vice president of ATM banking at Wells, "A lot of it is just trying to keep a dialogue open with customers," especially as they increasingly turn to electronic channels. The software works with a bank's CRM to identify customers who can be targeted by certain campaigns. The ATM application of CRM is primarily used to generate leads for further service usage by each customer. Trying to close sales at the ATM would be too difficult because the transaction, by definition, occurs too quickly.[52] Banks have the ability to send detailed personalized messages to their customers because of the amount of information they have on each customer. Companies in other industries, such as general merchandise retailing, may not be so lucky, since experiences with their customers may be sporadic and the transactional aspects of the relationship are not conducive to the collection of customer information.

Why have CRM systems been adopted and developed so quickly by financial institutions and readily accepted by their customers? The answer appears to be involvement. Consumers are more willing to engage in relationship-type behavior with products and services with which they are psychologically involved, and financial services are high-involvement services for most consumers. Involvement is a function of the perceived importance of the product or service in the life of the user. Price, complexity, and risk can directly impact perceived importance and, therefore, customer involvement. Most customers are more highly involved in their dealings with luxury hotels, banks, and medical centers than they are with the shoe section in the mass merchandise outlet.

THEORY IN ACTION

How a Customer Loyalty Program Increased Customer Visits

Harrah's Entertainment (now Caesars Entertainment) had a customer loyalty program that made it the envy of the industry. In 1994, the winner's information network (WINet), the industry's first national customer database, provided seamless recognition of customers across all of Harrah's properties. In 1997, Harrah's introduced a frequent-player card called Total Gold. It later introduced its Total Reward Program with platinum and diamond player levels, which included not only Harrah's chain but other Harrah's properties as well.

With its Total Reward Program, it achieved a 72 percent increase in the number of customers visiting more than one Harrah's property. Customizing offers enabled Harrah's to increase customers' visits from 1.2 to 1.9 times per month. Harrah's also used the data achieved from its CRM system to configure properties before building them.

J. Dyché, *The CRM Handbook: A Business Guide to Customer Relationship Management* (Boston, MA: Addison-Wesley, 2002).

THEORY IN ACTION

How Guests' Preferences Get Systematized at Ritz-Carlton

Ritz-Carlton has collected guest preferences of 120,000 individual guests over a three-year period. Anything a guest mentions gets in the system through an employee drop box. "No pickle on a sandwich" gets recorded as a guest's preference for all Ritz-Carlton's worldwide. A guest's anniversary or birthday also gets recorded.

K. C. Cooper, *The Relational Enterprise: Moving Beyond CRM to Maximize All Your Business Relationships* (New York: AMACOM, 2002).

Trying to engage low-involvement customers in a learning relationship will not benefit an organization—particularly if the exchanges they engage in are transactional. This is not to say that organizations should not conduct marketing research to determine why consumers are not more involved with their brand, particularly if the brand is in a high-involvement product category. A learning relationship provides continuous feedback from customers, while most marketing research studies are cross-sectional or "one-shot" studies and, therefore, fall far short of what a learning relationship entails.

One might hypothesize that specialty items, for which consumers will accept no substitute, would be high-involvement products (season tickets for the Chicago Bulls, a particular brand of automobile), whereas convenience goods (batteries, milk) would be low-involvement products. It is likely that companies marketing specialty items would benefit most from CRM systems, while companies marketing convenience goods would benefit the least. Wollan and Nunes provided an interesting way of looking at which types of companies benefit most and least from CRM systems (see Figure 1.4).

Their market profile positions companies on two dimensions:

1. Number of customers or customer interactions
2. The complexity of each interaction in terms of channels and type

Wollan and Nunes posited that those companies serving large numbers of customers through increasingly complex and frequent interactions—communications companies, retail banks, insurance companies, health care organizations, and utilities—stand to gain the most from CRM systems. Profitability can rise or fall dramatically with even small changes in the cost of serving their customers. Companies that engage in minimal interactions with each customer (auto dealers, government agencies) or companies with simple customer transactions (movie theaters, retail stores) would benefit the least from CRM systems. These companies would still benefit, but the dynamics of the marketplace would prevent the same returns on a comparable CRM system.

D. Peppers and M. Rogers took an interesting perspective on which companies will benefit most from a customer-centric or relationship marketing orientation. They claimed that companies with a "steep **skew**" will benefit more than other companies. When a company's customers' value varies widely, and their top customers account for the vast majority of the business, they are said to have a "steep skew."[53] Once identified, the company can treat its high-value customers to superior service.

When companies engage a customer in dialogue, they can use the growing amount of customer information to find or build a product or service that best satisfies the needs of that

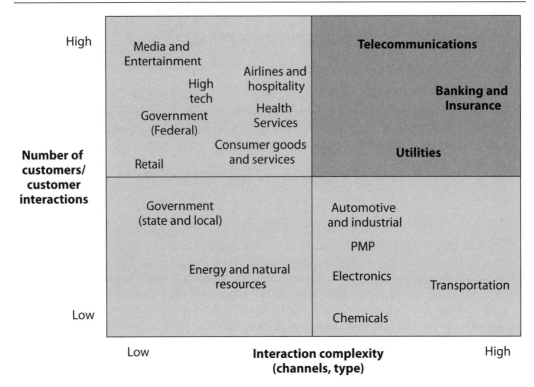

Figure 1.4 The Types of Companies Benefiting Most and Least from CRM Systems

Source: THE ULTIMATE CRM HANDBOOK: STRATEGIES AND CONCEPTS FOR BUILDING ENDURING CUSTOMER LOYALTY AND PROFITABILITY edited by John Freeland. Copyright (c) 2003 Accenture. New York: McGraw-Hill, p. 288. Reprinted by permission of The McGraw-Hill Companies.

particular customer. Whenever possible, companies should develop strategies and tactics that enable them to learn more about the needs of their customers. Individualized information is the basis of a learning relationship. Companies that interact infrequently with their customers will find it difficult to establish such a learning relationship. Staying in touch with customers on a regular basis is the key to attaining intimacy. Companies that offer a limited number of products whose margins are slight and that are purchased infrequently will find it difficult to reap the benefits of CRM systems.

B. B. Jackson said that CRM systems will be more beneficial for companies in "lost for good" situations than companies that are in "always a share" situations.[54] The latter characterizes customers who make purchases of some product category repeatedly and can easily switch all or part of their buying from one vendor to another (i.e., share patronage among multiple suppliers). Since such a buyer has a short time horizon in his or her ties with suppliers, their exchange is transactional. This is more likely to occur in noncontractual settings (department store purchases, catalog shopping) than in contractual settings (subscriptions to magazines, telephone services). In noncontractual settings, firms must ensure that the relationship stays alive because the customers typically split their category expenses among several firms.[55]

In the lost for good situation, the buyer is committed to only one vendor and faces high switching costs (purchasers of office automation systems, communications equipment). The buyer will view his or her commitment to a vendor as permanent and use a long time horizon in the relationship. The supplier will benefit from CRM investments that enable it to win new commitments, cross-sell, and up-sell.

Another factor in the productivity and return from a CRM system is economies of scale. If economies of scale are low, as they are for many types of services, closer relationships tend to generate more value than distant relationships. The more a firm is positioned toward offerings with low economies of scale, the stronger it must be in developing and keeping closer relationships.[56]

The benefits of CRM do not appear to vary, however, between firms that are for-profit or not-for-profit. While for-profit organizations want to drive profits, not-for-profit organizations want to reach people, retain people, and generate donations at the lowest cost possible. This has been a difficult thing for not-for-profits to achieve. Ten years ago they received more than $200 billion in donations but spent $160 billion on direct marketing efforts. According to the *Wall Street Journal*, the National Trust for Historic Preservation spent a total of about $25 on each new member using direct mail to generate a $20 membership fee. Membership renewal is the only way this will pay off.[57]

Making a single solicitation via direct mail or telephone costs $1 or more. Making a solicitation online costs only 20 cents, according to a McKinsey & Company study published in 2003. Even cheaper are "robo calls," the automatic, prerecorded telephone calls political candidates use to talk to voters. These cost as little as 2 cents per call or $1 for 50 calls.[58]

Ten years ago, the nonprofit sector was still learning what the Internet was all about, and barely two out of ten nonprofits were accepting donations online. They didn't engage their donors through e-mail and online marketing channels because they felt donors wouldn't accept it. Today, nonprofits are using social media channels to build relationships with the right markets and maintain communication—often free or at a very low cost.[59]

Chapter Summary

In this chapter we addressed the following questions: What is CRM? What are its benefits? Who uses CRM? Why has it been readily adopted and developed in some business sectors but not in others?

CRM is a defensive marketing strategy that focuses on managing the customer experience by better understanding their needs and purchase behavior. It is a systematic way to strengthen the relationship between a company and its customers, transforming acquaintances into friends and partners. This is done by building learning relationships—for example, through supermarket identification cards and loyalty programs. CRM adopts a customer focus that enables an organization to retain loyal customers and a greater share of the customer's wallet through cross-selling and up-selling. To do this effectively, an organization must master multichannel marketing and managing touch points. Companies attempt to increase CLV through such efforts coupled with personalization, customization, and effective customer profit projections based on measures such as RFM and newer measures taking purchase pacing into account.

All of this is done through technology components that create a CRM ecosystem or architecture. CRM architecture consists of an integrated front office; business intelligence systems (data warehouses, data marts, and data mining); business rules that transmit business intelligence to front-office personnel; physical links to back-office systems such as inventory control, accounts receivable, and so on; and performance metrics. Through the CRM ecosystem, an organization's front and back offices are integrated through the exchange of data, systems, and business processes.

Companies have adopted CRM because it can enhance productivity across the entire range of key marketing functions: identifying prospects, acquiring customers, developing customers through cross-selling and up-selling, managing customer migration, servicing, retaining, increasing loyalty, and winning back defectors. Many organizations have reaped the benefits of CRM: retaining and pleasing the right kind of customers, gaining repeat purchases, and increasing profitability.

Key Terms

360-degree view refers to a consistent view of the customer from beginning to end of the relationship available to all. The customer data must be integrated from all business areas, including billing, customer contact, marketing, and sales.

B2B stands for business-to-business commerce involving interactions with business firms, institutions, and government agencies that may consume or resell these products or services.

B2C stands for business-to-consumer commerce involving sales to individual or household markets for their personal consumption.

CCC is a customer contact center—formerly called a customer call center—that, in addition to incoming and outgoing company telephone calls, handles e-mail, Web, wireless, and written interactions with customers. CCCs may handle sales, service, and customer care.

Chief privacy officers are senior-level company executives charged with advocating and ensuring that customers' and prospects' privacy rights are maintained.

CSR is a customer service representative generally working in a CCC.

Customer lifetime value (CLV) is the net present value of the future profits to be received from a given number of newly acquired or existing customers during a specified period of years. CLV is calculated by identifying the revenue stream over time, applying a retention rate for each year, subtracting relevant costs, and then applying a discount rate to gross profit. CLV takes into account how much the customer spends on each purchase with the firm and the resulting profit, how often the customer purchases from the firm, how likely the customer is to remain a customer in the future, how much it costs to serve the customer, and the organization's discount rate.

Customer relationship management (CRM) is the initiation, enhancement, and maintenance of mutually beneficial customer and partner long-term relationships through business intelligence-generated strategies based on the capture, storage, and analysis of information gathered from all customer and partner touch points and transaction processing systems. CRM is a process that maximizes customer value through ongoing marketing activity founded on intimate customer knowledge established through collection, management, and leverage of customer information and contact history.

Customization exists when a manufacturer designs a product or website to suit a customer's individualized needs.

Data marts are subsets of a data warehouse that contain less depth or breadth of information, which allows for more efficient analysis by functional, business unit, or geographic divisions. It is generated from data gleaned from a specific function.

Data mining is the process of using statistical techniques to uncover patterns, trends, correlations, or other relationships among variables in the data warehouse or data mart. Data mining involves sophisticated software containing statistical analysis tools.

Data warehouse is the repository for all relevant customer and prospect information. Almost anything related to a marketing activity can be included in the data warehouse, including information from each touch point, sales force input, and perhaps even survey data. It is a collection of databases in one integrated relationship file that allows for data mining relational exploration. The data warehouse is a database that contains all relevant customer (primary and secondary data) information, including history, product information, product return activity, marketing promotion, and campaign data.

Lifetime value (LTV) is the net present value of a customer's profitability throughout the customer–firm relationship.

Mass customization is a manufacturing and communications technique companies use to produce individually differentiated goods or messages on a mass basis, usually through technological means.

Opt-in agreements are when companies ask their customers for permission to open communications. When it is granted, customers are "opting in." This means they are willing to let the organization market to them, use their data to learn more about them in order to create more attractive marketing offers, or actually sell their data to someone else for similar efforts. They are agreeing to have their behavior tracked and receive company promotional data.

Opt-out agreements are when companies provide their customers the option to terminate communications at any time. Companies must manage these agreements to prevent other areas of the company or other value chain members from contacting the individual.

Permission-based marketing is when a firm asks a current or prospective customer for permission to contact and make product offers (usually via e-mail).

Personalization exists when the customer is a creator or co-creator of website content. Personalization occurs when a customer modifies a company's website to suit his or her own purposes.

RFM stands for *recency, frequency, and monetary value* and is an approach to compute a score for each customer based on how recently the customer purchased, how frequently the customer purchases, and how much revenue or profit the customer generates. The score is used to predict the customer's likely response to future marketing expenditures and efforts.

Second lifetime value (SLTV) is the second lifetime value that can be computed for a lost customer after a company recaptures or regains him or her.

Skew describes the value of a company's customer base in terms of whether or not the top customers account for the vast amount of profits (steep skew) or whether customer value does not vary widely (flat skew).

Touch point is any point of contact that a customer or prospect has with the company, including phone inquiries, Web applications, e-mail, outbound advertising and promotion, direct sales contacts, CCC interactions, fulfillment centers, merchandise return desks, or in-person transactions. If we extend the meaning of *customer* to include suppliers, distributors, dealers, employees, and so on, the notion of a touch point can be extended to "transaction processing systems."

Transaction processing systems consist of inventory, order entry, billing, and accounts receivable information.

Questions

1. Why is CRM a difficult business practice to define?
2. Most agree that CRM systems must do what three things well?
3. CRM systems enable organizations to focus on relationships as opposed to transactions. What is meant by this?
4. Comment on the correctness or incorrectness of the following statement: "Companies should make it their goal to attract the greatest number of customers. After all, every customer counts, and growing market share is an important measure of success."

5. Comment on the correctness or incorrectness of the following statement: "CRM is concerned with managing one's current customer base and is not concerned with the process of acquiring new customers."

6. CRM is said to be the major bulwark used in "defensive marketing." What is meant by "defensive marketing," and how does it differ from offensive marketing?

7. CRM focuses on building relationships. There are actually three types of relationships that exist among acquaintances, friends, and partners. What are the characteristics of each of these types, and what can organizations do to move their customers from acquaintances to partners?

8. Why are so many companies and organizations developing CRM systems today?

9. According to Peppers and Rogers, there are four basic steps in CRM to establish learning relationships with your customer. What are these steps? In your answer, be sure to describe what a learning relationship is.

10. What is the CRM "ecosystem"?

11. What is multichannel marketing?

12. Define the following important CRM terms: touch points, 360-degree view, customer lifetime value, customization, personalization, RFM.

13. It is said that the companies that will benefit most from CRM systems are those that have a "steep skew" and those whose businesses are characterized by "lost for good" rather than "always a share" models. What is meant by "steep skew" and "lost for good"?

Exercises

1. Describe any exceptionally good or bad experiences that you have had with company contact personnel in person, over the phone, or over the Internet.

2. Are there any companies, stores, or brands that you have contact with that you think are interested in establishing a relationship with you as opposed to merely selling you a product or service in single transactions? What characterizes these companies, stores, or brands? What have they done to indicate that they are interested in your long-term business as opposed to one-time transactions?

3. Do you belong to any point, loyalty, or frequency programs? Are they effective in maintaining or increasing your business? Do they increase your feelings of loyalty toward the company?

4. Describe any exceptionally good and/or exceptionally bad company websites.

The History and Development of CRM

THE CORE CRM PROCESS

1. Identify prospects that are similar to your current high-value customers.
2. Develop an acquisition campaign.
3. Establish a dialogue or collaborative communication with each customer.
4. Learn more about each customer by capturing additional information from each exchange.
5. Integrate all of the customer information gathered from multiple touch points.
6. Provide internal access to relevant customer information to those who need it.
7. Use this information to retain customers and build each relationship.

2.1 The Origins of CRM

The origins of CRM are varied and diverse. One would think that it would be easy to pinpoint the origins of a field coming to the forefront of business in the mid- to late 1990s. Not so. There are many different views as to what led to CRM as we know it today. Most see the roots of CRM in the following areas.

2.1a Relationship Marketing

Relationship marketing (the subject of Chapter 3) focuses on maintaining a continuous relationship with customers and building long-term bonds. Over time, a company learns more about the customer's needs and wants and is, therefore, able to provide more personalized and relevant one-to-one service. Relationship marketing, with its focus on customer relationships as opposed to one-time transactions, has been viewed as a paradigm shift that has reshaped the entire field of marketing. There are paybacks for both company and customers in such relationships, and, consequently, marketers' focus on relationships is expected to be very long term.

Many forces drove marketers to focus so intently on customer (and partner) relationships. First, technological advances in information technology (IT) made relationship marketing feasible by enabling companies to record details from every transaction and enter into a dialogue with their customers. Second, the large-scale growth of direct marketing enabled more and more companies to enter into one-to-one relationships with their customers. Third, marketing academicians pointed out that acquiring customers was only the first stage in the marketing process and that retaining customers and improving service performance required more attention. Finally, consultants such as Frederick F. Reichheld wrote a number of very influential articles stating that customer retention was the key to corporate profitability and that downward migration was even a greater cause of company losses.

Marketers introduced the concepts of trust and commitment toward one's partner to supplement the concept of satisfaction in attempting to explain the dynamics underlying long-term relationships. The theory underlying relationship marketing and the relevance of the concepts it has introduced have led many to consider it a discipline within the field of marketing.

Even though relationship marketing involves establishing one-to-one relationships with customers, it is not the same as one-to-one marketing. The purpose of one-to-one marketing through mass customization focuses on adapting a product or offering for a customer and is, in actuality, a product-centric approach. Relationship marketing is always a customer-centric approach. Relationship marketing and CRM focus on the maintenance of long-term relationships between customers and partners, they involve analytical and operational components, and they extend beyond functional borders. They also need to be encompassed by the entire enterprise. It should be kept in mind that CRM may identify customers and customer segments with which a company may prefer not to establish relationships—for example, customers who are unprofitable due to the fact that they buy only what is on sale, require a great deal of sales or technical support, or consistently return merchandise. Relationship marketing focuses on customers with whom you want to maintain relationships.

2.1b Marketing Research

Some feel that CRM had its origins in marketing research's customer satisfaction studies of the late 1970s and its relationship with **total quality management (TQM)** in the late 1980s. Marketing researchers measured customer satisfaction, and others in the company continuously tried to improve quality through TQM techniques. Value-added flowcharts were developed and analyzed, and those areas promising the greatest payoff were reengineered.

Marketing researchers may have planted some of the seeds from which CRM grew, but they had little to do with the information technologies that made CRM possible. In addition, marketing researchers must maintain the anonymity of respondents, and they do this by focusing on market segments as opposed to individuals. Their demographic, product usage, and attitudinal questions are the basis of their analytical focus, not individual names or customer identification numbers.

2.1c B2B Relationships

The existence of productive relationships in high-contact services markets, and within organizations themselves, led some to see the underlying process as having potential value in consumer mass markets. The underlying process involved relationships in which the two parties were acquainted, and, through dialogue, the associations became stronger and deeper. Many claim that B2B interactions between companies and their suppliers are the origins of the B2C CRM models that are so prevalent in the market today. Mirroring such relationships on a mass-marketing basis, however, required advances in IT so that information from customer contact could be collected and updated on a real-time basis.

2.1d Materials Resource Planning, SAP, and Enterprise Resource Planning

CRM is so dependent on IT that some see CRM as primarily an exercise in technology implementation.[1] **IT**, initially in the form of the database, enabled marketers to capture and access customer information and to communicate with customers one-to-one.

In the mid-1980s, **materials resource planning (MRP)** was introduced, and companies began to construct customer databases. MRP is an earlier version of ERP (enterprise resource planning). MRP focuses on production planning and inventory systems in order to manage manufacturing processes. ERP automates a company's system integration through a software application. ERP manages information for finance/accounting, manufacturing, sales, CRM, inventories, and so forth. ERP is usually an integrated relational database system. In the early 1990s, a company called **SAP** integrated traditional MRP functions with accounting, and customer data warehouses were established. Once this occurred, companies had the demographic, behavioral, and contact data necessary for CRM. SAP or "systems, applications, and products in data processing" is an established product line of enterprise software from the German company SAP AG. The company's most popular product is SAP ERP, which is used to manage business operations and customer service.

2.1e Customer Contact Centers

The domain of CRM has always been marketing—in particular, customer service and sales. In the late 1980s, telemarketing technology was built into the customer call center (CCC). In the early 1990s, customer service and support applications were introduced as well. According to J. G. Freeland, the first CRM initiatives were launched in the early 1990s and focused on improvements to the call center.[2] Other new technologies and evaluation metrics were developed to improve the handling of customer inquiries. For example, by accessing "trouble tickets" that registered past customer complaints, customer contact personnel could solve similar complaints. Using "screen-pops," customer contact personnel can effectively cross-sell or up-sell to customers while they are on the phone. Using the Web, customers can keep track of their orders. The ability of customers to use the Internet to contact company call centers led to the name "customer contact center." The transformation to "customer interaction center" will be discussed in Chapter 3.

2.1f Sales Force Automation

The customer service CRM point solution was followed by sales force automation (SFA), another point solution. SFA tools were developed and introduced to improve the capture of customer and prospect information and to provide the sales force with real-time information.

According to Jill Dyché:

> CRM's metamorphosis from a focused application into an enterprise-wide business initiative has everything to do with its beginnings in sales force automation. Sales force automation products were originally meant to improve sales force productivity and encourage salespeople to document and communicate their field activities. However, sales force automation products are becoming increasingly focused on cultivating customer relationships and improving customer satisfaction.[3]

Successful salespeople developed more and more customer information. When they left the organization, the information often went with them. Today's SFA tools control follow-up with potential customers, allow sales teams to collaborate in real time, identify client decision makers, track customer account histories, and monitor leads and follow-up strategies. SFA products also provide sales personnel with company presentations, handbooks, proposal and contract forms, and so on that they need to manage their business. SFA functions now reside on headquarters' Web servers instead of salespeople's laptops to ensure the information is the most current possible.

2.1g Campaign Management Tools

Just as electric cars are being developed and introduced because of high oil prices, CRM campaign management tools were introduced to contain the excessive costs associated with media buys for mass-marketing promotional campaigns. Initial CRM campaign management techniques were based on customer lists containing variables that companies could target for smaller, more focused promotional campaigns. Companies could plan, target, schedule, and measure responses to each campaign and modify future campaigns based on the results.

THEORY IN ACTION

How Kimberly-Clark Uses CRM to Manage More Than 2,300 Promotional Events Each Year

Kimberly-Clark, one of the world's largest packaged goods companies, was running thousands of promotions annually with individual retailers but was unable to measure its effectiveness or break down results by individual customer, product, or shipment. Executives could not determine if promotions were effective—resulting in more retailer loyalty, increasing shelf space, and increasing sales—or if promotional dollars were going to waste.

Executives decided to experiment with CRM on a small, specifically focused problem: tracking the expense and results of individual promotional programs by integrating promotional investments with shipments. The software is now central to the company's sales and marketing efforts being used by salespeople to design promotional programs for specific retailers and by marketers to develop promotional strategies. Using the CRM system, key account reps can coordinate promotional plans with retailers by assessing the likely financial results.

The CRM program at Kimberly-Clark not only includes collaborative tools enabling them to design and plan promotional campaigns online with retailers, but it also puts real-time customer behavior online along with analytical tools, enabling them to predict payback for their retailers.

D. K. Rigby and D. Ledingham, "CRM Done Right," *Harvard Business Review*, 82, 11 (November 2004): 118–129.

2.1h The Web and Channel Integration

Most CRM systems started out as **point solutions** satisfying the needs of a single department or function (similar to the Kimberly-Clark promotional CRM solution). Departments and functions used local databases, and none were linked. The data warehouse, a centralized cross-functional database, was introduced to provide a single vision of the customer. The customer data comes from all business areas, providing what is referred to as a 360-degree view of the customer or an integrated view of the customer (IVOC). **CRM suite** solutions were developed to integrate all of the point solutions, but they must be consistently upgraded as well. For example, with the growth of multichannel users, the focus of CRM expanded to include the Internet and, more recently, mobile commerce (m-commerce).

THEORY IN ACTION

How Molex Corporation Keeps Track of 15,000 Sales Opportunities at Any One Time

Molex is an Illinois-based company that manufactures and sells electronic and fiber-optic interconnection systems worldwide. Finding that e-mail and spreadsheets were not sufficient to keep track of 15,000 potential orders and sales opportunities at any one time, Molex installed a CRM system to manage its order pipeline in 2002. Now the company can pursue leads having the highest potential and avoid having multiple parts of the company working on similar or related programs for the same customer at the same time without even knowing it! The CRM system has the following benefits for Molex:

- Improved order management
- More precise sales targets
- Better global coordination of inventory
- Better global coordination of pricing
- Earlier recognition of high-value sales opportunities
- Five percent increase in revenues
- Improved budget planning

D. K. Rigby and D. Ledingham, "CRM Done Right," *Harvard Business Review*, 82, 11 (November 2004): 118–129.

Much of today's CRM efforts include channel integration geared toward gathering customer information from each touch point and integrating it into the customer's profile to provide seamless service across all channels. Thus, companies have moved beyond the simple customer database into systems that link the database to call centers and Internet systems, allowing direct interaction with data capture, data updating, and data availability for future interactions. The Web has shaken up the ways that companies do business.

2.1i Diffusion of Personal Computers and Analytical CRM

The diffusion of the personal computer meant that every desktop had the capability to analyze customer data. This led to company divisions having the ability to manipulate their own customer data, develop their own marketing programs, and assess their own performance, without regard to what headquarters was doing. Divisions became empowered. While this did sometimes cause divisions to work at cross-purposes with one another and with headquarters, the diffusion of personal computers enabled those closest to the customer to develop and assess program and campaign performance in a new way.

As J. Peel discussed, statistical programs such as SPSS and SAS, in conjunction with the low costs of computing provided by the introduction of personal computers, laid the foundation for analytical CRM.[4] When bar codes and client-server architecture were introduced, analysts were able to study product movement by time of day, product's placement, and so on. *Data mining* was the term coined to describe analytical approaches to extracting information from data warehouses. The benefits of data warehouses were not limited to outbound marketing offers; they also enabled customer contact personnel to identify the value of each customer and treat them accordingly.

2.1j The Success of Direct-Response Marketing

Direct-response marketing efforts, such as toll-free calling and direct mail, provided for the identification of individual target prospects, personalized communications and messages, and measures of success. E-mail–based marketing followed directly in the footsteps of these earlier, successful techniques. Through direct marketing, not only personalized communication but dialogue was also possible.

2.1k Relational Databases

Relational databases allowed companies to identify, access, manipulate, and share customer information across departments. Databases contained customer transaction histories, all customer–company contacts, demographic and behavior information, and customer responses to company campaigns. Customer information could be supplemented with external information and analyzed quickly. Relational databases ushered in the age of **database marketing**, enabling firms outside the direct mail or direct marketing field to enter into relationships with their customers. Airlines established database marketing programs, followed by charge card and long-distance phone companies.[5] Database marketing was no longer confined to direct-mail organizations.

THEORY IN ACTION

How United Way Uses e-CRM to Personalize Relationships with Donors

United Way of Greater Toronto funds a network of 200 health and social service agencies and depends on campaigns to drive its fundraising and build donor relationships. To maximize funds available to social service agencies, United Way needs to minimize its expenditures on attracting donors and capturing donor dollars. United Way looked to e-CRM as a way to speed up the collection of donations and lower campaign expenditures, while at the same time improving relationships with donors through enhanced communication, interaction, and personalization.

United Way selected an e-business software solution that enables it to automate donor and follow-up campaigns. The software generates personalized campaign messages, processes online pledges, customizes thank-you messages, and processes donor feedback. Individual customer feedback is entered into a donor's profile, enabling United Way to customize individual customer contact completely. Continued dialogue with donors increases the likelihood of continued support.

D. E. Sharp, *Customer Relationship Management Systems Handbook* (New York: Auerbach Publications, 2003).

		Direct		Indirect
Interaction Frequency	High	EASY Banks, retail stores		INTERMEDIATE Packaged goods companies
	Low	INTERMEDIATE Computer stores		DIFFICULT Auto and furniture manufacturers
		Direct		Indirect
		Customer Interaction		

Figure 2.1 Difficulty or Ease of Database Construction

Source: Winer, R. S. (2001). "A Framework for Customer Relationship Management" in *California Management Review*, Vol. 43, No. 3 (2001), pp. 89–105. © 2001 by the The Regents of the University of California. Reprinted by permission of the University of California Press.

P. Kotler explains, "As customer database marketing grew, several different names came to describe it, including *individualized marketing, customer intimacy, technology-enabled marketing, dialogue marketing, interactive marketing, permission marketing*, and *one-to-one marketing*."[6]

Figure 2.1 provides a general framework regarding the ease or difficulty for companies attempting to construct customer databases. Database construction is easiest for organizations that have frequent and direct customer interaction (banks, retail stores) and most difficult for organizations that have infrequent and indirect customer interaction (auto and furniture manufacturers). It is of intermediate difficulty for companies that have frequent but indirect customer interactions (packaged goods companies) or for companies that have infrequent but direct customer interactions (computer stores).[7]

2.11 Industrial and Services Marketing

Some feel that CRM had its roots in the industrial and services marketing practice and literature. Industrial marketers looked at interaction theories and relationship building, focusing on trust and commitment issues. Service marketers looked at service quality, satisfaction, and the need to maintain one's customer base. Service marketers were also the first to offer a commonly adopted alternative to the 4 P's (product, place, promotion, and price) that had been the gold standard for decades. Service marketers added people, physical environment, and process to the mix. For CRM purposes, the addition of these extra P's is notable because they encompass the need for organizations to focus on them to generate repeat business from the current customer base.

2.2 CRM: Why Now?

2.2a The Increase in Competitors and Products

In the early 1990s, the managing director of Mitsubishi in the United States lamented that there was not only an increase in the number of competitors, but there also was an increase in the number of competitors that offered exceptionally high-quality automobiles. Benchmarking, Six Sigma, **CAD-CAM systems**, and cross-functional teams all contributed to the rising number of high-quality cars in the marketplace. Consumers not only faced an unlimited number of new choices but an unlimited number of new, *high-quality* choices. It was becoming more difficult for companies to stand out and differentiate themselves through their products and brands alone. And if they did, their differential advantage was short-lived given competitors' ability to match and exceed their product quality improvements.

Companies needed to do something to hold on to their customers in the face of increasing and higher-quality competition. That something was the creation of a bond between themselves and their customers that would instill loyalty. Loyalty would serve as a defense against the plethora of new, high-quality products continually being introduced by competitors, and CRM systems would be the technique that would enable these companies to help develop this bond with their customers. When one is loyal to a company's products, buying decisions become quicker and easier, and risk is reduced.

CRM can be implemented through the effective use of a number of strategies that are possible because of technology. CRM makes it possible for companies to distinguish themselves from their competitors in an area that cannot be easily copied, since it has its roots in corporate culture. CRM focuses on understanding customers so that identification, acquisition, development, and, when necessary, win-back can be developed and implemented effectively. In addition, CRM enables the most appropriate selection of distribution and information channels.

Identification refers to segmenting and then targeting certain markets. This can be done by analyzing one's customer database to profile the high-profit segments and then developing strategies to acquire similar prospects. Once acquired, companies can then "develop" their customer base by **cross-selling** and trading them up to higher-margin items. Encouraging referrals from this base is another aspect of development. If high-value customers defect, companies should have strategies in place that will help win them back. Often these win-back strategies are lower prices or higher-value offerings.

2.2b The Erosion of Traditional Marketing Communication Methods

The largest age-cohort market segment ever seen in the United States—baby boomers—came of age in the 1990s. Baby boomers were the first generation to grow up with television, along with its commercials, promotions, and, more recently, infomercials designed as noncommercial programming and product placements. Baby boomers experienced what no other segment had experienced en masse: information overload and a cynicism toward mass-marketing promises.

From the 1950s until the early 1980s, there were three major television networks in the United States. The evening news was the only outlet for information on international events and most "breaking" domestic stories. Today, of course, there are hundreds of channel alternatives to the "Big Three" networks. Likewise, print media has proliferated. Mass-media magazines from the 1950s, such as *Look, Life, Reader's Digest, Redbook*, and the *Saturday Evening Post*, have disappeared or transformed into more targeted audience publications. In the 1950s, mass-media magazines existed along with a few special-interest magazines. Today, there are over 20,000 hardcopy magazines available for the U.S. reader, and almost 25,000 magazines and journals can now be found online. Clearly, mass-media publications have been replaced with more targeted approaches toward ever-smaller market segments. Satellite radio had the same effect on radio station alternatives as well. With an abundance of these channel and print alternatives, all with their own hype, and given 40 to 60 years of such experience, baby boomers have had it with the monologue.

There is also a lot more "noise" in the marketplace today than ever before, and many feel that this makes it more difficult for a company to promote its new products and brands. For example, in addition to hypermarkets, boutiques, category busters, and kiosks, consumers can buy through home shopping networks and stores on the Internet. This implies that it is getting increasingly difficult for companies to establish and market new products and brands using traditional approaches. The consumer is bombarded with too much information from too many sources (both domestic and foreign) for a single message to make much difference.

To reach them, companies must engage customers in a dialogue. IT again comes into play because IT-enabled channels, such as the Internet, allow for such a dialogue. Some feel that technology-facilitated conversation and service will allow companies to cut through the market chaos and establish binding relationships with their customers.[8]

2.2c Changes in the Pace of Life

Dual-income households, which were a minority in the 1950s and 1960s, now comprise the vast majority of families. This has resulted in increased pressure on shopping time. The Internet has made it possible for consumers to become quickly educated on product and brand alternatives and their respective attributes. Automobile dealers are now faced with consumers who know exactly what their costs are and exactly how much they are willing to pay for an automobile. Banks are faced with consumers who know precisely what interest rates alternative charge cards carry and the interest rates that alternative mortgage brokers charge. Consumers are demanding quicker and better service.

2.2d The Internet and Multichannel Usage

Some expect the Internet to replace traditional channels in some industries because of cost advantages. For example, a bank saves 80 percent of its costs by doing business online. The more environments a company can provide, the richer its customers' experiences are likely to be.[9] Eddie Bauer found that customers who used the "channel triumvirate" of brick-and-mortar stores, catalogs, and the Internet bought five times more than others.[10] Websites and brick-and-mortar facilities reinforce each other. A company with a brick-and-click environment has an advantage over companies offering only one or the other. R. Verma, Z. Iqbal, and R. Baran found that e-brokerages that also have brick-and-mortar facilities (such as Charles Schwab) have a great deal more success than e-traders without such walk-in facilities.[11] C. K. Prahalad and V. Ramaswamy found that two-thirds of Schwab's customers are still recruited through its brick-and-mortar branches.[12]

Channels of communication are multiplying. 3G and 4G mobile technologies and social media are replacing fixed-line telephone and personal computers as the primary communication access channels for businesses. Companies today, however, are finding it difficult to manage even single channels. A study by Data Monitor found that nearly 9 percent of abandoned online transactions could have been salvaged. The abandonment caused a loss in e-commerce revenue of $10.9 billion.[13] Why were so many virtual shopping carts abandoned at checkout? A survey by PayPal found that nearly half (46%) claimed high shipping charges more than any other reason led to their abandoned carts. Many retailers have subsequently jumped on the free shipping bandwagon.[14]

E-mail is the preferred method of commercial communication by 74 percent of all online adults. Short message service (SMS) and wireless access protocol (WAP) have joined e-mail, and integrative devices, such as 3G and 4G phones, GPS technologies, and social networking, are becoming the primary ways companies and consumers keep in touch. Thus, companies must develop systems to handle effectively the number of channels their customers use to transact business. Some feel that portal software is the company's answer to the proliferation of channels used by their customers.[15] With a customer relationship portal, the various types of customer contacts are blended into a common cue. A **portal** provides a convergence of customer identification data, product and service information, and a customer's transaction history.

While a company's call center handles inbound and outbound calls and is generally viewed as a corporate cost center, companies are developing multichannel contact centers that provide customers with meaningful interactions. J. Peel argued that traditional call centers will diminish as IP-based communications become more and more common.[16] Thus, it becomes a basis for strategic advantage for the corporation. Companies need to be capable of handling any mode of communication the consumer chooses in both a synchronous and asynchronous manner, in live and automated formats. Multichannel customer contact is the key to CRM strategy focusing on the customer experience across the entire customer life cycle.

2.3 Organizations' Experiences with CRM

The best entry-level CRM software package is the one you actually use.
—Phil Arduzzi, a computer network software installer in Rocky River, Ohio

Have organizations been successful with their CRM programs and installations? When asked, companies have answered "yes," "no," and "don't know," with the last being the most common response. Success is difficult to determine if success metrics have not been determined in advance of CRM installation and implementation.

S. A. Brown and M. Gulycz reported on a business survey that showed that two-thirds of all companies lacked techniques to measure the business value of CRM, and nearly one-fourth defined CRM as a set of tools and techniques.[17] Without performance metrics, companies' claims that CRM does not work cannot be considered valid. In addition, defining CRM as only technology indicates that many business executives have a limited understanding of the CRM construct.

To improve their bottom lines, companies need to achieve the benefits of CRM (Table 2.1). While certain products claiming to provide CRM might be fads, the need for companies to communicate with and manage their customer base gets to the very core of any organization. Thus, CRM is not a fad but rather a business philosophy with proven benefits. Further, any company that

Table 2.1 **Quantitative Benefits of CRM Using Revenue Enhancement Metrics (Percent)**

Acquisition/prospect increase	27–45
Expense per convert decrease	30–60
Renewal rate increase	5–15
Cross-sell/up-sell rate increase	3–25
Share of wallet increase	3–25
Service and churn decrease	30–80
Campaign cycle time decrease	50–70
Campaign conversion increase	20–50
Win-back increase	25–33
Partners' market penetration increase	3–5
Mailing cost decrease	10–40
Marketing overhead decrease	8–10

S. A. Brown and M. Gulycz, *Performance-Driven CRM: How to Make Your Customer Relationship Management Vision a Reality* (Mississauga, Canada: John Wiley & Sons Canada, 2002).

does not have a CRM system is at a competitive disadvantage, for customers are beginning to expect it. If they cannot get the service they want from your organization, they will switch to an organization where they can. In addition, the implemented CRM programs can be all-encompassing and expensive, or they can focus on a single function. The returns on all-encompassing CRM systems are more difficult to determine. Even quantifying the costs of installation has proven challenging for many companies.

Companies, even Fortune 500 firms, can be naive when it comes to their CRM initiatives. For example, Gartner's Beth Eisenfeld cited a large telecommunications firm that spent $7 million on a CRM marketing and customer segmentation package and then did nothing to integrate the software into its business practices. It just sat back and waited for the benefits to show up.[18]

For many companies, CRM has meant nothing but massive outlays on information technology and the collection of ever-increasing customer data gathered from every touch point. What matters, however, is what companies do with the data. "At root, CRM is a business strategy which seeks to optimize value from customers," says John Radcliffe, vice president of research at Gartner.

Companies are frequently surveyed by institutions in the CRM field, and the findings provide further evidence of confusion about whether or not CRM has fulfilled its promise. More than half of all companies investing in CRM consider it a disappointment, according to several recent surveys.[19] In a study of 100 large companies, only 52 percent reported achieving their business goals.[20] Allegedly, 70 percent of all CRM projects fail.[21] Reports have also been disappointing with respect to specific-function CRM applications such as campaign management, call center management, and marketing analytics. According to a recent study, only 35 percent of the managers responsible for those operations were satisfied with attained objectives.[22]

The shortcomings in implementing CRM programs have become abundantly clear. Targeted revenue goals, for example, are often not achieved. Most expect at least a 10 percent improvement in revenue, but many U.S. corporations are experiencing half that. In addition, timetables are often not met, and budgeted costs have exceeded estimates by 300 percent in some cases. Failure to achieve revenue forecasts, budget overruns, and poor performance of CRM can lead employees to stop using the system, further eroding performance. This was the case at a leading computer wholesaler and retailer, where telephone sales representatives stopped entering data. Some companies have abandoned CRM initiatives as a result of such problems. Extensive research that we have conducted into this problem and reported in Table 2.2 indicates the major reasons companies fail in their CRM efforts.

Perhaps the majority of firms feel that the results achieved from their CRM efforts to date have been disappointing. It should be kept in mind, however, that their original expectations may have been too high and, with more CRM experience, they may achieve excellent results in the end. In addition, most companies have gone into CRM efforts without clearly stated goals, making their assessment of CRM failure somewhat specious, since there are no standards against which to measure results. Such business goals should be quantified and should include metrics dealing with acquiring more customers, reducing high-value customer defections, increasing revenue/profit from each customer, increasing the number of services each customer uses, squeezing value from the low-profit customers, and increasing cross-sell, among others.

Further, companies continue to introduce technology-based systems without first developing return on investment (ROI), user acceptability (both in-house and outside users), and customer satisfaction metrics. It has been reported that the success rate of CRM can be increased from 15 percent to 70 percent if a proper CRM strategy is adopted and CRM is "done right."[23] Nonetheless, the many reports of poor results are surprising given the advances made in data technology, new **middleware** software that can link disparate databases, e-commerce, and targeted marketing programs.

Table 2.2 **Reasons for Unsatisfactory Outcomes When CRM Solutions Are Used**

- Inadequate support from top management
- No CRM champion in the organization
- Inadequate financial commitment
- Supply chain partners not included in the effort
- No specification regarding who "owns" the data
- Poor data quality
- Technology becomes the focus instead of the customer
- Lack of establishment of performance metrics
- Lack of change-management initiatives
- Not "selling" the customer-centric vision to employees
- Not directing incentives to the sales force and others who are rewarded for immediate sales as opposed to developing relationships that may pay off in the future
- Not integrating the customer-centric vision into position descriptions, training programs, and mentoring efforts
- The company's CRM efforts don't create enough new value for customers
- Not applying basic CRM principles such as cost elimination for servicing low-profit customers and investing in high-value customers
- Trying to develop a grandiose 360-degree CRM system initially instead of developing quick-win CRM solutions for specific customers or campaigns and then building up
- Not viewing CRM as a process involving activities across all functional areas

There is another side to the issue of whether or not CRM systems have been successful. A CRM Community.com survey in August 2000 of over 900 of its members showed that 72 percent rated their CRM projects as "successful" or better. A 2004 study conducted by *InfoWorld* showed that the majority of respondents garnered between a 51 percent and a 500 percent return on their CRM investment and one-third reaped returns above 500 percent.[24] In a span of 18 months, Lowe's Home Improvement achieved a 265 percent ROI on its $11 million CRM investment. It is also reported that Charles Schwab recouped its large investment in CRM systems in less than two years. The Training and Development Agency for Schools raised inquiries about teaching by 50 percent through development of a CRM system.[25]

2.4 Implementing CRM and Overcoming Barriers

If I had to say what the Number One failure is, it's not having consensus of what CRM is and what it means to the organization. I walk into organizations and say, "What does CRM mean to you?" And they say, "Well, we're implementing X vendor's product." They don't give me why CRM is important.

—Elizabeth Roche, Vice President of Enterprise Application
Strategies Practice of Meta Group Incorporated

Introducing CRM systems into any organization requires and creates a great deal of change. The implications of such change for the organization and its stakeholders should not be underestimated. Global studies of companies that use CRM usually show that technology, the need to replace or integrate existing systems, or extensive setup times are not major barriers to effective

CRM implementation. Rather, the real barriers appear to be corporate culture, employee attitudes, organizational structure, and the lack of a strategic plan for the CRM system. Included in the last factor are the lack of quantifiable goals and objectives, integration with business unit strategies, and the lack of program-performance metrics. Thus, the main problems companies have with effective CRM implementation reside with the "software" side of the business (skills, strategy, structure, and style) as opposed to the "hardware."

CRM will affect the ways that things have been traditionally done. For example, a **customer-centric** orientation replaces the mass-marketing ideology of the past 50 years. Market share as an effectiveness measure must be replaced by customer profitability. Certain traditional market segments may be deemphasized or eliminated if they prove to lack profit potential. Market researchers must begin focusing more on mining internal as opposed to external sources of data. Marketing managers must begin focusing on bonding efforts as opposed to only acquisition efforts. Mass marketing may be deemphasized in favor of direct marketing efforts. The focus on synchronous customer satisfaction requires a much different organizational structure than the one in the past.

CRM systems arguably interface with a larger group of stakeholders with more diverse needs than any other business system. This stakeholder group makes it more difficult for the organization to effect the many cultural, psychological, and structural changes needed for successful CRM implementation. Executives worry about the system's payback, managers worry about the CRM implementation process, salespeople are skeptical about yet another solution du jour, and customers worry about privacy. Everyone worries about learning the system while carrying out day-to-day activities.

The following are the major ways organizations can overcome the barriers to effective CRM implementation:

1. Communication
2. Integration
3. Foresight in relating CRM functions to the tactics that drive success in their industry

Communication includes the following components:

1. The organization must adopt a relationship marketing philosophy. This philosophy must become embedded in the minds of managers, departments, functions, and employees.
2. The organization must detail the benefits of the CRM system to its employees and also detail what they personally will gain from it.
3. The top executive must communicate his or her support at the start of the CRM initiative and maintain support throughout the development and implementation stages.

Integration includes the following components:

1. Business strategies must be integrated and serve as drivers of the CRM initiative rather than the other way around.
2. If separate "quick-results" CRM projects are initiated, they should be coordinated and integrated into a single CRM vision.
3. IT and business managers must be integrated into start-up teams and work together throughout the development of the CRM system.
4. Customer data must be integrated.

Tactical considerations include the following components:

1. Customer contact center issues must be clearly addressed in the form of service blueprints, hiring, training, and image maintenance.
2. Product selection
3. Customer analytics

THEORY IN ACTION

One Company's Experience with CRM

ENMAX Energy distributes electricity to more than 400,000 residential and commercial customers in Alberta, Canada. In a newly deregulated environment, the company faced competition for the first time. It had to become customer-centric and increase customer satisfaction and loyalty by providing an excellent experience for customers every time they made contact with the company. How did it proceed?

First, ENMAX established a new corporate vision that focused on excellence and core values such as a customer focus, innovation, and employee support. Second, ENMAX decided to roll out its CRM system in a single area first—sales—since it was the most critical area in the business. Third, to encourage quick adoption, ENMAX assigned a CRM champion—the top sales executive—to encourage usage. Fourth, ENMAX selected a CRM product to meet its specific business-process requirements. Fifth, ENMAX tracks customer information no matter which touch point the customer uses to contact the company and records the information. This enables them to engage each customer individually.

D. E. Sharp, *Customer Relationship Management Systems Handbook* (New York: Auerbach Publications, 2003).

2.4a The Relationship Marketing Philosophy

THEORY IN ACTION

To a United Pilot, The Friendly Skies Are a Point of Pride

Captain Denny Flanagan is a rare bird in today's frustration-filled air travel world—a pilot who goes out of his way to make flying fun for passengers. When pets travel in cargo compartments, the United Airlines veteran snaps pictures of them with his cell phone camera, then shows owners that their animals are on board. In the air, he has flight attendants raffle off 10 percent discount coupons and unopened bottles of wine. He writes notes to first-class passengers and elite-level frequent flyers on the back of his business cards, addressing them by name and thanking them for their business. If flights are delayed or diverted to other cities because of storms, Flanagan tries to find a McDonald's where he can order 200 hamburgers or a snack shop that has apples or bananas he can hand out. And when unaccompanied children are on his flights, he personally calls parents with reassuring updates.

United has supported Flanagan's efforts. The airline supplies the airplane trading cards he hands out as passengers board, plus books, wine, and discount coupons he has flight attendants give away. "He's a great ambassador for the company," says Graham Atkinson, United's executive vice and president and "Chief Customer Officer," who is leading an effort to boost customer service. He hopes more pilots and airport workers will adopt some of Flanagan's techniques.

S. McCartney, "To a United Pilot, The Friendly Skies Are a Pilot of Pride," *Wall Street Journal* (August 28, 2007), A1.

All of the databases and technological systems in the world cannot instill the necessary customer focus in employees. This focus must be engendered from the day employees of all levels join the organization. Unfortunately, it is sometimes easier to create a culture from scratch than it is to change the culture.

CRM systems often face stiff resistance, since the CRM system instills a different focus: a focus on individual customers. Shifting the focus from products to customers is a major challenge because most companies have a product manager system and their sales force has incentives based on selling products as opposed to servicing customers.

Many companies that have introduced CRM systems obtain valuable information through their customer contact centers: information regarding customer opinion of the brand or product and even suggestions for improvement. This is a CRM success only if marketing, sales, and engineering personnel act on the data. One of America's largest manufacturing firms, selling thousands of products to consumers and industrial buyers alike, cannot compute the value of individual industrial customers because the data resides in product as opposed to customer silos and cannot be merged under current corporate systems.

In some organizations, those who should use CRM information do not. Some point to the lack of marketer interest in the data generated by their own customer contact centers. In other organizations, political infighting precludes the dissemination of information to those who want it. As previously discussed, customer data should be available to everyone in the organization who can benefit by having access to it. Many organizations have expanded such stakeholders to include anyone in the distribution channel (suppliers, distributors, and dealers) as well as customers themselves.

M. Georgiadis and K. Lane of McKinsey & Company offer numerous suggestions on how to implement CRM in the organization to make it a high-performing customer-centric endeavor. Senior management must ensure adequate funding and integrate CRM activities across businesses and geographies, while determining the amount of empowerment frontline groups should have in dealings with customers. They recommend that a centrally located statistical group analyze customer data to identify opportunities in cross-selling, customer life cycle management, and channel management, and then decentralized tactical groups monitor the success of individual programs and conduct tests to improve program impact. Then, pivotal "integrators" develop the actual CRM-based programs based on statistical findings from the centralized statistical group. Once the structure is in place, customer-centric skills must be developed throughout the organization, which can be accomplished through recruiting, training, and compensation linked to customer-specific metrics. These metrics should also be embedded in performance reviews. Finally, processes should be in place to ensure that CSRs have access to all information relevant to a customer who calls and incentives given to increasing the value of high-value customers.[26]

2.4b How Organizations Should Communicate the Benefits of CRM

More than half of all companies are dissatisfied with their CRM system. Many feel the major problem is that companies do not attend to the organizational challenges with the CRM initiative. The wide variety of stakeholders who must work together to define needs and ensure that the CRM system serves the entire enterprise makes implementation a daunting task.

Organizations should commit from the top but motivate from the bottom. This means that communication from the top down is imperative for CRM success. If managers and their staff have to be retrained, if legacy systems have to be scratched in favor of new databases and procedures, and if many are asked to perform new roles in different departments, they must be told how such changes will be mutually beneficial. If marketing and sales bonuses will now be based on retained customers' profitability as opposed to just the number of new acquisitions, then the case for such a strategic change must be well laid out. Involve everyone throughout the project, and foster enthusiasm by working with key influencers in each department.

Communication is not a one-way street, and bottom-up information should be encouraged and examined carefully. CRM developers' responsiveness to user requests can lead to favorable assessments of the CRM configuration and willingness to adopt the system. Gaining user approval is necessary, since user resistance is one of the major reasons enterprise resource planning (ERP) implementations failed.[27] According to McKinsey & Company, CRM configuration problems account for an estimated two-thirds of CRM project failures.

Organizational behavior suggests that employees will change only if they know why an effort is important and what is in it for them. For example, salespeople must be shown how a CRM initiative could reduce the number of processes they deal with and target successful salespeople as early adopters. Their success gives the CRM effort the credibility that drives widespread adoption.[28] Companies must consider adding support programs as well as helping employees during what, for many, will be a difficult transition.

2.4c Top Executive Support

Top management must be involved from the very beginning in setting philosophy, managing culture change, and presenting a detailed case for CRM benefits. Obviously, to do all of this work, they must "buy into" the future promised by a CRM orientation. A survey released in July 2002 by the New York Office of Accenture showed that CRM software failed to work effectively because of inadequate support from top management. Three-fourths of executives surveyed felt that CRM fails because of flawed planning. One of the reasons most frequently cited for the shortfall of CRM programs was no long-term CRM vision. Many feel that failures in CRM implementation and usage are actually failures in communication. The top executive most effectively communicates the case for CRM, as communication should begin and be maintained at this level. The success of Harrah's CRM efforts was attributed, in part, to the fact that Harrah's CEO had a CRM person reporting directly to him.

Things never go completely smoothly when installing such complex systems, and the benefits may take time to accrue even once they are running. Therefore, it is important that top executives not become disillusioned and begin to question their decision to implement such a system. Reducing the scope or not signing off on budgetary requests will only make others question the decision for CRM system adoption.

2.4d Business Strategies

It may seem strange that business strategy often does not precede the development of CRM systems, given that these systems may cost tens of millions of dollars and take years to complete.

Companies develop strategies before developing new products that cost much less than this. However, many companies already had in place a variety of systems and procedures that were forerunners of CRM systems, even though they were not called that. Functional heads within the organization (sales, marketing, customer service, and marketing research) primarily developed these systems, and they were intended to be function-specific. None were corporate-wide, and the top executive seldom got involved with these approaches. When vendors started selling CRM solutions and CRM "suites," companies became vulnerable to putting the technological cart before the strategic horse.

IT is a tool, but too often in the area of CRM, it becomes the plan. Early CRM initiatives were built by technical specialists and focused on platform technology rather than on solving managers' problems. Processes and strategies must be in place to determine the type of system needed, what data to collect and analyze, and how to analyze it. The customer relationship strategic gap (i.e., where the company currently is and where the company wants to be) must be calculated. This can best be done by conducting a specific type of exploratory research called a "situational analysis," which consists of in-depth interviews with a representative sample of people inside and outside the organization who deal with customers. The latter would include distributors, dealers, suppliers, and anyone else who can add to customer service.

Most organizations lack a central enterprise-wide CRM strategy and, therefore, become focused on the problems faced by individual departments. They then introduce a plethora of functional solutions that do not really relate to one another and do not provide the institutional synergy that should be the goal. A CRM business plan should be developed, and a business analysis should be conducted showing how CRM system features will relate to each business goal and enable each goal to be accomplished. As an example, the following list might be business goals in the business plan:

- Increasing the profit from each customer
- Increasing the number of items sold annually to each customer
- Increasing the acceptance of new products by the customer base
- Increasing customer satisfaction
- Improving response rates to promotional campaigns
- Increasing the speed of campaign development
- Decreasing the costs involved in campaign development and assessment
- Decreasing the number of employees and time involved in solving problem tickets
- Improving the percent of the customer base that trades up to the next item

Keep in mind that business and marketing strategies are most effective when tied into the dynamics of the industry. For example, mobile phone service providers concentrate on "**feeding the funnel**" and on developing strategies based on acquiring new customers. Only later do they implement strategies to retain customers and reduce **churn**. Mass merchandisers, retail banks, and airlines already have a large base of customers. Consequently, they develop strategies based on maintaining customer loyalty, cross-selling, and **up-selling**.

2.4e "Quick-Results" CRM Projects

While technical integration is important, it does not guarantee performance integration. Organizations must integrate technologically, structurally, and strategically in order to possess a CRM system that benefits all—including, of course, customers. The ultimate goal of CRM systems is to increase the value of the customer relationship. Too many CRM installations lose sight of this. The focus is often on systems, techniques, and technologies instead. Marketing, sales, customer service, advertising, and IT departments may all want different things from their CRM system, things that must be integrated into a system that is compatible for everyone.

The issue of whether an organization should introduce and develop its CRM system in the form of a one-shot "big bang" or CRM suite solution versus a series of "quick hits" or manageable pieces is debatable. Recent opinions seem to favor the latter approach. If the piecemeal, quick-hit, or phased approach is used, then the key to successful implementation is integration and coordination of all the pieces.

THEORY IN ACTION

Verizon Successfully Introduced CRM by Starting Small

When Verizon adopted CRM, they started with small projects in small regions. The former senior vice president and CMO of Verizon's retail markets group, Maura Breen, had this to say:

> An important question we had to answer was how to size CRM for a $22 billion business with 25 million customers without boiling the ocean. We're taking a phased approach, defining manageable projects in specific geographies that can be measured for ROI, and then using the learning to expand the effort. The first phase creates an experience for high-value customers in the call center, our most heavily trafficked channel. We're looking at how to make it easier to provide more of Verizon's products and services on one call to customers who need them.
>
> The lesson is clear: Start with a limited customer group (high-value customers), a single business process (the call center), and a limited area (specific geographies), all selected so that they can be measured for ROI.

F. Newell, *Why CRM Doesn't Work: How to Win By Letting Customers Manage the Relationship* (Princeton, NJ: Bloomberg, 2003).

CRM's complexity is due to the range of usage—the number of departments that will be using it—and the quantity of functions.[29] Regarding the quantity of functions, campaign management and SFA are difficult because of the number of functions each requires. Computing customer value, developing customer profiles, monitoring call center effectiveness, and so on—although not easy to compute—are easier in the sense that the domain of each is more restricted. If the phased approach is used, the development initiatives determining the sequence of work should be based on cost, benefit, feasibility, and time to produce. SFA, campaign management, and customer contact center productivity measurement software pit sales against marketing against customer service in terms of who gets theirs first. While a cost-benefit analysis can help prioritize the phasing in of these CRM functions, the problem of integrating them remains.

The "quick results" term is used when CRM functions, once developed, are released incrementally. This phased introduction sequence benefits the organization in a number of ways. First, it combats disenchantment that can set in when CRM results are not forthcoming within a reasonable time frame. Second, users get to sample and gain experience with small sections of the CRM system. This avoids information overload and culture shock. Third, users can provide input that can help develop future CRM modules.

2.4f Including Both IT and Business Unit Managers

Poor returns on many companies' CRM systems cannot be blamed on CRM systems per se but rather on the general difficulty of cross-functional IT integration. Sales and marketing personnel have often felt that there was a "disconnect" between what they expected from IT and what they actually received. Not only is it difficult to integrate systems and technologies, which generally results in missed deadlines, but the sales and marketing culture is different from IT culture, which makes communication difficult.

When evaluating companies' success or lack of success with their CRM systems, it is valuable to compare it with companies' success or lack of success with their IT projects in general. K. Thompson, L. Ryals, S. Knox, and S. Maklan reported on a series of studies concerning the success or failure of IT systems. In one study, only about 10 percent of the 400 firms interviewed said their IT installation had been successful. Another study found that three-fourths of IT projects were either not completed or not used when they were completed.[30] A report in *IEEE Software* found that approximately 15 percent of all company IT projects were cancelled before they delivered anything, and between 17 percent and 22 percent were considered unsuccessful. On the other hand, between 48 percent and 55 percent of delivered IT projects were considered successful.[31]

McKinsey & Company pointed out that executives with other primary responsibilities are often assigned to take charge of the CRM effort on a temporary basis.[32] Just as product managers cannot be expected to take charge temporarily of a new product under development effectively, managers with bottom-line responsibility will not have the resources to lead a CRM installation. A variety of people representing numerous business functions must collaborate to define, deliver, and deploy a CRM system effectively.

Experience has shown that simply relying on IT personnel to get everything right is foolish. Likewise, overcompensating with a team comprised primarily of business specialists will not work either. McKinsey & Company suggested that instead of holding businesspeople accountable for determining the requirements of a CRM system and IT personnel for developing it, companies should make both parties responsible for all aspects. A "receiving team," consisting of IT and business personnel, should provide the business case and the usability requirements. The "sending team" defines a solution and delivers it and should consist of IT and business personnel. Implicit in this approach is the continuous involvement of future CRM system users as opposed to their being involved only at the beginning and end of the project.[33]

J. Dyché suggested that a program management office (PMO) be formed to expedite and coordinate the development of an organization's CRM system. The function of the PMO, generally located in the IT department, is to divide the project into manageable chunks containing repetitive tasks (coding, design, testing) and assign each chunk to a project manager. Each project manager is responsible for the goals, budget, and deliverables in his or her area. By putting a PMO in charge of coordination, individual project teams can concentrate on their specific deliverables.[34]

Whether the McKinsey approach or the PMO approach is used, the effort should be preceded by an impact analysis that studies the impact the CRM system will have on current ones (**legacy systems**). Then, the IT staff can develop the appropriate linkages necessary for data to be exchanged across corporate systems.

As companies move toward a customer-centric approach, IT has a major role to play in developing the systems that will monitor sales activity, collect and analyze customer data, and provide decision support to marketing and sales. Marketing and sales, however, must provide functional direction to IT in terms of what customer data to collect, where to collect it, and how it needs to be integrated across products, channels, and markets. In addition, marketing and sales must work closely with IT to specify the modeling, forecasting, pattern detection, and segmenting needs that must be met so that the appropriate analytical tools can be applied to information residing in the data warehouse and data marts.

2.4g Customer Data

The Gartner Group cites poor data quality as the single greatest inhibitor to successful CRM implementation. Since contact data erodes at a rate of 33 percent per year, without proper attention, data can become incorrect, unusable, and ultimately untrustworthy.[35] Certain types of customer information and data are typically collected and input into CRM systems (Table 2.3). **Customer data integration (CDI)** enables an organization to accrue knowledge about the customer, a necessary antecedent for an effective CRM strategy. CDI allows for the creation of a consolidated view of the customer from multiple customer data stores. All customer touch points are linked, and CDI continuously accesses and upgrades the customer information. Although most organizations believe that a single, integrated view of the customer is critical, only a few currently have this. A number of challenges present themselves as organizations attempt to create the single customer view so critical to CRM. They must consolidate and resolve the problems resulting from the following:

- Disparate databases
- Multiple touch points
- Departmental disparity
- Dissimilar applications
- Inconsistent customer data

CDI is the process of managing the customer response or activity related to all possible touch points. For example, a consumer can make a telephone call to the organization, access the organization's Web pages, or communicate via traditional channels such as the mail, point of sale (POS) transactions, surveys, returns, and warranty. The CRM system must be capable of identifying the source, capturing the information, and recording it for future use.

2.4h Building a Case and Conducting an Analysis

Since some CRM initiatives in major corporations could cost well over $80 million and take three years to complete, a business case should be built and a business analysis should be conducted.

Table 2.3 Customer Information and Data Used in CRM Systems

Type	Consists of
Customer transaction history information	What was purchased, date of purchase, where it was purchased (online or in-store transaction), price, payment history, returns, length of time as customer, customer referrals
Customer demographic and life-stage information	Age, gender, income, occupation, marital status, number of children, age of children, address, type of dwelling unit
Profitability information	RFM and CLV scores that are computed to indicate the value of the customer to the company

These should provide the business rationale for the CRM development and estimate costs and payback. The analysis should assess your various markets and the competition you face in each market, in addition to the value of each market segment.

On a tactical level, the analysis should offer approaches dealing with multichannel communication and the decreasing productivity of mass-marketing efforts. The competitive analysis should include competitors' usage of CRM and a determination of whether your company should introduce CRM on a project-by-project basis or as an all-encompassing system (a wraparound CRM suite).

Another option available to companies today is simply to subscribe to a "hosted" CRM service over the Internet at a low monthly fee. Delivering software over the Internet is designed to reduce the large initial investment and lengthy installation process companies adopting CRM face. The online CRM product delivers all of the standard CRM functions such as lead management, campaign management, and customer service management. Users need only standard Web browsers to use the service. Research and analysis firm IDC projects that soon one-third of all business software will be delivered from the Cloud.

According to IDC, the software as a service (SaaS) market achieved worldwide revenues of $13.1 billion in 2009. IDC predicts the SaaS market to reach $40.5 billion by 2014, representing a compound annual growth rate of 25.3 percent. By 2014, approximately 34 percent of all new business software purchases will be procured via SaaS, and SaaS delivery will constitute about 14.5 percent of worldwide software spending across all primary markets. IDC also indicates that business applications will account for just over half of the market revenue. The rest of the market growth will occur on cloud platforms as businesses begin to purchase cloud services instead of hosted services. Market research firm ABI Research forecasts that the global market for hosted services will exceed $34 billion in 2012, of which the North American market will account for $11.6 billion.

2.4i Using Success Metrics

Put quite simply, the best CRM system is the one the company actually uses. The most basic CRM success metric is whether the company actually uses the system once it is developed. The second indication of success is whether or not the system provides real, tangible benefits for your customers. Third, has the company benefited from the CRM effort? Has it realized greater value from its customer relationship orientation?

Success metrics are often the missing link in CRM systems but are necessary to assess the effectiveness of CRM efforts and to serve as a scorecard for performance. Changes in revenue, acquisition, usage, customer satisfaction, time to market, campaign effectiveness, and margins all serve as indicators of whether the effort in establishing the CRM system was worthwhile. Surprisingly, many companies have not bothered to create metrics for evaluating the success or lack of success of their CRM systems. A survey among the Fortune 1000 companies conducted by the Forrester Group found that 39 percent had no metrics for evaluating their CRM projects.[36] Success metrics are discussed in Chapter 12.

THEORY IN ACTION

Wells Fargo and Customer Churn Rates

In 2006, Wells Fargo had 84 businesses, 23 million customers, and 6,250 branch offices and stores. Wells Fargo has a strong sales culture and an effective chief marketing officer (CMO), and it is an Internet pioneer. Wells Fargo has more data than the Library of Congress and five times more data volume. How can Wells Fargo continue growing at a double-digit annual clip as it has over the past 20 years? According to David Holvey, they must retain its customers while at the same time supplementing its sales culture with modern marketing strategy; when sales increase, so does the customer churn rate. The key to growth is keeping customers, but that is becoming increasingly difficult. A measure of success is reduction in the customer churn rate.

Presentation by David Holvey, Senior Vice President of Consumer Banking, Wells Fargo & Company at the MSI conference "Taking Stock of Customer Relationships" (March 2, 2006).

2.5 Developing CRM from a Tactical Perspective

2.5a Checklist for Customer Service Success

The importance of the customer contact center ([CCC]; often referred to today as the customer interaction center [CIC]) cannot be underestimated. For many companies, the CCC is the main customer touch point. CCC personnel are often both the voice and the face of the company, product, or brand. In addition, they are the ears of the organization, providing critical customer feedback in areas such as product deficiencies, customer likes and dislikes, reasons for acquisition and attrition, and customer reactions toward new promotions and campaigns. As such, CCC personnel are critical links in any company's CRM process. Unfortunately, CCCs in many organizations have not been recognized as the critical warehouses of customer marketing information that they are. This could be due to their recent prominence or the tendency of brand, product, and marketing managers to rely on more traditional sources of information, such as advertising and marketing research firms.

Because of the importance of CCC personnel and the functions they perform, it is important that those involved with CRM do the following to ensure customer support success:

- Develop a profiling technique that enables you to hire the best applicants. When Ritz-Carlton places an ad, it selects the best 100 applicants, reduces the number to 10, and then hires one of them.
- Provide your CCC personnel with complete customer profiles and be willing to adjust the information contained in these profiles based on their requests. This means that information must be captured and coordinated from all channels. Gartner found that lack of channel integration was one of the key weaknesses of failed CRM implementations.
- Put process blueprints in place (business process reengineering) to enable them to increase sales for individual products, cross-sell, and up-sell, and to enable them to differentiate high-value from low-value customers. An example of the former is providing them with guaranteed room availability, no blackout dates, and preemptive service. Process blueprints are particularly important when trying to market new products and services to your customer base, and they can also ensure that your CCC personnel are projecting the image of your company, product, or brand. Singapore Airlines' "Singapore Girls," for instance, have been an important factor in their being rated the number one airline in the world for many years.

Remember the saying: "What gets measured gets done." Establish success metrics for acquisition, development, retention, and win back, and do not skimp on training.

2.5b Customer Analytics

What are the key lessons that practitioners have learned regarding CRM analytics to date?

- Use your current customer database more effectively. Auto insurance companies such as GEICO and Progressive Insurance are experts at using customer data to direct policy offerings. CRM efforts allow GEICO to direct offerings to low-risk motorists, while Progressive effectively targets high-risk motorists.
- Segment in order to discriminate. If your database contains the information necessary to differentiate offers to your various customer segments—do it! Consider United Airlines Mileage Plus program. United has the flight history of each passenger at its disposal and offers incentives to its best customers accordingly. United differentiates based on miles flown and revenue earned per customer.
- Identify the value of market segments. Most industries have key factors that represent customer leverage points. In the credit card industry, for example, those factors would be the monthly profit margin of a customer, the longevity of a customer, and customer acquisition costs. Capital One has learned that encouraging existing customers to increase their charge volume produces higher returns than attracting new customers. The real focus for the industry is customer lifetime value.
- Build customer relationships. Too often, we focus our attention on the size of customer databases. Consider Safeway's database for frequent shoppers. Although it exceeds 28 million households, Safeway's promotional efforts tend to be transaction focused and not relationship oriented.

2.5c Product Selection

The organization's needs and CRM goals that are outlined in the CRM business plan should be the drivers for CRM product selection. The product decision should not drive the CRM effort (often called the bottom-up approach) because this approach will hinder communication, integration, and usage. If no consensus is reached regarding the goals of CRM, then the technology solution (CRM products) purchased may contain features that will never be used or will focus only on low-priority issues. If the technology solution is purchased without considering how it will be integrated with existing legacy systems, then the company runs the risk that it will never be used. And if the technology purchase is based simply on features a single user or department desires, then the CRM solution is departmental rather than company-wide. Clearly, CRM products must be selected based on the company's need to provide greater value to its customer base.

CRM technology need not be expensive. While global corporations have spent tens of millions of dollars on individual systems, sole proprietors who do not need data-sharing tools with others in their company can spend as little as $250 for a system that will manage contacts, leads, referrals, and opportunities. Even large companies with a geographically dispersed sales force can find inexpensive CRM solutions by using a hosted system instead of investing in an intranet or Web server. Low-cost CRM systems are not generally sufficient for companies involved in complex transactions involving multiple departments or for use in managing marketing campaigns or automating the customer service process. They are, however, sufficient for account management applications.[37] Table 2.4 is a timeline summary of CRM activities.

Table 2.4 Six-Step Timeline of CRM Activities

1. Establish a strategic plan for CRM system activities quantifying goals and objectives.
- Establish a central enterprise-wide CRM strategy tied into industry dynamics.
- Conduct a situation analysis with all those providing customer service, including distributors, dealers, suppliers, and those internal to the organization.
- Determine whether the key objective is acquisition, maintenance, or both.
- Clearly state goals and objectives for the CRM system in terms of ROI/user acceptability/ customer satisfaction metrics.
- Estimate the business value of CRM: costs and payback. Include the value of each market segment, keeping in mind competition, target return goals, and estimated costs.
- Highlight the business strategies that will drive the CRM system.
- Integrate business unit strategies with the CRM system.

2. Estimate the impacts on ongoing structure: executive, managerial, sales, and customer contact center levels.
- Develop integration procedures for marketing, sales, and engineering personnel with CCC.
- Consider sharing CCC information with channel partners.
- Retrain managers and staff in their new roles and use of new CRM systems as opposed to legacy systems.

3. Communicate the relationship marketing philosophy from the top down to managers, department heads, functional departments, and employees.
- Work with key influencers in each department to gain user commitment and approval before the final CRM configuration.
- Detail the CRM system benefits to employees and how they will personally benefit from it.
- Consider bonus systems for sales, marketing, and others based on retained customer profitability.
- Communicate continuously throughout the CRM development and implementation process.
- Reallocate resources (both budgetary and human) based on customer segment value.

4. Build the CRM platform technology to solve the problems faced by managers, including processes, strategies, necessary data, and analysis necessities.
- Determine if a CRM suite or an approach based on the buildup and integration of components is most suitable.
- Ensure complete integration of all functional components: customer value, customer profiling, monitoring CCC effectiveness, SFA, campaign management, modeling, forecasting, pattern detection, and segmentation.
- Determine the sequence of work using cost-benefit analysis.
- Integrate customer data linking all customer touch points.
- Consider integrating "quick-results" strategies into the overall CRM development effort.

5. Organize to expedite the development of the CRM system.
- Consider establishing a PMO to coordinate development.
- Integrate IT and business managers into start-up teams.
- Divide the project into manageable tasks and assign each to a project manager.

6. Establish CRM program metrics to measure the effectiveness of performance.
- Be prepared to measure changes in revenue, acquisition, usage, development, customer satisfaction, time to market, campaign effectiveness, and profit margins.

2.6 Extending the Meaning and Application of CRM

While customer interactions are often said to be the core of CRM, if a college or university followed such a restrictive view, it would focus only on its students and neglect its alumni and other potential donors from whom the students could also benefit in terms of grants and donations. A more expansive notion of CRM includes more constituencies than merely customers.

Although a relatively new concept, the customer focus of CRM has been extended to include all members of the channel who might find it beneficial to collaborate. This includes suppliers, distributors, and facilitating agencies. CRM approaches can benefit each member in the supply chain, including equipment manufacturers, raw material suppliers, wholesalers, retail stores, industrial suppliers, household customers, and industrial customers. While CRM systems are valuable for **vertically aligned networks (VANs)**, they have also been used by **value-added partnerships (VAPs)**, which work closely together to manage the flow of goods and services along the supply chain. This is called partner relationship management (PRM). Suffice it to say that every relationship is dependent on the quality, relevance, consistency, and value of interactions. This implies that everyone in the organization, and outside stakeholders, can be a beneficiary of a CRM system.

Chapter Summary

The roots of CRM are diverse. Relationship marketing, with its focus on maintaining a continuous relationship with customers and building long-term bonds, certainly provides a strategic foundation for CRM. Service and industrial marketing contributed the concepts of satisfaction, trust, and commitment to the marketer's lexicon, along with ways to measure customer satisfaction and the strength of customer–company bonds. CCCs and SFA tools allowed marketers to capture customer and prospect information for use in customer databases. This, in turn, enabled companies to develop campaign management tools that reduced the high costs associated with mass-marketing campaigns. Channel integration, geared toward gathering customer information from each touch point, facilitated more proactive customer service. Direct-response marketing techniques enabled companies to target prospects one-on-one. Finally, relational databases made it possible for companies to identify, access, manipulate, and share customer information across departments.

CRM is a tool for differentiation now that product parity exists in many sectors. CRM enables companies to reduce the costs of expensive mass-marketing efforts and increase results from their communication efforts. It allows companies to deal effectively with the multichannel usage to which consumers have become accustomed.

Not all companies have successfully implemented CRM. Targeted revenue goals are often not achieved, and budget overruns are common. Some companies have even abandoned their CRM efforts. There are many barriers to the successful implementation of CRM systems, but they can be overcome. First, the organization must adopt a relationship marketing philosophy across all functional areas. Top management must communicate the benefits of a CRM orientation to all employees and support the effort throughout its development. A business plan and business strategies must precede CRM development, not the opposite. All-encompassing CRM suites must be viewed with caution. CRM success metrics should be developed before it is implemented. And finally, CRM start-up teams should consist of IT as well as business unit managers.

Key Terms

CAD-CAM systems are computer-aided design and computer-aided manufacturing systems.

Churn is the same as customer turnover or attrition. CRM is geared to reduce churn. Some churn is inevitable, however, due to customer changes in life cycle and life stage.

CRM suite is an enterprise-wide CRM solution in the form of a single package or "suite" that claims to provide all the necessary CRM functions, such as SFA, campaign management, customer profile and value analysis, and CCC programs.

Cross-selling is a marketing and sales strategy focused on selling related products or services to customers.

Customer-centric means focusing on customers rather than products or brands. This includes focusing on customer profitability and share of wallet as opposed to market share and one-to-one relationships as opposed to mass marketing.

Customer data integration (CDI) enables an organization to accrue knowledge about the customer in a consolidated manner from all possible touch points. It is the process of managing the customer response or activity related to all possible touch points. All customer touch points are linked, and CDI continuously accesses and upgrades customer information.

Database marketing develops targeted promotions to customers and prospects based on the likelihood that they will respond to the tailored messages and establish long-term ties with the organization.

"Feeding the funnel" means acquiring new customers—the first step in CRM. This is more necessary in industries where churn is high.

IT is analytical procedures to gain information from customer databases.

Legacy systems are historical systems originally developed to serve the needs of individual departments or functions such as sales, billing, inventory, and customer service. They have been useful, and departmental and functional users feel comfortable using them. They may need to be replaced or modified, however, as a company develops enterprise-wide systems.

Materials resource planning (MRP) is a relationship between suppliers and customers oriented toward the reduction of costs and improvement of quality.

Middleware is software that allows disparate databases to work as a single integrated database. It allows a company's various legacy systems to be coordinated with one another to build an enterprise-wide CRM system.

Point solutions are CRM systems that satisfy the needs of only a single department or function.

Portal, in the Internet context, is a website that offers entry to multiple data sources. In a broader sense, a portal now refers to any set of consolidated services accessible via a Web browser available to customers, employees, or partners.

Relational databases are accumulated computer-based data that is arranged to facilitate retrieval, making it possible for companies to identify, access, manipulate, and share customer information across departments. A relational structure integrates data across multiple tables based on data already existing in the tables.

Relationship marketing is a focus on the relationships between the firm and its customers based on cooperation and collaboration. According to J. Compton, it is "the ongoing process of engaging in cooperative and collaborative activities and programs with immediate and end-user customers to create or enhance mutual economic value at reduced cost"[38] and "the process of identifying and establishing, maintaining, enhancing, and, when necessary, terminating relationships with customers and other stakeholders, at a profit, so that the objectives of all parties involved are met, where this is done by a mutual giving and fulfillment of promises."[39] Relationship marketing includes affinity marketing, loyalty marketing, cobranding, personalized one-to-one relationships, and key account management.[40]

SAP is a leading software company in enterprise resource planning (ERP) and CRM marketplaces, integrating middleware and portal functionality.

Total quality management (TQM) is a management philosophy based on improving quality while reducing costs throughout the value chain.

Up-selling/trading up is a marketing and sales strategy focused on selling a higher-priced item to a customer owning or considering buying a lower-priced item—for example, a Volvo dealer pointing out the advantages of owning the more expensive S80 model to a customer looking at the less expensive S60 model. Maintenance of the relationship is achieved if the higher-priced item is also the better value (i.e., its additional benefits exceed the additional cost).

Value-added partnerships (VAPs) are efficiencies of VANs obtained in a channel by independent companies.

Vertically aligned networks (VANs) are channels in which all institutions work together to provide more effective and efficient service for final customers. They can be corporate-owned (Sherwin-Williams), wholesaler-sponsored (True Value), retailer-sponsored (IGA), or franchised (McDonald's) store systems. Efficiencies are a result of shared information, purchasing, promotion, and operational expertise.

Questions

1. Some say the origins of CRM are in the concept of relationship marketing. Describe the concept of relationship marketing.
2. What were the forces that drove marketers to begin to focus so intently on customer relationships?
3. What led to CRM as we know it today—in other words, what are the roots of CRM?
4. Mass-marketing techniques worked well for nearly three-quarters of a century. What caused current organizations to change their focus to one-to-one or CRM?
5. Have organizations experienced success or failure with CRM systems?
6. What major challenges do companies encounter when trying to implement a CRM system?
7. Although still very young, the field of CRM is already being extended both in meaning and practice. How so?

Exercises

1. Conduct research on the concept of relationship marketing, and discuss how it has changed the focus of marketers and the field of marketing itself. Compare and contrast the differences between customer-centric marketing and product/brand-oriented marketing.
2. Conduct research on the two major corporate-wide systems of the 1990s: materials resource planning and enterprise resource planning. Compare and contrast them with today's CRM systems. Which systems are likely to remain viable over the long term?
3. Research relational databases and determine why they advanced companies' ability to integrate customer information.
4. Contact a company you have a relationship with via multichannels. Contact a competitor in the same industry using the same query and decide which has the better CRM system.

5. Through research, find an example of a company experiencing success in developing and using its CRM system. Find a company experiencing failure. Compare and contrast the differences in implementation of the two systems.

6. Through research, find a company or companies that have been able to develop close relationships with their customers via CRM systems. Are their experiences applicable to other companies?

7. Research examples of companies that have successfully extended their CRM systems to include channel members or partners.

Chapter 3

Relationship Marketing and CRM

Relationship marketing is the biggest paradigmatic shift marketing theory and practice has seen during the last 50 years. It is taking marketing thought back to its roots.

—C. Grönroos, "Relationship Marketing: Strategic and Tactical Implications,"
Management Decision, *34*, 3 (1996): 5–14.

Relationship marketing has the aim of building mutually satisfying long-term relationships with key parties—customers, suppliers, distributors, and other marketing partners—in order to earn and retain their business.

—P. Kotler and K. L. Keller, *Marketing Management*, 12th ed.
(Upper Saddle River, NJ: Prentice Hall, 2005).

3.1 The Roots of Relationship Marketing

Until the early 1980s, most marketers focused on the acquisition of customers by attempting to develop a better **marketing mix** than the competition—the marketing mix being the blending of optimal product, place, promotion, and price for the targeted market segment (the 4 P's). Using mass media, the same basic messages were sent to everyone. Products and their prices were developed to attract the average consumer, and distribution outlets were standardized. The focus was on developing economies of scale, where cost economies were realized through repetition as opposed to customization. Companies focused on feeding the pipeline with ever more customers, and once prospects became customers, companies would market to them via promotions that, other than the name and address, were not personalized. As C. Grönroos commented, this was an approach that was entirely suitable for the North American packaged goods industry.

This would change as marketing "revolutionized" (as many called the shift) due to a variety of factors, some of which had been incubating for years. Marketers began shifting focus from acquisition of new customers to maintenance, enhancement, and retention of customers through numerous strategies and tactics called customer relationship management (CRM).

At the same time, companies began working with other members in the value chain to provide more value to customers, often in the form of vertically aligned networks, strategic alliances, joint ventures, and so forth. As a result, marketers extended their CRM techniques to include partner relationship management (PRM). These "partners" could be "input publics" (employees, board members, investors, security analysts), "output publics" (channel members closer to the final customer, customers, and final customers themselves), or "sanctioning publics" (legal, political, and regulatory agencies, and the general public—whether they are customers or not).

THEORY IN ACTION

The Future of CRM

With CRM technologies evolving, one of the most important selling points has been the ability of CRM systems to provide a 360-degree view of the customer. Having an integrated view of the customer has helped organizations to keep all departments (sales, service, finance, etc.) on the same page and thus in turn provide a consistent service to the customer. Essentially, what has been captured in the 360-degree view is the transactional behavior of the customer.

Transactional data has been mainly classified under three subcategories: transaction data like sales orders, billing, receivables, and warranties; account data like receivables, outstanding balances, account hierarchies, and credit histories; and interaction data that essentially captures communication from all customer touch points like e-mails, chat rooms, and call centers.

It is now time to add another subcategory that I call "behavioral metrics," which fundamentally captures customers' social behavioral patterns. A lot of information is available on the social network that can be utilized to improve customer views in the organization. With a growing number of success stories, the time has come for organizations that already have implemented a 360-degree customer view in their systems to improve it and look beyond the transactional behavior of the customer. Organizations now must ready themselves for obtaining customer information through new sources and build new columns in their database tables to capture this information.

Integrating the traditional CRM systems with social media tools is very important, or the CRM system could end up becoming a middleware solution that stores only the transactional behavior of the customer. A 360-degree view needs to be redefined to capture the social behaviors of, and to forge more meaningful and effective relationships with, customers.

Posted by Subodh Rane on March 7, 2012. Published on Customer Think (http://www.customerthink.com)

When the word *customer* is used in relation to CRM, many interpret it as including partners as well. As pointed out by P. R. Timm and C. G Jones, CRM is not just oriented toward customers; it has an important role for key constituencies within a company as well. In addition to marketing, CRM impacts sales, customer service, customer contact personnel (CCP), and Internet-based commerce. CRM provides contact and lead management for the sales force, cross-selling and up-selling opportunities for marketers, product weaknesses for CCP to forward to engineering, and Web design opportunities for Internet marketers. In fact, CRM impacts any customer-oriented department, including R&D, purchasing, manufacturing, sales, logistics, accounting, finance, public relations, information technology (IT), and marketing.[1]

What are the forces driving marketers to begin focusing so intently on customer and partner relationships? First, advances in IT made relationship marketing feasible. Companies could develop customer transaction histories in the form of customer relational databases that recorded information about every transaction between a company and its customers. Relational databases became widespread in the 1980s, enabling companies to combine their customer data with internal and external customer data. Analytical capabilities were becoming widespread, relatively easy to use, and relevant. Companies could now individualize their 4 P's based on customer reactions to their marketing mix. Through statistical analysis of customer transaction data in the form of data mining, companies were able to design, develop, and implement promotional pieces, product/service modification, pricing, and distribution at the individual level as opposed to delivering an undifferentiated mix to the masses. In addition, two-way communication between customers and companies provided for dialogue—a necessary ingredient in relationship marketing. Many labels described this new paradigm: learning relationships, one-to-one marketing, interactive marketing, dialogue marketing, and so on. The label that appears to be most commonly used, however, is relationship marketing.

Second, direct marketing continued to grow because of 800 numbers and the wide distribution of credit cards to Americans. By the mid-1970s, bank credit cards were primarily in the hands of credit-worthy consumers after numerous failed attempts to get cards to the masses starting in the late 1960s. It was now easy for consumers to order direct. Companies had demographic information from customer credit files and applications and behavioral data from customer purchase histories. Further, they were in a position to communicate one-to-one with their customer base. With large-scale growth of direct marketing, more and more companies could enter one-to-one relationships with their customers. Most viewed direct marketing as more targeted and less wasteful than traditional mass marketing. Manufacturers, retailers, and B2B organizations, in addition to firms in the direct mail industry, were now using customer information. Companies were now able to market to individual customers as opposed to mass markets.[2]

Third, marketing academicians and researchers began to point out the need for companies not only to acquire new customers but also to continue to market to current customers. L. L. Berry stressed that attracting new customers is only the first stage in the marketing process. Companies must then continue their marketing efforts by developing and implementing strategies that form strong bonds between company and customers.[3] He pointed out, however, that marketers before him, dating back to the late 1970s, noted that companies paid insufficient attention to encouraging customer loyalty, engaging in reselling efforts, and improving service personnel performance to retain customers.[4] It became apparent that since relational databases could identify and track individual purchase behavior and direct marketing could personalize communication with customers, the building of relationships was as feasible in B2C as in B2B markets.

Fourth, consultants such as F. Reichheld wrote a number of influential articles in the early 1990s based on analysis of client data. The findings were quite startling at the time. For example, they reported that companies with the highest retention rates earned the best profits and that customer retention explained company profits better than the more traditional explanations of market share or economies of scale.[5] Consultants at McKinsey & Company pointed out that while retention was important, downward migration was a two to four times greater driver of company losses than customer defection.[6] It was also noted that acquiring a new customer could cost up to five times more than retaining a current customer.

These four forces ushered in a new era for marketing—the era of relationship marketing.

THEORY IN ACTION

Can Relationship Marketing Create Truly Meaningful Relationships?

Can a multibillion-dollar company establish a meaningful relationship with an individual customer? You be the judge after reading this true story.

It was December 1995. Bangkok was bustling and glowing in celebration of the king's birthday on December 5th and the upcoming Christmas holiday. Twenty-five college students from Chicago on a foreign study seminar were checking into the Grand Hyatt Erawan Hotel, when a student informed the seminar leader that one of them was extremely ill. The lobby was busy and the front desk packed when the student informed the leader that he was a diabetic taking a rare type of insulin, which he had left in a hotel in Vientiane, Laos, the group's previous stop. He said that if he did not get his insulin soon, he would be in serious shape.

The Grand Hyatt Hotels have some of the best-trained concierges in the world, and the Erawan's concierge was doing his best, without success, to locate a hospital that had the rare type of insulin. Holding his American Express card in his hand to guarantee hotel expenses for the group, the leader had an idea. He called American Express and explained the circumstances. The American Express rep, no doubt looking at his pop-up chart, could see that the group leader had charged well over $150,000 in the past five years, a result of numerous overseas seminars. She asked him to stay near the phone. Within 20 minutes, she called back to inform him that she had located the one hospital in Bangkok that had the rare type of insulin and that they were waiting for the student's arrival. She provided directions to the hospital and added, "By the way, you can charge the insulin on your American Express card!"

The student arrived at the hospital, and the staff was waiting in the lobby. He received his insulin and soon after was able to enjoy the rest of the seminar. Do you think that for the student and the seminar leader, American Express is just another multibillion-dollar company?

Companies realized that it was in their best business interest to adopt a customer focus as opposed to focusing on brands. For example, Procter & Gamble, a standard for marketing practitioners, renamed its marketing department Customer Business Development; it focuses on large retail and supermarket customers.[7] It is predicted that companies will soon have vice presidents of data—a position charged with analyzing customer data contained in company databases in order to better understand consumer behavior. Companies such as United Airlines have created new posts such as vice president for the customer experience. Such positions attempt to relate customer experiences to return on investment, as discussed in the "Top 5" Theory in Action feature.

THEORY IN ACTION

Top 5 ROI Benefits of Customer Experience Management

In the customer experience space, *return on investment* (ROI) is a term often thrown around but rarely defined. That lack of clarity can be problematic, especially when businesses are considering different customer feedback programs or trying to make the most out of the one currently in use.

The purpose of this article is to help frame ROI analysis around specific measures and outcomes in order to quantify the fully loaded economics of customer-centricity: increased sales to existing customers, lower staff turnover costs, increased brand value, and more.

We will flesh out a few different definitions of ROI as it relates to customer experience management (CEM) and offer examples of the ROI that real companies have achieved using CEM programs.

Reduce At-Risk Revenue and Recover Potentially Lost Customers

The CEM program should allow businesses to "close the loop" with customers, identifying those who are at risk of defecting in time to pull them back into the fold. Consider this example of a customer at a leading luxury hotel.

During his visit, a businessman had a string of poor service transactions with one receptionist, from delays at check-in to a missed wake-up call. Frustrated and angry, the customer had decided to never stay at that hotel again if he could avoid it.

The day after his stay ended, a link to an online survey arrived in his inbox. Though he was busy, the customer took the time to fill it out, naming the offending employee. Not 24 hours later, he received a call from the hotel manager apologizing sincerely and offering him a free night's stay the next time he was in town. Delighted, the customer accepted the offer and renewed his loyalty to that hotel brand.

What the hotel chain lost in revenue from offering the customer a free night it more than made up in the ROI of future visits the customer is likely to make, as well as any referrals he may make to friends and family based on one outstanding act of service recovery.

Engage Existing Customers as a Sustainable Engine for Growth

Good CEM programs allow businesses to identify their biggest customer fans and single them out for loyalty rewards and promotional offers. The ROI of these actions translates into more future visits and more money spent.

Data collected by Medallia shows that in a single transaction at a top apparel chain, the strongest brand advocates of the business spend 15 percent more and buy 15 percent more items than brand nonadvocates. That activity is also an indication of future behavior—within three months of responding to the survey, fans will make 10 to 15 percent more visits and spend 10 to 15 percent more than those who were less thrilled with their shopping experience.

The bottom line is that fans of your business will spend more money and spend it more frequently. Using CEM tools to engage them and market specifically to them further increases the ROI of these programs.

Reduce the Costs of New Customer Acquisition

When positive buzz about your company abounds, new customers tend to follow. Think Apple or Southwest. CEM can help businesses follow in the footsteps of these iconic companies and attract new customers almost effortlessly. By tracking various CEM metrics such as likelihood to recommend, businesses can see how many "wow" customer stories they're generating over time and compare that to the number of "ouch" stories circulating. One level deeper, businesses can identify the trends behind the numbers— for example, using verbatim analysis of open-ended comments correlated with positive or negative scores. Finally, businesses can facilitate fan word of mouth by pointing promoters to social media sites like TripAdvisor, Facebook, and Twitter.

Reduce Staff Turnover and the Cost of Hiring

Businesses can also use CEM programs to measure satisfaction and engagement among employees and take steps to improve them if necessary. Common metrics include employee satisfaction score and employee churn rate.

A body of research—as well as our experience—demonstrates that engaged employees are less likely to quit, even for more money, and are more likely to refer friends and family to apply to work for their companies. This in turn reduces the cost of recruiting, hiring, and training new employees.

Reduce the Cost of the Customer and Employee Feedback Infrastructure

Businesses are switching in droves from more traditional customer satisfaction programs offered by market research vendors to technology-enabled real-time CEM programs. CEM surveys should be short and to the point, attracting customer response through ease of use. In addition, once implemented, the best CEM programs require very little support, and businesses can run their own analysis using the platform.

"Top 5 ROI Benefits of Customer Experience Management," by David Strom. www.readwriteweb.com

Thus, understanding and managing a firm's customer base have become as important for a firm as managing its 4 P's. The customer or relationship marketing concept has achieved the status formerly reserved for the marketing mix concept. Companies and organizations are focusing on managing their customer relationships, and the field of marketing has an important new discipline: relationship marketing.

3.2 Relationship Marketing and Its Domain

Why Relationship Marketing Works!

The more relationships the customer has with the firm, the higher the real and psychological switching costs, and the greater the profits. The more relationships the firm has with the customer, the more the firm has an opportunity to learn about the customer's behavior. Good predictors are even better with behavioral data.

—Presentation by Richard Staelin at the MSI conference
"Taking Stock of Customer Relationships"
(March 3, 2006).

Relationship marketing focuses on maintaining a continuous relationship with customers by providing value that increases their **commitment** to the company, leading to increases in customer retention, customer lifetime value (CLV), and greater share of wallet. Its distinguishing characteristic is its focus on building long-term rather than short-term relationships with customers. Relationship marketing attempts to create a bond between the customer and a company or its brands. It consists of initiating, enhancing, and maintaining relationships with one's "customers," broadly defined. According to L. O'Malley, M. Patterson, and M. J. Evans, relationship marketing "involves the identification, specification, initiation, maintenance, and (where appropriate) dissolution of long-term relationships with key customers and other parties, through mutual exchange, fulfillment of promises, and adherence to relationship norms in order to satisfy the objectives and enhance the experience of the parties concerned."[8]

Relationship marketing has three basic features: relational databases, integrated marketing communications, and capabilities for dialogue. A company's database enables it to identify customers, track purchasing behavior, calculate CLV, and personalize communication. Company systems must be in place to collect customer information from all touch points, disseminate the information within the company to all relevant parties, and generate coordinated communications with the customer. Underlying this is the need for privacy.

A key concept of relationship marketing is the development of an individualized, one-to-one relationship with a customer that becomes increasingly relevant and focused as the organization learns about the customer's needs and wants over time. This is one of the three aspects unique to relationship marketing, according to J. N. Sheth and A. Parvatiyar. The other two, they state, are that it is an interactive process, rather than a transaction exchange, and that it is a value-added activity between suppliers and customers.[9]

As with any new and significant concept, there are numerous definitions and conceptualizations. M. J. Harker found 26 different definitions of *relationship marketing*,[10] while Sheth and Parvatiyar noted that there is no current consensus on a definition:

> Relationship marketing has proliferated with many definitions and many programs. It includes **affinity marketing**, loyalty marketing, **co-branding**, co-marketing, and customer–supplier partnering. In professional services, it includes personalized one-to-one relationships with individual clients and dedication of the organization's resources to the individual relationship. In business-to-business marketing, it includes key account management and solution selling.[11]

Table 3.1 details some of the more prominent definitions of relationship marketing.

72 CRM Theory and Development

Table 3.1 Definitions of Relationship Marketing

Shani and Chalasani (1992): "An integrated effort to identify, maintain, and build up a network with individual consumers and to continuously strengthen the network for the mutual benefit of both sides, through interactive, individualized, and value-added contacts over a long period of time."

Jackson (1985): "Marketing oriented toward strong, lasting relationships with individual accounts" (referring to relationship marketing as practices by industrial marketers).

Hoekstra, Leeflang, and Wittink (1995): "The customer concept is the new marketing concept. It is a management orientation which maintains that firms establish relationships with selected individual target customers with whom superior customer values are designed, offered, redefined, and realized in close cooperation with other partners in the marketing system, such as suppliers and intermediaries, in order to realize long-term profits through customer satisfaction, partner, and employee satisfaction" (referring to relationship management as the "customer concept").

Grönroos (1996): "Relationship marketing is to identify and establish, maintain, and enhance relationships with customers and other stakeholders, at a profit, so that the objectives of all parties involved are met" and "that this is done by a mutual exchange and fulfillment of promises."

Morgan and Hunt (1994): "Relationship marketing may be used to describe a plethora of marketing relationships, such as those between a firm and its buyers, suppliers, employees, and regulators."

C. Grönroos, "Relationship Marketing: Strategic and Tactical Implications," *Management Decision, 34*, 3 (1996): 5–14.
J. Hoekstra, P. Leeflang, and D. Wittink, "The Customer Concept: The Basis for a New Marketing Paradigm," *Journal of the Academy of Marketing Science, 23*, 4 (1995): 255–271.
B. B. Jackson, "Build Customer Relationships That Last," *Harvard Business Review, 63*, 6 (1985): 120–128.
R. M. Morgan and S. D. Hunt, "The Commitment-Trust Theory of Relationship Marketing," *Journal of Marketing, 58*, 3 (July 1994): 20–38.
D. Shani and S. Chalasani, "Exploiting Niches Using Relationship Marketing," *Journal of Consumer Marketing, 9*, 3 (1992): 33–42.

Note the expansion of relationship marketing's domain in the definitions in Table 3.1. Relationship marketing was first defined in terms of lasting bonds between a company and its customers. Next, it was defined in terms of lasting bonds between an entire marketing channel (a company and its distributors and dealers) and its customers. Finally, it was defined as being applicable to a firm and all of its relationships: partnerships with suppliers, buyers, lateral occupants of the value chain, and those within the company (Table 3.2). R. M. Morgan and S. D. Hunt pointed out that relationship marketing is applicable on at least ten different levels:[12]

Table 3.2 Companies Do Not Just Relate to Customers Anymore

- IBM is believed to have more than 500 strategic alliances with other companies.
- Hilton Hotels Corporation has over 50 airline partners.
- P&G has employees who have been permanently assigned to work at Walmart's headquarters.
- United Airlines has over 100 Mileage Plus partners.
- DePaul University partners with over 40 overseas universities.
- UB-Haworth is a joint venture consisting of Taiwanese, U.S., and Thai partners who must relate to one another while being cognizant of cultural differences that exist among them.
- In order to penetrate simultaneously major markets around the globe with new product innovations, General Electric, Matsushita, and Phillips formed a strategic alliance. Ordinarily competitors, they relate as partners in numerous endeavors.

Relational exchanges in network competition take place between firms and their:

1. Goods suppliers
2. Service providers
3. Competitors (as in strategic alliances)
4. Nonprofit organizations
5. Government entities (as in joint R&D)
6. Ultimate customers
7. Intermediate customers (as in franchising and other distribution channels)
8. Functional departments
9. Employees
10. Business units (as in cooperation across corporate divisions, subsidiaries, or other strategic groupings)

There are merits for including relationships other than company–customer in relationship marketing; however, customers continue to be the primary focus of relationship marketing in that companies' raison d'être is satisfying customers at a profit. As Peter Drucker wrote, the basic purpose of any business is not to sell products but to create and keep customers.[13]

A. R. Zablah, D. N. Bellenger, and W. J. Johnston state that when Leonard L. Berry initially coined the term "relationship marketing" in 1983, he defined it as "attracting, maintaining, and . . . enhancing customer relationships."[14] Berry, in 2002, suggests that relationship marketing can also be viewed as a philosophy and not just a strategy and that it is a way of thinking about customers, marketing, and value creation, not just a set of techniques, tools, and tactics.[15]

3.3 Relationship Marketing as a Paradigm Shift

> Relationship marketing is much like a marriage—a connection between equal partners, characterized by trust, commitment, communication, and sharing, which results in the mutual achievement of goals.
> —L. O'Malley and C. Tynan, "Reframing Relationship Marketing for Consumer Markets," *Interactive Marketing*, 2, 3 (2001): 240–246.

> Wells Fargo developed its KUAR model as a way to standardize and guide its view of the bank–customer exchange. KUAR is what the customer expects from Wells Fargo:
>
> Know me
> Understand me
> Appreciate me
> Reward me
>
> Information flows from the customer to the bank through the KU activities.
> Information flows from the bank to the customer through the AR activities.
> —David Holvey, Senior Vice President of Consumer Banking, Wells Fargo & Company

Relationship marketing—with its focus on customers as opposed to prospects, with its focus on relationships rather than one-time transactions, with its focus on individuals as opposed to masses, and with its attempt to improve the company's offerings to each individual by learning more about each individual's needs—has not only been viewed as a paradigm shift,[16] but F. E. Webster Jr. believes it is reshaping the entire field of marketing.[17] For relationship marketing to have caused such an impact, it must be offering something significant to each party in the relationship. Let us now explore the benefits that it provides the company and those at the other end of the exchange.

Sheth and Parvatiyar[18] posited a number of reasons why consumers may want to engage in relationship marketing. The reasons relate to personal factors (1, 2, 3, and 4), sociological factors (5, 6), and institutional influence factors (7):

1. To achieve greater efficiency in their decision making
2. To reduce the task of information processing
3. To achieve more cognitive consistency in their decisions
4. To reduce the perceived risks associated with future choices
5. To adhere to norms of behavior set by family members
6. To adhere to the influence of peer groups (e.g., social class and reference groups)
7. To adhere to government mandates, religious tenets, employer influences, and marketer-induced policies

THEORY IN ACTION

Beyond Cause Marketing: Emotive Customer Bonding

The landscape is littered with cause marketing campaigns—so much so that it is tough for any one campaign to stand out. We are bombarded wherever we shop and whatever media we consume. What is the answer to this cause clutter?

According to Jason Saul, a leading expert on strategy and performance measurement in the social sector and author of the new book *Social Innovation, Inc.: 5 Strategies for Driving Business Growth Through Social Change*, businesses and causes must move to a totally different model for linking social good and good business. Saul states that most companies think about society as a "responsibility" and focus on mitigating risks by doing good (charity) and not doing bad (risk management). But he urges businesses to embrace social strategies as the powerful business strategies that they can be. Saul, sounding very much the social entrepreneur, says that some of humanity's biggest problems, such as lack of health care, poor funding for education, and the deteriorating environment, are today's biggest business opportunities.

"Emotive customer bonding" is one of Saul's five strategies for changing the way business approaches social change. Such bonding is "a powerful new form of customer loyalty" that leverages the customer experience "to address meaningful social problems," thereby building an almost "familial allegiance" to a brand. Saul uses OfficeMax and its "A Day Made Better" (ADMB) initiative as an example of emotive customer bonding.

OfficeMax first asked customers what social issue was most important for the company to focus on. The answer was education. During its research of educational issues, OfficeMax discovered just how often teachers bought school supplies for their students out of their own pockets—to the tune of about $4 billion a year. The company decided to raise awareness of this problem and provide free supplies to teachers. Thus was born "A Day Made Better."

The company picked 1,200 U.S. schools, and on October 1, 2009, it sent 4,000 OfficeMax employee volunteers to classrooms, surprising teachers and students with free supplies worth about $1,200. These included staples such as paper and pencils but also digital cameras, supply carts, and furniture.

OfficeMax partnered with Adopt-a-Classroom, a nonprofit that matches donors with classrooms to offset the personal expenses that teachers shoulder in order to equip their classrooms. Adopt-a-Classroom helped OfficeMax identify deserving schools near 1,000 OfficeMax locations and recruit worthy teachers. Several celebrities, ranging from Penny Marshall to Dakota Fanning to Dustin Hoffman, helped bring attention to the effort.

OfficeMax designed this campaign to both benefit the business and inspire a national movement of grassroots support for teachers. You can imagine the delight of teachers and schools. One school principal quoted in Saul's book said, "A Day Made Better improves teacher morale, provides more supplies for our children and our classrooms, and ultimately impacts the quality of education we offer." The campaign resulted in an 832 percent increase in new classroom adoptions by Adopt-a-Classroom and a torrent of media coverage.

But the commercial outcome was just as important to OfficeMax. The company sought especially to influence a "prototypical customer" called "Eve." Eve, not surprisingly, is a 30- or 40-something woman who purchases office supplies and is likely a mom, a teacher, or both. She cares deeply about education and is emotionally attached to efforts to improve education. ADMB was designed to create an emotional connection with the thousands of Eves who drive much of the market for office supplies.

The commercial outcome was a big increase in website traffic after the promotion; the redemption of coupons included in brochures as part of ADMB, which generated revenue; and OfficeMax won several bid contracts with school districts as a direct result of the campaign. In addition, ADMB gave meaning to the thousands of employees involved in ADMB from packing boxes of supplies to delivering them to the teachers during the event.

ADMB is now an annual event and has become identified with OfficeMax's brand and culture. The program even escaped the budget cuts that were made during the recession because, as Saul says, "The company recognized the deep value the program has brought to its target market and the company itself by forging deep emotional connections to ADMB and OfficeMax more broadly, all while addressing an important social problem."

What makes ADMB such an unqualified success? Saul points out four attributes that make it work:

- It has a clear business objective. It has to drive real return on investment and focus on a key business priority. It is not a short-term sales promotion.
- It leverages the core business. It uses the primary engine of the business to solve a social problem.
- It creates new value. It uses emotional connections to tap latent value in the social capital market. It creates customer loyalty and engages employees.
- It makes a meaningful social impact. Donating a few cents from a product sale to a charity doesn't cut it. It has to create a meaningful bond and make a meaningful difference. As Saul so well puts it, "It's no longer enough just to 'associate' with a good cause—even one that makes sense for your company. . . . Emotion requires intensity, and intensity requires deep, meaningful engagement."

Joanne Fritz, About.com, http://nonprofit.about.com

Sheth and Parvatiyar feel that since relationship marketing reduces risk in the minds of consumers and the number of choices, it simplifies decision making.[19] It is important to remember that additional benefits consumers reap from relationship marketing are the recognition and rewards they accrue from loyalty programs—two of the most visible manifestations of relationship marketing.

Many also feel that customers satisfy social needs through relationship marketing. By having one-to-one relationships with service providers, customers can be made to feel important. Through repeated encounters they receive more personalized and customized attention, which leads to greater satisfaction and loyalty to the supplier. P. Guenzi and O. Pelloni discuss the importance of social bonds in customer–employee relationships and how they lead to and may be more important than loyalty toward companies and brands.[20] As detailed by Guenzi and Pelloni, Marvin Jolson claimed:

> Relationship selling focuses on the building of mutual trust within the buyer/seller dyad with a delivery of anticipated long-term, value-added benefits to buyers [in order to] create long-term relationships, alliances, and collaborative arrangements with selected customers whenever possible.[21]

It is well known that sales personnel frequently establish social relationships with their customers, and these affect the quality of the relationship between the buyer and the seller company, increasing customer **satisfaction**, loyalty, and **trust**. Studies have found that in a retail context, relationships are primarily between customers and salespersons rather than between customers and the firm, although customer loyalty partially transfers to the firm.[22] Gummesson, for example, points out that a customer's overall perception of quality of the service provider is strongly influenced by the customer's relationship with frontline employees.[23]

Bagozzi, on the other hand, feels that consumers enter marketing relationships for a variety of reasons and that, ultimately, while the decision to remain loyal to a single company reduces choices, it would not be the motivation for a singular relationship in the first place.[24] Bagozzi feels that consumers enter marketing relationships to fulfill a goal through the acquisition of a product or service. Peterson feels that since most consumers do not limit themselves to a single relationship with a product or service provider, it is an indicator that customers don't need or want to reduce choices when entering into a marketing relationship.[25]

What is the payback to companies for their relationship marketing efforts? As discussed throughout this book, the payback is in many forms, including lower cost of retaining versus acquiring customers, greater share of customers' wallets, opportunities for cross-selling and up-selling, retaining customers and their positive impact on profits, positive recommendations resulting in a greater customer base, more satisfied employees and a consequent improvement in service quality, and the ability to aim marketing efforts at higher profit segments, among others.

Sheth and Parvatiyar claim that by making marketing more effective and efficient, relationship marketing will lead to greater marketing productivity for companies, which in turn will encourage them to make greater efforts to maintain long-term relationships with consumers.[26] They write that relationship marketing will make marketing more *effective* by:

1. Enabling marketers to learn more and more about individual customers and, through this organizational memory, develop customized products and services
2. Allowing customers to help design and develop the product
3. Minimizing opportunities for negative images of marketing

They write that relationship marketing will make marketing more *efficient* by:

1. Enabling companies to retain customers (retention being the major driver of company profits)
2. Reducing mass-marketing wastes
3. Having consumers do much of the marketer's work, such as order processing and product design

Payoffs such as these will ensure that relationship marketing, as implemented through CRM systems, will remain a basic tenet in the field of marketing.

3.4 When Relationship Marketing Is Most Applicable

Until now, we have avoided addressing one important issue: will relationship marketing benefit every company in dealings with every customer? We can envision relationship marketing's potential for auto manufacturers, pet food manufacturers, luxury goods producers, restaurants, airlines, hotel chains, and even universities in establishing bonds with customers, but what are the benefits for manufacturers of pencils, pasta sauce, or shoelaces? For companies to understand the parameters of their customer relationships, they must go beyond the superficial questions and answers of qualitative surveys and attempt, through quantitative means, to understand the place of their company and products in their customers' lives.

If buyer–seller exchanges are put on a continuum, one could argue that some exchanges are merely discrete and functional transactions (e.g., buying shoelaces), while others are continuous, collaborative, relational, and emotional (the doctor–patient relationship). With the former, it is unlikely that either party to the exchange is interested in establishing and maintaining a relationship; however, for the latter, both parties are emotionally involved. Relationship marketing has a critical place in relationship maintenance and development (Figure 3.1).

Regarding the products and services on the continuum, their exact placement depends on how the consumer views the product or service and the buying situation at hand. For a tourist, a hotel may just be a place to sleep (a functional position). For a businessperson, a hotel may be a place to live (a relational position). For some, an automobile is just transportation (unemotional). For others, it is an expression of personality (emotional). The closer your product or service is to the right of the continuum, the greater benefits you will glean from relationship marketing.

There are many ways products can be arrayed on a continuum. One way is to position "commodities" on one end and "customized/individualized" products on the other. At first glance, it would appear less beneficial to build relationship marketing strategies around commodities than around customized/individualized products. Individuals are less emotionally involved with commodities and most often buy them on the basis of price. What opportunities for relationship marketing efforts exist for commodities? The answer is plenty, if one uses the Extended Product Model in Figure 3.2 to look for opportunities. The **Extended Product Model** states that a product is much more than simply its physical characteristics. It consists of maintenance, service, installation, training, warranties, delivery, and image, all of which offer companies the opportunities for creating value for the customer over time.

Discrete Functional Unemotional		**Continuous Relational Emotional**
Shoelaces	Hotels	Professional Services
Meat Sauce	Airlines	Sports Teams
Office Supplies	Automobiles	Luxury Products

Figure 3.1 Exchange Continuum

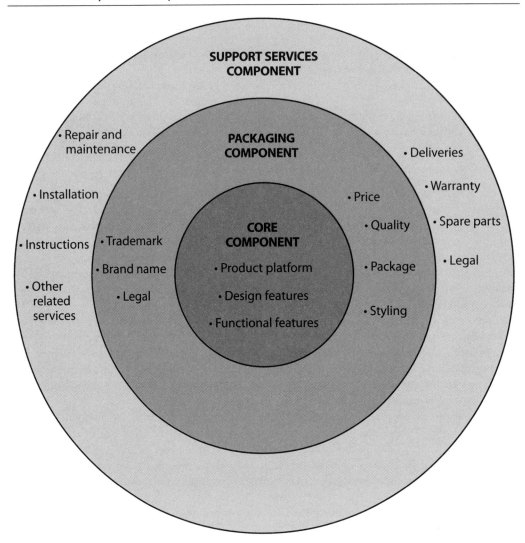

Figure 3.2 Extended Product Model

Source: Cateora, P. & Graham, J. (1999) International Marketing, 10th Edition. New York: McGraw-Hill, p. 368. Reprinted with permission of The McGraw-Hill Companies.

THEORY IN ACTION

Glenlivet Scotch—an Emotional Relationship for Some

Glenlivet is one of the world's foremost producers of single-malt scotch. It has formed a society for single-malt scotch drinkers that consists of special events, trips, and personalized mailings. For most, single-malt scotch is just another drink—one that they may not prefer, at that—clearly belonging on the left side of the continuum. So why has Glenlivet spent so much money on its relationship marketing efforts? It is because an increasingly large niche of alcoholic beverage drinkers consider single-malt scotch a pastime they are willing to spend a great deal of money pursuing. For them, single-malt scotch is far right on the continuum.

Customers do not want deep relationships with every company they are involved with; that is untenable and unwarranted. Instead, they want relationships with companies that provide them with products and services with which they are highly involved. Therefore, this means that most companies will have both transactional and relational customers. If only relational customers warrant relationship marketing strategies, should companies eliminate their transactional customer base and concentrate on the latter? As numerous authors have argued, the problem with transactional customers is not that a company has them but rather that companies have a tendency to continue to spend too much money on them after it is clear a relationship cannot be built.[27] Consequently, companies should not try to eliminate transactional customers from the fold; rather, they should keep them profitable by staying within a minimal marketing budget when marketing to them. Charles Schwab decided to direct low-value brokerage customers to lower-cost automated channels so it could free up personalized services to its more profitable customers. This differentiated cost-servicing structure ensures that both customer segments remain profitable.[28]

L. L. Berry posited that there are three levels of relationship marketing and that the level of relationship marketing must match the strength of bond appropriate for each type of customer:

1. Level one relationship marketing relies primarily on pricing incentives and is most appropriately aimed at customers toward the transactional end of the continuum.
2. Level two relationship marketing relies primarily on social bonds involving personalization and customization aimed at customers toward the relationship end of the continuum. Retailers such as Macy's provide their best customers with parties, fashion events, educational seminars, rewards, and so on.
3. Level three relationship marketing is also aimed at customers toward the relationship end of the continuum, but bonds are established by structural solutions as opposed to the personalized and recognition-of-status solutions used in level two. Structural solutions could include providing customers with computer terminals and software to track their orders (FedEx), imaging equipment to customize clothing, and so on.[29]

In one of their landmark articles, W. J. Reinartz and V. Kumar provided an interesting typology of customers based on their profitability and their projected duration with a company (Figure 3.3).[30] Once a company determines into which quadrant a customer belongs, it can determine the amount it should spend on their relationship efforts.

They suggested that since Butterflies are high-profit/short-term customers, the mistake that most companies make is investing too much money over too long of a time period in relationship

		Butterflies		True Friends
Profitability	High			
	Low	Strangers		Barnacles
		Short-Term		Long-Term
		Customers		

Figure 3.3 Choosing a Loyalty Strategy

marketing. The key with Butterflies is to maximize transactional profit through short-term promotional blitzes and not to attempt a long-term relationship. Because True Friends offer the greatest profit over the longest time period, companies must foster this relationship more than the others but not overwhelm these customers with constant communications.

Since Strangers are low-profit/short-term customers, no investment should be made, and companies should seek profit on every transaction. Never expect that offering them loss-leaders will lead them to trade up. They are loyal only to low prices and will not change. Barnacles are long-term/low-profit customers. They may be low profit either because their wallets are small or because you have a small share of their wallet. Companies should try to increase profits from this group by cross-selling and trading up. If this fails, assume their wallets are small and minimize relationship marketing expenses.

Customers can serve as proponents or opponents of a company, and because of the importance of referrals and word-of-mouth advertising on future business, they can have an extraordinary impact on company profits. T. O. Jones and W. E. Sasser Jr.[31] developed a typology consisting of four types of customers:

Loyalists serve as great ambassadors for your company. Companies should spend the greatest amount of relationship management resources on this group.

Mercenaries are only loyal to low prices on fashion/novelty items. They are transaction specific with no intention of establishing a relationship with a company no matter how superior the service or attention. Mercenaries can be costly for unaware companies.

Hostages are customers who are "stuck" with you for any number of reasons (e.g., contractual obligations or company policy dictating usage). You may need to treat them well, however, because when alternatives become available, they may provide negative word of mouth if you do not. Companies should direct the second greatest amount of CRM dollars at this group.

Defectors consist of various categories of dissatisfied former customers. The most dissatisfied can do a lot of damage to your company.

J. Barnes arrayed company–customer relationships on a continuum based on relationship strength.

Intimate Relationships	For example, patient and doctor
Face-to-Face Customer Relationships	For example, customers and retail stores
Distant Relationships	For example, interactions over phone or online
No Relationships	For example, manufacturers with final customers who buy through the distributor–dealer channel or service providers who only have contact with their customers through their sales force[32]

It should be pointed out that all four relationships offer opportunities for relationship marketing, since each may contain high-value customers. Companies having intimate or face-to-face relationships with their customers can easily establish customer databases because personal information generally has to be disclosed before treatment or for credit cards or delivery. FedEx, American Express, L. L. Bean, and Fidelity Investments are just a few of the companies that have established valuable relationship marketing initiatives with distant customers. How can manufacturers or service providers with little or no contact with the final customer establish a relationship? Here are two examples.

HOW MARY KAY ESTABLISHES RELATIONSHIPS WITH CUSTOMERS

Mary Kay beauty consultants establish close relationships with their customers. When they leave Mary Kay, the customers often go with them. Mary Kay needs to hold onto these customers because the turnover of beauty consultants is quite high. They do this by providing their beauty consultants with a personalized beauty analysis for their customers IF the consultants provide their customers' names and addresses. Mary Kay is thus able to build a customer database that the beauty consultants cannot take with them if they leave the company.

R. C. Blattberg and J. Deighton, "Interactive Marketing: Exploiting the Age of Addressability," *Sloan Management Review, 33,* 1 (1991): 5–14.

HOW HUGGIES ESTABLISHES RELATIONSHIPS WITH CUSTOMERS

Huggies spent over $10 million establishing a database that contains the names of three-quarters of the expectant mothers in the United States. During pregnancy, Huggies develops strong bonds with them through personalized baby magazines and letters. Per-baby expenditures on disposable diapers average over $1,400 annually (they are much higher today).

J. R. Copulsky and M. J. Wolf, "Relationship Marketing: Positioning for the Future," *Journal of Business Strategy, 11,* 4 (July/August 1990): 16–20.

3.5 Relationship Marketing and the Characteristics of a Relationship

The objective of relationship marketing is to increase a customer's commitment to the organization through the process of offering better value on a continuous basis at a reduced cost.
—J. N. Sheth and A. Parvatiyar, "Relationship Marketing in Consumer Markets: Antecedents and Consequences," *Journal of the Academy of Marketing Science, 23,* 4 (1995): 255–271.

If the purpose of marketing is to establish, maintain, and enhance relationships (under the new rubric of relationship marketing) rather than satisfy customer needs at a profit (as marketing used to be defined), then the focus is on relationships rather than the marketing mix. Just as marketing academicians defined the marketing mix as the 4 P's and spent volumes describing how to manage each element, relationship marketers need to define the nature of a relationship and then focus on how to manage each relationship component.

The discipline of services marketing introduced the concept of customer satisfaction. Measuring customer satisfaction was viewed as an important predictor of future behavior. Researchers have defined two types of satisfaction: overall or cumulative satisfaction, which describes overall experiences with a company or product, and transaction-specific satisfaction, which describes feelings about a single recent transaction. With the recognized importance of relationship marketing, satisfaction as a variable appeared too weak to describe strength and depth of a relationship, and other variables were introduced to predict future behavior.

Table 3.3 **What Is a Relationship?**

Caring	Understanding
Support	Desire to maintain a long-term relationship
Loyalty	Interacting over time
Placing priority on the other's interests	Benefits accruing to both parties
Honesty	Not criticizing publicly
Communication	Liking
Respect	Reciprocation
Affection	Trustworthiness
Helpfulness	Working through disagreements
Maintaining privacy	Keeping confidence
Trust	Commitment

The literature is quite vast in suggesting what these variables are. This is not surprising, since relationships are studied in many fields, including social psychology, industrial marketing, services marketing, marriage and the family, and even religion. Consequently, numerous variables must be examined. Table 3.3 lists the required variables for a true relationship.

As Table 3.3 demonstrates, many elements make up a relationship, but the literature on the subject singles out trust and commitment between both parties as being critical. R. M. Morgan and S. D. Hunt, in their theory of relationship marketing, state that trust and commitment are essential because they encourage partners to:

1. Preserve the relationship through cooperation
2. Resist attractive short-term alternatives in lieu of expected long-term benefits
3. Take risks, since they are confident their partner will not act opportunistically[33]

With trust, one partner will rely on another because they have confidence in their integrity, durability, and their ability to work out problems they will face in the marketplace. Commitment refers to both parties' understanding that they are in the market together for the long run. They are willing to make sacrifices for their partner because they are mutually dependent on each other in their quest to achieve long-term returns on their psychological and financial investments.

The implications of relationship marketing get to the very heart of a company and its marketing efforts. The sales force must adopt a problem-solving orientation in its prospecting and client maintenance efforts. By nature, this will be long term, and results should be lasting. The marketing department must focus on uncovering unmet needs in the market and developing and introducing products and services that meet these needs. Finally, marketing researchers must develop techniques to measure trust and commitment, just as they have developed numerous measures of satisfaction.

3.6 Relationship Marketing and CRM

What Is Customer Relationship Management?

CRM can be thought of as a set of business practices designed to put an enterprise into closer and closer touch with its customers in order to learn more about each one and to deliver greater and greater value to each one with the overall goal of making each one more valuable to the firm.

—D. Peppers and M. Rogers, *Managing Customer Relationships: A Strategic Framework* (Hoboken, NJ: John Wiley & Sons, 2004).

CRM aligns business processes with customer strategies to build customer loyalty and increase profits over time.

—D. K. Rigby, F. F. Reichheld, and P. Schefter, "Avoid the Four Perils of CRM," *Harvard Business Review, 80*, 2 (February 2002): 101–109.

Customer relationship management—collecting and using data about your customers' buying histories, service histories, profitability, and so forth, to offer an exceptional customer experience.

—P. R. Timm and C. G. Jones, *Technology and Customer Service: Profitable Relationship Building* (Upper Saddle River, NJ: Prentice Hall, 2005).

Customer Relationship Management. This is the process of managing detailed information about individual customers and carefully managing all customer "touch points" to maximize customer loyalty.

—P. Kotler and K. L. Keller, *Marketing Management*, 12th ed. (Upper Saddle River, NJ: Prentice Hall, 2005).

CRM is concerned with the creation of market intelligence that firms can leverage to build and sustain a profit-maximizing portfolio of customer relationships.

—A. R. Zablah, D. N. Bellenger, and W. J. Johnston, "An Evaluation of Divergent Perspectives on Customer Relationship Management: Towards a Common Understanding of an Emerging Phenomenon," *Industrial Marketing Management, 33*, 6 (2004): 475–489.

Is there a difference between relationship marketing and CRM? The two have more similarities than differences. Although it is true that relationship marketing refers to relationships with both customers and partners and the acronym CRM refers only to customers, many have expanded the notion of CRM to include relationships with partners. In addition, both relationship marketing and CRM are enterprise-wide business strategies not restricted to the traditional, centralized marketing department. Further, CRM must be integrated into all corporate functions to be successful, and relationship marketing is a way of thinking that is applicable throughout all departments as well.

Zablah, Bellenger, and Johnston feel that there is a difference between relationship marketing and CRM—namely that relationship marketing focuses on the establishment and maintenance of close relationships with customers, whereas CRM is concerned with developing a portfolio of profit-maximizing customer relationships that will exclude having relationships with low- or no-profit customers. Thus, they view relationship marketing activities as a subprocess within the CRM rubric.[34] The goal of CRM is not to establish close, intense, and costly relationships with all customers but rather with the profitable ones. Less profitable customers would receive less personalized and less costly service and no-profit customers would receive no personalized service at all. In other words, a customer's lifetime value determines the amount of relationship resources a firm should expend on the customer.

Conceptually, CRM focuses more than relationship marketing on the operational components of relationships. As discussed by R. T. Rust, K. N. Lemon, and D. Narayandas:

> CRM technologies are enabled by a systems architecture with three distinct pieces of software functionality: operational, analytical and collaborative. . . . Operational functionality includes integration of front and back office products and activities. . . . Analytical functionality relies on . . . a CRM implementation [that] keeps data in consolidated databases, making data collection and analysis much easier. CRM creates multiple customer touch point opportunities by enabling various communications channels.[35]

The preceding statement illustrates that CRM includes aspects of systems architecture as well as strategies made possible by maintaining and mining databases. We submit that relationship marketing is implemented through CRM systems. The ultimate goal of relationship marketing is to build bonds between parties based on satisfaction, trust, and commitment that will lead to mutually satisfying transactions.

Relationship marketing does not need to rely on a customer database to be operational. A good example is how customer service is handled at The Inn at Little Washington in Virginia's Shenandoah Valley, a restaurant voted number one in North America by *Travel + Leisure* magazine and listed among the top ten in the world by the *International Herald Tribune*. After guests are seated, the waiter assesses the group's collective mood and rates it from 1 to 10. This score appears at each work station throughout the restaurant. The goal is that no guest should leave with a score lower than 9. The waiter identifies who at the table appears most irritable, and the individual is granted extra attention. The table's score is updated after each interaction, and the staff works together to elevate mood ratings to a 9 or 10.[36]

3.7 The Impact of CRM

Are marketers losing ground as the focal point for organizing all of the company's customer contacts? The answer, both "yes" and "no," is based on some complex forces. As discussed in the first section of this chapter, marketing thought underlies the concept of relationship marketing, and CRM is an integral part of relationship marketing. So "yes" marketers have assumed an important role in the CRM arena. In contrast, the marketing functions in today's companies are no longer centralized within marketing departments. Everyone in the company must embrace marketing principles. Some traditional marketing functions, such as advertising, sales promotion, and marketing research, may continue to be centralized within a "marketing" department, but the customer-centric focus has diffused throughout departments.

We argue that marketing is becoming so important that it can no longer be confined within departmental walls. It is becoming decentralized throughout the organization. Following is a discussion of the important forces at work in this regard.

3.7a "Marketing Is Far Too Important to Leave to the Marketing Department" (the late David Packard of Hewlett-Packard)

Line managers often feel that because they are closer to their customers, they should have greater control in managing marketing efforts. Many departments established customer databases that enabled them to stay in direct touch with their customers. A technically oriented person who was there during construction regularly managed these databases, which, while not terribly complex, required some time and effort to understand. Centralized marketing department personnel were often supportive of line management control of these databases.

Line management then worked closely with direct-mail organizations to develop marketing and sales promotion pieces. Using the new databases, they also experimented with different promotional pieces to see which were most effective. They then began their own target marketing campaigns, often in conjunction with these direct-mail agencies. Marketers, schooled in mass media, were often content to leave these targeted marketing efforts in the hands of line management. As these efforts have led directly to today's CRM systems, many of the marketing efforts aimed at companies' customer bases have been assumed by line personnel performing marketing functions formerly carried out by centralized marketers.

This shift does not denote a diminished need for marketers; rather, it is consistent with a customer-centric, as opposed to a functional-centric, shift taking place across firms in the United States.

3.7b Companies Today Are Increasingly Being Organized Across Functional Lines

Total quality control, enterprise resource planning, and in-house venture groups that develop new products and services are some of the developments that are centered on providing more value to the customer. Many of these customer-centric efforts began in areas such as industrial engineering, IT, manufacturing, and line departments. These areas were often aided by outside facilitating agencies that assisted with tactical marketing plans and implementation. There was no need to bring in centralized marketing department personnel to interface between line personnel and customers.

These departments had the database, the analytical techniques, the procedures needed to plan and implement, the ability to measure results, and, through outside facilitating agencies, the ability to create their own sales promotion materials. They were closer to their customers and understood the systems better, so it was difficult for centralized marketers to claim responsibility for these efforts. Marketing was not becoming less important; rather, marketing functions were being taken over by those who were closer to the customer. The marketing staff was beginning to be seen as a group that should work on corporate marketing issues such as developing the corporate brand and the business-unit marketing plans.

Cross-functional teams are becoming more important in all areas of the corporation, but CRM is a leading area. Cross-functional CRM teams have to deal with issues as diverse as hardware, technology, and business systems on the one hand and managing acquisition, retention, development, migration, loyalty, win-back, and privacy strategies on the other. Will the traditional marketing function tackle these efforts, or will they fall to IT or the line division? Or, as is increasingly possible, will companies create new organizational structures that contain vice presidents of customer relationships? It does not really matter as long as the most effective and efficient group is performing the marketing function.

3.7c Transactional Marketing Is Being Replaced by Relationship Marketing

Product and brand managers have traditionally specialized in "push" marketing: pushing the product through the channel, onto the shelves, and into the customers' hands. Traditional mass-marketing efforts created awareness of the product or brand, created positive feelings and preference, and moved the product off the shelves through point-of-purchase (POP) displays and sales promotion activities such as games, contests, and sweepstakes. Everyone was exposed to the same advertising and sales promotion.

These efforts were the antithesis of efforts required to build a one-to-one relationship with customers, which are based on dialogues. Often, brand and product manager training did not stress this, and some have suggested the development of a new position: the "customer" manager, who is responsible for overseeing the relationship with the customer.[37]

During the U.S. recession of the early 1990s, marketing staff experienced pressure to justify their mass-media spending. Mass-media results were difficult, if not impossible, to measure. IT-supported approaches such as direct mail, telephone, and Internet communications were far less expensive, could reach masses of people individually, and, perhaps most importantly, could produce measurable results.

Business has developed new promotional techniques over the past ten years as mass media has fragmented. Their results are less predictable and still not measurable. Product placement has become a common marketing promotional tool, as has guerilla marketing. Internet-based viral marketing has been effective for many industries. With one-to-one communication feasible on the Internet and through text messaging, companies will possibly continue to put their promotional dollars behind such efforts to the detriment of mass-media–related firms. Will marketing department personnel or CRM personnel be the drivers of these new efforts? Whatever the answer, it is increasingly likely that sales and marketing systems will attach themselves to CRM systems. Whether an IT or marketing person heads CRM is likely to be based on capabilities rather than in which department the person originated.

What is apparent is that forces that will not abate are changing the dynamics of business across the globe: customers can personally access increasingly greater amounts of information. They now go car shopping knowing more about competitive prices than the salesperson. This information, gleaned from the Internet, has obvious implications for the future of informational-type advertising. Since customers are using the Internet more and more to handle information search and product transactions, companies must learn new techniques to uncover customer needs and measure results of their efforts.

Some feel that CRM's future not only will include traditional mass marketing but also will absorb the functions of the traditional brand manager.[38] We feel that it is highly unlikely that CRM, with its focus on one-to-one relationships, would ever include mass-marketing strategy development and implementation. Whether CRM's realm will include brand management is moot. Brand or customer managers will make increasing use of CRM to build bonds between the brand and its customers.

Mass-media advertising campaigns are increasingly being replaced by interactions with the user that help to enhance the brand. Such approaches can create differentiation and excitement, greatly boosting a brand's leadership and popularity. Furthermore, both the company and customer can briskly move up the learning curve with regard to each other. Some have actually defined CRM in terms of the brand.[39] T. Gokey and H. Yin state:

> So what really is CRM? CRM is all about building a strong brand. It does so by creating the right blend of organization systems and processes that allow your people to understand your customers as individuals, and potentially to tailor every interaction with a customer to their specific needs.[40]

CRM systems can provide customers with added brand value by doing the four things that brands are supposed to do: provide value, save time, provide convenience, and allow for customization. Customers can now design their own jeans, shoes, gardens, and investment advisory services.

Today, customers are increasingly initiating interactions with companies. Companies need to develop techniques to monitor customer use of their websites and deliver content depending on individual needs. For example, the Thailand Tourism Board can monitor an individual's use of its website and ultimately detect whether the person is oriented toward five-star hotels or hostels. It can then customize its offerings to the individual. Similarly, if a website user is interested in food, particular sports, particular parts of the country, islands and snorkeling, visiting during a particular time of year, shopping, or simply finding the best bargains, the Thailand Tourism Board can customize its offerings or let users personalize their own site.

Some have gone so far as to say that the 4 P's—the standard image of marketing for 50 years— have outlived their usefulness. J. Peel suggests they be replaced with the **4 C's** (as laid out by the Gartner Group): content, context, collaboration, and community.[41] D. Peppers and M. Rogers also use the 4 C's acronym but use a different mix of C's. They state that companies need to deliver customer value, lower costs, better convenience, and better communications.[42] T. Osenton argues that the 4 P's acronym be kept but updated to people, preferences, permission, and precision—all characteristics of CRM.[43]

Others feel that mass-media advertising will not disappear, since it is necessary to "feed the funnel" and get prospects into the pipeline. Actually, what has occurred with CRM is that another level of marketing and communications planning has been opened. Joining mass marketing, with its emphasis on broadcast TV and radio, newspapers, and general interest magazines, and niche marketing, with its emphasis on special interest magazines and subscription TV, is relationship marketing. The latter emphasizes in-person interactions, telephone and e-mail correspondence, and direct mail.

Whatever the case, many feel that marketing and CRM are not coordinated and that companies have not applied CRM concepts and techniques to marketing. What is probably true is that marketing planners and strategists have not used the new strategies available as a result of CRM; however, companies are improving their coordination efforts.

3.7d The Customer Interaction Center is Becoming the Nexus for Customer, Sales, and Management Information

Some, but not all, companies today are making effective use of their customer interaction centers (CICs), realizing that their CICs provide them with data that is impossible to obtain through any other method. Some product and marketing staff have never visited their CIC, and yet the CIC is the key source for information about the customer and the company's products—for example, deficiencies, strengths, suggested improvements, and new product ideas. The CIC should not be isolated from marketing because it provides unbiased feedback from customers. Along with the customer database, the CIC should be the nexus for collecting marketing research information.

Relationship marketing has its basis in a dialogue between a company and its customers. As such, it must not simply send messages to individuals; rather, it must engage them in dialogue. CIC personnel are perhaps in the best position to obtain customer feedback concerning company service, product quality, and impressions of new products and ideas. Difficulties with instructions, directions, and product usage will reach CIC personnel first. Company frontliners can also decipher intensity of feeling. CIC personnel gather a wealth of marketing research information each week—perhaps not the standard types, but important information nonetheless. Those in marketing management, sales, marketing research, and product design functions could continuously benefit from CIC's information.

3.7e CRM Creates Useful Measures of Purchase Behavior and Customer Segments

Marketing researchers have always been able to collect information on customers' wants and needs, attitudes, and brand purchase behavior; however, brand purchase behavior measures were based on memory or diaries maintained by a few panel members. As such, they merely provided a broad

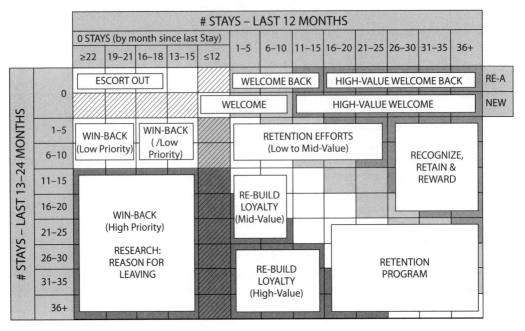

Figure 3.4 Hilton 13 Segment Matrix

Source: Jim Von Derheide, VP, CRM Strategy, Hilton Hotels Corporation Presentation at MSI Conference: Taking Stock of Customer Relationships, March 1, 2006. Used by permission of Jim VonDerheide.

gauge of a company's marketing effectiveness. CRM systems enable companies to measure many other aspects of a customer's interface with the company, such as customer purchase cycle (i.e., the time between a customer's repeat purchase of goods and services), customer channel usage, and the concurrent opportunities it provides for a company's interaction with the customer.

In addition, analytical processing techniques allow companies to manage the development and retention of customers, which results in defining new types of market segments. Managing migration, while always a broad theoretical construct, has become highly actionable because it relies on readily available customer records in the data warehouse. McKinsey & Company define **migration** as the change in customer value over time and claim that managing migration can represent two to four times more value than managing attrition.[44] Further, the available data, when analyzed properly, can become a warning system, allowing marketers to take action before certain customers defect. Hilton Hotels Corporation developed a matrix based on customer recency and frequency of stays. They identify 13 segments, each receiving different types of promotional appeals with different attached objectives (Figure 3.4).

3.8 Reorganizing Marketing to Maximizing the Benefits of CRM

Companies today are, for the most part, organized around products, markets, sales, or channels; therefore, a company's move toward CRM, with its focus on the customer, almost always involves trauma because organizational charts have to be redrawn. Since CRM belongs to the enterprise and not exclusively to IT, CCC, sales, or marketing, CRM will cause changes in the way companies are organized. For example, the traditional product management system has worked for years; however, it is not built around one-to-one relationships. Product managers have been responsible for monitoring customer needs, developing and modifying the product/service offering to meet those needs, coordinating advertising and sales promotion at all levels within the channel, and selling as much as possible. Their tools and mental marketing sets are based on mass transactions as opposed to relationships.

The parameters of the product management system did not often include feedback from customers as an intrinsic product manager input (except through marketing research reports), much less include dialogues with millions of customers. Customer service representatives conduct such dialogues, however, and their findings are valuable.

Just as companies are beginning to organize around customer segments rather than product lines, globalization is effecting change within companies organized on geographic regions. Global hotel chains would find their efforts disjointed if they managed each geographic region independently. Which would be responsible for managing the global customer? With CRM systems, the management focus *is* the customer, and the centralized CRM system has no problem managing relationships with regional or global customers. Companies that focus on managing their channels are forced to hire more and more people, in this age of channel proliferation, in order to staff each new channel. Clearly, this is a costly and ineffective organizational structure for most companies.

Few companies attempt to measure the cumulative effect of the promotion messages they aim at consumers. Since consumers today are bombarded with messages from a multitude of sources, it is important that a company interacts with its customers in a continuous but unobtrusive way. This means that its messages must be relevant within the dialogue it has established with its customers. The messages must also be consistent across all customer touch points, whether the gift wrapper in the retail store, the delivery personnel, or the customer service representative, and all media channels, whether home pages on the Internet, television commercials, or messages on the ATM.

With product, channel, and media proliferation and fractionalization, and with more and more companies dealing in the global marketplace, it is likely that current organizational structures will undergo significant modification. Some have suggested that companies organize themselves around their customers in the form of customer portfolios run by "segment managers." These segment managers would be responsible for optimizing the profitability and loyalty of their customer portfolios. They would be responsible for acquiring, developing, and retaining customers, while product managers would be responsible for developing the products that satisfy each segment's needs. Segment managers would become the coordinators of marketing communications and channel management.[45]

Another organizational possibility is the rise of the separate CRM department, which would become the perfect conduit for converting customer needs into marketing imperatives. As such, the CRM department would become the driving force behind product development and marketing efforts. It would be best positioned to decipher channel placement, since it monitors customer channel preferences. It would manage customer service, since it controls the CIC. The department would even be in a good position to develop and initiate acquisition efforts, since it could match existing customer profiles with similar prospects. The best situation would see marketing and CRM departments working in tandem to process customer information, develop strategies, and measure results.

A paradigm put forth by C. Moorman and R. T. Rust, based, in part, on some of the work of George Day and Frederick Webster, offered insights into the future organizational relationship between marketing and CRM. They state that the marketing function should play a role in connecting the customer with the product, service delivery, and financial accountability systems. The traditional role of marketing has been to link the customer with the product, while the other two connections are fairly new and primarily due to advances in IT. CRM has facilitated these two connections, between customers and service delivery, and customers and financial accountability.[46]

By looking at marketing with respect to these three connections, one can conclude that marketing may own the customer–product connection, while CRM will own the other two. The department managing the customer–product connection will be responsible for product strategy, branding strategy, price, and promotion—traditional marketing department functions. The customer–service delivery department will be responsible for improving customer satisfaction and loyalty through management of loyalty and retention programs. The customer–financial accountability department will be responsible for managing customer profitability through data mining and determining the profitability of marketing initiatives. These two departments' existence is based on CRM inputs.

For the marketing/CRM interface, the implications of such a paradigm are critical. The 4 P's are acquisition variables and important in feeding the pipeline. The customer–service delivery function revolves around CRM and is focused on satisfying customers and creating customer loyalty—a relationship as opposed to a transaction orientation. It will be interesting to see how organizations structure themselves in order to exploit customer acquisition and maintenance, maximizing the benefits that will accrue through a smooth marketing/CRM interface.

Chapter Summary

Marketers have started shifting their focus from acquisition of new customers to maintenance, enhancement, and retention of customers through numerous strategies called CRM. What are the forces driving marketers to focus so intently on customer and partner relationships? IT enables companies to develop and analyze customer transaction histories. The development of 800 numbers and nationwide customer acceptance of charge cards led to dramatic growth in direct marketing. And marketers believed they could increase profits by serving existing customers, increasing their retention, and managing downward migration.

This led to the development of relationship marketing—a focus on relationships rather than one-time transactions; a focus on individuals rather than mass-market segments; and a connection between the company and the customer, characterized by communication and commitment, resulting in a mutual achievement of goals. Relationship marketing attempts to strengthen the company–customer bond, moving from a simple transactional focus to social bonding to a partnership based, perhaps, on a structural solution. Relationship marketing realizes that not all customers should be targeted equally. "True Friends" rank high and "Strangers" should be brought into the fold, but companies must be careful about spending on "Butterflies" and "Barnacles." According to relationship marketers, customer satisfaction as a variable may be too weak to describe the strength and depth of a relationship, and trust and commitment are better predictors of future behavior. Trust and commitment can be achieved through problem solving, uncovering unmet needs in the market, and developing products and services to meet these needs.

If the purpose of marketing is to establish, maintain, and enhance relationships, then relationship marketing creates many issues for traditional marketing. For example, if the focus is on relationships, how does this affect the marketing mix? If marketing is far too important to leave to the marketing department, where does that leave the marketing department? If marketing becomes decentralized, what happens to the centralized marketing department?

Relationship marketing makes marketing more effective and efficient. It will lead to greater marketing productivity, encouraging companies to engage in even greater efforts to maintain long-term relationships with customers.

Key Terms

4 C's are a modern adaptation of the 4 P's, consisting of customer value, better convenience, lower costs, and better communications. The 4 C's describe the marketing mix from the customer's viewpoint as opposed to the company's viewpoint.

Affinity marketing is developing programs or promotions for well-defined groups such as alumni, professional, or demographic segments. The Notre Dame Visa Card is an example of an affinity program. Affinity marketing is used primarily to differentiate commodity-type products or services.

Co-branding involves combining two brand names—for example, the Ford Explorer Eddie Bauer Edition or Intel's co-branding with IBM and Compaq.

Commitment refers to one's desire and effort to maintain a long-term relationship.

Extended Product Model is also called the Product Component Model. The model extends the core component of a product (function, style, design, features, and need satisfaction) to include a packaging component consisting of price, quality, styling, and branding, as well as a support services component consisting of installation, delivery, servicing, and repair and maintenance.

Marketing mix is mixing the four key marketing variables—4 P's, or product, place, promotion, and price—in the best way possible to satisfy your target markets better than the competition.

Migration refers to an upward or downward change in customer value over time. Companies manage migration by developing databases that make them aware of customers who are becoming less profitable. Downward migration is considered a greater source of company losses than defection.

Satisfaction can be overall or cumulative satisfaction, which describes overall experiences with a company or product over time, and transaction-specific satisfaction, which describes feelings about a single recent transaction.

Trust refers to one's confidence in a partner's reliability, honesty, and integrity and the belief that a partner's actions are in one's best interest. Trust is a function of a partner's credibility (reputation for fairness and satisfaction with outcomes) and benevolence (caring and sacrificing for one's partner).

Questions

1. What forces drove marketers to begin focusing so intently on customer and partner relationships?
2. Describe relationship marketing and its domain.
3. Relationship marketing is applicable on at least ten different levels. What are some of these levels?
4. How does relationship marketing benefit consumers? Companies?
5. Will relationship marketing benefit every company in its dealings with every customer? If not, which companies would benefit most from relationship marketing efforts?
6. Trust and commitment are central to successful relationship marketing. What is meant by trust and commitment, and why are they so important to long-term relationships?
7. Is there a difference between relationship marketing and customer relationship management?
8. It can be argued that marketing is becoming so important that its practice must be decentralized throughout all departments, not just the marketing department. What are some of the causes of this?
9. How will CRM affect traditional company organization?

Exercises

1. Research how direct mail and direct marketing helped influence the creation of CRM.
2. Companies such as Procter & Gamble have started to organize around customers. What other companies have done so, and what have been their experiences?

3. We have discussed CRM systems with a focus on a company and its customers. Describe the value of CRM systems between a manufacturer and its:
    a. Suppliers
    b. Wholesalers
    c. Retailers
    d. Sales force
    e. Employees
4. Develop a list of companies (or types of companies) for which CRM systems would be extremely valuable. Develop a list of companies (or types of companies) for which CRM systems would not have much value. Explain why companies made each list.
5. How can companies develop social bonds with their customers? How can companies develop structural bonds with their customers?
6. What companies would classify you as a True Friend? Butterfly? Barnacle? Stranger? What could the companies that classify you as a Butterfly, Barnacle, or Stranger do, if anything, to make you a True Friend?
7. Companies used to organize and manage around the 4 P's: product, place, promotion, and price. Today, some suggest that companies should organize and manage around the 4 C's: customer value, lower costs, better convenience, and better communications. Discuss the causes and the benefits of such a shift in focus.

Chapter 4

Organization and CRM

4.1 Introduction

This chapter examines how organizational dynamics impact, both positively and negatively, the CRM initiative. The chapter is intended to raise awareness of those areas to be addressed when contemplating implementation of a CRM environment or just performing an evaluation of a current CRM initiative. Each area mentioned could itself be the topic of several chapters, so depth is limited. The reader will soon determine that people, organizational structures, and value chain relationships are areas that precipitate the largest challenges when discussing CRM initiatives. CRM technology solutions alone are, with few exceptions, a proven commodity that, if implemented and maintained properly, are not a major cause for concern from a performance perspective. Technology can become a concern, however, if the other dimensions are not optimally managed. This does not make light of the complexity of CRM technology, but most CRM technology solutions are optimal if used appropriately. The chapter concludes with a table that suggests approaches to implementing and maintaining CRM implementation. This table is intended to provide the reader with an overall perspective of areas to be considered and is not intended to be an all-inclusive implementation plan. Specific technology issues are discussed later in the text.

The process of defining an effective CRM strategy must take into consideration the reality of the organizational environment. This should include all of the organizations in the organization's value chain. As organizations intensify their focus on their core competencies, it is extremely important that they examine the entire value chain when defining a CRM strategy, as the strategy will only be as effective as the weakest link in the chain.

A multidimensional thought process is also necessary when discussing CRM within the context of organizational and channel structures and forces. There is a business dimension, a technological dimension, and a human dimension. A change to one will impact the others. Underlying all three is the dimension of time. According to a survey conducted by online resource center CRM Forum, when asked what went wrong with their CRM projects, 4 percent of the managers cited software problems, and 1 percent said they received bad advice, but 87 percent pinned the failure of their CRM programs on the lack of adequate change management.[1]

Typically, change management efforts include the identification of the leaders of change, the change agents, targets of change, and those that may resist change. These principles apply to the changes required when moving to a CRM-focused environment. Thomas H. Davenport states that the most important organizational change issues in any systems initiative have to do with education and training. His research has shown that organizations spend between 25 and 50 percent of project budgets on educational and skills development issues. Davenport also identifies the following examples of change required:

- Technical people need to learn the nature of the software, the hardware, and the networking requirements needed to run the system, as well as the system's overall performance characteristics.
- Process designers need to learn what process designs the system is capable of supporting and what the implications of seeking a change in the configuration would be.
- Each business user needs to learn the day-to-day use of the system, how the system supports the process that he/she performs, and how it affects the broader organization each time he/she presses a key.
- Senior executives need to learn the implications of the system for strategy, organization, and business processes, in addition to how the newly enabled organization can compete more effectively using the system.[2]

A program is a tactical strategy. If a CRM program effort is not an integrated extension of the overall vision, it may be unpredictably or unsustainably successful. Optimally, a CRM vision is created at the highest level of an organization, followed by goals, objectives, strategies, and plans. In reality, however, sometimes a simple CRM initiative creates momentum from success. As senior leadership sees that success, it can create the CRM vision for the entire organization. In fact, this may be the most prudent approach with regard to organization and business environment dynamics. The reality is that organizations consist of people, and it is people who make decisions and who work in areas critical to implementing and sustaining a CRM environment. This chapter generates thoughts on organizational environment forces that affect efforts to build and sustain an optimal CRM environment in the organization and, in some instances, the value chain.

4.2 The Human Factor

4.2a Leadership

I am well versed in the subject of CRM. I feel comfortable with our CRM goals and objectives. The plan to implement CRM is well thought out and fits a "textbook" strategy. However, I am very concerned about our ability to execute the strategy. The main obstacle as I see it is unfortunately our own organization. Outside my area, there does not seem to be the same excitement and understanding of the benefits of implementing a CRM strategy. Our leadership just does not seem to "get it."

—Director of Marketing for a Fortune 1000 organization

The preceding quote demonstrates a typical challenge. CRM initiatives rarely start as company-wide, top-down initiatives from executive management. In order to be sustainable and successful, CRM must be treated as a business methodology that the entire organization and value chain adopt. In many instances, it is a radical change to the way an organization conducts business.

Organizations must reinvent themselves as having a business process that focuses on the customer and on developing customer loyalty. Failure to achieve total adoption may lead to some success, but the initiative as a whole will not be optimal. In fact, inconsistent adoption of CRM can confuse the customer. CRM requires an organization to create a total customer-centric mentality.

Research on the CRM implementation efforts of three separate organizations by H. W. Kim and S. L. Pan demonstrated that for a CRM implementation to succeed, it needs continuity of champion activity and strong leadership and influence from the champion until project completion.[3] The organizations stuthed were in the same industry and similar in many aspects, which minimized variances in the research. Out of the three organizations studied, one successfully implemented a CRM environment, while the other two had less than optimal experiences and results. In the case where an organization successfully implemented CRM, the CEO invested huge resources to the effort and continued on as its champion. In the second organization, the CEO allocated substantial budgetary resources but was unable to sustain his personal commitment to the project. Getting leadership from other senior management was not successful. As a result, business department managers perceived the project as a typical systems development project. In the third organization, the CEO recruited CRM experts, which were marketing experts. The CEO then delegated all responsibilities of development to this new CRM team, which was structured under the marketing department. The absence of a champion made it extremely difficult for the new team to gain support across business and IT teams.

While leadership at the CEO or high executive level is critical to success for a self-contained CRM implementation, it is mandatory for when other organizations are part of the CRM blueprint, which is usually the norm.

4.2b Human Resource Capacity

> I understand the importance of CRM and agree that our organization needs to leverage these types of marketing efforts to sustain and grow our business in our increasingly competitive marketplace. My concern is we have limited resources and conflicts in setting priorities. On top of this, my staff is not current in CRM technical best practices. I am worried that this CRM effort could fail and the opportunity costs are high.
>
> —Chief technology officer for a midsize manufacturer

This quote illustrates a common problem: limited human resources. With CRM adoption, human resources can be categorized as CRM enablers and CRM users. The enablers are skilled technologists. The users are employees who use the CRM technical infrastructure to support their CRM efforts. The enablers' primary focus is support of the organization's operational infrastructure. They are usually consumed in development, implementation, and maintenance of the organization's core operational system environments. A CRM imitative is usually perceived as a noncritical system component and may not get the attention it deserves. Enablers must be shown CRM's inherent value. They must be given time to become proficient in CRM technology or be given additional support from outside the organization, either temporarily or permanently.

Outsourcing some or all of the enabling effort reduces direct labor costs and eliminates the risk for finding, motivating, and retaining talented people. The advent of "cloud-computing" technology methods and "paying as you go" or leasing-enabling services has also contributed to more organizations choosing to outsource these functions. Outsourcing, however, increases the risk of lesser quality and adherence to the organization's CRM strategy.

THEORY IN ACTION

Hitachi

In many of the CRM projects that failed in the financial industry in Japan, we found an organizational and operational barrier between customer contact points and back-end analysts and/or marketers. For instance, even though marketers create a campaign program based on customer information analysis, front-end officers, such as bank sales representatives, sometimes do not understand why they should communicate specific messages to their customers. Rather, front-end officers will stick to their own customer information base (such as self-developed spreadsheet macros) and show a significant resistance to use CRM new technology because they feel that "changes in operations" will just cause painful moments for them.

CRM itself will not work if it is not used at the customer front end (i.e., customer contact points). It is important to let the customer front end "willingly" use the CRM infrastructure in order to ensure the success of CRM implementation. For that purpose, the CRM system should prove itself that it will contribute to the revenue generation for the front end before organization-wide rollout, and the real success story is important even if the level of success is small initially. In many cases, executives tend to require a quick return on investment (ROI), and it sometimes reinforces a large-scale rollout from the beginning without proving the concept at all. These cases lead to total disaster and a waste of money. It is critical to prove that the CRM system actually works, and all staff involved in CRM activities need to be educated.

Many cases in Japan have proved that "accumulation of small successes will finally lead to huge success." The entire organization should understand this conventional wisdom when they want to have a CRM environment that works.

Toshiya Cho, Senior Vice President, Financial Information Systems Division, Hitachi, Ltd.

CRM users must also be given time to learn and practice CRM techniques. Imagine a store clerk spending time with a valued customer while simultaneously looking over the customer's shoulder as the line of waiting customers grows. CRM must consider the number of employees and the time each expects to spend with a customer. Investments must be made in training and motivating customer contact employees in the art of CRM. This increases labor costs and places pressure on employee retention efforts.

4.2c Communication

This whole project has turned into a disaster. It really is a shame. We were 60 percent complete on designing the CRM data collection and data warehouse design when we found out that our customer's marketing area was not aware of their own corporate initiative to implement a company-wide ERP environment. The creation of a separate CRM system does not make sense at this point. They have spent over 1 million dollars to date on an environment that cannot be used. I guess there was a failure to communicate.

—Project leader for a major consulting firm

Unfortunately, the previous observation is all too common. It is important to communicate the potential adoption of a CRM methodology throughout the organization before formulating a specific strategy. This typically precipitates positive and negative reactions, as well as opportunities and constraints across multiple dimensions, including financial, technology, competitive environment, and value chain issues. This input is critical to the CRM strategy process. A realistic CRM objective follows the overall CRM strategy. A tactical strategy to achieve that objective is defined and a plan to accomplish the strategy enacted. Each phase of this process must be communicated at the outset and throughout implementation to everyone impacted. Communication should include value chain members, who are likely part of the organization's operational processes as buyers, suppliers, or enablers.

As part of its CRM initiative, the company must also balance respective business profitability and strategic objectives, while building and maintaining customer loyalty. The organization relies on people, processes, and technology to support its CRM initiative. To fulfill requirements and adhere to any constraints, nearly all areas are impacted or have an impact, including value chain members.

4.2d Cooperation

Our corporate team has made the decision to proceed with a CRM strategy throughout our properties. Two of our properties are within a short distance of each other and compete for the same customers at times. One of the property managers is reluctant to share customer and prospect information with the corporation. Someone needs to make a decision.

—Vice President of Marketing for Casino Operations

The preceding quote raises the issue of strategic business unit (SBU) conflict. When two or more SBUs are in competition, corporate leadership must induce cooperation. This problem can occur at various levels, requiring essentially the same solution. The CRM strategy will only be successful if the SBUs (in this case) understand their role and the benefits involved. The solution in this case was to create a "communication" customer warehouse. Each SBU provided all relevant information on current and prospective customers, which was then organized to facilitate access. One SBU, however, could only access nonidentifying data for the other SBU's customers. It could analyze the information, but it would require the other SBU's permission to initiate customer communication. This strategy fostered cooperation. Each SBU had the benefit of a common database. Through analysis, they gained a better understanding of their customers and prospects. Communication to customers and prospects was more efficient and reduced the risk of overcommunication. The company as a whole benefited financially from economies of scale and from a competitive standpoint. Similar strategies can be created for divisional and departmental scenarios.

4.2e People

We have invested a tremendous amount of money to implement what appears to be an excellent CRM environment. One thing we discovered was that the people in our organization that have the biggest impact on our CRM effort are the lowest-paid employees who also have the least amount of information and a lack of direction on our effort. We need to fix this immediately!

—Director of Marketing for a major consumer cataloger

People are instrumental in forming and sustaining relationships, which is important to CRM success. Although telemarketers do not receive high compensation, they nevertheless are a key component of a CRM strategy.

At the outset, current employees' CRM knowledge should be evaluated to identify skill gaps. Dialogues should take place with any employees who may be involved with the CRM initiative. Observations of customer–employee interactions should be made and recorded. These dialogues and observations may raise issues, constraints, and opportunities that are useful to strategy formulation.

CRM benefits for both the customer and the employee should be communicated to the employee. While information sessions and meetings are important for CRM dissemination, they are not nearly as effective as having the employee involved. Some organizations have created workshops with simulations and role-playing, not only to introduce the CRM concepts but also to start building a buy-in from the employee. For example, the creation of an interactive website or an 800 number for employees to access as if they were a customer, either as a simulation or an employees-only business application, has been implemented by many companies. The employee may purchase a product, for example, and a follow-up workshop or survey is used to solicit the experience from the employee. By having the employee involved in the process, it is easier to disseminate the knowledge and to encourage buy-ins.

Interactive activities may also include rewards. One organization had a 100-question exam posted on its company intranet. The exam covered basic CRM concepts as well as applications of CRM specific to the organization. Taking the exam was mandatory, but practice tests, aimed at helping employees learn about the system, were made available. Final test scores were posted on the intranet. Soon, office buzz centered on CRM. This example is extreme, but it shows that employee involvement is critical.

Employee role or objective conflict is another area that requires addressing. CRM may be a drastic change for some organizations, requiring a certain level of employee empowerment. That is where the conflict surfaces. An employee accustomed to complying with service standards with no room for modification may be hesitant or incapable because of conflict. To get around this, for example, a high-end retailer allows its employees, as representatives of the company, to absorb up to $100 in costs to satisfy a customer. This removes the employee's conflict and increases the effectiveness of the transaction. Employees' behavior often needs modification when CRM is in practice.

An additional skill, albeit one that is harder to train and learn, is customer selection. Having employees well versed in how to spend time and money on the "right" customers will help optimize the return on a CRM investment because they minimize or eliminate costs incurred with the "wrong" customer. This may sound harsh, but the reality is that there are limited resources that must be utilized effectively. Empowering the employee with information at the time of customer contact is the way one retail organization supported this concept. By providing color-coded icons on a point-of-sale (POS) screen as a result of a customer inquiry, the employee was able to determine quickly whether the customer they were about to spend considerable time with was in fact the "right" customer. The icon was green if the customer was profitable, yellow if not enough information or potential existed for profitability, and red for the "wrong" customer. Which color appeared resulted from transactional history, including not only products purchased and their respective margins but also whether they were purchased on sale and how much postsale time was spent with the customer (returns, etc.). This process helped ensure that the employee spent the right amount of time with the "right" customer and minimized time spent with the "wrong" customer. The employee increased his or her commission and felt good about the process, thus building momentum.

THEORY IN ACTION

OakLawn Marketing

OakLawn Marketing is one of the most successful direct marketing companies in Japan. Started by Robert Roche from Oak Lawn, Illinois, OakLawn Marketing has grown rapidly in the 11 years since its conception. It is so successful that it is preparing to expand into neighboring countries. Its primary business is selling goods, the majority of which it does not make, to Japanese consumers over the Web and over the phone via its inbound telemarketing staff. Customers can order 24 hours a day, 7 days a week. Its employees work from a customer call center (CCC) in Nagoya, Japan. Most employees are part time, some working only three hours a day. OakLawn Marketing is sensitive to the local culture and provides flexibility in scheduling and thorough training (initial and ongoing), and it is extremely supportive of its employees' needs. The company provides each employee in the CCC with the same merchandise that it sells to customers. Harry Hill, chief operating officer, believes that providing the employee products for home use enriches the selling proposition when they talk with customers. Employees then speak from experience and in a manner similar to friends suggesting products. Hill adds that an ancillary benefit is unbiased hands-on feedback from its employees, who share both good and bad product experiences with their employer as well as with the customer. The employee feedback is a critical input to the process of determining which products to sell, as Japan has strict guidelines with regard to selling products that do not match product description. The result is more depth of sales for fewer products, greater customer satisfaction, and reduced costs. The employees sell more products, they are enthusiastic about what they sell, and they buy into the process. Everyone is a winner!

That said, employees should not totally eliminate the "wrong" customer. People do change, and it may be prudent to attempt to build a profitable relationship occasionally. Perhaps scheduling an appointment with the "wrong" customer at an off-peak time could reduce or eliminate any costs lost not spending time with the "right" customer and potentially lead to some conversion of "wrong" customers. At the very least, it would give the employee an opportunity to experiment with new CRM techniques.

Organizations sometimes fall into traps when training and supporting their employees in CRM utilization. One major mistake is to get employees enthusiastic, provide some initial training, and offer positive reinforcement about results, and then either stop or fail to reinforce the CRM momentum. This confuses both employees and customers as they quickly see through noncommitment strategies. They will also be harder to encourage in the future.

Organizations that reinforce the initiative must ensure that it is progressive, has variety, and is used optimally. Too much of a good thing may have a negative impact. Employees usually learn quickly if they have a buy-in. If a CRM strategy does not move them along a curve, they will become bored, fail to see relevancy, and possibly lose a current buy-in. The strategy should be progressive, leading to increasing success with the customer, which should then lead to an employee's success (e.g., commissions, recognition, and advancement). A strategy that fails to incorporate variety or is used too often may induce a robotic effect.

Research conducted by M. D. Hartline and D. Bejou has shown that there is growing momentum in linking human resources to market performance. Thus, internal marketing and internal customer relationship strategies enhance the CRM efforts with external customers.[4] A lesson gained from this research is to establish relationships with and in between employees first to increase chances for success with the overall CRM initiative.

THEORY IN ACTION

A "Not-So-Good Story"

The retail grocery business is extremely competitive. Grocers are implementing subtle CRM techniques across all levels because most of their employees come into direct contact with customers throughout the store. This is a good thing. In one major grocery chain's effort to control the messages they envisioned their employees communicating to their customers, everyone was instructed to say the same thing after a customer interaction: "Thank you for shopping at Grocery X. We appreciate your business. Have a nice day!" Sounds good, right? But look at the customer impact. Customers buy groceries every week. They usually go at the same time and take the same route and make the same stops throughout the store. Let us walk with a customer during a typical store visit. The customer is greeted at the cart corral, at a coffee bar near the entrance, at the deli counter, at the meat counter, at the fish counter, at the pharmacy counter, at the film counter, at the checkout counter by the cashier and the bagger, and finally at a stop by customer service. This customer heard the same greeting at least 10 times. If the customer shops weekly, that is an average of 130 greetings over a three-month period (13 weeks × 10 greetings per weekly visit), which was the life of this particular effort. At what point did the greeting lose its effectiveness? The customer probably was unaffected and may have become annoyed or insulted by the impersonal, repetitive greeting. This problem was compounded by the employees' monotonous tone because they became tired of saying the same greeting over and over as well. In fact, some employees even laughed when saying the greeting. This organization needs variety and mystery shopping to see the impact of a strategy that sounded good in a marketing planning session but was ineffective. Additionally, employees will look on any new effort with suspicion. As one employee mentioned with regard to the customer greeting, "This is the flavor of the month."

4.3 Organization Environment

4.3a Culture

Each organization has a distinct culture. The culture is an intangible variable that has its own effects on the organization. The following are some indicators of a culture that may lead to a suboptimal CRM initiative:

- A reward structure that favors adherence to hard, nonflexible standards
- A production-orientated organization with a heavy concentration of financial, accounting, technological, or engineering leaders (This is not always true but can indicate potential issues.)

- A foreign-owned business where executive management resides in a different country than that of the intended CRM initiative
- Leadership that believes technology is CRM
- Executive leadership that has little customer involvement
- An organization that does not promote reasonable risk taking
- Predominately top-down decision making and information flow
- An internal competitive work methodology and reward systems not aligned within the CRM strategy

Just because an organization has some of these characteristics, it does not necessarily mean that CRM will be inhibited. Conversely, an organization may exhibit none of the characteristics and still create an inhibitive-type CRM culture. For example, a worldwide, highly successful high-tech company was led by a progressive CEO who had instilled an intense internal competitive culture. He felt that out of competitiveness comes greatness, and he was right. A lot of ideas that helped support the company's continued success came directly as a result of internal competitiveness. Employees even had to compete for their own jobs every 18 months. The financial community and the organization's own leadership felt a large part of their success was due to this type of culture. This type of environment, however, left little room for cooperation and collaboration with regard to customer relationships, both internal and external. Culture can be intangible, but it is present, and its impact on a CRM initiative should be defined and assessed before proceeding. The assessment will determine boundaries and allow for a more realistic set of objectives and method of implementation.

Gartner researchers E. Thompson and M. Goldman found that effective CRM requires a fresh view of corporate culture, behavior, and collaboration, and they defined ten best practices (Table 4.1) to help an organization achieve this behavioral change and collaboration.[5] The key findings of their research indicate that change management is critical and requires support beyond the completed implementation of a CRM solution.

4.3b Size

Size is not a determinant of an organization's level of success in adopting a CRM methodology. However, different sizes do precipitate advantages and disadvantages. In many cases, an advantage

---

Table 4.1 **Ten Best Practices to Make CRM Project Change Management More Effective**

1. Adhere to Gartner's five key elements needed to effect behavioral change:
   a. Define the imperative or case for change.
   b. Leaders recognize imperative.
   c. Levers are tools used to encourage behavior change.
   d. Those affected by change must support and adapt.
   e. Buoys are for people to cling to when buffeted by massive change.
2. Know the amount of change before starting.
3. Be sure which key employee and stakeholders need to buy in, and when.
4. Align organizational structure with the customer viewpoint.
5. Communicate how everyone affects the customer experience.
6. Choose the right incentive.
7. Create the environment for collaboration.
8. Don't confuse change management with training.
9. Communicate objectives and performance achievements.
10. Monitor and enhance staff satisfaction.

for one is a disadvantage for the other. Table 4.2 lists some of the advantages and disadvantages of size for large organizations adopting a CRM methodology.

4.3c Structure

Major organizational structure categories include functional, product/service or brand alignment, geographic, key account management, industry category, matrix, and customer based. Each of these structures was probably built to achieve specific strategic objectives. The following discussions provide insight into each structure and how organizations have adapted to a CRM initiative. What must also be considered, which may not be as evident, are the organizational business complexity, organizational culture and politics, and respective exogenous variables.

4.3c.1 Functional Structure

Most organizations structure themselves by business functions. There is a hierarchy structure for each function sometimes referred to as **"silo"** based. This is not desirable, for example, when trying to

Table 4.2 **Advantages and Disadvantages of an Organization's Size**

Advantages	Disadvantages
More financial resources or easier access to those resources	Many are functionally structured with silos
Economies of scale with respect to technology and human resources	Increased complexity in training and implementing CRM
Potentially deeper levels of CRM expertise or easier access to expertise	Customer and prospect data may proliferate without thoughts to a single view of the customer
Readily available technology and CRM consultative suppliers	Difficulty in creating a single, accurate view of the customer
Appropriate funding dollars generated from high-margin customer base	Difficulty in consolidating customer data and transferring it into a single, accurate view of the customer
Large amount of customer and prospect information	Increased likelihood that one part of the organization might use one customer approach, while another part uses a different approach
	Difficulty integrating new technology into existing technical infrastructure without major impacts to other parts of the business
	Complexity of implementing culture change requirements on a large scale
	Increased complexity of implementation and ongoing maintenance and support of CRM business and technical initiatives
	Difficulty in coordinating multiple value chain partners

respond quickly to a customer. It violates the CRM principle that requires internal CRM be implemented first, as a satisfied employee is better equipped to satisfy the customer. The situation may be better or worse if the functional area in question is not within the organization but is instead a value chain member. This will be elaborated upon later in this chapter when value chain members and channel management are discussed. The silo structure type is usually not conducive to successful CRM strategies and can paralyze the organization with respect to customer management. But it is not realistic to think that most organizations will change their entire business structure to adopt a CRM strategy—at least not all at once. McKinsey & Company professionals A. Agarwal, W. E. Pietraszek, and M. Singer propose using a case management approach (i.e., the ability to track sales leads and complex service requests across silos) to bridge these functional areas. They have found that improving a company's case management capabilities through relatively modest changes in processes, technology, and organization can increase cross-channel revenues by 10 to 20 percent while reducing customer churn by 5 to 10 percent. This can be accomplished with minor changes and completed rather quickly, but the main obstacle is a failure to recognize the potential and act on it.[6]

4.3c.2 Product/Service or Brand Alignment Structure

Organizing around a specific brand is common in the packaged goods industry and those manufacturing industries that create a large number of brands or sub-brands. The CRM challenge in this type of environment is to build a holistic view of the customer by combining transaction information across all brands. This information can then demonstrate, for example, which brands are synergistic and inform the respective brand manager of the consumer's current and optimal baskets of goods. Ancillary benefits include more efficient and optimal communication to the consumer. Challenges arise due to brand management reward structures and fear of customer cannibalization.

4.3c.3 Geographic Structure

The more decentralized an organization's customer interactions, the greater the challenges it may have practicing CRM. The following are some of the major challenges:

- Communicating CRM strategies and best practices throughout all customer interaction points
- Timely and accurate disseminating of relative customer and prospect information from all customer interaction touch points, ability to process this data, and timely and accurate reverse information flow
- Flexibility in changing CRM strategy to optimize specific geographic opportunities or adjust to geographic nuances, requirements, or other constraints
- Integrating value chain members across geographic boundaries, including optimal utilization of local versus national partners
- Sustaining the CRM momentum to decentralized employees
- Adopting input from decentralized employees and incorporating that input into the CRM strategy for the specific geographic location or all locations in line with best practices
- Providing supportive organization entities for all different time zone customers, including Internet and phone interactions

4.3c.4 Key Account Management Structure

Suppliers may organize themselves around certain key customers or accounts. These accounts are selected for strategic reasons.

The person or team that manages a key account is probably developing relationships already and to a certain extent is practicing some form of CRM. Account teams usually rely on CRM-enabling software such as Salesforce.com, CDC Software's Pivotal CRM, and Oracle's Seibel CRM to support their CRM efforts.

4.3c.5 Industry Category Structure

Organizations may need to take into account the inherent structure of their industry. Organizational structures are usually formed over time and take on a design that allows companies to operate efficiently in their respective industry. How they interface with their suppliers and buyers usually is an acceptable best practice, as each member in an industry's value chain will tend to adopt the most efficient method of integration and make that method a standard means of operation. If an organization in the value chain sees a major benefit in changing its structure to support its adopted CRM strategy, it must take into account the impact the structure change will have on its value chain partners. There are several considerations in this scenario. For example, the current structure change will invariably lead to some change in how the company conducts business with its value chain partners. If the impact on its partners results in reduced efficiency of its current process, partners will resist change or possibly discontinue the relationship. Similarly, if the impact is too much to absorb, the opportunity costs may create resistance.

4.3c.6 Matrix Structure

A matrix structure can facilitate a customer-centric strategy. It allows a variety of functional skills to be focused on the customer. This structure basically "tags" everyone to the customer and enables these individuals to move and act more freely across functional boundaries. It reduces bureaucracy and "fiefdom" emergence. It decreases internal reaction time, which reduces customer response time.

4.3c.7 Customer-Based Structure

If customers are clustered, there are economies of scale with respect to serving the customer. If customers are fragmented, CRM costs may increase. CRM efforts, however, may include a strategy to focus on "segments of one," where each individual or household is targeted separately with potentially unique value propositions. Do the segment differences dictate multiple versions of CRM strategies and capabilities? Organizations need to determine what, if any, economies of scale can be utilized across multiple customer or prospect segments.

4.3d Technology

CRM efforts are most successful when all technology functions in the organization are integrated. When traditional brick-and-mortar retailers began selling products on the Internet, the customer demand function quickly made the current order-processing technology obsolete. The order-processing system had been designed to provide optimal internal and external service levels in line with customer satisfaction. If a customer ordered a product via a mail-in catalog order form, she would be satisfied if the product was received within 10 to 14 days. A customer who orders a product on the Internet, however, expects receipt within one week or less. Additionally, batch orders provided some buffer of time and control. Internet orders are dynamic, and customers will hold organizations to their delivery promise. Another issue is the technology needed for dynamic demand fluctuations in support of the actual Web pages. Changing the order-processing system to manage real-time orders in addition to normal batch orders is no easy task. The systems that have integrated suppliers and respective retailer product destinations (catalog pickup, home delivery) must also be changed. While the change takes place, the current environment must still be supported and maintained. This puts a tremendous burden on the technical staff. Outsourcing some or all of the work becomes an option. This would require the organization to reinvent itself in terms of how it was leveraging technology. In some cases, the magnitude of these proposed changes has precipitated strategic discussions across executive management teams, including boards of directors, due to the cost and risks of integrating technology throughout the organization and the possibility of outsourcing support and maintenance.

There are two other considerations relative to technology. First, many organizational technology environments are not compatible enough to enable CRM effectively. Some of the reasons for incompatibility or suboptimal environments are as follows:

- A variety of software and hardware platforms from the same or different original equipment manufacturers (**OEMs**)
- Different levels of the same software used in various parts of the organization
- Varying hardware versions or capabilities, including hardware from the same OEM
- Different licenses, leases, or contractual terms for the same or different OEMs
- Organizational silo-based decision making
- Budget constraints
- Lack of strategic and technical understanding and leadership
- High skill-level employee turnover
- Changes in technology solutions over time
- Resistance to frequent change of business process rapid technology adoption causes

Most organizations do not intend to become suboptimal or dysfunctional, but they can easily fall into this trap due to the preceding reasons. Several chapters in this text discuss types of technology used to support CRM objectives. Organizations must determine to what extent their existing employees can evaluate, implement, and support CRM technology. In many cases, the optimal solution is one where the technical activity is a joint effort between IT employees wishing to employ a CRM objective and employees of firms providing technology solutions and technology resources.

Second, an organization merger or acquisition usually creates major technical challenges. Multiply the reasons listed for suboptimal environments by the number of organizations merging or being acquired to illuminate potential issues.

4.3e Process

Your call is important to us. Your wait time will be approximately 20 minutes.

> —Message received by a person at work on their lunch break
> (the company service line was not available after 5:00 p.m.)

I am sorry, but you can't return merchandise here in the store. Since you purchased it on the Internet, you need to send it to the address shown on our Web page and wait for a return acknowledgement of credit.

> —Said to a first-time Web purchaser

The person who can answer your question is currently at lunch, and, unfortunately, there is no one else available who can answer your question at this time. Can you come back in 45 minutes or so?

—Response to a woman with two crying children in a retail store

You have reached our technical support hotline. Our hours are 6:00 a.m. Eastern until 8:00 p.m. Eastern. Please leave a message, and a representative will get back to you during our regular hours.

—A new purchaser of personal computer hardware

These examples may sound familiar, as most consumers incur these experiences frequently. Providing employees with a process that supports CRM is critical to the success of the CRM effort.

In the first example, the long wait stemmed from limited human resources at the time of the call. Organizations can resolve this by outsourcing the call center function. Based on the service-level agreement (**SLA**), call centers can provide the organization with unlimited inbound call capacity, which is attractive to organizations. Additionally, it may cost less because the call center provides economies of scale. The trade-off is loss of control with regard to employee flexibility when interacting with the customer. The call center will require **hard standards** to ensure compliance with the organization's business objective. By staffing its own call center, an organization may incur higher costs; however, these costs may be offset by increased revenue from more satisfied customers.

An interesting phenomenon developed with the advent of the Internet. When existing brick-and-mortar companies incorporated the Internet, many intentionally separated the Web-based business from the traditional retail brick-and-mortar–based business, creating silos. Some reasons for this separation were:

- Financial reporting
- Risk management
- A feeling that different types of individuals were needed to run the e-commerce side of the business
- A perception that online business was entirely different from a traditional brick-and-mortar business

In the second example, creating Internet versus non-Internet silos was not an optimal method of integrating the two channels, as this particular scenario could be the result of poor or nonexistent communication between the organization's silos. Unfortunately, the employee has dissatisfied the customer due to a process constraint. A subtle outcome, if this continues, is employee dissatisfaction. Plus, one has to wonder if the first-time Web purchaser will purchase from either channel again.

In the third example, cost containment pressures may have created the temporary shortage of knowledgeable personnel. The last thing that woman needed to hear was to come back later. A knowledge-based system may be of help in this situation. If an employee does not have the knowledge to answer a question, a system that could provide the answer would lead to customer satisfaction. The system could be software at POS that allows the employee to search for the answer, a call to an internal support pool of knowledgeable personnel, or some combination of the two.

In the last example, the company made a conscious decision not to provide technical support after a certain hour. The reasons that a company may choose to do this may be cost containment, shortage of qualified people willing to work certain hours of the day, or perhaps statistical results that show minimal need after a certain time frame. With cost containment, the organization makes a decision, hopefully knowing the negative impact on customer relationships. A shortage of people precipitates the question "Why is there a shortage?" Is it because there are not enough people, or is it because there are enough people but they will not work later hours? Looking at different geographic regions for people could solve this problem. The last reason, statistical results, is a numbers game. The organization has to decide whether a fewer number of potential customer calls justifies the cost of manning personnel.

So what is the right process? Whatever it is, it should not be one that prevents the employee from satisfying the customer. While many industries have what can be considered best practices, possibly the best approach to define optimal process is to work backward from the customer's perspective. The company should define as many customer interaction scenarios as possible. From a customer relationship–building standpoint, the company must determine the optimal process or justify a suboptimal process, including risk assessment. While outsourcing a process makes it easier to implement and is usually an attractive direct cost reduction, a company must also consider the indirect and opportunity costs of outsourcing.

4.4 Value Chain Organization and Considerations

An organization's well-planned CRM strategy can fail if it does not take into account the capabilities and willingness of its value chain members. Each function may have multiple subfunctions and multiple organizations providing these subfunctions. They may also leverage vendor-managed inventory (VMI), just-in-time (JIT) supply and demand aggregators, and exchanges. As organizations move to increase efficiencies and reduce cost, these function interactions have increased in number and complexity as some have been eliminated and new ones have been added. Across the whole chain, there has been an infusion of strategic collaboration. Radio-frequency identification (RFID) and self-service technologies each are creating new partners and processes. Internet and mobile commerce have created opportunities but require in-depth expertise, usually provided by partners. The following examples illustrate current changes in value chain organizations and methods.

- *Scenario 1*: An installer and maintenance subcontractor for a major appliance retailer is currently servicing a customer. He determines that he will need to return to finish the maintenance work and sets up a time with the customer. At the same time, the retailer's salesperson completes a sale in the same market area as the subcontractor and, after looking at the subcontractor's schedule in her POS system, schedules an installation for the same time the subcontractor just promised for his maintenance call completion. At the very least, one or both customers will be inconvenienced. The subcontractor may also be inconvenienced, depending on the distance between the two customers.
- *Scenario 2*: Part of a cruise line company's CRM strategy included recognizing loyal customers on the gangplank, ensuring they were assigned their favorite cabin location, and providing perks such as favorite fruits in their complimentary fruit basket. Unfortunately, the travel agency that made the reservations was reluctant to share specific customer information.
- *Scenario 3*: A construction company's major challenge was the coordination of building supplies and tradespeople. It wanted to keep its delivery date promises but struggled to deliver within 30 days of the promised date.

A major U.S. landline communications company provides high-speed Internet access to its customers as an additional option to their home phone line service. They partnered with another company that provided a device to enable wireless connectivity within the home, The communication line and the wireless enabling device were dependent upon each other. The landline communication company handled all sale transactions, including billing and customer service, but if there was a problem with the wireless device, the customer was instructed to deal with the wireless device provider directly.

It happened that a customer had to replace the wireless device as it was the wrong model for her configuration. The landline communication company arranged for delivery of a replacement device. When received, the customer would place the incorrect device in the same box and return it, using a mailing label and tracking number provided. The landline company handled billing, so the customer would be charged a second time for the new device. The customer would receive credit within sixty days once the returned device arrived at the wireless company, which would in turn notify the landline company to credit the customer's account. The customer would have to monitor her credit card bill to make sure she received the credit. However, until her card was reimbursed, she would lose the use of the amount of money that it cost for the wireless device unless she paid interest on the credit card bill.The landline company apologized but explained that is the way the system works. The irony is that it was the land line's mistake when they ordered the original device, but the customer absorbed the cost.

Figure 4.1 **Channel Integration Example 1**

Each of these scenarios demonstrates the need for a value chain strategy to support CRM objectives. In the first scenario, the retailer and subcontractor need to coordinate their customer interactions in as close to real time as possible. A wireless connection between the retailer's POS system and a mobile communication device with the subcontractor should prevent scheduling problems. In the second scenario, the cruise line and the travel agency need to share information. Customer ownership is most likely the issue, as the travel agency may fear losing ownership of its customer's relationship to the cruise line company. This can lead to the customer perceiving the travel agency's value as reduced or not necessary; meanwhile, the customer's relationship with the cruise company strengthens.

Integrating channels is essential to an organization's CRM efforts. It is not easy to integrate technically, and it is even harder to ensure that all employees across the chain have the same training and stake in the strategy. Figures 4.1 and 4.2 illustrate failed attempts.

Sometimes a more formal approach is required when integrating CRM strategies. The following example illustrates what one company did to ensure an optimal cultural exchange between itself and its strategic partner.

An alcoholic beverage manufacturer managed partner relationships to support its CRM efforts. The manufacturer's partners included a CRM technology organization responsible for customer data management and an advertising company that developed value propositions for its customers. Each organization dedicated a team of people responsible for the CRM environment. Each had different expertise, but they all understood their role, the CRM objectives, and their required participation in the effort. At the beginning of the relationship, the manufacturer conducted a cultural education class. The technology enabler and the advertising agency were introduced to the manufacturer's culture, work methods, and decision-making processes. Every month, each team would travel to a respective partner's site to better understand that partner's day-to-day working environment. This could not be communicated via meetings, and it supported team bonding. These minor steps minimized organizational differences while building trust to dedicated teams.

A mattress and box spring delivery was scheduled for the morning. Steve waited all day. At 5:30 p.m., as he looked out the window, he saw a delivery truck pass his house slowly with a bewildered look on the driver's face. Steve ran out as the truck was passing by the second time and waved it down. The driver confirmed the address and that a mattress was to be delivered, but asked if he could look to see where it would be put in the house. As he walked through the house he said, "I didn't think so!" The invoice listed delivery of twelve mattresses, so he was expecting a nursing home or some type of multi-dwelling unit such as a new condominium complex. He and Steve agreed that Steve's order was not on the truck. In fact, the reason for the arrival delay was that they put the largest order in the back of the truck. Steve worked from home that day, so he did not waste a vacation day, but he was disappointed. It did not help when the driver said, "Yeah, they never get it right," and proceeded to tell Steve a few delivery horror stories. Steve thought, "Who is 'They'?" As Steve signed the invoice acknowledging wrong delivery, he harbored negative thoughts about the retailer. He was thinking of purchasing a large, expensive appliance from them as well but started having second thoughts. In addition to the delivery mix-up, Steve had a bad experience with a service call on an appliance that he bought from the same retailer several years ago. The service was performed by a subcontractor that the retailer used for appliance installation and maintenance. The retailer risks losing a loyal customer and potential negative word-of-mouth. To make matters worse, the retailer was never informed of the botched delivery because the product flow was between the manufacturer and the distributor. There are three parties associated with the poor delivery service: the manufacturer, the local distributor, and the retailer. The problem started at the POS when the salesperson placed the order and confirmed Steve's information along with delivery day and time. While the information was entered correctly, the technology the manufacturer used transposed the items on the order. There was no check-and-balance at any end of the transaction. Value chain member integration creates opportunities as well as risks.

Figure 4.2 Channel Integration Example 2

In summary, the company's position and role in its value chain present opportunities and risks. If it provides information flow, a key component of CRM strategy, advances in digitizing data pose a major risk. Companies are slowly replacing physical forms of receiving and transferring data, such as warranty cards, surveys, and order forms, with digital forms using the Internet, POS system entry forms, and wireless applications. A data entry firm, therefore, will see a declining need for its services. Companies may implement their own CRM strategy, but they are likely part of another organization's CRM strategy as well.

4.5 Other Considerations

4.5a Knowledge Management

When transformed into knowledge, information can be a key CRM enabler. Information gathering and usage can be informal and unplanned. Employees' experiences can help empower them in their customer interactions. Their cognitive process can transform this accumulated information into a knowledge base that they can leverage, consciously or subconsciously, in their CRM efforts. However, it may or may not be shared either as a best practice or as a link to a continuum information flow on a particular customer. The art of formally capturing information and transferring it into knowledge that can be shared within the organization or value chain is called knowledge

Table 4.3 CRM Component Stages

Category	Stage 1	Stage 2	Stage 3	Stage 4
CRM planning	Limited budget	Annual planning with required budget	Planning incorporated into corporate strategy	Value chain inclusion in corporate CRM planning
Market research	None	Focus groups, surveys	Batch transaction analysis	Integrated analysis, including real-time activity
CRM orientation	Mass market	Segments	Customization by segments	Customization by individual
CRM channel management	None	Basic internal SLAs tied to CRM strategy	Basic external SLAs tied to CRM strategy	Integrated CRM strategy tied to end customer value proposition
Communication	Disparate	Coordinated internally	Coordinated internally and with external partners	Channel integrated dialogue with end customer
Marketing organization	Sales orientation	Sales and marketing	Complete organization coordination across all functions	Value chain member integration
CRM methodology training	None	Sales and marketing	Cross-organizational	Value chain coordination
Employee recognition	None tied to CRM	Informal based on "atta boys"	Formal based on predefined metrics	Tied directly to internal and external customer satisfaction and loyalty
Customer relationship	None	Efficient complaint handling	Hard standards for customer interaction	Empowerment with **soft standards**
Technology	Basic and disparate	Internal customer state-of-the-art	External customer state-of-the-art	Value chain integration

management (KM). KM is a methodology and is considered a process as well as a system. It is important not to confuse the system that enables the process to be KM. Technology used to enable KM is referred to as KM systems.

Traditionally, companies use KM to increase efficiency and reduce cost. However, a CRM strategy can take advantage of such a system to satisfy the customer. For example, an engineer developing a new design for a customer can tap an internal KM system to decrease design time. This improves efficiency and reduces cost, and it benefits the customer as well. Customer service and customer technical support centers can answer customer questions efficiently and with a better level of accuracy if they have access to a KM environment. KM is an asset that increases in value as it ages because it is continuously enriched with new information.

KM is not only applicable to the private sector but also to the government as well. Li-Hsing Ho and Chen-Chia Chuang found in their research that the most pressing requirements of government institutions today are the establishment of a CRM system, the enhancement of the core capability and performance, and the effective reflection of the public's hopes and expectations toward government services. These are all enabled in part by a sound KM environment. They also state that increased competition, a bleak economy, industrial restructuring, and a high unemployment rate have placed greater importance on building a good communication with their customers.[7]

4.5b Financial Challenges

> We understand the importance of implementing a CRM strategy. Our main obstacle is financial. Competitive pressures have created an environment where the last area of differentiation is our relationships with customers. It is a catch-22. We need to proceed with a CRM strategy to increase profitability. But the money is not there to implement the strategy.
>
> —Marketing executive for a major retailer

Metrics and ROI are covered later in the text. Initial and ongoing financial investment, however, is a major challenge for companies. Public organizations have an obligation to their shareholders. CRM is not a low-cost endeavor. Costs can be reduced with phased implementations, but there is still cost. If the right metrics are not in place, it is hard to justify continuing investments in CRM. Private organizations may have a slight advantage, all other things being equal, as they do not have a formal obligation to shareholders in a public forum. They do, however, have obligations to their employees, board of directors, investors, and themselves.

Chapter Summary

The organization must approach CRM realistically. Areas mentioned to address, evaluate, and change where appropriate may not be easily corrected. Market forces combined with organizational resources may dictate a step-by-step approach to address changes. Table 4.3 places parameters around specific areas of potential change and the different stages for each area. How an organization chooses to approach each stage is unique to its environment. A stage in one category may require that another category be at a certain stage level.

Key Terms

Hard standards are specific rules and policies that govern an employee's action with the customer. Hard standards ensure compliance with the organization's CRM strategies but inhibit the employee from customizing the action in an effort to optimize the specific customer engagement.

OEM is an acronym for original equipment manufacturer (e.g., Intel, Microsoft, Caterpillar, and Whirlpool).

Silo is a term frequently used to describe a vertical hierarchy organization structure that is based on specific functions. Silos can inhibit communication and efficiency due to the respective reporting and procedure policies.

SLA is an acronym for service-level agreement. An SLA is a contractual arrangement whereby a buyer and a provider of services agree to perform certain levels of service. The buyer and seller both have obligations, but it is usually the seller or provider of the service that bears the brunt of the agreement.

Soft standards are rules and policies that lay the foundation for what an employee can and cannot do, while allowing the employee flexibility in support of any specific CRM initiative. This allows for a more effective CRM strategy because it empowers the employee. It requires training, however, so the employee knows the boundaries.

Questions

1. What are some of the challenges a manufacturer would face with the forward part of its value chain when implementing a CRM strategy with the end consumer?
2. What benefits relative to CRM effectiveness might an organization give up if it outsources its telemarketing function?
3. What challenges must a silo-structured organization overcome when attempting to implement a CRM environment?
4. Why would firms such as FedEx and UPS be critical to an organization's CRM efforts?

Exercises

1. Select an organization and identify advantages and disadvantages relative to CRM effectiveness based on its size.
2. At CRM adoption, a major packaged goods manufacturer has instructed its brand managers to reevaluate their advertising spending in an effort to shift funding from mass advertising to interactive marketing. The brand managers are comfortable in their current mode of operation and are resisting this effort. How can the manufacturer persuade brand managers to support the CRM effort?
3. Select an organization and identify its value chain members, at least by function. Identify the critical CRM requirements each value chain member has in the company's CRM efforts.
4. A manufacturer of computer chips has been unable to convince her dealers to give her the names and addresses of the end consumer. She understands CRM and wants to implement a plan that includes both the dealers and the end users. Define an approach that the manufacturer can take to build a CRM environment that provides optimal flow of all relative information in support of company–consumer relationships.

Section 2

Data Management and Technology

CRM and Data Management

5.1 Introduction

Data management is a key CRM enabler. Creating a single, accurate, and consolidated view of a customer establishes a foundation that supports all CRM efforts. Data integration is a series of steps, each one critical to achieve a technical environment that can support the CRM effort. This chapter illustrates the process of data collection and transformation of data into information and knowledge, as well as how it enables CRM. It includes a discussion of customer and prospect touch point identification and "primary data" capture techniques, conversion of disparate data into consolidated information, transformation of information into knowledge, knowledge leveraging to support CRM effort, and secondary data acquisition.

THEORY IN ACTION

Obtaining an accurate view of each customer across the enterprise is key to the success of CRM efforts. This is the foundation on which to base decision and drive interactions. To achieve this accurate and complete view, an organization must integrate many different data sources, linking individual transactions through complex processes to create customer profiles. Today, CRM demands an even higher level of data-integration accuracy as enterprise-wide strategies and digital marketing increase a company's exposure and opportunities with each customer interaction.

Chandos Quill, Vice President of Marketing, Experian Marketing Services

> Understanding and influencing customer behavior is at the heart of scientific, insight-driven marketing approaches. Generating actionable customer insights derived from customer characteristics, attitudes, and behaviors requires accurate and complete data that is consolidated from multiple sources. Customer data integration (CDI) is fundamental to providing cleansed, integrated data that forms the raw material for creating predictive customer insights that drive downstream marketing strategies, programs, and tactics. If the data feeding descriptive and predictive analytic processes is inaccurate and/or fragmented, the ripple effect throughout each marketing program can significantly degrade program performance, ROI, and the ability to accurately measure marketing impact.
>
> The Allant Group

5.2 Managing Customer Interactions

The success of a business–customer relationship is determined by the quality of the interactions. It is during these interactions that a customer takes measure of the business and determines the level and type of relationship he or she will forge with the organization. Whether the interaction occurs via the telephone, direct mail, website, or any other channel, the customer's experience—whether good or bad—is squarely in the company's hands. It is a time when a company can create loyalty, differentiate itself from its competitors, and increase the value of the relationship. If managed improperly, the experience can undermine the success of that relationship. CRM strives to manage the customer interaction effectively from an enterprise point of view.

The digital age has introduced a more discerning customer who expects much from his/her interactions with a business. More often than not, these expectations are not met because the business lacks a complete and up-to-date view of the customer's information. The goal of **customer data integration (CDI)** is meeting customer expectations by enabling relevant information to flow freely throughout an organization to the point of the interaction.

Today, a more frequently used term to describe a single, accurate view of a customer is *master data management*. This methodology is not CRM but is an enabler of CRM. Organizations are using this term and, in some cases, actual methods to create a single, accurate view of the customer across the enterprise. Gartner, a world leader in information technology research and advisory organization, publishes a "magic quadrant" for different areas in this and other marketing- and technology-related disciplines. Some examples of quadrant areas of coverage include data integration, master data management, customer contact centers, CRM services, CRM multichannels, CRM social media, lead management, and other related disciplines.

Magic quadrants depict markets in the middle phases of their life cycle by using a two-dimensional matrix that evaluates vendors based on their completeness of vision and ability to execute. The magic quadrant has 15 weighted criteria that plot vendors based on their relative strengths in the market. This model is well suited for high-growth and consolidating markets where market and vendor differentiations are distinct. Emerging or mature market participants are illustrated via other methodologies, such as Gartner's MarketScopes. A generic example of the magic quadrant is illustrated in Figure 5.1. Magic quadrants provide a graphical competitive positioning of four types of technology providers, where market growth is high and provider differentiation is distinct:

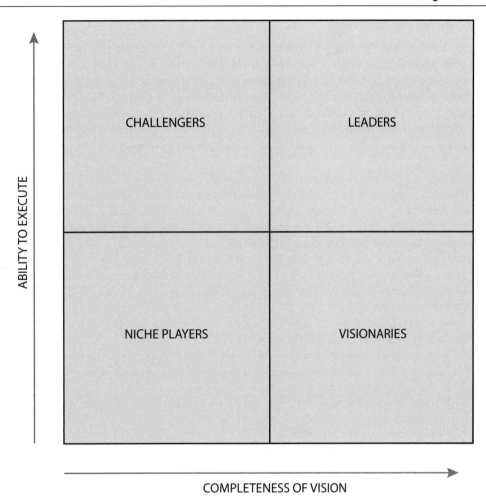

Figure 5.1 Gartner Magic Quadrant Example

Reprinted with permission of Gartner, Inc. www.gartner.com/technology/research/methodologies/research_mq.jsp. Gartner does not endorse any vendor, product or service depicted in its research publications, and does not advise technology users to select only those vendors with the highest ratings. Gartner research publications consist of the opinions of Gartner's research organization and should not be construed as statements of fact. Gartner disclaims all warranties, expressed or implied, with respect to this research, including any warranties of merchantability or fitness for a particular purpose.

- **Leaders** execute well against their current vision and are well positioned for tomorrow.
- **Visionaries** understand where the market is going or have a vision for changing market rules but do not yet execute well.
- **Niche players** focus successfully on a small segment or are unfocused and do not outinnovate or outperform others.
- **Challengers** execute well today or may dominate a large segment but do not demonstrate an understanding of market direction.

Few firms, however, can implement such systems, so a more simplified version and often less costly approach of data integration is usually their optimal solution. To illustrate the impact of CDI, consider the scene described in the next section.

5.2a Customer Service Fiasco[1]

The scene opens in Bob Sanderson's kitchen. Bob is seated at the table with the telephone to his ear, on hold again for the third time in the last two weeks. Bob is trying to speak to a representative from a company with whom he's had a three-year relationship. This time, he is trying to straighten out an order he made recently. A muzak version of "Jumpin' Jack Flash" is playing on the line as Bob waits. The music is interrupted by a markedly nasal, unemotional voice: "Thank you for waiting. Your call is very important to us. Please do not hang up, as all calls are answered in the order they are received. Your estimated wait time is now three minutes." Finally, Janet, a company representative, answers.

Janet: "Thank you for holding. My name is Janet. How may I help you today?"

Bob (frustration apparent in his voice): "I placed my service order online a few weeks ago, but I just received an offer in the mail for 50 percent off on the $198 installation fee. You have not installed the service yet, so I wanted to make sure I could get the discount on the installation."

Janet: "May I have your last name and ZIP code?"

Bob: "Sanderson. S-a-n-d-e-r-s-o-n. My ZIP code is 80038."

Janet (after a five-second pause): "OK. I have your order in front of me. I have you signed up for the high-level service with a one-year service term, which requires a $198 installation fee for new customers."

Bob (more frustrated): "I am not a new customer. I currently have your 'at home' service and spend over $1,000 per year with your company."

Janet: "I'll go ahead and cancel the current order. I can then transfer you to the new service number, and they can process your request with the installation discount. This will probably take about five minutes to process your information."

Bob (with frustration turning to apathy): "I have been a customer for three years. I am quite sure you have my information."

Janet (somewhat annoyed): "I'm sorry, sir. There is nothing that I can do. My system doesn't have the ability to access that information."

Bob (apathetic): "Well, why don't you call me when it does? By the way, you can just go ahead and cancel my 'at home' service while you're at it."

Janet (annoyed): "I'm sorry, but you'll have to dial the 'at home' customer service line in order to do that. Their number is 800-555-5555."

Bob (offers a sigh, knowing he's been beaten): "Great, I'll do that."

Scenes such as this occur too commonly in corporations today. Without access to proper information, Janet really had no chance to help Bob. In this case, the company failed the customer in three ways that real-time integration of customer data would have solved. The company should have been aware of the following:

- The customer was a long-time, high-value customer, deserving of extra attention. He should not have had to wait on hold for 20 minutes.
- There were several offers made to the customer for the same service. He should not have had to call to receive the best offer.
- Information for the customer interaction was already available in another customer-facing application. He should not have had to repeat the information-gathering process.

Corporations understand the problematic nature of interactions such as these, and yet they struggle to solve the underlying issues that plague the delivery of CRM.

5.3 The Customer Integration Problem

Corporations have been capturing and storing volumes of customer information for a number of years. This information is generally stored in a database specific to a particular business process case. Typically, these cases can be differentiated by process type (customer service, billing, fulfill-ment), channel type (telephone, mail, Internet), and product type.

This process-centric method of data capture and storage results in customer data existing in a number of different databases across the corporation (Figure 5.2). Often, there are variances in the capture and storage process such that the specific capture of a customer's contact information is not the same.

For example:

Joe Smith	Joseph Smith
714-444-5656	456 Oak Way
Orinda, CA 95051	
Joseph Smith	J. Smith
123 Main Street	100 Pleasant Drive
Orange, CA 92868	Denver, CO 80218
J. Smith	jsmith@aol.com
132 Main Street	
Orange, CA 92886	

To enable CRM effectively, disparate customer data must be integrated into a cohesive informa-tion flow so that all data can be available during any customer interaction. The integration challenge is daunting, but as frustrating as it is for corporations, customers are equally frust-rated. Solving the challenge of nonintegrated data helps solve the failures of CRM execution.

Corporations have been investing in the development of customer-centric views of their data for years. Different approaches have had limited success. The most common approaches include mar-keting database development and data warehousing. These applications typically utilize batch processes that prepare data for offline applications such as mail stream generation, modeling, and

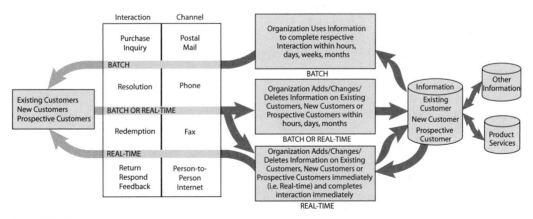

Figure 5.2 **Data Capture Process**

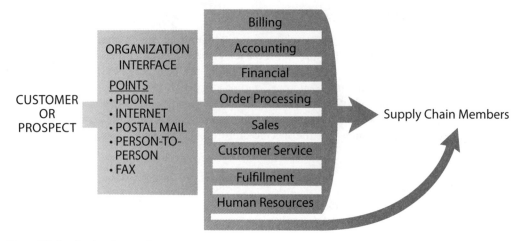

Figure 5.3 Application Integration

decision support. These technologies and methods were developed before the new requirement of real-time interaction management and thus lack the appropriate "backbone" to deliver customer information to all points of interaction in real time.

Another integration approach involves the development of interfaces that allow the applications that manage customer data to interact. This approach can be successful when only a few applications are involved, but it can become unmanageable when faced with many applications (Figure 5.3). In most organizations, the latter is common, as customer data can reside in dozens of systems (billing, accounting, CRM).

Using these approaches to create the single customer view causes a number of symptoms to appear within the practice of CRM, including the following:

- *Data latency.* **Data latency** results from architectures that have adopted traditional extraction, transformation, deduplication, and distribution methods to facilitate movement of customer information. Processing large volumes of data through these typically batch processes takes time and often ages the data unnecessarily, which can have a direct impact on the CRM effort. In Figure 5.4a, Jennifer made a conscious effort to inform the organization of her desire to be removed from future solicitations. Her expectation is set when she checks the "Do Not Solicit" box on the organization's Web page. Due to the latency of data being updated to the database, however, a telemarketer in the organization's telemarketing department, unaware of Jennifer's request, calls her to promote an extended warranty.
- *Lack of data and distribution standards.* Virtually every database supporting a business case is developed in isolation, capturing and storing data in different ways without linking customer information across sources. As a result, there is no standard means to integrate customer data at the point of contact.
- *Inaccuracy.* Failure to create a consistent customer view is inevitable when comparing customer data from different systems using imperfect matching techniques. Although traditional matching techniques continue to improve, they are not accurate enough for CRM applications because customers present themselves uniquely to companies. These symptoms do not occur because of a failure in the existing systems but rather because these methods cannot cure the real-time, enterprise-wide integration problem (Figure 5.4b). The cure requires a different approach: CDI.

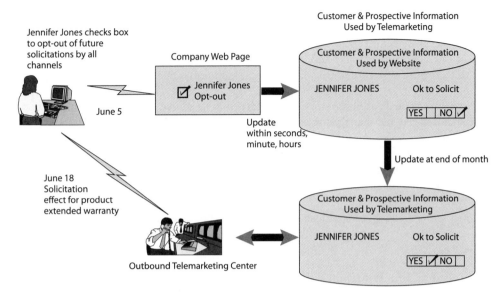

Figure 5.4a **Data Latency**

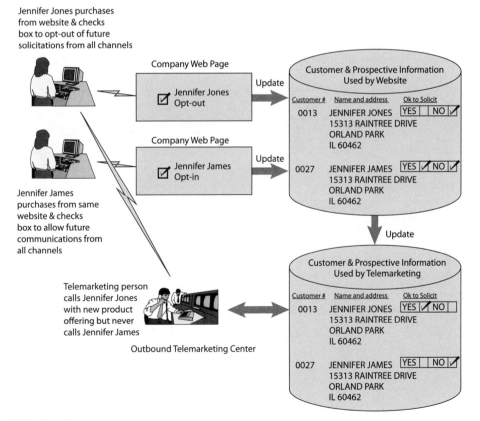

Figure 5.4b **Data Inaccuracy**

5.4 Customer Data Integration Definition and Requirements

CDI is a data management process where all prospect and customer data can be distributed to points of interaction in a timely and accurate manner. With this definition, the unique requirements of CDI must be well understood when considering the overall CRM objective:

- *Distributed.* The distribution of customer data from its source to all points of interaction must be standardized and managed through a single corporate point of reference.
- *Points of interaction.* All points of customer and business user interaction that determine the nature of the relationship must have access to relevant customer data.
- *Timely.* All customer data needed for decision making must be delivered in a time frame appropriate to the needs of each point of interaction.
- *Accurate.* Customer data delivered must consistently and accurately represent a given consumer entity, including individuals, households, or businesses.

5.4a The Solution

To meet the real-time, transaction-oriented CDI needs of a corporation, a revolutionary solution is needed. CDI is, in fact, a revolution, creating a foundation for integrating customer data where all information can be managed and distributed in real time throughout the corporation. CDI is based on three components:

1. *Enabling technology components, which control data management and distribution.* This technology is designed to operate within the framework of existing data warehousing and database marketing systems, providing the means to access and distribute relevant data from each system.
2. *The introduction of a reference database to provide customer links through a referential matching process.* The reference database is impartial, providing links between all captured instances of a customer.

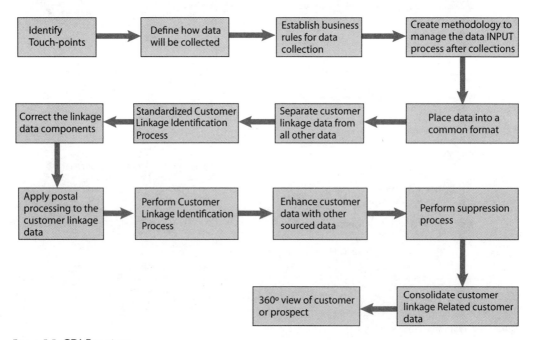

Figure 5.5 CDI Functions

3. *The corporate-wide adoption of both the technology and the reference database.* Establishing relationships with customers requires an organization to have a certain amount of knowledge about a particular customer. When an organization understands its customers, it can attempt to form a relationship with them. An organization can create a customer knowledge base by meticulously collecting data from multiple customer interactions with the organization and its value chain members. Once data is accumulated, it can be transformed into knowledge through a series of functions to create a consolidated view of the customer (Figure 5.5). Due to a variety of constraints, such as financial, technical, or strategic, organizations may not be able to implement a real-time CDI environment. Functions are shown in serial format. It is important that the logic demonstrated in the function be included; however, system design differences and technological advances may alter the sequence and function components to the point where some functions may be combined or occur simultaneously. The CRM strategist should ensure that the function objectives are met.

5.5 Householding Concepts

Individuals with the same last name living at the same address may be defined as one **household**. Individuals with different last names living at the same address may be defined as separate households.

Bob Smith	1247 State Street	Chicago	IL	60601
Mary Smith	1247 State Street	Chicago	IL	60601
Steven Smith	1247 State Street	Chicago	IL	60601
Julie Smith	1247 State Street	Chicago	IL	60601
David Carter	1247 State Street	Chicago	IL	60601

Bob, Mary, Steven, and Julie are in the same household. David Carter, although living at the same address, is a separate household because he has a different last name. If Steven moves to a new address, a decision must be made as to whether he now belongs to his existing household or a new one. For example, if Steven moves away to college, he will technically have a new address for residence. This may be temporary in that he intends to conduct some or all of his organization relationships at his home address. He probably plans to move back to his home address during semester and summer breaks and perhaps briefly after graduation. In this example, Steven would be kept in his original household. If Steven moves into an apartment to live independently, however, he may be defined as a new household because he will have different needs living independently, and his behavior and decisions may change. With regard to David Carter, we may not know his relationship to the Smiths, but he has a different last name and thus is defined as a separate household.

For the purpose of logistical tracking through the CDI process, each individual is assigned a unique individual identification number. Each individual in the same household shares a second identifier: a unique household identification number.

Household #	Individual #	
0230	001	Bob Smith, 1247 State Street, Chicago, IL 60601
0230	002	Mary Smith, 1247 State Street, Chicago, IL 60601
0230	003	Steven Smith, 1247 State Street, Chicago, IL 60601
0230	003	Steven Smith, 423 College Drive, Champaign, IL 61820
0230	004	Julie Smith, 1247 State Street, Chicago, IL 60601
0344	001	David Carter, 1247 State Street, Chicago, IL 60601

To continue with the Smiths, Bob and Mary have flexible work schedules, so they decided to purchase a condominium in Arizona and live there periodically throughout the year. Their consumer behavior will be transparent regardless of their current residence. This adds complexity to the household tracking because an organization needs to know which address to use for what reason. They also need to accumulate information on Bob and Mary from either location in order to sustain the CRM effort. The organization assigns Bob and Mary each a unique identifier that remains the same no matter what Bob or Mary does with regard to address or name changes. The same process is applied to everyone in the database. So if Julie leaves the residence to marry and changes her name, her unique identifier will point to all interactions she has had with the organization. This provides a complete profile of an individual that bridges name or address changes.

Unique #	HH #	Ind. #	
224567	0230	001	Bob Smith, 1247 State Street, Chicago, IL 60601
224567	0230	001	Bob Smith, 77 Sunset Strip, Sedona, AZ 86336
224568	0230	002	Mary Smith, 77 Sunset Strip, Sedona, AZ 86336
224568	0230	002	Mary Smith, 1247 State Street, Chicago, IL 60601
224569	0230	003	Steven Smith, 1247 State Street, Chicago, IL 60601
224569	0230	003	Steven Smith, 423 College Drive, Champaign, IL 61820
224562	0230	004	Julie Smith, 1247 State Street, Chicago, IL 60601
224562	0577	002	Julie (Smith) Jones, 77 Kenmore Road, Chicago, IL 60632
224561	0344	001	David Carter, 1247 State Street, Chicago, IL 60601

This methodology is gaining acceptance by organizations. Many companies provide this methodology as an additional service to an organization's CRM effort. Several large data providers have developed identifying solutions that manage all of a customer's current and historical identifying information in different ways, but the results are similar.

5.6 Customer Data Integration Steps

5.6a Identify Touch Points

The organization needs to identify all areas in which it is possible to interact with current and prospective customers. Every interaction generates a transaction or some type of relative information. These interaction areas or **touch points** will vary depending on an organization's vertical market and business function within that market. Examples of touch points include the Web, the telephone, written documents, kiosks, and face-to-face. Tables 5.1 and 5.2 contain examples of touch points in a business-to-consumer (B2C) and a business-to-business (B2B) environment.

These table entries are for illustration purposes. They are not all-inclusive, are somewhat generic, and can be applied to a variety of vertical markets. For example, in the hotel industry, a large majority of a customer's transactions conducted on the hotel property may be captured via the guest account if the transactions are charged to the room. However, if a patron makes a purchase within a nonhotel entity on the property, such as a retail vendor leasing space, that transaction will not be easily captured by the hotel. The hotel may look into building a relationship with the respective retailer to share customer information via a reciprocal arrangement.

Many B2C touch points are similar to B2B touch points. For instance, an employee, as part of his or her organizational responsibility, searches a company's website for information on a new

Table 5.1 Retail Business-to-Consumer Data

Data Touch Point Source Examples	Possible Data Element Examples
Point-of-sale (retail brick-and-mortar, catalog, Web, inbound/outbound telemarketing, kiosks, fax) products/services across multiple vertical markets	Name, address (home/work), phone number (home/work/cell), e-mail address (home/work/other), checking account number, credit/debit card number, age, gender, ship-to address, gift recipient name/address/phone number/e-mail address, item(s) purchased (number of items, product code, SKU), purchase price (item, total, tax), coupons, rebates, gift certificates, purchase location, Web (URL) entry point, inquiry request
Customer service (retail brick-and-mortar, catalog, Web, inbound/outbound telemarketing, kiosks, fax)	Item(s) returned/exchanged, date of purchase, purchase location, return location, reason(s) for return, name, address (home/work), phone number (home/work/cell), e-mail address (home/work/other), checking account number, credit/debit card number, account/customer number, purchase price (item, total, tax), coupons, rebates, gift certificates, purchase location, Web (URL) entry point
Scheduled and unscheduled technical support (retail brick-and-mortar, Web, inbound/outbound telemarketing, kiosks, fax)	Account/customer number, name, address (home/work), phone number (home/work/cell), e-mail address, product type owned, service type owned
Solicited and unsolicited postal "mail-in"	Name, address (home/work), phone number (home/work/cell), e-mail address (home/work/other), checking account number, credit/debit card number, age, gender, ship-to address, gift recipient name/address/phone number/e-mail address, item(s) purchased (number of items, product code, SKU), purchase price (item, total, tax), coupons, rebates, gift certificates, purchase location, website (URL), other demographic/psychographic information, information related to warranty, rebate, survey, payment, catalog order, subscription order, financial instruments, service order, inquiry, appointment
Non-country of origin (all of the above)	All of the above, including complexity of language and potentially dissimilar contact information, product/service transaction data

product. Data gathered by the website owner while the employee searches the site is similar to a consumer browsing a retailer or cataloger's Web page.

There are additional touch points in a B2B environment that would normally not appear in a B2C environment. For example, two organizations have linked themselves through an extranet, which in this case is a network or connection where two companies utilize the same Web pages to conduct business. It is a closed environment, as only two organizations have access to the respective Web pages. This touch point is predefined, and all interaction activity has a purpose.

Although not included, a table for a business-to-business-to-consumer (B2B2C) environment would include a combination of Tables 5.1 and 5.2. In a B2B2C environment, for instance, a manufacturer may have "information-only" Web pages available for consumers, who access the Web pages for information on the company and its products or services but do not interact with that company for any other reason. The consumer would likely conduct some business transaction

Table 5.2 **Business-to-Business Data**

Touch Point Source Examples	Possible Data Element Examples
Point-of-sale (retail brick-and-mortar, catalog, Web, inbound/outbound telemarketing, kiosks, fax) products/services across multiple vertical markets	Name/address/phone number/fax/e-mail address of company/subsidiary/division/department, individual(s) within above (name/address/phone/fax/e-mail address), customer number, account number, credit card number, ship-to information, item(s)/services purchased (number of items, product code, SKU, types of services), purchase price (item, total, tax), discounts, purchase location, Web (URL) entry point, inquiry request, requisition number, purchase order number
Customer service (retail brick-and-mortar, catalog, Web, inbound/outbound telemarketing)	Item(s) returned/exchanged, date of purchase, purchase location, return location, reason(s) for return, name/address/phone number/fax/e-mail address of company/subsidiary/division/department, individual(s) within above (name/address/phone number/fax/e-mail address), customer number, account number, credit card number, purchase price (item, total, tax), discounts, credit, purchase location, Web (URL) entry point
Scheduled and unscheduled technical support (retail brick-and-mortar, Web, inbound/outbound telemarketing, kiosks, fax, in-person)	Account/customer number, name, address (home/work), phone number (home/work/cell), e-mail address, product type owned, service type owned
Solicited and unsolicited postal "mail-in"	Name, address (home/work), phone number (home/work/cell), e-mail address (home/work/other), checking account number, credit/debit card number, age, gender, ship-to address, gift recipient name/address/phone number/e-mail address, item(s) purchased (number of items, product code, SKU), purchase price (item, total, tax), coupons, rebates, gift certificates, purchase location, website (URL), other demographic/psychographic information, information related to warranty, rebate, survey, payment, catalog order, subscription order, financial instruments, service order, inquiry, appointment
Non-country of origin (all of the above)	All of the above, including complexity of language and potentially dissimilar contact information, product/service transaction data
Peer-to-peer interaction	Account/customer number, name, address (home/work), phone number (home/work/cell), e-mail address, project management software entries, contracts, service-level agreements

with another member in that manufacturer's value chain, such as a retailer, distributor, or reseller. The interaction and/or touch points that the consumer would have with that intermediary may be critical for the manufacturer and should be categorized as a touch point. The challenge would be to connect the information gathered from the consumer touch point interaction with the manufacturer's Web page to that of the subsequent interaction(s) with another member in the value chain (Figure 5.6).

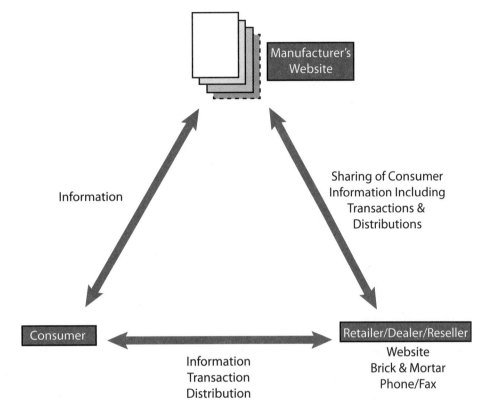

Figure 5.6 **B2B2C Touch Point Interaction**

Even if the manufacturer overcomes its challenge of identifying multiple touch points with multiple value chain members, it must also solicit, from the respective members, information gathered at those touch points and validate the touch point interaction. In this case, while it may be somewhat easy to identify the touch points with an intermediary, gathering information may be difficult or prohibited. Sharing consumer information among members in the same value chain may vary in terms of depth and breadth of information shared as well as the frequency. A classic example is retail grocery stores, which rarely provide specific consumer contact information to manufacturers.

5.6b Define How Data Will Be Collected

Once touch points have been identified, a method of collecting information from interaction at a specific touch point must be defined. Data may be collected from a human-to-human interaction (e.g., retail sales counter, telemarketer), human-to-technology interaction (e.g., kiosk, computer telephony, Web), or technology-to-technology interaction (e.g., RFID, fax, voice mail exchange).

5.6c Establish Business Rules for Data Collection

Each touch point will precipitate the capture of one or more data variables. In many instances, the same information may be captured from more than one touch point. A company must first determine which variables will be captured and then determine and define a priority setting for each variable. For example, if a person enters his or her age in more than one touch point and the age is different, a business should determine which touch point will be used as a source for age.

Table 5.3 illustrates a priority setting made by a catalog company for data capture on several consumer demographic variables. In an effort to better understand its customers, the catalog company has attempted to capture as many demographic variables on its customers as possible from a variety of sources. In some cases, the data is primary (i.e., submitted by the customer), and in other instances, it was inferred via observation or by product purchased. Of course, primary data will always be deemed more accurate as long as the method of capture has not been negatively compromised. The company has decided that information from Touch Point A will have a priority of 1, and if information for a respective variable is missing or conflicts, Touch Point A will always be used because it is considered the most trusted source. The exception is when information across the touch points differs, but two or more touch points other than Touch Point A have like data. Under those circumstances, the data from the agreeing touch points is used in place of that from Touch Point A.

Table 5.4 is an example of a business rule priority table for a B2B environment. A company that produces and sells industrial cleaning solvents segments its market based on square footage and respective sales revenue in order to package and price its products optimally. It captures relative information from industry researchers, potential customers' websites, its sales personnel, and industry trade publications.

Table 5.4 assigns the following priority for the Annual Revenue variable: always use the Industry Research touch point source if available. If it is not available or if it is present but all other sources have the same value and differ from Industry Research, use the other variables' value. If Industry Research is not available, use Sales Personnel regardless of other sources. Use Websites third and Trade Publications fourth. For Plant Square Footage, use Sales Personnel first, Trade Publications

Table 5.3 Business Rule Priority Table—Consumer Example

Data Element	Touch Point A	Touch Point B	Touch Point C	Touch Point D	Data Used
Income	$65K–$70K	$120K	N/A	$65K	$65K
Age	35–40	37	37	34	37
Occupation	Professional	Other	Unskilled	N/A	Professional
Homeowner	N/A	N/A	Yes	Yes	Yes
Children	N/A	2 (4–8 years)	1 @ 4 years, 1 @ 3 years	1 @ 6 years, 1 @ 8 years	2 (4–8 years)

Table 5.4 Business Rule Priority Table—Business Example

Element	Industry Research	Websites	Sales Personnel	Trade Publications	Data Used
Annual Revenue	$10MM	$11–$13MM	$10MM	N/A	$10MM
Plant Square Footage	4,000	5,500	3,500–4,000	3,800–4,200	4,000

second, Industry Research third, and Websites fourth. If information is present from more than one source, use the value present in the majority of sources.

5.6d Create a Methodology for Managing the Data Input Process after Collection

The data input process consists of all the steps required to move data from the point of collection to a place where it can be readied for input into a process for transforming each variable into a common format. This process should be coordinated to meet the timing requirements of other processes, ensure security, and be consistent and accurate.

5.6d.1 Timeliness

Organizations should establish a check-and-balance to ensure that all required inputs have been made available to the next process. If unavailable, technically the next process should not begin. Organizations have made rules for this, however, as it is inevitable that some inputs, for whatever reason, will not be made available. The creation of and adherence to a data flow schedule are critical to the CRM effort. For example, an organization's website may state that it will honor a customer's request to be taken off its e-mail mailing list within 24 hours of receipt of that request. The Web transaction by which the customer submits the request will need to update the e-mail address data repository used for e-mail promotions within 24 hours.

5.6d.2 Security

The data must be secure. There are several dimensions to security. First, the data must not be "dropped" (i.e., lost in data transmission, a file or database deleted or rendered unreadable, or a hard copy physically lost). Second, data must be processed in a way that ensures only authorized employees of the organization and/or its partners can access it.

5.6d.3 Consistency and Accuracy

Inconsistent data is perhaps worse than inaccurate or absent data. When there is no data, no information is generated, and subsequently nothing is available for input for the next step of placing the data into a common format. It is more problematic when the data input is available, but the data elements are inconsistent. This could mean that a data field may contain blanks when it was a required field (i.e., should have contained nonblank characters) or a numeric is imbedded in what should have been an alpha field. Remember that one can plan for inaccurate data as long as it is consistently inaccurate.

5.6e Place the Data into a Common Format

Customer or prospect personal identification information may be captured by the organization or its value chain members in a variety of formats from different touch points. Table 5.5 illustrates types of personal data collected at touch points.

The information in Table 5.5 may be collected as a result of an inquiry, a transaction, or another type of communication (e.g., a follow-up to an order, a complaint, a suggestion, or a reimbursement). Notice that there may be three or more sources of the same type of information for each variable captured. Principal Residence refers to an individual's home. Business may be an employer or the individual's own business if he or she is self-employed. The variable Other can represent a number of situations. It may be contact information for a gift recipient, in which case it is possible

Table 5.5 **Touch Point Data Collection Example**

Variable	Principal Residence	Business	Other
Title			
Prefix			
First Name			
Middle Name or Initial			
Last Name			
Organization Name			
Apt. #/Unit #/Suite/Department/Floor/Office			
Address Line 1			
Address Line 2			
City			
State			
County			
ZIP Code (5 digits)			
ZIP+4 (9 digits)			
Country			
Phone # Home			
Phone # Work			
Cell Phone #			
Fax #			
E-mail Address 1			
E-mail Address 2			

that information may appear in multiple columns for the same transaction. Other may also represent a person's secondary residence, a part-time business, or an individual's dependent, such as a college student away at school. These are just a few examples. The number of contacts may exceed three for one type of customer interaction, but one or two is usually the norm.

Each variable may not be the same length (i.e., the number of possible characters allowed per variable) from each touch point. For instance, a person entering his first name on a Web form may have up to 13 spaces to fit his name (Figure 5.7). The same organization, however, may have a paper form that allows a person to enter up to 15 characters for his first name. This scenario may exist for all of the above variables. In Figure 5.7, data present in the Web and POS transactions will be placed in the standard format. The standard format will ensure that all data has the same justification and filler characters and contains the proper character type (e.g., alpha, numeric, special characters). Advances in software logic and design have, in some cases, eliminated the need for a standard format. In these cases, each subsequent step that references the data must be given the data's current format so it can interpret it correctly.

5.6f Separate Customer Linkage Data from All Other Data

Data collected from touch points can be placed in two categories. The first category represents "nonlinkage information," which is any element that is not used to identify contact information. Product(s) purchased, price paid, or date of purchase would be examples of nonlinkage

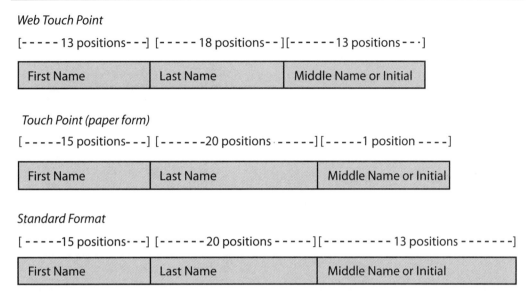

Web Touch Point

[- - - - - 13 positions- - -] [- - - - - 18 positions- -][- - - - - -13 positions - - ·]

First Name	Last Name	Middle Name or Initial

Touch Point (paper form)

[- - - - -15 positions- - -] [- - - - - -20 positions · - - - - -] [- - - - -1 position - - - -]

First Name	Last Name	Middle Name or Initial

Standard Format

[- - - - -15 positions· - -] [- - - - - -20 positions - - - - -] [- - - - - - - - 13 positions - - - - - - -]

First Name	Last Name	Middle Name or Initial

Figure 5.7 **Standard Format**

information. The second category can be called "linkage information." This is the type of information that can be used to identify a person, business, or household. In a consumer context, a household can be defined as those individuals who make up a consumer family (including nontraditional or extended) who live at the same location. There are variances to this definition, such as the student temporarily living away at college discussed earlier in this chapter. A business household is usually more complex than a consumer household because it may be defined a little differently each time. Some general rules, however, apply. Organizations may have multiple locations. They are usually "compartmentalized" (e.g., divisions, business units, departments, sections, territories, and other entity divisions or structures). Within each of these entities, individuals must be defined as part of that respective entity. Just as in the consumer environment, variances exist here as well. For example, individuals move frequently within an organization, their titles change, they leave the organization, and new individuals are hired. Rules should be established to determine which of an organization's structure entities will be used as linkage criteria. Management of these variances and a more detailed discussion of households are covered later in this chapter.

Whether in a consumer or business environment, linkage information will vary by the touch point at which it was gathered. A not-all-inclusive list of customer or prospect linkage information in a consumer retail environment may have some or all of the following for each touch point: customer number, credit card number, name, address (home/work/delivery), phone number (home/cell/work/other), e-mail address, delivery information, gift recipient contact information, personal check number, and driver's license number.

A brief example of the different types of information for a retail organization and the likely source is shown in Table 5.6. Subsequent steps in this chapter will demonstrate the tasks of matching individuals and/or households. Information not relative to this matching effort is not needed at this time but will be brought back later in the process.

With data in a common format in the last process, the effort to split the information is a relatively simple task (Figure 5.8). As the contact information is split from all other information, a unique sequence number must be assigned to both data segments to properly join them together later. Based on software design, this may not be an actual physical split of data. The splitting discussed here illustrates the logic being performed.

Table 5.6 Retail Touch Point Data Example

Source (Touch Point)	Possible Information
Point of sale (POS)	Linkage information, product SKU, service type/ description, price, payment type, payment amount, purchase date, delivery/pickup date, order number, warranty, rebate/ coupon, product exchange, inquiry information
Customer service (face-to-face, on-site home/work, or phone contact)	Linkage information, product SKU, service type, price, date, warranty and/or guarantee information, rebate/ coupon, "reason for return," complaint information, product exchange information, inquiry information, phone number called*
Website	Linkage information, product SKU, service type, price, date, warranty and/or guarantee information, rebate/ coupon, "reason for return," complaint information, product exchange information, inquiry information, external link source, external non-Web source*

*One easy way to track advertising effectiveness is to have separate phone numbers or Web links advertised in different advertisement sources. The phone number used or Web page accessed is captured and points to the original advertising source.

The "unique sequence numbers" are the same for both linkage and nonlinkage information. The linkage and nonlinkage information is then split. Linkage information is input to the "Standardized Customer Linkage Data" step. Nonlinkage information is temporarily removed and held from the linkage process and then brought back to be matched to the linkage information in the "Consolidate All Relative Customer Linkage and Related Customer Data" step. Figure 5.9 depicts this linkage/nonlinkage split.

Bill Smith visited the same retailer four times in May. The first time he returned merchandise. As part of the return process, he was asked to fill out a form with his name and address information. Since the original purchase was made with his credit card, he needed to provide the retailer with the credit card again to receive credit. The merchandise was scanned for SKU information, and that data was also tied to the return transaction. Bill's daughter borrowed her father's customer preferred card to take advantage of a special sale for preferred customers. She used cash for the purchase. Bill's preferred card along with the respective product SKUs were scanned and tied to that transaction. Even though Bill was not the purchaser, these two transactions were tied to his preferred card number. Bill returned to the store at the end of the month and purchased a product but did not use his preferred card. He used the same credit card to make the purchase. At month's end, the retailer performed a CDI process on all transactions from that month. Bill Smith's transactions were split into linkage data and nonlinkage data. Sequence numbers were assigned to each transaction so that the process could bring the nonlinkage data back to Bill Smith. Linkage processing was performed on the respective linkage data, which linked all of Bill's transactions together. For that month, the data warehouse would indicate Bill's net monthly purchase activity as $90.99. Note that $21.88 of this total was actually attributed to his daughter. But in this scenario, the retailer could not distinguish between purchasers because the customer preferred card was used as the link.

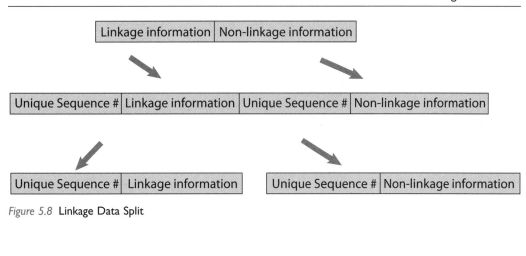

Figure 5.8 Linkage Data Split

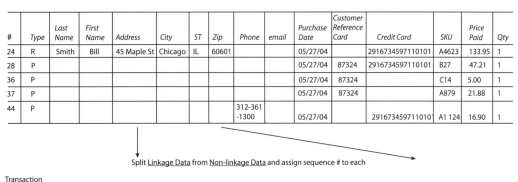

#	Type	Last Name	First Name	Address	City	ST	Zip	Phone	email	Purchase Date	Customer Reference Card	Credit Card	SKU	Price Paid	Qty
24	R	Smith	Bill	45 Maple St	Chicago	IL	60601			05/27/04		2916734597110101	A4623	133.95	1
28	P									05/27/04	87324	2916734597110101	B27	47.21	1
36	P									05/27/04	87324		C14	5.00	1
37	P									05/27/04	87324		A879	21.88	1
44	P							312-361 -1300		05/27/04		2916734597110101	A1 124	16.90	1

Split <u>Linkage Data</u> from <u>Non-linkage Data</u> and assign sequence # to each

Transaction

Sec #	#	Type	Last Name	First Name	Address	City	ST	Zip	Customer Prefered Card	Credit Card
001	24	R	Smith	Bill	45 Maple St	Chicago	IL	60601	87324	29167345-
002	28	P							87324	-
003	36	P							87324	-
004	37	P							87324	-
005	44	P								2916734597110101

Seq #	Puchase Date	SKU	Price Paid	QTY
001	05/27/04	A4623	33.95	1
002	05/27/04	B27	147.21	1
003	05/27/04	C14	5.00	1
004	05/27/04	A879	21.88	1
005	05/27/04	A1 124	16.90	1

Figure 5.9 Linkage Data Split Example

5.6g Standardize Customer Linkage Data

The linkage data elements captured from multiple touch points may differ in their format. In some instances, data coming from the same touch point may vary in format as well. Format can be defined as the number of characters (i.e., the length of a field that contains data). The length of a data record or row can also vary. Additionally, the contents of a particular data field may vary by its type. Data types are shown in Table 5.7.

Why is this important? In order to facilitate corrections where applicable to the input data, the relevant data should be consistent in format and position. That is, software is used to analyze each data element, and it will expect that data element to be in a certain format and have the same length between records. Let us look at an example. John Q. Adams Sr. lives at 15345 South La Grange Road, Apartment #2, in Orland Park, Illinois, with a ZIP code of 60462. John Adams purchases a

Table 5.7 **Data Types**

Alpha Characters	A, b, c, d, . . .
Numeric Characters	1, 2, 3, 4, . . .
Special Characters (usually used as delimiters)	;, :, ., ,, &, /, . . .
Case Sensitive	Upper, lower A, a, B, b, . . .
Character Position Justification	Left justified, right justified, center justified
Absence of Above Characters (i.e., null character)	Blanks, zeroes, special characters
Length Variance	Data field, record

digital camera on a manufacturer's website. He fills out his name, home address, and other contact and delivery information. John pays for the camera with his credit card and enters the credit card number and expiration date. When the digital camera is delivered to his home, he sees, fills out, and mails in a warranty card for the camera. As John reads through the information supplied with the camera, he sees a reference in an accompanying brochure to an optional camera case that is far superior to the case he received with his camera. He calls the manufacturer's phone number referenced and orders the case. He purchases the camera case with the same credit card and provides delivery information to the manufacturer representative taking the order. John's activity generated three transactions, each coming back to the manufacturer through a different touch point. The manufacturer uses optimal means for the receipt and transfer of John's transaction data. However, the format of the data captured varies by touch point source for valid reasons, as each touch point is using an optimal method of data capture for that respective location. Using a portion of this data, name, and address information, Figure 5.10 illustrates the importance of standardizing this data input.

Information gathered from John Adams is similar across these three transactions. Software compressed data gathered from the Web so there were no trailing spaces or blanks in the transaction record, and each logical field was separated by one space that contained an asterisk. The asterisk was used as a delimiter—that is, the presence of the asterisk indicated the ending of one logical field. John Adams filled out the warranty information via a form and sent it in the mail to a post office box number. The manufacturer contracted with a **data entry organization** to enter all of the hard copy information into a designed computer screen form.

The Web page form did not allow for a middle name or initial, so John entered that information into the first name field. It also allowed for two address lines. The warranty form allowed for a title and a prefix (e.g., Mr., Mrs., Ms.) and a suffix (e.g., Sr., Jr., II), but since John did not enter anything in these fields, the data entry process did not include those fields. The warranty form had one address line field for input. John entered the state in the same field as the city field, and the data entry allowed that to continue through their process (i.e., they were not separating fields but just entering the fields as they were entered by the consumer). John also used "ILL" as the abbreviation for the state of Illinois and not the correct abbreviation of "IL." The Web page had a drop-down list for state abbreviations to prevent someone from entering an incorrect one. A customer service representative entered the phone transaction data via a computer screen with predefined entry fields for each element. The representative prompted John Adams for information and entered it as he responded. The screens used in the phone interaction were the same as those on the Web page form with an additional field for a phone number.

Faced with different formats, the organization has two options. The next step, "Correct the Linkage Data Components," will examine each addressable component and make corrections where appropriate based on digitized postal information. The correct linkage software may have an option whereby the organization can illuminate the presence of each address component by type of transaction source. The software can then find each address component and understand how each address field is formatted. A second option is to convert each of the transactions into one format. The software can then treat each transaction the same way (i.e., the length of the transaction record as well as the length of each date element and each element's format). Figure 5.11 shows the result of the conversion into one common format.

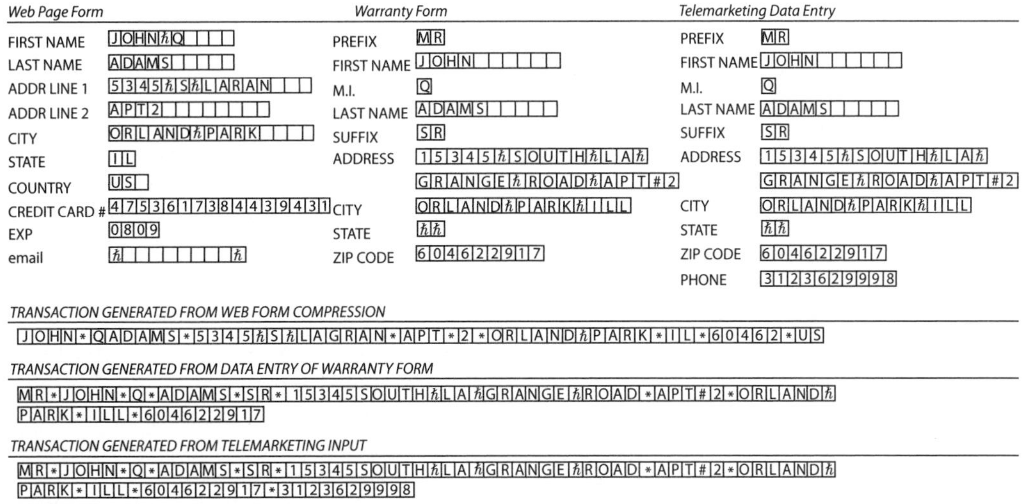

Figure 5.10 Data Standardization

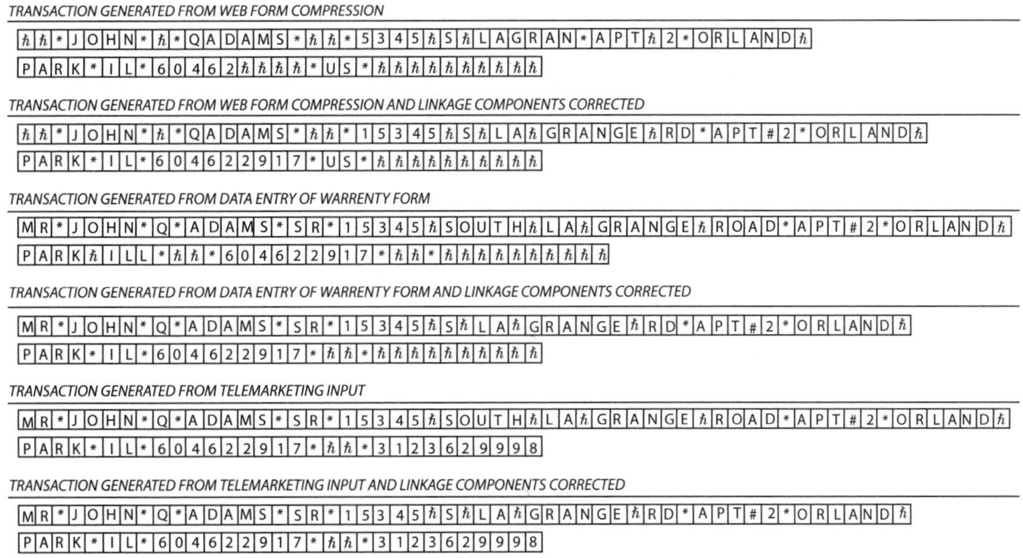

Figure 5.11 Common Format Conversion

Web transaction		
Before correction	5347 S. LARANG	60462-bbbb
After correction	15345 S. La Grange Rd	60462-2917
Warranty card		
Before correction	15345 South La Grange	60432
After correction	15345 S. La Grange Rd	60462-2917

Figure 5.12 Web Transaction Address Corrections

5.6h Correct the Linkage Data Components

Correcting any errors in the linkage components will enhance all subsequent steps. Software is commercially available for purchase by companies wishing to manage this process themselves. There are also organizations that perform this step using the same or similar software as a service to organizations. The software examines each geographic linkage component for errors and makes the corrections where applicable. The software is very sophisticated but is only as good as its current level. It uses a database of geographically defined points, as almost every addressable point in the United States has been digitized. If any of these points have changed, the software will lose its accuracy; therefore, currency in the software is critical to managing the integrity of the data environment successfully. Not all countries can provide accurate digitized addressable points for their respective geographic area. When working with customers outside the United States, it is important to partner with organizations that provide this type of service, if possible. Examples can be found at the end of the chapter.

With regard to John Adams's Web transaction (Figure 5.12), he omitted the first digit of the street address. He also misspelled the street name and omitted the address suffix "Road." The software accesses databases, files, and tables that contain information on every delivery point in the country. In this case, the software identifies "5345" as being outside the range of valid street numbers for that street and ZIP code. It used logic and tables of valid streets within ZIP codes to determine that La Grange was misspelled (see Figure 5.9). It also knew that "La Grange" is a road in that ZIP code. The software also added ZIP+4 digits to make the addressability more accurate. On the warranty form, John Adams printed the complete word "South" for directional information and left off "Road." The software truncated the directional to "S" and added "RD" for "Road." It also added ZIP+4 digits.

Address correction software can be used in a batch or real-time environment. The latter is more expensive and somewhat more difficult to implement and maintain, but it does expedite the process. The batch environment is less costly and easier to maintain, but it adds time to the process.

5.6i Apply Postal Processing to the Customer Linkage Data

To ensure accurate, timely, and cost-effective delivery of mail to customers and prospects, both U.S. and non-U.S. organizations need to utilize many of the products and services provided by the U.S. Postal Service (USPS) and the International Postal Union (UPU). Of particular importance to U.S. organizations with regards to CDI are the USPS products and services offered in their Address Quality Management (AQM) solutions, which can be found on the USPS website (http://www.usps.com). Some of these products are listed by category in Table 5.8. It is suggested that the USPS website be checked for more detail as well as changes. The USPS is constantly striving to improve its services.

CRM and Data Management   137

Table 5.8 **Manage Address Quality**

Address Information Systems Products (AIS)	AIS products are raw database files made available to enhance address standardization and/or obtain detailed address information. AIS Viewer (interactive DVD), Carrier Route, City State, Delivery Statistics, Five-Digit ZIP®, eLOT®, Z4Change, Zip+4®, ZIPMove.
Address Management Products	Tools for addressing software solutions (Computerized Delivery Sequence, DPV®, Delivery Sequence File Second Generation, Labeling Lists, RDI™, Modern Service Standards, National Zone Charts Matrix, TIGER/ ZIP + 4®, Z4INFO)
Address Management Publications	USPS provided publications on Address Management products and services
Address Quality Services	Maximize address quality and minimize mailing costs. Services include Address Element Correction & AEC II®, Address List Sequencing, ADVANCE Notification & Tracking, Confirm®, Electronic Address Sequencing, Electronic Publication Watch, LACSLink®, Special Services
Certification Programs	Evaluate the accuracy of software and equipment offered by Vendors and Licensees that provide mailing services. Certification programs include CASS™, Delivery Confirmation™, MAC™, MAC Batch™, MASS™, Periodicals Accuracy, PAVE™, Zone Analysis, CASS & MASS certified vendors
Move Update	Mailing list updating methods for presort or automation rate mailings (ACS Service, Ancillary Service endorsements, FASTforward® System, NCOALink® systems)

All of the products and services offered by postal entities have an impact on efficiency and awareness of whom and where the customer is, which enables the CRM effort. In particular, postal processing utilizes information provided by the USPS to ensure that the customer's or prospect's most current address is available in a company's CRM data environment. Every year, over 40 million Americans change addresses.[2] There are two ways for an organization to find out if a person changes their address. First, the person can tell the organization directly. Second, the organization can attempt to find out using other means when the person does not tell them. The former is preferred. It ensures timely and accurate updates. It also demonstrates that the customer relationship is strong, as the person chooses to tell an organization about a move in order to continue the relationship. To facilitate the customer volunteering notification of a change in address, the organization should make it easy and convenient for the customer to communicate the change. Many organizations place a change-of-address section on the envelope the customer uses to send payment or other communication back to the organization. Telephone operators in customer service may verify the current address. Web pages usually have an option highlighted for any changes to e-mail or postal address. Free industry trade publications usually require individuals to confirm and/or change address information every 6 to 12 months to guarantee future delivery.

Customers and prospects rarely inform the organization that their address is changing unless there is a financial relationship, however, and even then it may not be their priority. Therefore, organizations must have a method of finding the consumer's new address to maintain the relationship. In the United States, people who are moving can fill out an Address Change Request Form at the post office so future mail is sent to their new address. The USPS makes these address changes available to organizations by updating a national database of all persons and their respective mailing addresses.

5.6j Perform the Customer Linkage Identification Process[3]

The customer linkage identification process, sometimes referred to as **merge/purge**, is a method of linking records of individuals or businesses that appear more than once in any set of data. The intent of this record linkage process is not to perform any type of consolidation of information but to identify each appearance of an individual or business and to assign an identifier to each record occurrence.

Record linkage methods fall into three broad categories: manual, deterministic, and probabilistic:

- Manual matching is the oldest, most time-consuming, and costliest method and is not a feasible option when large databases or files are involved.
- Deterministic record linkage links pairs of records on the basis of whether they match or agree on certain variables. For example, an organization may wish to link records that match on surname, initial, address, birth date, and gender, or some combination thereof.
- Probabilistic record linkage uses probabilities to determine whether a pair of records refers to the same individual. Weights are calculated based on these probabilities in order to quantify the likelihood that a pair of records is a true match. A weight is assigned to every record pair examined, based on the information obtained from the comparison of the fields used in the linkage. The value of the total weight is used to assess whether the linked pair is a true match, a nonmatch, or a probable match.

All record linkage software must take into account special, or situational, matching scenarios. These situational matches are the result of valid record pairs based on specific business rules that cannot be captured in either deterministic or probabilistic routines. Examples would be matching a married woman's and an unmarried woman's surnames. Alisha Jones and Alisha Smith would never match based on last name. However, given that both reside at the same address and that the address is a single-family dwelling, a business rule is invoked forcing the pair to become a duplicate. Similarly, Bob Smith at P.O. Box 53 and Bob Smith of 123 Main Street in the same town can be effectively forced to be duplicates based on a similar business rule.

The Alisha Jones/Alisha Smith example introduces another very important concept of record linkage: the use of external information to help make a match/no-match decision for a pair of records. In the married/unmarried name match, the system relied on two additional pieces of information: gender and address type. It is fairly obvious that for a married/unmarried match to be valid, both records should have a female gender first name (and that the names must be equal). It might not be as obvious that the business rule can only be effective if both records are from the same single-family dwelling address. Imagine if the address had pointed to a business address that housed over 100 employees. It would be very possible that there were actually two unique individuals named Alisha Jones and Alisha Smith working for the firm. Given this information, combining these records would have resulted in an overkill or false positive error.

To help determine any situational business rule and additional data element dependencies, it is common to establish and use a match (or linkage) grid to aid in defining matching rules. In these grids, organizations must specify if an element is present and matches (PM), present and does not match (PNM), or does not enter into the decision process. Once the organization has provided all the various match scenarios in a grid, the record linkage process can allow for a reduction of the rules into a set of agreement and disagreement rules for precise implementation. Tables 5.9 and 5.10 are examples of a household grid and an individual linkage grid, respectively.

To determine if a set of match rules and weights are effective in any given record linkage, metrics can be used to measure and grade a resulting record linkage process objectively. A few definitions follow.

True Match—Occurs when two linked records relate to the same entity

False Negative (Underkill)—Occurs when two records relating to the same entity are not linked

False Positive (Overkill)—Occurs when two linked records do not relate to the same entity

True Negative—The number of record pairs unlinked correctly

True Positive—The number of record pairs linked correctly. Once the previous metrics have been assessed, one can determine a series of mathematical measurements using them in various combinations.

False Negative (Underkill) Match Rate—The number of false-negative matches ÷ The total number of true matches

False Positive (Overkill) Match Rate—The number of false-positive matches ÷ The total number of true matches

Gross Matching Error—The number of false negatives + The number of false positives

Sensitivity—The number of correctly linked record pairs ÷ The total number of true match record pairs

Specificity—The number of correctly unlinked record pairs ÷ The total number of true non-match record pairs

Overall Match Rate—The total number of linked record pairs ÷ The total number of true match record pairs

Positive Predictive Value (PPV)—The number of correctly linked record pairs ÷ The total number of linked record pairs

Table 5.9 Household Qualification Grid

Household Qualification

Case #	Zip	Addr	Acct #	SS #	Last Name	First Name	Mid Init	DOB	Gender	HH	Match Type
1	PM	PM			PM	PM				Y	N & A
3	PM	PM	PM							Y	ACCT
4	PM	PM		PM						Y	SSN
5			PM	PM						Y	ACCT
6					PM	PM		PM	PM	Y	N & DOB
7	PM				PM	PM		PM	PM	Y	N & DOB

PM	–	Data Present/Match; Condition based on equal and nonblank/nonzero presence
PNM	–	Data Present/No Match; Condition based on nonequal and nonblank/nonzero presence
Y	–	Yes, put in same household
N	–	No, do not put in same household
Addr	–	80 percent or higher score of similarity of significant address. Insignificant addresses include those that are blank, those in multiple dwellings with no apartment or unit, those on rural routes with no P.O. Box number, and those that have only a street name.
Names	–	Phonetic (spellings can be different but still result in a match based on phonetics)
First Init	–	Records have only first initial

Source: S D. Sieloff, Senior Systems Architect for The Allant Group, Inc., in Naperville, Illinois.

Table 5.10 Individual Qualification Grid

Individual Qualification Identifies Each Unique Individual within a Household

Case #	Last Name	FName/ FInit	Mid Init	Gender	Suffix	Aprx DOB	SSN	Individual
1	PM	PM	PM	PM	PM	PM	PM	Y
2	PM	PM	PM			PM	PM	Y
3	PNM	XM					XM	N
4	PNM	XM						N
5	PNM	XM					XM	N
6	PM	PNM		XM		XM	XM	N
7	PM	PNM						N

PM	–	Data Present/Match; Condition based on equal and non-blank/non-zero presence
XM	–	Data Present/Match or only one record has a value
PNM	–	Data Present/No-match; Condition based on non-equal and non-blank/non-zero presence
Y	–	Yes, identify as same individual within household being processed
N	–	No, would not be considered to be same individual
Addr	–	80 percent or higher score of similarity of significant address. Insignificant addresses include those that are blank, those in multiple dwellings with no apartment or unit, those on rural routes with no P.O. Box number, and those that have only a street name.
Names	–	Phonetic (spellings can be different); Match condition requires that M/F gender also match when present
First Init	–	Records have only first initial
Approx. DOB-1	–	Month is equal, year is within eight years, day does not need to be equal
2	–	Day and year are equal
3	–	Match on year alone is OK where Acct, last name, and first name are equal

Source: S. D. Sieloff, Senior Systems Architect for The Allant Group, Inc. in Naperville, Illinois.

Two other performance measures widely used in the information retrieval research field are precision and recall. Precision measures how well a search avoids returning results that are not relevant, while recall refers to retrieval completeness of relevant items. For record linkage, precision can be defined, in terms of matches, as the number of correctly linked record pairs divided by the total number of linked record pairs. Therefore, precision is equivalent to the positive predictive value (PPV). Similarly, recall is defined, in terms of matches, as the number of correctly linked record pairs divided by the total number of true match record pairs. Therefore, recall is equivalent to sensitivity. Precision and recall can also be defined in terms of nonmatches. Alternatively, combined measures of precision and recall can be defined in terms of overall record pairs correctly classified (matches and nonmatches).

It is important to note that the degree of acceptable overkill or underkill can vary depending on the use of the final file. For instance, individuals listed in the resulting clean file were to receive a $250 discount coupon for an automobile. The mailer would be well advised to accept a higher degree of overkill, as this would ensure only one coupon per unique customer by overcombining pairs of records. Conversely, if the resulting use of the clean file was a prospecting catalog, promoting a higher degree of underkill to maximize the penetration of catalogs to potential prospects might be appropriate.

5.6j.1 Phonemic Name Compression[4]

In record linkage, name compression codes are used for grouping together variants of surnames for the purposes of blocking and searching so that effective match comparisons can occur using both the full name and other identifying data, despite misspelled or misreported names. Considerable attention has been given to the ways in which surnames are captured, and algorithmic methods reduce or eliminate the effects of variations in spelling and reporting and compress names into fixed-length codes. Common phonetic codes include **Russell-Soundex**, Metaphone, Dolby, ONCA, and NYSIIS. These codes have been optimized for specific populations of names and a specific type of English pronunciation.

Here are some other name variants that influence record linkage:

1. Punctuation (e.g., "Owens Corning" vs. "Owens-Corning"; "IBM" vs. "I.B.M.")
2. Capitalization (e.g., "citibank" vs. "Citibank"; "SMITH" vs. "Smith")
3. Spacing (e.g., "J.C. Penney" vs. "J. C. Penney")
4. Qualifiers (e.g., "Jim Jones" vs. "Jim Jones d.b.a. Jones Enterprises")
5. Organizational terms (e.g., "corporation" vs. "incorporated")
6. Acronym (e.g., "General Motors" vs. "GM")
7. Misspellings
   a. Omissions (e.g., "Collin" vs. "Colin")
   b. Additions (e.g., "McDonald" vs. "MacDonald")
   c. Substitutions (e.g., "Smyth" vs. "Smith")
   d. Letter reversals (e.g., "Peirce" vs. "Pierce")
8. Word omissions (e.g., "National Electrical Benefit Fund and its Trustees" vs. "National Electrical Benefit Fund")
9. Word permutations (e.g., "State of Missouri District Attorney" vs. "District Attorney, State of Missouri")
10. Word order (e.g., "Dewey, Cheatem, and Howe" vs. "Howe, Dewey, and Cheatem")
11. Word concatenation (e.g., "Peter O. Tool" vs. "Peter O'Tool")
12. Compound/hyphenated words (e.g., "Mary Smith" vs. "Mary Smith-Jones")
13. Nicknames/Aliases (e.g., "Richard Jones" vs. "Dick Jones"; "3M" vs. "Minnesota Mining and Manufacturing")
14. Acronyms (e.g., "IBM" vs. "International Business Machines"; "AOL" vs. "America Online")
15. Abbreviations (e.g., "cooperative" vs. "coop"; "CommEd" vs. "Commonwealth Edison")
16. Semantically equivalent words (e.g., "Joe's Cement" vs. "Joe's Concrete"; "John's Diner" vs. "John's Restaurant")

5.6j.2 Customer Linkage Approaches

There is a spectrum of logical approach options to customer linkage. The spectrum can range from a very "tight" logical approach to a very "loose" logical approach. A very tight approach requires almost every character in every field of each record to be an exact match to be labeled a duplicate record or match.

In Figure 5.13, records #1 and #2 would not be declared a duplicate under a very tight logical approach. A very loose logical approach, however, may declare these two records a match, perhaps due to a phonetic similarity. A "middle" approach, halfway between very tight and very loose, may find records #1 and #3 to be the same person at the same address but not record #2 because the last name is spelled differently and there is no middle initial. In this case, a decision was made to have a name match carry more weight than an address match, even if the first name was only an initial. There can be more than three levels of approach, which can vary based on the fields being examined. We can refer to this variance as customer linkage identification elasticity. A very tight approach can be called inelastic, while a very loose approach can be called elastic. And there will be degrees of elasticity depending on each organization's data environment. The creation of the logical approach is usually referred to as business rule definition. Several things must be considered when defining business rules for duplication identification.

First, each industry and each organization in each industry has certain nuances in its data that will have an effect on the elasticity of matching. Certain industries have historically been efficient in their data capture and editing efforts. Financial services have for decades been a collector and manipulator of data, since transactions are at the core of their business. This is the same for catalogers, who collect payment and deliver product.

Second, the ramifications of error may be more severe in one industry than another. An error in matching a person's financial transaction can lead to a liability regarding the pure operational aspect of the business and also provide the marketer with erroneous historical data if the person is incorrectly matched. Sending a person an extra catalog will not create a liable situation. However, it may have a negative impact on the CRM effort, since two identical catalogs sent to the same person tells that person that the organization is either inefficient in its distribution process or may have that person listed differently in its database and hence think the person is two different people.

Third, the organization structure must be considered. An organization that collects and processes data centrally will have more control over the business rule definition. An organization that has decentralized data capture and duplication identification processing may create a situation where it is performing duplication identification in various areas and at different levels of elasticity. If different areas in an organization apply various approaches to duplication identification, it will be difficult to aggregate the data from each respective area, as they may have used different elasticity methods. Thus, it is important to standardize the business rules across all areas of the organization.

Fourth, once the business rules for duplication identification have been defined and implemented, they should not be changed. If they are, the integrity of the current matched records has been jeopardized. Refer back to Figure 5.13. If the original rule was loose in its matching application, it may find records #1 and #2 to be the same individual. Exact match on name and address is not a requirement for considering the individual the same. Therefore, the names John M. Symthe and J. Smith, while different, will be identified as the same person because their street address, city, state, and ZIP code are the same, even though one has a secondary address present, Apt. #3, and the other does not. Now the organization decides to change the rule on duplication identification. It decides the current rule is too loose and that the record match just shown is

Record 1	Record 2	Record 3
John M. Symthe	J. Smith	J. Smythe
123 Dresser Dr.	123 Dresser Dr.	123 Dresser Dr.
Apt. #3		Apt. #3
Oak Lawn IL 60451	Oak Lawn IL 60451	Oak Lawn IL 60451

Figure 5.13 Customer Linkage Approach

inaccurate. This conclusion may have resulted from customer feedback or an internal marketing audit. Now, if a subsequent transaction comes in for John M. Symthe, it will be accurately defined as different from J. Smith, and Symthe's transaction information will be correctly linked to him. J. Smith's transaction will be more accurately assigned as well.

While the rule change may result in more accurate identification proceeding, it presents a challenge with regard to understanding the customer history. So what happens to the historical information gathered to this point? The organization has three options: (1) do nothing with historical data prior to this rule change, (2) apply the historical information to one of the customers and not the other, and (3) split the historical information appropriately (i.e., correctly assign John M. Symthe his history and the same for J. Smith). Selecting an option is highly dependent on what the organization has done in the first rule identification process. The first and second options do not support the CRM effort. If an organization is trying to build or sustain a relationship with a customer, the customer's past is critical input to understanding that customer's needs, wants, and demands. Doing nothing will cause J. Smith to have John M. Symthe's history, up to the rule change, attached to him. Going forward, historical information will be managed accurately, but all of John M. Symthe's history prior to the rule change will be missing from his account. Also, J. Smith's history is inaccurate prior to the change. For example, let us say that in some prior interaction, John M. Symthe indicated, via a Web page, that he did not want to be bothered with any promotional material either via the Web, postal mail, or a telemarketer's phone call. Additionally, he mentioned that he did want to receive communication when a certain product category has been updated with new product versions. With that history now excluded from his account, a future marketing effort may violate that agreement, which is not a good option for a marketer building customer lifetime value.

5.6k Enhance the Customer Data with Other Sourced Data

Sourced data (secondary data) is usually purchased or made available from a source other than the customer (primary data). The data is usually purchased from a government institution or from companies that collect and sell data as their core competency. The former has become more restrictive due to heightened privacy concerns.

Adding the purchased data to existing customers or prospects requires software algorithms that match a customer or prospect to a person on the purchased data. When a match occurs, the purchased data elements are added to the customer or prospect data. Additional data can only enrich subsequent CRM initiatives because the more one knows about a person, the better the effort will be at building or sustaining a relationship.

There are other benefits to adding information at this point. First, it improves the **suppression** process. For example, if a person is found to be less than 13 years of age, the suppression process can mark that person's record as a "do not solicit." Data can be maintained for analysis purposes, but until that person reaches a certain age, he or she should not be solicited for ethical as well as legal reasons. Once enhanced with an age variable, however, that field can be updated each year and a trigger set so when that person reaches an appropriate age, he or she can be marked for marketing communication.

Second, it improves the consolidation process. Suppose that Mary Smith had three different transactions with a company over a one-year period. Each transaction contained slightly different information. Before these records were consolidated, external files with enhanced data matched Mary differently, which resulted in data being appended to each of Mary's transactions. If the data enhancement process were to occur after the consolidation, not all information may have been added. Also, placing all relevant data in Mary Smith's records allows the consolidation process to reconcile all information at once and execute business decision rules per variable.

5.61 Perform a Suppression Process on the Data

There are reasons for not establishing a relationship with a customer or prospect that depend on the nature of the business. Some reasons to suppress a person in the organization's customer records are that he or she is deceased, a minor, in prison, in the military, in an area unable to serve the product or service, on the "Do Not Call" or "Do Not Mail" files, or has told the organization not to send further communication (i.e., has opted out of any communication). Table 5.11 lists sample data suppression sources.

Some data enhancement and data suppression providers are Infogroup, Equifax, Epsilon, Experian, Polk, Acxiom, and Nielsen Claritas, just to name a few. The industry is dynamic, and

Table 5.11 Example of Data Suppression Sources

Mail Preference Service (MPS)	Managed by the Direct Marketing Association, includes people who have opted not to receive advertising mail
Deceased Master File Suppression	Flags addresses whose primary residents have died within the past 48 months
Deceased/SSA Deathmaster	Social Security Administration
Prison Suppression	From the American Correctional Association, compares list data against a national directory of addresses identified as prisons
Pander Files (do not mail, do not call)	Uses written requests from outside organizations to have a name and address removed from mailing lists (Direct Marketing Association)
Business/Shopping Center Addresses	Compiled from regional White Pages listings
College Addresses	Compares addresses in lists to a database of approximately 220 ZIP codes assigned to colleges or universities
Military ZIP Codes	Flags addresses with ZIP codes corresponding to military installations
Nursing Homes	Matches addresses against those that have been identified as nursing homes
Relative Input of Another's Death	Similar to Deceased Master File Suppression, but consisting of written do-not-mail notifications from a relative of a deceased person
Retirement Homes	Similar to Nursing Homes Suppression, this service isolates addresses that have been identified as retirement homes
Mobile Home Park	Flags mobile home/trailer park addresses
Customer's Debtors	
Prior Mail Suppression	
Customer/Prospect Opt-Out	Customer/prospect notification to organization

new providers enter the marketplace with new solutions rather frequently, especially with the advent of numerous new data sources precipitated by social media activity. One place to look for these providers is online. A more prudent and less risky approach to identifying data providers is to attend industry conferences. The Direct Marketing Association (http://www.newdma.org) is a good place to start a search. The National Center for Direct Marketing also hosts annual events (http://www.ncdmevents.com) that data providers attend and sponsor.

5.6m Consolidate Customer Linkage and Related Customer Data

Figure 5.8 illustrates the separation of linkage data from nonlinkage data. Each record at that time had been assigned a unique sequence number. Both linkage and nonlinkage data are reunited and consolidated by household and individual via their respective sequence numbers.

In reality, the actual process will vary based on the type of software design. All relevant customer information will now be tied to the linkage component precipitating a single consolidated view of the customer. This was the CDI objective. To make this information actionable, it must update those data repositories that will use this information. Chapters 6 and 7 discuss different approaches to updating data repositories.

Chapter Summary

CDI is a key success factor of CRM efforts. It is a meticulous and time-consuming process. CDI is a dynamic area due to changes in software and hardware advancements as well as approach innovation. However, performing the following steps, regardless of whether they are combined or replaced with new methods, increases the probability of a successful CRM undertaking, provides ancillary benefits such as fraud detection, precipitates data collection areas that need improvement, and possibly uncovers new data collection areas of opportunity:
(1) identify touch points for data collection,
(2) define how the data will be collected,
(3) establish business rules for the data collection process,
(4) create a methodology to manage the data input process after the data is collected,
(5) place the data into a common format,
(6) separate customer linkage data from all other data,
(7) standardize customer linkage data,
(8) correct the linkage data components,
(9) apply postal processing to the customer linkage data,
(10) perform the customer linkage identification process,
(11) enhance customer data,
(12) perform suppression,
(13) consolidate the linkage data with the related customer data, and
(14) create a 360-degree view of the customer.

Key Terms

Customer data integration (CDI) is a data management process where all prospect and customer data can be distributed to points of interaction in a timely and accurate manner.

Data entry organization is a company that generates digital data from nondigital text by using a person to read text and enter the text into digital format or scanning the text into a digital format.

Data latency is the concept that data, once captured, may not be readily available for leverage in support of a CRM effort.

Household can be defined as those individuals who make up a consumer family (including nontraditional or extended) who live at the same location. A business household is comprised of employees who work in the same organization, but the actual group of employees may vary by organization entity, department, or location.

Merge/purge is to combine two or more sets of data in such a way that the resulting data has the same organization as the two individual sets of data. During the merge process, duplicate sets of data are deleted or purged.

Reference database serves as an impartial reference, providing links between all captured instances of a customer.

Russell-Soundex is a phonetic algorithm for indexing names by their sound when pronounced in English.

Suppression is the exclusion of an individual or household, either business or consumer, from being input into a process dependent on relative criteria, such as suppressing deceased consumers from a marketing promotion.

Touch point is a specific area where an organization and a customer or prospect may interact. Examples of touch points include the telephone, the Internet, face-to-face, kiosk, and wireless device.

Questions

1. Explain how data latency can inhibit an organization's CRM effort with a customer.
2. Why is it important to understand the extent to which data is "populated"?
3. What is the purpose of customer linkage data?
4. Why should organizations enhance their data with secondary information?
5. Why would an organization maintain data on a customer but suppress that customer from any CRM effort?

Exercises

1. The larger the organization, the more likely disparate data will occur. What are the implications of disparate data in an organization relative to the CRM effort?
2. Select an organization that you purchase products or services from and identify the organization's touch points. Are they effective? Can they be improved? If so, how?
3. Give an example of how "householding" data can enhance a B2C, B2B, and B2B2C CRM effort.
4. Fill out a form requesting information from a company. Leave out some address information (e.g., directional, suffix such as boulevard/street/road/avenue), misspell your first name if common (e.g., Robrt instead of Robert), and then submit the request. Examine this linkage information when the company responds to see what, if any, changes its software made to your address and name information.

Appendix

The quadrants are usually updated quarterly to include a company's new competencies in the respective discipline, a reduction competency capability, an elimination of a competency, or new companies. Companies appearing in the top right quadrant are at the forefront of the respective discipline—that is, they are probably the most innovative and have good insight to future approaches and are also excellent at execution. A company in the top left quadrant is excellent at execution but may be classified as a follower in the industry. Companies that fall into the bottom left of the quadrant usually reflect new entrants who are building their competencies or companies struggling to build a competency. Companies may appear in the lower right quadrant for a limited time. They may be innovators who are in the process of building their competency or may have temporarily encountered a setback in their ability to execute. The setback usually is due to unexpected macro environment events or uncertainty.

Chapter 6

Technology and Data Platforms

TOPICS

6.1 Introduction

6.2 Technology Evolution

6.3 Marketing Technology Development Path

6.4 Other Emerging Technology Influencers

6.5 CRM Providers

6.1 Introduction

This chapter provides readers with an understanding of technology concepts, specifically how they are related to CRM in a business context. The field of technology is dynamic and complex and is filled with acronyms. We have, however, chosen not to overwhelm the reader with these acronyms or with technical details. Our approach should leave the reader with a firm grasp of the areas to be addressed and the types of decisions that need to be made regarding the CRM initiative. We also include a list of CRM technology–enabling companies. As this is a dynamic industry, information may change from the time of printing; the textbook website (www.routledge.com/9780415896573) contains links to more in-depth and current information.

6.2 Technology Evolution

It is important to understand the evolution of CRM technology for a number of reasons. First, some organizations still use the same technology and methods that were widely used for the past several decades. If the intent is to migrate to more recent best practices, understanding the current methods will help ensure that marketing objectives are sustained during migration. Second, understanding the current technology will help facilitate the tactical migration to different technology environments by reducing risks and identifying some steps in business methods that may be candidates for change. Third, the nature of competitiveness in CRM technology–enabling organizations has posed a risk in that it creates an environment of overwhelming and sometimes confusing solutions in the marketplace.

In some cases, technology solutions may be positioned so well that the marketer may believe the implementation of technology is actually the CRM solution. There is no doubt that these organizations have created efficient, CRM technical solutions, but marketers must be careful when evaluating technology and how it can be leveraged to support their CRM strategy. As one CRM director stated, "Do I really need a Ferrari to drive to the convenience store to pick up a gallon of milk?" The approach this chapter takes demonstrates the leveraged value and leaves the specific technical-provider choices up to the marketer.

Another reason to understand the evolution of CRM technical solutions is that each phase of this evolution is not necessarily replaced by those in subsequent phases. In fact, best practices may be carried over and maintained, albeit in a different form. Additionally, financial constraints may prohibit an all-encompassing solution. Technology is gradually phased in, but organizations entering new phases of CRM implementation must sometimes integrate different generations of technology to complete the process. Finally, we can learn a lot from the evolution of CRM technology and, thus, potentially avoid the mistakes of earlier technologies and methods.

6.3 Marketing Technology Development Path

One can look at the evolution of marketing and technology across three major phases. There is no distinct division between phases; each one has certain strengths that may be carried over into subsequent phases. Numerous organizations use technologies from different evolutionary phases concurrently. Many organizations prior to the early 1990s used simple techniques to gain and sustain relationships with their customers. Their marketing efforts required the collaboration and use of highly skilled technology professionals who employed sophisticated but laborious techniques to achieve the simplest CRM objective. Table 6.1 demonstrates the phases of technology related to customer acquisition and retention via building and sustaining customer relationships.

Table 6.1 **Marketing Technology Development Phases**

	Mass Communication	*Database Marketing*	*Integrated Marketing*
Characteristics	– Lists – Offers – Creative program emphasis – Buy/use names – Data hygiene – Telemarketing – Households – Testing	– Individuals – Dialogue – Feedback – Segmentation – Forecasting – Segment market research – Batch – Some real time	– Channel enhancement – Service and quality management – Inventory control – Value chain evaluation – Media coordination – Production control – Individual market research – Distribution – Real time
Measurement Methods	– Programs	– Programs – Models	– Lifetime value – Word of mouth
Customer/ Prospect Behavior	– Predict	– Predict – Change	– Change
Technology	– Primitive – Laborious – Reliance on technology professionals – Centralized processing – Long lead times – Limited data communication	– Some technology distributed – Technology more advanced – Marketing tools becoming available – Data communication improving – Some online processing	– Technology integrated across business disciplines and with external value chain members – Marketing tools prevalent – Data communication very efficient – Data storage cheap and readily available

(Continued)

Table 6.1 (Continued)

	Mass Communication	Database Marketing	Integrated Marketing
Technology	– Batch processing – Limited disk data storage capability – Strong reliance on technical professionals for execution	– Still relying on technology professionals for execution but ability to self-execute growing	– Greatly reduced reliance on technology professionals for day-to-day but heavy reliance for technology planning – Overall technology costs decreasing and technology effectiveness and capabilities increasing – Customer service/sales/Web/marketing integration

1960s <--->2000s

6.3a Mass Communication

For many years, organizations communicated to the masses by compiling lists of names or households. They gathered this information from their existing customers or would purchase or rent the names and contact information (e.g., address, phone number) from other organizations. Certain organizations were developed for the sole purpose of buying and renting names and contact information. Alternatively, an organization would sell or rent its customers' names and contact information to other companies or share that information with other entities in the same organization, such as a subsidiary. The list rental process used data preparation methods described in Chapter 5. This technique is still practiced by some organizations.

6.3b Database Marketing

As previously discussed, there is no definitive separation between technology-enabling phases. The hardware and software improved simultaneously. Figure 6.1 shows a fully functional database marketing environment as it had evolved by the 1990s. It demonstrates a complete cycle of information and transaction flow between a consumer and an organization.

6.3b.1 Data Preparation

Data preparation ("dataprep") describes the data integration steps defined in Chapter 5. During this process, the data is being prepared to update data repositories such as an operational data store, a **data warehouse**, or a **data mart**. Dataprep occurs twice in Figure 6.1. The first occurrence, represented by the elongated icon taking in information from a variety of sources, is usually a **batch process** of all the dataprep steps. This process may be performed once data from all sources is available, on-demand as sources are available, or on a source-by-source predetermined schedule with specific "cutoff" processing scheduled time/dates to ensure compliance with customer information processing flows.

The second occurrence of dataprep is related to online access by either the Internet Web page software or a telemarketer ("TM" in the illustration) using a computer screen. Both situations usually require dataprep before the software, Web or otherwise, can access the operational data store. This second instance of dataprep is basically performing the same functions as the first, except that one is performing it in a controlled and scheduled sequential batch environment, while the other is executed in real time on-demand.

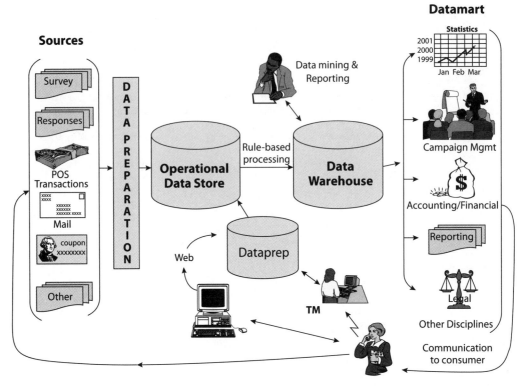

Figure 6.1 **Data Flow Environment**

6.3b.2 *Operational Data Store*

An **operational data store (ODS)** is a type of data repository or database that is designed for quick read/write access on-demand to and from multiple sources and types of technology. Quick read/write access means that a person can expect a quick response upon entering information or selecting information from any software or via the telephone to access the ODS. An ODS is designed to contain a limited amount of information, which supports those time-sensitive interactions between the customer and an organization that contribute to an overall CRM strategy. Two examples of the types of sources accessing this entity are a telemarketer who needs to look up information for a customer and a customer accessing the ODS via a Web page as he searches for information. The latter is transparent to the customer, as all he knows is that information is displayed on the Web page. The Web page is actually being supplied information from an ODS. The information in the ODS is current, time sensitive, and usually tied to a specific customer–organization interaction. It does not contain all of a customer's history with an organization, only that information needed to facilitate a "point-in-time" interaction. History, if present, is combined with the present. Therefore, five years of transaction information may be present as one total dollar amount. Some examples of a typical customer-initiated "point-in-time" interaction are a purchase transaction; a merchandise return; a complaint; or an inquiry such as order status, inventory verification, or product/service information. The organization may also initiate interaction to facilitate a customer or potential customer's transaction or request for information. A postpurchase survey, product shipment acknowledgment, and product availability notice are all types of communication initiated by an organization. Additionally, it may be a scheduled communication as part of the customer's opt-in agreement under the guise of a permission marketing strategy.

It is important that the ODS is designed to facilitate the flow of information accurately and efficiently, and it must be technically compatible with a variety of software that may access it. If a person calls an inbound 800 number for customer support to check on her back order for a product, the customer service representative will need to access the most up-to-date information as quickly as possible. Here is an example of the value of a well-designed ODS:

> David and Jenine Carter just moved into their new home. The previous residents left a washer and dryer, but the dryer did not work. David determined that it needed a new part and, while at work, used his retailer customer preferred credit card to order the part from the retailer's website. David's order information was now in the ODS.
>
> Later that same day, Jenine, unbeknownst to David and unaware of David's online part purchase, called the retailer's 800 number and talked with an inbound retailer telemarketer. She decided to order a new dryer to surprise David. The telemarketer asked for Jenine's ZIP code and last name. That information was linked internally to another ODS to determine if the Carters were existing customers. There was a match because the retailer performed postal processing. David and Jenine had notified the United States Postal Service (USPS) when they moved, and that information flowed to the NCOALink (national change-of-address) service provider the retailer used. The telemarketer also noticed David's recent transaction in the ODS and informed Jenine of David's order. She was grateful to the telemarketer and decided not to purchase a dryer. However, the telemarketer sold her a tool kit for David to make installing the part easier and asked about other needs. The telemarketer sold other household merchandise to Jenine and, in the ensuing conversation, arranged for an interior decorator to come to the Carter home the following week.

Software that retrieves information from the ODS and updates the data warehouse may access the ODS on a scheduled or, more infrequently, ad hoc basis. The marketer, in conjunction with a technical architect, must determine the timing of retrieval and the types of information retrieved. The technical architect ensures that the marketer's requirements can be technically fulfilled. For example, there may be situations where the amount of information to be retrieved and subsequently updated to the data warehouse could not meet the marketer's requirements no matter how much money and technical hardware and software were used.

6.3b.3 Data Warehouse

The term *data warehouse* (DW) is appropriate for this entity's purpose. A DW is used as a repository for all relevant customer and prospect information over an extended period of time. This information is more extensive than that related to a "point-in-time" interaction, as we saw with the operational data store. But what is relevant information, and for how long should information be kept? The following is a brief, noninclusive list of the types of consumer and company information that a DW may maintain:

- Customer and/or prospect name, address(es), phone number(s), e-mail address(es), business contact information (if applicable), demographics, psychographics, and lifestyle data
- Customer transaction history by period of time and aggregated as data is aged
- Other customer activity (e.g., return, inquiry, complaint, gift purchase, and recipient contact information)
- Customer preferences and/or restrictions (e.g., products, services, channels, privacy, method of payment)
- Suppression and privacy rules
- Organization product and/or service information by periods of time (for synchronization with customer or prospect activity)
- Marketing metrics (e.g., lifetime value, return on investment, customer equity)

- Marketing activity (e.g., campaigns, promotions) and marketing collateral used, by periods of time (for synchronization with customer or prospect activity)
- Supplier and/or other value chain partners such as agencies, by periods of time (for synchronization with customer or prospect activity)
- Relevant macro environmental exogenous data (political, economical, demographic, natural resources, technological), by periods of time (for synchronization with customer or prospect activity)
- Relevant competitive information, by periods of time (for synchronization with customer or prospect activity)
- Derived (calculated) variables (i.e., new information generated by performing calculations on data previously described)
- Marketing model data (e.g., behavioral, predictive, change)

In some industries, there may be hundreds of data elements defined but not populated in the DW. There are several different approaches relative to choosing fields used. A field is a set of characters in a database, usually a data element. The terms *data element* and *field* are often used interchangeably. One approach is to define every possible variable that may be captured, and define a field to hold that information in the DW even though it is not present. Then, over time, slowly eliminate the unused fields from the DW. The second approach is the opposite: define those fields for the data variables that are important and that will be captured. Then, as needed, evaluate which new fields should be added. There is no right or wrong approach; however, technical design issues should be defined and decisions made with the appropriate technical designers to determine the optimal approach.

The question of how much identified data is to be kept in the DW is also pertinent. *Depth* refers to the amount of detail for a particular variable, whereas *breadth* refers to the number of variables. If the database contained six different demographic variables in addition to products purchased, there would be a width of 7 variables. If the products purchased variable contained 12 different product codes, which were purchased over a period of time, then that variable would have a depth of 12 elements. For example, a customer bought 44 products over a four-year period in four product categories through three different channels. The customer used two different credit cards as well as paid with cash. The customer took advantage of several promotions and rebates and also returned three products. On two occasions, the products purchased were gifts for different people, and the customer provided both gift recipients' addresses for delivery of the products. Detailed information for all of these transactions may be included in the DW, with some detail in aggregate form. For example, maintaining ten years' worth of customer transaction history increases storage costs and requires more processing when attempting to calculate customer revenue. Usually the last several years of customer transaction detail are relevant, with the remaining years only requiring a summation or aggregation of revenue, such as an eight-year total revenue. This will vary by industry and respective company needs. Decisions regarding the depth and breadth of information to be stored should be made prior to the DW design.

The DW is updated with information acquired in the ODS. It may also be updated with information from other sources such as product information or value chain information. The DW can be accessed by a variety of different methods, the most common being structured query language (SQL), which requires the user to learn the language syntax it uses. Some companies have created what is referred to as "front-end tools," which are basically well-written programs that generate SQL from a Windows-based or other operating system–based set of screens. The user does not need to learn SQL but instead interacts with user-friendly screens. Pull-down and point-and-click methods are then used to create a query for the DW. The programs executed by the respective screens generate the SQL, perform the respective action on the DW, and return the results to the user in an easy-to-read format. The SQL process can be quick if the query is simple, or it may be laborious, taking hours to complete, if the query is complex. While the need to search the entire DW for information may be valid, it is not something that should be done regularly. The situation becomes more complex when there are multiple users performing queries simultaneously.

6.3b.4 Data Marts

Data marts are an alternative and more frequently used method of accessing information that is present in the data warehouse. Data is extracted from the DW and stored in a data mart, which can be thought of as a subset of a DW. Data marts contain less depth or breadth of information than a DW. Data marts usually differ in design and content based on the business function(s) they are intended to support. They are designed to optimize the specific software the individual will use to access and manipulate its contents. Software used to access a data mart is generally different from that used to access the DW and may be classified as a decision support system (DSS). The software analyzes and makes decisions based on a subset of data. The following are some software functions that comprise DSS:

- Campaign management software
- Spreadsheet software
- Statistical software
- Data mining software (discussed in Chapter 7)

More information on suppliers of DSS can be found at the textbook product support website (www.routledge.com/9780415896573).

Data marts typically allow for ease of use and fast access capabilities while the users interact with the data by browsing the data looking for patterns or correlations, or performing specific analysis on the data. Customers—current or prospective—may, for example, be selected from the data mart for a targeted marketing effort. The ability to write data to the data mart is also generally required. Following are two examples of the use of data marts:

- *Example 1*: A marketer wants to measure her monthly marketing effort to increase the average sales to 18- to 25-year-old female customers from $25 to $30 over a one-year period. She wants to analyze the transaction purchase activities, including types of products and SKU (stock keeping unit) numbers over the time frame. She also needs to monitor the merchandise return activity as well as any feedback from the customer. The company's DW contains detailed transaction activity, both purchases and returns, on all customers for the last two years. (Any data older than two years has been aggregated to a level higher than the specific transaction level.) To enable the marketer to easily access the specific information she needs, the relative information can be copied from the DW into the data mart on a scheduled or requested basis. The marketer then accesses the data mart by using software that analyzes the data relevant to her effort. Her access to data is, therefore, quick, as her software is designed to perform the specific analysis she needs.
- *Example 2*: A major appliance manufacturer sells, among other things, gas ranges and the hoses for gas connections. The legal department wants to maintain a list of all customers who purchase a gas range or a connector hose in the event of a recall. Due to the potential danger to the consumer and also the ensuing liability, they have asked that a customer's contact information be current, accurate, and available as soon as possible after the sale. All sales data is updated to the DW. To meet the legal department's need, immediately after the DW is updated, a process is automatically executed to select all customer and product data related to

the purchase of the gas range or connector hose (e.g., contact information and product serial number) and send this information to the legal department's data mart.

There are usually multiple data marts used throughout an organization, each designed and updated to meet a specific business need. The type of software used to access a data mart will vary by business discipline.

6.3b.5 Logical Data Model

Building a database, whether it be the ODS, DW, or data mart, is a two-step process similar to building a house. First the house is designed, and then it is physically created. When building a house, an architect works closely with the builder or owner on the conceptual design: appearance of the house, size of rooms, number of floors, locations of windows and doors, and so on. Once the architect and the builder/owner agree on the layout and inclusions, the next step is final drawings and a last-minute walk-through before the contractors begin physical construction.

Database creation follows the same steps. The database owner knows what should be included in the database and how it will be used. The database architect creates a **logical data model (LDM)**, which is the equivalent of a house blueprint. Figure 6.2 is an example of part of an LDM (the entire LDM can contain several hundred pages of drawings). Each box represents a logical entity. One arrow is used to demonstrate one occurrence, and two arrows depict two or more occurrences, or "many." Hence, when discussing the creation of an LDM, the phrases "one-to-many," "one-to-one," or "many-to-many" relationships are involved. One marketing campaign, for example, may comprise many promotions, and each specific promotion may have more than one subpromotion within a campaign. The database architect does not have this information. The business owner must ensure that all relative knowledge owners in the organization have been interviewed by the database architect for their input into the LDM creation process. Depending on the magnitude of the database to be created, this process can take anywhere from 30 days to 6 months. Once the LDM is complete, a final walk-through is usually required to ensure compliance with all business requirements.

Concurrent with the LDM process, business owners must address other areas as well prior to the physical build process. The factors they need to consider may include the following:

- Number of individuals accessing the database concurrently
- Access requirements related to speed and the display
- Export requirements for accessed data (e.g., print format, visual format, compatibility for export to other software or hardware)
- Security and privacy requirements
- Data add, delete, and update requirements
- Data recovery and contingency requirements
- Scalability requirements for information breadth and depth growth

With a completed LDM and answers to the points previously listed, the physical build process can begin.

6.3c Integrated Marketing

This is the third and most current phase of the marketing and technology development path. In an attempt to gain a competitive advantage, companies have started integrating their marketing

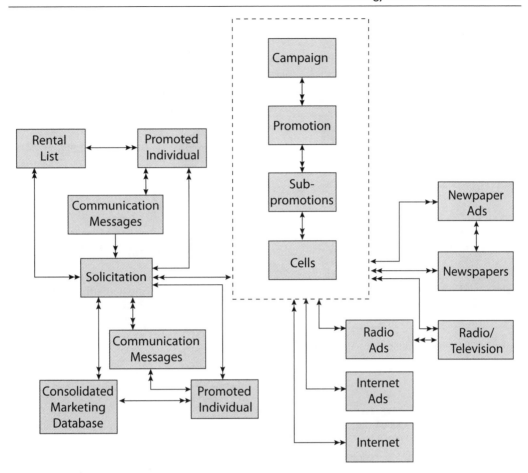

Figure 6.2 Sample Logical Data Model

strategy both throughout their organization and with their value chain partners. The companies that have put marketing and CRM in the forefront have placed a strategic emphasis on integrating technology both internally and with their value chain partners. The standardization of software and the Internet has also made it easier to create and maintain these types of environments. Figure 6.3 provides a high-level overview of this environment.

As Figure 6.3 shows, there are three main areas of activity within integrated marketing. The first area is the collaborative environment, which supports the customer interface activity. Computer telephony, Web pages, telemarketing, **kiosks**, and point of sale (POS) are applications that today enable the interface between a customer and an organization. The advent of social media has required companies to create and implement software that interfaces with these new means of collaboration. Some CRM technology providers are creating or have modified or are currently modifying their current solutions to interface with social media tools such as Facebook, Twitter, LinkedIn, Google Blog Search, and InsideView. Applications using radio frequency identification imbedded in mobile devices including automotive accessories and robotics will soon be used.

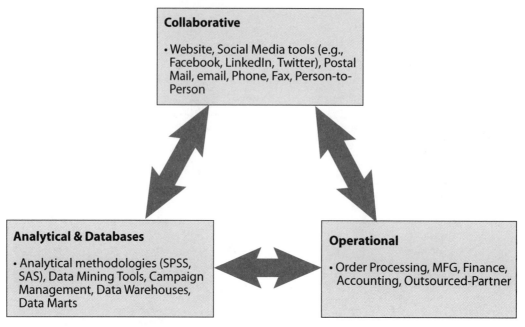

Figure 6.3 Technology Component Overview

The second area of integrated marketing is the analytical environment. Information is analyzed and acted upon via most of the database marketing applications previously mentioned, including the use of data marts, DSS, and data mining, which support the marketing effort.

The third area is the operational area of the enterprise. This includes the core business applications (e.g., accounting, finance, sales, order processing, inventory management, manufacturing and distribution, supplier integration); prior marketing systems, often referred to as "legacy systems" that need to be accessed; and interfaces with value chain members. The last one is a growing need as organizations optimize their business process by outsourcing non–core competency activities and creating a competitive value chain. Some organizations have implemented **enterprise resource planning (ERP)** systems to run their operational environment. Companies such as SAP from Germany and Oracle in the United States are the leading providers of ERP systems. ERP systems are designed in a way that allows a company to integrate all of its business activity into a single software platform for the purpose of reducing information duplication while increasing data flow and management. ERP is a CRM enabler, since one of its benefits is the creation of a single source of information for customer information. The major challenges for companies that adopt ERP systems are the cost, the time to implement, and the requirement to adopt its business standards and information flows.

The arrows connecting each of these three main areas of activity represent middleware technology (i.e., software and hardware that is in the middle of two or more functional areas). Numerous organizations provide a variety of middleware offerings. The technical architects ensure that the middleware used optimizes the receipt and use of information from two or more areas of activity. For example, if there is a Web page for the consumer to access her current account information, the middleware used to connect the operational environment with the collaborative environment must be timely so as to satisfy the consumer's request for information. Having to wait for more than a few seconds for a response is usually not acceptable to the consumer and inhibits any CRM initiative with that individual. The following examples illustrate the advantage of integrating all of these environments.

- *Example 1*: A pet supply manufacturer noticed an unusually high number of online coupon requests for dog food by the same individual. These requests were continuous for the last seven months. In the absence of other information, an assumption could be made that the individual was downloading these coupons for resale. In actuality, the individual was an administrative person working in a veterinarian's office. The veterinarian preferred this manufacturer's product and found it contained the optimal nutritional balance for dogs at an affordable price. She made it a habit to give each of her customers a coupon when they visited to entice them to use this product. The data captured in the ODS that was used for Web interaction was fed to the DW on a weekly schedule. A person performing data mining on the DW came across the anomaly. Because the DW was enhanced with additional demographic data, the marketer was able to identify the cause and turn what would have been thought of as a fraud incident into a marketing effort with all veterinarians.
- *Example 2*: The director of marketing for a major boat manufacturer had compiled customer purchase data on boats and accessories. He had segmented his customers into five deciles based on revenue and margins. His marketing efforts were different for each of these segments. However, once he was able to integrate accessory return and boat warranty usage data from disparate databases within his organization, he found that approximately 15 percent of his previously defined "profitable" customers were not as profitable as originally calculated. In fact, once he consolidated and analyzed all relevant interactions, he discovered he was losing money on 3 percent of those customers.
- *Example 3*: A telecommunications company provided its outbound staff with existing customer name and phone numbers for an up-sell marketing promotion. The company had recently experienced a variety of service problems, but the severity of the problems was not evident until the telemarketers started to report the reasons customers did not want to discuss purchase of any new service or product in their database. The call center manager immediately implemented a plan to integrate the ODS that captured customer complaint information and the ODS that was updated with a call report from service technicians. Both were integrated real time into the call center so a telemarketer's customer call list could be flagged up until seconds before a call. The customer would receive a follow-up service satisfaction call instead and be suppressed from solicitations until the customer received uninterrupted and problem-free service for 90 days.

These are but a few examples of integrating data entities in an organization relative to CRM efforts. The permutations are endless. Most organizations could do more to improve their efforts by carefully examining current data capture areas and optimizing relevant marketing data flow.

6.4 Other Emerging Technology Influencers

6.4a Computer Telephony

Computer telephony (CT) describes the hardware and software technologies that enable communication of voice and information via the phone. Basic CT functions include the ability to send and receive messages, the routing of calls, and the performance of some activity based on the

Table 6.2 Computer Telephony Applications

External Customers	Internal Customers
• Order entry	• Benefits enrollment
• Inventory availability	• Employee scheduling
• Account inquiry	• Job postings
• Claim status	• Remote payroll entry
• Dealer locator	
• Product locator	
• Shipment tracing	
• Warranty registration	
• Product and service information	
• Student registration	
• Rate quote	
• Loan calculator	
• Talking classified ads	
• Event schedules	
• Music sampler	
• Voice dialing	
• Automated paging	
• Integrated voice messaging	
• International callback service	
• Prepaid calling service	

information provided during the call. Table 6.2 contains a list of potential applications for both external and internal customers.[1]

Figure 6.4 is an example of the savings an organization received by incorporating CT and screen pops into its inbound telemarketing operation. A screen pop is text displayed on a telemarketer's computer screen generated by an inbound phone call. That call prompts a database to read information and display it on the telemarketer's screen before he or she speaks with the caller. The organization identified all cost drivers associated with the operations of their inbound telemarketing center and allocated or "loaded" these costs across all inbound calls. For example, some of these costs included the cost of utilities for the telemarketing center, rent, telemarketers' benefits and wages, equipment costs, software costs, and a small allocation for future system development and R&D. This organization averages 100 inbound calls per day.

A McKinsey analysis identified the most recent call center improvements (Table 6.3), which should yield substantial benefits if accompanied by the necessary changes in management, incentives, and behavior.[2]

6.4b Radio Frequency Identification

Radio frequency identification (RFID) is a technology that uses radio waves to communicate between two objects. There are several major components in an RFID environment. An RFID tag is a miniature computer chip containing specific information. It can be called the transponder. An antenna affixed to a similar device can be the transceiver. Tags can be passive or active. A passive tag

---

Telemarketing Costs:

$7 per inbound telemarketing call handled by person

$0.80 per call when using only CT

$0.25 per web transaction, which replaces all functions of inbound calls

Telemarketing personnel time savings with CT screen pops and routing is 1 minute per transaction

Scenario with No CT or Web Applied

100 calls per day @ $7/call = $700 daily cost

Scenario with CT Applied to 20 Transactions and Web Applied to 5 Transactions

75 calls per day @ $7/call = $525 daily cost

20 calls routed to CT IVR @ $0.80/transaction = $16 daily cost

5 transactions migrated to Web @ $0.25/transaction = $1.25 daily cost

1 minute savings per transaction due to screen pops applied to 20 calls per day
    @ $0.25 and assuming $15/hour labor cost = $5.00 savings per day

Total daily cost without CT	= $700
Total daily cost with CT and Web	= $537.25
Total daily savings using CT and Web	= $162.75
Annual savings = 365 days × $162.75/day	= $59,403.75

Figure 6.4 Technology Utilization Cost Savings

has no power but draws its power via its antenna, which picks up power from electromagnetic waves emitted by a transceiver. An active tag has a battery and can receive and emit signals, similar to a cell phone. A transceiver can constantly emit an electromagnetic field or utilize a sensor to identify the presence of a tag and, once identified, initiate some read/write action. When the transponder enters that field or is identified by a sensor, it can be activated. The transceiver can read and/or write information to and from the transponder. Many security devices, such as a plastic clip attached to clothing in a store, are RFID tags. If someone takes a tagged article through an electromagnetic field (usually established with a set of parallel bars through which a customer must pass to exit the store), the transceiver's sensor identifies the tag and triggers an alarm. Tollways use the same technology to read the transponder in vehicles passing through the tollbooth. The transceiver reads the transponder and then communicates in real time to a networked computer, the transponder identifier. This is linked to an individual's account residing on some networked computer, which contains all transponders' information, and the appropriate toll amount is subtracted from the account. The transceiver can also alert the driver instantly to a shortage of funds in his or her account by activating a signal light.

So how can one leverage this technology for a CRM effort? The technology has been around for over 50 years. Previously, cost prohibited much consumer use, but costs are decreasing. But how does this relate to CRM? Rather than just using RFID tags on clothing for security reasons, a manufacturer can imbed RFID tags in the clothing and retail stores can install scanners. When the second-to-last sweater is taken off the shelf, the scanner immediately detects the number remaining and signals the store personnel to replenish sweaters. Or a winemaker can tag each bottle of wine with an RFID tag at the time of bottling. The tag maintains a history of temperature exposure. Or fish tagged with RFID can be tracked for temperature exposure to frozen, thawed,

Table 6.3 **Center Improvements**

	Technology	Inefficient Use	Efficient Use
Automate where possible	Automated voice technology	Touchtone responses required; conversion of data to voice is awkward and limited	More effective voice recognition lets system handle more calls; easier to convert transactional data to speech
Fix at the front line	Better middleware and agent desktop	Agent's screen showed limited information; complex interfaces to different operational systems	Improved middleware delivers a simplified agent desktop, presenting relevant customer data during call
	CRM data	Incomplete customer information extracted from multiple systems	Integrated prioritized customer information is presented to the agent when needed
Match staff with demand	Better call distribution	Hardware-based system to route calls between call centers using traditional telephone circuit switching	More sophisticated routing software balances calls smoothly across centers, while improvements in VoIP (voice over Internet protocol) technology lower transmission costs
	Workforce scheduling	Staffing projections for individual call centers based on historical call volume and handling time	New scheduling systems accept more variables to improve projections and schedule multiple call centers, including outsourced ones; allows real-time adjustment of staffing projections

and refrozen scenarios. All the items in a grocery store can be tagged with RFID. The customer merely walks through a scanning area, and all the products to be purchased are read and totaled, eliminating the need for cashiers to handle merchandise and move it across bar code scanners. Another potential future application of RFID could be a restaurant menu tagged with nutritional information. A device could be programmed with a person's personal nutritional diet, and as the diner scans the menu, the relevant nutritional data for that meal would come up. From an operational perspective, retailers are pressuring their suppliers to ship only product pallets that are RFID enabled. This is becoming increasingly common.

Unfortunately, this technology has not yet been perfected. Some scanner-read interference issues remain. The foil wrapping on a cigarette box, for example, can hamper the scanner's ability to read.

Such issues are being addressed, however, so expect this technology to be a major CRM enabler in the near future.

6.5 CRM Providers

The information in this section provides the reader with examples of some CRM providers, organized by the technology they offer. We are not implying that these are necessarily the best organizations or solutions, and the order of their appearance is not in relation to their performance. An effort was simply made to list the "top-of-mind" solution providers. There are, however, plenty of other organizations capable of delivering superior CRM technology solutions. Depending on your organization's needs, you will need to thoroughly research the various solutions available at the time.

6.5a Database and Data Warehouse Providers

A database or data warehouse is the foundation of any CRM system environment. There are many different providers of database software and hardware. These providers vary in the markets that they serve, as well as in their ability to deliver both hardware and software and customized solutions. They tend to have well-documented information, including case studies, white papers, and solution descriptions available on their website. Much knowledge can be gained from reading their information and downloading white papers. Taking into account the recent trend in acquisitions and consolidation in this industry, some of the major providers in this category include IBM, Oracle, Teradata, Sybase (SAP), EMC/Greenplum, Microsoft, Ingres, Vertica, Aster Data, Kognitio, ParAccel, Infobright, and SAND Technology.

6.5b CRM Service Providers

Some of the leading organizations that provide CRM consulting and implementation services are IBM Global Business Services, Accenture, Deloitte, Capgemini, Cognizant, Infosys Technologies, Hitachi Consulting, Tata Consultancy Services, Wipro Technologies, CSC, Pricewaterhouse Coopers, HCK Technologies, and Patni Computer Systems. Other organizations supply these services, but the preceding organizations are currently the most active in the area of CRM services. This industry is very dynamic, so new entrants are common and their ability to execute varies over time.

6.5c Sales Force Automation

Sales force automation (SFA) is becoming an increasingly critical competitive advantage strategy when trying to enhance the CRM effort. SFA tools enable organizations to reduce costs and optimize flow of information internally as well as with partners (externally). This subject is covered in more detail in Chapter 8, but some SFA providers are Salesforce.com, Microsoft, Oracle, SAP, Sage, NetSuite, CDC (Pivotal CRM), and Zoho.

6.5d Social Media Technology

Much attention is being placed on social media and the opportunities it presents to CRM efforts as consumers gravitate to this communication medium. While in its infancy, two firms seem to be emerging as leaders in the area of social media applications: Jive and Lithium. Jive provides applications in the areas of collaboration, corporate communication, social marketing communities, sales enablement, customer support communities, social media monitoring, and open government (making it easier for people to work with government). Lithium provides solutions in brand advocacy, social commerce, and social support. There are 50 or more other organizations entering this technology space, all of which currently have a certain niche but are sure to grow in capability. More discussion on this new area is covered in Chapter 13.

6.5e Cloud-Based Technology

Cloud-based technology is an evolving technology that is under serious consideration by many organizations as they look to the future. CRM enablers are already providing CRM cloud solutions. For example, salesforce.com offers its "Sales Cloud" solution to its customers. Cloud technology allows for a virtual data repository so all sources of relevant information are captured, disseminated, and packaged for updates into a virtual environment that can be accessed from anywhere at any time with many different types of mobile devices. This greatly empowers that sales team because they can access the most current information when it is needed. Many other companies are incorporating cloud technology into their CRM tools. Companies such as IBM provide the core engines for CRM enablers to incorporate into their CRM solutions, such as with their IBM SmartCloud Entry solution, which is a starter kit for cloud. Chapter 14 discusses this new generation of data management in more detail.

Chapter Summary

Not every organization needs a complex and expensive data integration environment. Organizations should build CRM technical environments based on:

- The amount of data being captured
- The frequency of data capture
- The amount of data enhancement activity (i.e., size and frequency)
- The amount of information to be kept and made available
- The frequency of access by organization personnel and partnering organizations
- The number of organizational personnel accessing the information and response times
- Human and financial resources for the purpose of development, training, implementation, and maintenance and support of the environment
- Customer requirements for inquiry and transaction activity
- CRM strategic objectives

Creating an efficient and dynamic marketing and technology environment within respective financial constraints is very difficult in today's enterprise. Ownership of specific tasks and the overall strategic direction and function of a system can create challenges across business entities, including partner organizations. The organizations that can, over time, continuously balance the marketing and business needs with the appropriate financial and technology resources under the guise of executive or owner leadership have a good chance of creating a competitive CRM environment.

Key Terms

Batch processing is the noninteractive execution of predefined software steps that act on files and databases. Each step usually creates predefined outputs, some of which may be simple changes to the inputs.

Computer telephony (CT) is hardware and software technology that enables communication of voice and information via the phone.

Data mart is a database that is a subset of a larger database, usually a data warehouse or an operational data store. It is usually accessed by specific business applications for decision making.

Data warehouse is a database that contains all relevant customer and marketing information. It is usually static in nature and is a source of data from data marts.

Enterprise resource planning (ERP) is a business management system that integrates all facets of the business, including planning, manufacturing, sales, and marketing.

Kiosk is a booth providing a computer-related service, such as an automated teller machine (ATM).

Logical data model (LDM) is a logical view of a database or some file structure.

Operational data store (ODS) is a database designed to allow quick read/write access to and from multiple sources and types of technology dynamically. It contains a limited amount of information, which is usually required for a specific customer interaction such as a product purchase order. It is used as a source of data to update other databases such as data warehouses and data marts.

Radio frequency identification (RFID) is a technology that consists of an antenna and a transceiver that read the radio frequency and transfer the information to a processing device, and a transponder or tag that is an integrated circuit containing the RF circuitry and information to be transmitted.

Questions

1. Define the characteristics and technology used to sustain an organization's mass-communication activity in support of its CRM effort. Do the same for database marketing activity and integrated marketing activity. Refer to Table 6.1.
2. Using a real-life experience, define how an ODS can be utilized in support of the organization's CRM effort.
3. Give an example of the type of variables a catalog sales organization such as Lands' End or L. L. Bean would keep in a DW.
4. Provide two examples of how a data mart could support a CRM effort.
5. Why is an LDM critical to the creation of an ODS, a DW, or a data mart?

Exercises

1. Search a list rental source, select a list, and create a scenario for how the selected list could be used in a customer acquisition effort.
2. Provide an example, using a recent experience, of information flow between Collaborative, Operational, and Analytical functional areas. Refer to Figure 6.3.
3. Discuss your most recent experience interfacing with CT. Elaborate on what you think was happening in the organization with respect to an ODS and a DW. If applicable, discuss any dataprep that you think may have occurred.
4. A small hardware business owner with approximately 5,000 customers, both business tradespeople and consumers, wants to create an ODS, a DW, and several data marts. Is this feasible? What would you do?

Chapter 7

Database and Customer Data Development

7.1 Introduction

Organizations have become extremely proficient at generating data. This mass infusion of data has created unlimited opportunities for building relationships with customers. The Internet has accelerated this data generation and challenged organizations to determine how to leverage this data in an effort to sustain and grow relationships with their customers. Unfortunately, it has also created many opportunities to hinder relationship growth or destroy what may have been a good relationship.

> Have you ever heard of a person sending flowers to their florist? I really love my florist, honest I do. She has saved me several times. Here is what I mean. I receive an e-mail to my work e-mail address 10 days in advance of dates for occasions that I have purchased flowers for my wife in the past. This includes wedding anniversary, birthday, Valentine's Day, Mother's Day, and a few other one-time occurrences. I usually ignore the latter, as they are not recurring, such as when my wife received a community award. But when our anniversary is coming up, for example, I receive an e-mail telling me the date and what I purchased the last several times. The e-mail also provides me with three suggestions for this anniversary. It also takes into account those special anniversary dates—5 year, 10 year, and so on, each with its own theme. The e-mail has a hyperlink to the order page that contains all of my information, so all I need to do is enter or confirm my credit card number, change the day and time of delivery if not the same as the last, check one of the suggestions or select something different, and I am done. I love my florist!
>
> —A loving husband

This florist is an excellent example of converting data into information that was then used to maintain an excellent relationship with an existing customer.

> Every year I receive a solicitation from a university asking me if I am interested in pursuing a bachelor's degree. The letter is very well written. It contains my first name throughout the letter and explains that I can get credit for my life experiences, thereby reducing the time it will take to earn the degree. There is only one problem: I am a full-time professor at that same university, and I have been for years. The irony of this is that the letter includes my title and the name of the department I am in, in both the address and the opening salutation in the letter. I guess the shoemaker's children really do go barefoot.
>
> —A bewildered professor of marketing at a major U.S. university

This example demonstrates the importance of the customer selection process, which ensures that the target aligns with the appropriate value proposition. The university had valid data, but the information should have indicated that this professor was the wrong target and therefore should not have received this type of communication.

> As I browsed through the newly arrived issue of a national weekly news magazine to which I subscribe, I was surprised to see a full-page advertisement for a nearby private high school. I have two sons—one who attends this school and one who is in the seventh grade. They were amazed at the coincidence when I showed them the ad. *Was* this a coincidence?
>
> —An interested dad

The high school acquired the correct data and used the information to attempt to build, via a first step of awareness, a relationship with a potential customer. If the high school could determine that this family was a candidate for its services, however, it should also have noted that this customer already had a child in that school. However, an argument could be made that the school knew this and used the advertising to sustain the relationship. Alternately, it may not have known that the recipient was an existing, not a prospective, customer.

> I admit that I am a demanding customer, but I pay for attention. I make an appointment to shop every so often at a very exclusive retailer. When I arrive, they hand me a cup of my favorite tea, we conduct a few minutes of small talk to discuss my needs, and then I proceed to shop. My personal salesperson is not always the same person, but whatever salesperson assists me, she always knows my preferences. It is a pleasure to shop there.
>
> —A very satisfied customer

The exclusive retail shopper is a good example of retail "clienteling." Retailers have an excellent opportunity to build a relationship with a customer in a face-to-face setting. This effort can be enhanced if the retail person has relevant information about the customer at his or her disposal while working with the customer, assuming the customer does not perceive the vehicle for disseminating that information and the type of information used as invasive.

The widespread sending of credit card offers to individuals is an interesting phenomenon. If vast amounts of data are available, it should not be too difficult to discern that lack of consumer response after multiple attempts probably means that the targeted consumer is unlikely to respond in the future. Yet, organizations continue to mail solicitations to these same people. One explanation may be that it is cheaper to "blanket" the population continually with solicitations in the hopes of achieving a certain rate of response rather than spending money trying to understand each consumer's unique needs. Once the recipient of such an offer does become a customer, the company should suppress that person from future solicitations.

Hopefully, these examples have generated thought on the subject of data and data use. Let's take a more in-depth look at the differences between data and information and how organizations can leverage that information to support their CRM efforts.

7.2 Data Defined

Data is a series of numbers, characters, and/or pixels, and, logically assembled, they represent information. For example, a list of only people's names with no other information can be called a set of data.

7.2a Primary, Secondary, and Derived Data

Within the context of our discussion, data can fall into three major categories: primary, secondary, and derived. Primary data is acquired directly from the original source. For example, if a consumer walks into a retailer, fills out a form with her personal information, and returns it to the retailer, that retailer now has primary data on the consumer. If a telemarketing firm calls a consumer at home and asks for and receives personal information, that data is primary data to the telemarketing firm.

Secondary data is acquired from some party other than the party for which the data represents. If a telemarketing firm gives or sells consumer information to a retailer, the retailer would treat it as secondary data because it was not acquired directly from the original source.

Derived data is information created from other data. It can be inferred or implied. An inferred income based on an analysis of spending patterns, demographic characteristics, and other data elements that, when analyzed together, create a view of potential income for a person is an example of derived data. Derived data may or may not be reliable. A company that purchases inferred data should attempt to validate that data.

7.2b Individual and Household Data

In Chapter 5, we discussed the method of managing household and individual data. Individual data is data attributed to a specific person. A traditional family may have four individuals: a husband, a wife, and two children. Each individual may generate data in a variety of transactions with a variety of organizations. If these individuals are identified as one household via a data integration process, it is then possible to capture and maintain individual data while allowing a view of data from a household perspective. For example, if each of the parents spent approximately $250 with a cataloger, and one of the children, a teenager with her own credit card, spent $100 in the same time period, the total household expenditures for that period were $600. There are many possible permutations of the individual spending patterns, so an organization needs to assign transaction credit to the best of its ability. If the teenager used her mother's credit card number, name, and mailing address, the company may tabulate the mother's total expenditure as $350 and $0 for the daughter. Someone analyzing the data may not be aware that part of the mother's behavior actually reflected the daughter's behavior, which would result in a wrong assumption and an erroneous action taken. In some industries, such as financial services and credit card solicitations, most data is captured and analyzed at the individual level. A consumer's credit rating and subsequent maximum allowable charge amounts are based on the individual, not the household. Another consideration, and one reason why companies maintain data at both levels, is when an individual leaves home and forms a new household, such as a college graduate going out on his or her own or a child getting married. In both cases, the individual is now a new household. Decisions will be made based on the new household's needs. Individual data collected while the individual was part of the previous household may still be relevant and should be available. But in either household, this transition should be recognized and resultant transactions included or excluded for analysis based on the specific marketing effort.

7.3 Data Capture and Allocation

7.3a Touch Points

In Chapter 5, identifying touch points was one of the key steps of the customer data integration process. This process must be in direct correlation to a marketer's strategy. One of the challenges most marketers face when they enter a new environment is finding where the data relevant to their effort is located and whether it is currently being captured. If it is not currently being captured, then it must be determined whether it can be and, if so, what the timing and resource requirements are. If it is being captured, the quality of the data must be evaluated in light of the marketer's requirements. For example, saying that a file contains a customer phone number field is one thing, but what percentage of the files have that field populated, and what percentage of the phone numbers are accurate and consistent?

A marketer who wishes to determine the quality of existing data may create a grid that includes decision trees as well as timing information. Timing information would include the availability of the data and where the data goes. For example, if a person returns a product and during the return indicates extreme dissatisfaction with the retailer, he or she would not want to be solicited for a promotion for some time after the return. That information should be entered into the database for organization members or value chain members' use to prevent immediate solicitation. The organization may use the information as part of a follow-up customer service call to acknowledge dissatisfaction and mend the relationship. In this case, timing is critical; the customer service call should be made within 24 hours of the customer interaction. The following examples illustrate how manufacturers have approached the management of touch point interaction between the manufacturer's value chain partner and the customer.

An advertising company ran a national, 60-day promotion in a variety of restaurants, bars, and wine emporiums. The promotion included contests and prizes. The advertiser and manufacturer were interested in tracking the promotion continually for the purpose of adjusting the promotion when applicable. If a participating retailer did not have Internet access, the advertising company provided it for the length of the promotion. Custom Web pages were developed as part of an extranet, and the retailers were instructed on how to enter the desired information into the Web pages. Consequently, both the advertiser and the manufacturer were able to track, in real time, all activity from each retailer for the length of the promotion, thus providing specific management of the data as it was obtained.

Manufacturers partnered with retail grocers to create a real-time interaction with the customer as he or she shopped in the grocery store. An interactive flat panel device attached to the grocery cart recognized the individual when he/she scanned the grocer's loyalty card. Sensors located throughout the store sensed the presence of the cart and displayed promotions as the customer pushed the cart through the store. Manufacturers bought time on the display similar to advertising. The sensors also captured the customer movement throughout the store visit, which gave the store manager shopping pattern information. Manufacturers were still limited in their interaction, but this was the closet they were able to come to interacting with a customer at a retailer's site.

7.3b Real Time versus Batch

Timing of information capture and use decisions are critical to any CRM initiative. Marketers need data to be captured and disseminated at different times for different situations. In some cases, data captured at a touch point may need to be processed and action taken as soon as possible. A customer order given over the phone or via the Web should be processed as soon as possible from an operational perspective. However, the marketer may not need to know that information until a trend or pattern has emerged. The order expedition process may happen in or as close to real time as possible. The record of that transaction, however, may be saved and input to a batch process at the end of the week. The results of the weekly batch process may create input to a data mart or appear on a report. In general, activity required to support the customer should be as close to real time as possible, although organizational timing needs for data captured at a touch point will vary.

If possible, it is a good idea to be consistent with the customer with regard to different touch points. For example, when a person fills out a magazine insert for a subscription, it usually takes four to six weeks for delivery. The time to fulfill a phone order or process a Web transaction will usually be substantially less than the mail-in card. In either case, the organization should not send an e-mail solicitation until it feels comfortable with the subscription being activated and the customer is satisfied. The timing of this subsequent contact will vary greatly depending on the method used for the subscription.

7.3c Side Note: How Much Data?

Organizations approach data collection in one of two ways. The first is to collect as much data as possible. The organization may not be certain what data they should collect, so by collecting everything possible at the beginning, they ensure that nothing is missed. Relevancy can be determined later. The process of determining relevancy comes with a cost, as the human and computer resources that determine which data to keep and which to discard are probably not optimal. In the alternative approach, organizations are extremely discriminatory in data collection. They then add new data as relevancy is determined. One approach is not necessarily better or worse than the other. Which method an organization uses depends on its knowledge of data and resource availability.

7.4 Data Transformation

Data is critical to operational processes. In its raw form, however, it is not very useful to marketers. Transforming data into information is one of two steps that must be executed before the marketer can leverage the data. Once the data is transformed into information, it can then be analyzed, or "mined," to determine if there is inherent value. The information may then be used to support a CRM effort. This is transforming data into information and knowledge, which can lead to action.

$$\text{Data} \;\rightarrow\; \text{Information} \;\rightarrow\; \text{Knowledge}$$

7.4a Converting Data into Information

The marketer must be heavily involved in determining which data should be transformed and how. Here is an example of transaction data (Table 7.1) converted into information:

> Customer information: John Smith, 147 Highland Avenue, Downers Grove, IL 60515
> Customer #: 0234434
> Total purchase dollars for week of July 16, 2012: $106.47
> Number of products purchased: 5
> Promotions utilized: (A23, B49)
> Responder to mail promotion A23: Yes
> Responder to mail promotion A24: No
> Responder to mail promotion B49: Yes

Table 7.1 Point-of-Sale Transaction Data

Customer #	Purchase Date	Product SKU	Quantity Purchased	Price Paid (each)	Promotion Code
0234434	071612	2333	1	19.98	A23
0234434	071612	1844	1	29.97	
0234434	071812	8279	2	23.88	B49
0234434	071812	6554	1	8.76	

Table 7.1 lists point-of-sale (POS) transactions generated by John Smith. In this example, he used a customer loyalty card for each transaction. The transactions were stored in an operational data store (ODS). (Refer to Chapter 6 for a discussion of operational data stores, data warehouses, and data marts.) At the end of the week, the transactions in the ODS were input to a predefined process, which updated a data warehouse (DW) (Table 7.2). In this process, the customer number linked the transaction data to the customer, John Smith, in the DW. The transaction data for customers is kept at the same detail level that was generated in the POS system. In addition, some fields in the DW that were not in the transactions—for example, "Total YTD $ Pur."—were updated by adding the purchase dollars in the transaction records to a total field. (The actual format of this data will be different in a DW, but it is presented in this way for illustration purposes.) The current information on John Smith in this organization's DW is shown in Table 7.2.

Table 7.2 Data Warehouse Transaction Update

ODS (POS Transactions) Update	Data Warehouse
	Before Update
0234434 071612 2333 1 1998 A23	0234434
0234434 071612 1844 1 2997	John Smith
0234434 071812 8279 2 2388 B49	147 Highland Avenue
0234434 071812 6554 1 876	Downers Grove, IL 60515
	Phone: 630.555.8000
	Age = 37
	Own Home = Yes
	Gender = Male
	Income = $60,000
	Promo Codes = A11
	Last Pur. Date = 042812
	Total YTD $ Pur. = $324.50
	Current Year Trans. (descending)
	042812
	041012
	. . .
	. . .

(Continued)

Table 7.2 *(Continued)*

ODS (POS Transactions) Update	Data Warehouse
	After Update
0234434 071612 2333 1 1998 A23	0234434
0234434 071612 1844 1 2997	John Smith
0234434 071812 8279 2 2388 B49	147 Highland Avenue
0234434 071812 6544 1 876	Downers Grove, IL 60515
	Phone: 630.555.8000
	Age = 37
	Own Home = Yes
	Gender = Male
	Income = $60,000
	Promo Codes = A11, A23, B49
	Last Pur. Date = 071812
	Total YTD $ Pur. = $430.97
	Current Year Trans. (descending)
	071812
	071812
	071612
	071612
	042812
	041012
	. . .
	. . .

In reality, many DWs contain extensive information on customers—in some instances, well over 100 unique elements. Some of the demographic data was probably provided by John Smith (primary data) as part of the loyalty card sign-up process. Other information such as gender, age, or income may have been volunteered by Smith, but it was probably acquired from a secondary source. The organization has an opportunity to collect more information about John or receive updated primary data from John himself at any touch point or from secondary sources. Whatever the source, the information would normally be obtained within some type of transaction. The system that creates that transaction should create it for input into the DW update process. The DW can hold as much relevant information about the customer as is available. The DW also contains all relevant noncustomer marketing information, such as promotion descriptions, product or service detail, pricing information, advertising information, and other information related to CRM efforts. This information will be relevant later in the data mining process.

7.4b Information Aging

Information aging—what information to keep, in what form (aggregate, summary, or detail), and for how long—will vary by industry. To a lesser extent, the organization's position in that industry, resources (human, computer, and financial), and macro-environmental forces also have an effect on information-aging strategy. A discussion of industry characteristics, which follows, can better illustrate information-aging issues. Some of the recommendations for specific industry characteristics are open ended for potential CRM efforts and will be elaborated upon later.

Either by the nature of their business or by their specific product or service, firms may need to maintain detailed transaction histories over time. Government or industry regulations or potential liability constraints may require a firm to keep detailed customer transaction information for extended periods of time—in some cases, since the initial transaction. Financial services, insurance firms, and manufacturers of infrequently purchased durable goods may fall into this category.

No matter the industry, detailed transaction histories that are more than several years old may be irrelevant. Usually, organizations will start to aggregate the transaction data as it ages. Each industry has its own unique characteristics. Financial services organizations may keep detailed transactions for decades due to regulations and financial best practices. For marketing purposes, 8-year-old transaction details may not mean anything. However, total transaction amounts by year for the last 8 years may show a trend. Conversely, a company selling durable goods with a life cycle of 10 years would need transaction information for the last 30 years to look at three purchase scenarios for a customer. Determining what information to keep or discard, what information is missing, and what information needs to be aggregated is vital when analyzing the information.

The CRM effort would usually not require details on credit card usage older than two years. Anything older is usually aggregated, as totals are relevant for lifetime value (LTV) trends and patterns. Any firm that sells a product or service that carries with it a liability, such as insurance or products under warranty, usually keeps detailed transaction records until the liability expires. From a CRM perspective, high-level information (what was purchased, how much the customer spent, and the cost of servicing that customer) and customer behavior information may be relevant and kept for a longer period of time. Transaction details for high-priced, infrequently purchased goods such as PCs, high-definition televisions, and stereos are usually needed for warranty purposes. Transaction details on the last purchase should be maintained to support potential CRM efforts. A person may not buy a furnace or air conditioning unit for ten years. This information, albeit ten years old, is the last set of purchase information for that category and may be of value to the dealer or installer and the manufacturer. For high-tech and consumer electronics, detailed transaction history may need to be kept for at least one purchase cycle. For example, a consumer who purchases a PC may not purchase another PC for another three to four years, but the transaction history should be kept regardless.

7.5 Data Mining

Information alone may be interesting, but it is not actionable. One must decipher what the information is saying: the process of turning information into knowledge. Data mining is the most common method for performing this activity.

7.5a Data Mining Methodologies

Data mining is a sometimes overused phrase, so it is important to understand the context within which it is used. Browsing through transactional data records may be appropriate to find a specific piece of information for some operational purpose, but it is not conducive to identifying a relationship with other data elements or for pattern recognition. When data has been transformed into information, data mining is effective. Several methodologies are sometimes included in

Table 7.3 **Data Mining Methodologies and Their Characteristics**

Decision Support Systems

- List current inventory, predict sales of products to be promoted, and list inventory requirements by store.
- Determine who were responders and nonresponders for the last promotion.
- Print a report from customer service that lists the customers who returned merchandise in the last week and send these individuals a satisfaction survey.
- Identify nonresponders from the last promotion and send them a second promotional offer using a different advertising copy.
- Each week, update the legal department's data mart with customers who purchased an LP gas connector for their gas range to facilitate a product recall in the event of a problem and to maintain risk assessment information.

Executive Information Systems

- Provide a report by 7:30 a.m. every day showing department sales by retail store in all regions.
- Provide ROI results for all sales promotions for the last 60 days.
- Create a spreadsheet populated with sales by product category from the Web, catalog, and retail outlet; allow for simple data manipulation for the purpose of creating trend reports.
- Identify market share gains and losses by market area and provide supporting detail and respective action plans.
- Provide alerts when supplier service level slippage is probable.

Enterprise Resource Planning

- Process all online orders within 12 hours; alert quality and control when time limit is exceeded.
- Automatically notify supplier to restock when inventory depletes to a certain level.
- Update customer service ODS with current customer order status information.
- Provide alerts when supplier service level slippage is probable.
- Update accounting and finance systems with all relevant operational data dynamically to facilitate cash-flow analysis.

Data Mining

- Identify the most profitable customers by household level for the last 24 months and create a recognition strategy at different incremental levels based on profitability level.
- Determine which customers have purchased for their own consumer needs versus their company's needs; create a profitability index for each.
- Identify lost customers, analyze their behavior for the last several years, and create a profile; overlay this profile on existing customers in an effort to increase retention.
- Examine customer purchase history and build a channel preference profile for each customer that includes time variations, such as in the case of "snowbirds."
- Identify B2B customers; determine who are influencers, gatekeepers, and decision makers, and create a coordinated contact strategy for each.
- Identify customers who are transaction buyers and ensure their suppression from future marketing efforts.

discussions of data mining. Decision support systems (DSSs), executive information systems (EISs), and enterprise resource planning (ERP) systems can support CRM efforts and are extremely valuable. Technically, though, they are not data mining. Table 7.3 outlines the key characteristics of both these systems and data mining as they might be applied in the case of an appliance manufacturer. This serves to illustrate the similarities and differences between the methods and how they might be used. Decision support systems, executive information systems, and ERP are not formally defined as data mining tools, but they do allow organizations to perform what may be called "quasi data mining" because they can provide insight into information.

7.5b Types of Data Mining Systems

7.5b.1 Decision Support Systems in Data Mining

DSSs are frequently used to support a tactical operation. They are software systems designed for a specific purpose, for any of a variety of business disciplines. The systems are easy to use, with graphical user interfaces, and their functions can be partially or fully automated. They may allow for ad hoc inquiry in addition to functional operations. An example would be a campaign management tool used to manage marketing campaigns by assigning promotion and campaign codes to groups of customers or prospects. These tools maintain a history of campaigns and allow the marketer to manage, report on, and analyze the campaigns. They normally include ROI capabilities and usually access data marts for their information.

7.5b.2 Executive Information Systems in Data Mining

EISs are designed to provide information for higher-level decision making, usually through the use of "dashboards." Within a marketing context, a **dashboard** is analogous to an automobile dashboard and represents the different gauges that provide the information necessary to operate the vehicle properly, and nothing more. This information is usually aggregated but can be detailed at any time if requested. These systems provide an extremely easy-to-use interface and allow for some data manipulation.

7.5b.3 Enterprise Resource Planning Systems in Data Mining

ERP systems integrate most, if not all, businesses functions. Order processing, manufacturing, distribution, human resources, accounting, finance, and value chain members are some of the functions and areas integrated. Integration benefits are minimal transaction generation and flow, less redundancy, improved data integrity, and efficient organization-wide flow of information. These systems are now incorporating relevant marketing information as well. The challenge of implementing ERP systems is tremendous, but the returns justify the effort. A major issue for organizations that implement these systems is that they need to adapt their business process to the ERP system's design.

7.5b.4 Data Mining

The data mining process can be envisioned as the catalyst for turning information into knowledge. In Chapter 6, data was depicted as residing in several entities. The ODS was the repository for data captured as part of an operational process. Usually on a scheduled basis, the data in the ODS was processed by software for the purpose of updating a DW. The update process placed the data into a more usable format and usually transformed some of the data into information. A person's detailed transaction may be present in the DW, but a field containing transaction purchase dollars-to-date may also have been updated during the process. That field is informational, as it presents the person viewing it with information. By itself, that information may or not be useful. But if the purchase-to-date field indicates a loyal customer, that is now knowledge.

The DW contains information from other sources as well. Company-sourced information such as product or service information, marketing communication information (past, current, and planned), survey information, and pricing may be present in the DW. External information on value chain members may be relevant, such as a subcontractor who provides feedback on the customer after a completed job. Secondary information on customers is also usually present in the DW, including demographic and psychographic information. It may also contain relevant **exogenous** (i.e., outside the core business process and that organizations have little control over) information (economic, political, legal, natural resources, and environmental) or an occurrence that may have an effect on the customer, prospect, or business being analyzed. Each company defines "prospect" differently, but it is usually a person, a household, or a company that is not currently a customer. Former customers may be considered prospects based on the time elapsed since their last interaction. This varies but, in general, information in the DW on a customer who has not had interaction for a substantial amount of time is rendered stale and not conducive to use for marketing decisions. An approach taken with a former customer (i.e., a win-back strategy), however, may be more of a "reacquainting" versus an introductory approach taken with someone who has had no prior interaction with the company. Identifying patterns, variable relationships, and trends is the initial step in data mining.

7.5c Location and Access Considerations

Where to access information for data mining depends on the objective of the data mining effort. Data may reside in the operational data store (ODS), the data warehouse (DW), or the data mart (DM). These were discussed at length in Chapter 6, but following is a review with specific details on how data mining is accomplished within them.

7.5c.1 Operational Data Store

This is a dynamic data repository. It usually is designed and operates in a way that supports specific business functions, most of which are dynamic. Telemarketers, the Web, and POS systems are usually adding, updating, changing, and deleting data in an ODS in or close to real time. Tactical and decision report applications may access this information regardless of its dynamics, as their objective is usually execution of predefined rules on some parameters meeting a certain level. Ad hoc inquiry of information in an ODS is usually performed to get a picture of some phenomena.

7.5c.2 Data Warehouse

The DW is more static than an ODS. While it changes with updates from an ODS (i.e., additions, changes, and deletions), it is not as dynamic as an ODS. If the timing of updates is known, a data mining exercise may be successful if performed between updates or if it is accessing the part of a DW that will not change with an update. The DW contains data and information as part of its update process. It usually contains all relevant data and information. It may, however, contain substantially more information than is required for data mining. It may restrict the mining effort to certain times and access methods. For example, a person may need to learn a query language in order to perform a data mining exercise. Or the software used to perform the data mining may not be optimal and may possibly lengthen the effort and hamper other resources' DW access efforts. If the data mining exercise requires many iterations of queries based on the last set of information, it could take several hours, which may not be optimal.

7.5c.3 Data Mart

While there may be times when access to all information is required, many times a subset of the DW is sufficient for data mining efforts. The subset is referred to as a data mart (DM). Most data mining efforts use a DM as their source for data and information. The DM's dynamic status is usually controlled by the data miner. It allows for efficiency because it only contains relative data, in amounts almost assuredly less than in the DW. The DM is usually designed to optimize the analysis software. For example, a person may use SAS (statistical analysis system) software, which is a grouping of software modules integrated throughout the organization, to produce optimal business information flow and reduced information redundancy, access the DW but use PC SAS (a version of SAS that enables the marketer to use the software on the PC without executing the software on a large server and accessing large amounts of data in a DW), or access a data mart, which is basically a subset of the DW that was placed on a PC or on a server that the PC accesses.

7.5d Data Mining Techniques

Many different techniques are used to "mine" information. The number of companies providing the tools to perform mining, as well as the companies that provide mining services, is growing. Additionally, their product or service offerings are constantly being improved, with noneffective approaches eliminated. Some of the more prominent data mining providers include IBM (SPSS, Unica), SAS, Teradata (Aprimo), Oracle (Seibel), Neolane, and Responsys. At times, traditional statistical techniques fall under the umbrella of data mining discussions, as they can also provide insight into information. Three primary techniques used in data mining—the recency, frequency, and monetary value (RFM) approach; decision trees; and cluster analysis—are discussed in greater detail following.

7.5d.1 Recency, Frequency, and Monetary

RFM is a relatively easy and inexpensive technique that facilitates a better understanding of customer behavior and creates segment strategies based on the customer's likely future actions. RFM is not a "true" data mining approach. It uses historical information from three data categories, and the user makes an assumption that past behavior is a good predictor of future behavior. It only includes revenue and excludes costs to serve the customer, including cost of goods sold. It is a first step in placing customers into categories, and since it is inexpensive and easy to execute (an Excel spreadsheet can be used), it is a prudent first step to understanding customer data. It may be used as a first step to identify best customer segments for specific marketing strategies. The outputs of this process can then be input to more sophisticated techniques. As the name suggests, it relies on three variables: recency, frequency, and monetary value. Recency is the date of the most recent customer transaction. Frequency is the number of customer transactions with the organization within a specific period of time. Monetary value is the amount spent within the same specific time period.

We will use the florist example at the beginning of this chapter to demonstrate the RFM technique. The florist has approximately 5,000 customers in a customer database (Figure 7.1). Each

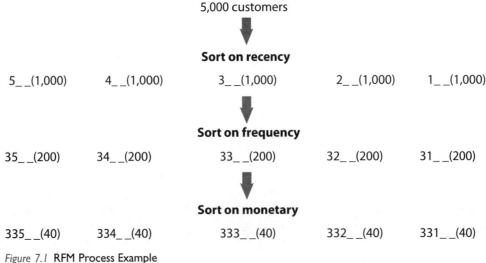

Figure 7.1 **RFM Process Example**

has a unique numeric customer number that links back to the customer's identification and detailed product purchase information. The time period measured will be the past 12 months.

RFM is basically a sorting procedure. The file will first be sorted on recency, and the results will place all of the 5,000 customers in an ascending order sequence, with the most recent date being the first record. That sorted output will be segmented into quintiles. Each quintile will be assigned a three-digit identifier. The top 20 percent of customers based on recent purchases will be assigned a "5" as the first three-digit identifier. The second quintile will be assigned a "4," and so on, with the quintile representing the oldest set of customers based upon recent purchase assigned a "1." Each quintile will contain 1,000 customers. The middle quintile from the recency sort will have a cell identification of "3_ _," with the last two digits not yet assigned.

Sorting these quintile cells on frequency and dividing the result into quintiles again will yield five groups, or cells, of 200 customers each for each of the recency quintiles. In ascending order of frequency, these cells will have their second digit assigned. The same procedure applies to all the cells, but for illustration of this and the next sort (monetary), we will use only the middle cell. The middle quintile from the frequency sort will contain 200 customers and will have a cell identification of "33_," with the last digit not yet assigned.

Sorting this cell on monetary and dividing the result into quintiles again will yield five groups, or cells, of 40 customers each. In ascending order of monetary, these cells will have their final digit assigned. Running this process for all cells will generate a total of 500 cells. The cell containing the 40 most recent purchasers who purchased the most frequently and spent the most money within the last 12 months will be identified in cell #555. These are the most loyal customers. The least loyal customers will appear in cell #111. They are the 40 customers whose purchase dates are the oldest, who have the most infrequent amount of purchases, and who have spent the least amount of money. Every other customer falls somewhere in between. A snapshot of the results may look like Table 7.4.

From this RFM sorting, the florist will create a file that contains the customer number, the date of the most recent customer purchase, and the number and total dollar amount of purchases over the last 12 months (Table 7.5).

The florist can easily see which cells are worth marketing. The file can also help define what type of marketing and how much money should be spent on customers in each cell. The customers in cells 112 and 111 do not appear to be responsive. The organization should probably not incur any expense to market to these individuals.

7.5d.2 Decision Trees

Decision trees are structured like a tree, where the leaves represent classifications and the branches represent conjunctions of features that lead to those classifications. A decision tree can be

Table 7.4 **Snapshot of RFM Sort**

Cell	Sales Dollars
555	$400
554	380
554	325
554	250
113	50
112	12
111	8

Table 7.5 **RFM Results Example**

Customer #	Cell #	Recency (12 mo.)	Frequency (12 mo.)	Monetary Value (12 mo.)
0001	555	12360	5	$340
0002	555	12350	5	330
0003	555	12340	5	330
0004	554	12300	4	300
0005	500	12280	4	250
0006	455	12230	4	200
0007	333	12160	3	150
0008	253	12075	2	40
0009	112	12020	2	12
0010	111	12010	1	8

created by splitting the source set into subsets based on an attribute value test. This process is repeated on each derived subset in a recursive manner. The recursion is completed when splitting is either not feasible or a singular classification can be applied to each element of the derived subset. A random forest classifier uses a number of decision trees to improve the classification rate. **Classification and regression trees (CART)** and **Chi-squared automatic interaction detectors (CHAIDs)** are commonly used decision tree methods to classify a data set. You would apply the results of these methods to an unclassified set of information to predict outcomes. CART usually requires less data than CHAID. A good introduction to these methodologies can be found at the SAS website (www.sas.com). SAS is a leading industry provider of data mining tools.

7.5d.3 Cluster Analysis

Cluster analysis in the context of data mining is the process of placing customers or prospects into groups such that everyone in a group has similar traits. The traits can be represented by variables. There are several categories of variables related to clustering relative to the context of data mining. The following are the categories and examples of the variables in each:

- *Demographics:* Age, gender, sexual orientation, family size, household size, family life cycle, income, occupation, education, home ownership, socioeconomic status, religion, nationality
- *Psychographics:* Personality, lifestyle, values, attitudes
- *Behavior:* Benefit sought, buy status, product usage rate, purchase frequency
- *Geographic:* Country, state, county, city, ZIP code, climate

In many instances, an organization will solicit the assistance of a company specializing in clustering, such as Claritas. The organization would make its data available to Claritas, which would then apply its techniques to help the organization answer questions such as:

- *Who* are my customers?
- *What* are they like?
- *What* do they buy?
- *Where* can I find them?

- *How* can I reach them?
- *How* can I keep them?

Other companies active in this area include Equifax, TransUnion, Esri, Acxiom, and Experian.

Clustering may not always be the ultimate solution. Just because two individuals live on the same block and share similar demographic profiles does not mean they are similar in a behavior variable such as risk taking. However, the cluster effort could create a base of people that may meet basic requirements, with risk level to be determined.

7.5d.4 Other Data Mining Techniques

There are a variety of data mining approaches, and there is a fine line between data mining and statistics. The former is actually a derivative of the latter, and semantics can make understanding the difference, if there is a need to differentiate, confusing. Refer to Appendix A at the end of the chapter.

7.5e Data Mining Benefits and Challenges

As it becomes easier to duplicate products and services, it becomes harder for organizations to differentiate themselves to the consumer. Data mining can enable organizations to leverage their limited resources to strengthen relationships with customers and prospects in their efforts to sustain long-term predictive profitable growth. By adding the modeling component, organizations can turn data mining results into an optimal, cost-justified, measurable action in fulfillment of customer acquisition, retention, customer-centric selling, inquiry routing, online shopping, staffing scheduling, prospect identification (e.g., Web mining), and growth strategies. Ancillary benefits include fraud detection, consumer fatigue prevention, and identification of new market opportunities. Consumer fatigue is especially prominent when multiple areas in the same organization communicate to the customer, each unaware of the other's activity. A specific area may have good control over its communication efforts, but it cannot control other areas' efforts. Thus, the consumer may receive too much communication, resulting in "consumer fatigue."

Even though data mining has many benefits, there are challenges as well. Following are some of the issues in data mining:

- Organizational obstacles to attaining data for transformation
- Political and societal pressure regarding privacy
- Sustained secondary data availability
- Cost versus benefit, which also requires ability to measure
- Impact on performance of one or more source applications
- Ability to perform all of the data transformations into knowledge in real time
- Knowledge and experience of implementation personnel
- Interpretation of information and turning knowledge into action
- Inability to capture customer transactions
- Organization expertise and retention of expertise
- Getting "too smart" with the information and offending or giving the consumer the perception of invasiveness

7.6 Enabling CRM

The following industry examples help illustrate how data capture, transformation, and mining help enable CRM.

7.6a Manufacturer Tools Products

A data mining effort by a tools manufacturer advanced some valuable information. The manufacturer was analyzing purchase information of its products through a major home improvement retail chain. It was able to differentiate between tradespeople purchases and consumer purchases. It also linked tradespeople's transactions with their personal (consumer) purchases. Frequency and amount of purchase, products purchased, and days and times of purchases enabled the manufacturer to define promotional strategies to these customers. The manufacturer shared its results and worked with the retailer to implement a coordinated promotion campaign to these tradespeople. The effort increased sales over prior periods as a result of cross-sell and up-sell efforts.

7.6b Entertainment and Hotel

A major gaming corporation owned a hotel and a casino that were within close proximity of each other. Although they were part of the same corporation and had different ambiances, they were competing for customers. The corporation understood the importance of data capture and mining, but the general managers of each property were hesitant to share data, fearing cannibalization of their customer base. The corporation included all information from both properties in a common DW and identified the customer's preferred property, which determined the property "ownership" of that particular customer. Each property had total marketing control over the customers it "owned." They could also access the other property's customer information, excluding identification information for the purpose of analysis. If they wanted to market to a specific individual "owned" by the other property, they would ask permission. This enhanced the analysis, as a marketer wishing to better understand, for example, slot players who liked to golf had a larger pool of consumers to include in its data analysis effort. It minimized cannibalization and optimized customer communication by avoiding "customer fatigue." Within the corporation, data mining was critical to several major strategies. The casino business is one of the best examples of dynamic CRM. Its success is directly tied to DSS and data mining. A few examples follow:

- Collecting and using a customer's demographic and lifestyle information provide input into the type of compensation given to a person during a losing streak. Seats to a show with a couple's favorite performer, reservations at their favorite restaurant, a bottle of their favorite wine, and a new set of clothes for each waiting in their room when they return from the casino floor are not uncommon for high rollers. Data mining can accurately define an individual's tolerance range. Once a person loses too much money, he or she may not return to that property. Data mining sets up the tolerance levels, and a real-time DSS can perform the execution.
- Applying a profile of loyal customers who bet frequently to hotel guests who do not gamble in the casino enhances that property's effort in turning hotel patrons into gamblers. The more often a person stays in the hotel, the more chances the organization has to market to them and sustain the relationship. It also keeps them away from the competitor. Additionally, identifying good gambling customers who do not stay in the hotel can create an opportunity to solicit them to stay.
- Tracking the profitability of customers, not just revenue, by travel agency allows an organization to determine which agencies send the most valuable customers. This is interesting because sometimes the agencies that send more customers to a property actually contribute less to the profit line. The agency that sends fewer but more profitable customers should receive better rewards. In fact, sending more people can create an opportunity cost by filling up the property with less profitable customers.

7.6c Financial Services

Organizations in financial services are usually data mining leaders. The nature of their business has generated countless transactions, and their need to process transactions in fulfillment of their service has produced data management competencies that far exceed other industries. A good example is a retention strategy. By analyzing past behavior of lost customers, these organizations build a predictive model on lost customers and overlay that model on existing customers. This enables them to identify those current customers most likely to discontinue use of the organization's services. Once identified, the organization can develop marketing efforts to minimize attrition. These results are also used as input to their acquisition strategies and help with their customer selection effort. One cautionary note with regard to mixing financial and marketing information: Controls have been established in the United States via the Gramm-Leach-Bliley (GLB) Act, enacted July 1, 2001. (Chapter 11 discusses issues related to regulation and privacy.)

THEORY IN ACTION

Capital One

Capital One, a financial services company, pioneered fact-based decision making, based on analysis of large data sets, in its lending operations. In the past, credit cards were issued to only those customers who had a sound history of repayment, and loans were extended to borrowers who could secure their loans with collateral. Capital One changed the rules of the game by using data to determine creditworthiness. Its strategy was based on the premise that customers who had no credit history could have the potential to be good borrowers. A typical example is a recent college graduate with limited means and a large student debt who could eventually succeed in business. Capital One has created a huge DW with information relevant for subprime lending. It uses this information to conduct experiments to find financially sound offers for its various segments.

7.6d Toy Manufacturers

Any organization with diversified businesses has an opportunity to gather information from a brand or product category perspective. This information can prove valuable to other entities in the organization. Take, for example, a toy manufacturer with several major businesses. The first is making and selling toys for toddlers. The second makes and sells dolls, toy cars, and models. The third sells educational and computer games for young adults. If data is captured on sales of toddler products and profiles are enhanced with demographic data, it is not difficult to predict when the children in a household have outgrown toddler products and entered the market for dolls, toy cars, and models. Mining the data provides the organization with periodic updates to segments. This may be a combination of age change and reduction in sales for the respective product category. As the child nears the end of the life cycle for a set of products, the manufacturer can begin to introduce that child or household to products in the next category. This same process would continue when the child moves from dolls to computer games. Even when the child has outgrown the last product category, maintaining a relationship with some young adult interests may be feasible, as that person will eventually have his or her own household and potentially begin the cycle again.

7.6e Infant Formula Manufacturer

Once an infant formula and infant product manufacturer learns a woman is pregnant, it begins an information-sharing relationship with the expectant mother. The woman would normally fall into one of two segments: one who has given birth before and one who has not. The needs of both are different. In the latter case, there are sometimes more questions than answers. For the duration of the pregnancy, the manufacturer will conduct a dialogue with this person. Both parties will share information. In the end, if the manufacturer has been successful, the woman will ask her pediatrician for the manufacturer's products, if possible. The Web has advanced this effort tremendously from the days of direct mail. Information gathered on a woman will help the manufacturer with the next dialogue as it continues to update its information on the Web and in a database for response to questions.

Another opportunity that arises from the data accumulation process is recognizing when a person in the household purchases a product for someone outside the household. When this occurs, the manufacturer has gained information on a potential new customer. Adding secondary data helps build a profile on this new household, and a relationship-building effort can commence. Another opportunity is relatives of the household. This information can be gathered from a variety of sources, including the household itself.

7.6f Apparel Cataloger

Monitoring the number and types of purchases customers make can help a cataloger understand the optimal mix of catalogs to send to the customer. This reduces the cost of printing and mailing catalogs that are irrelevant to a customer. It also controls the amount of communication to the customer. Identifying a person as a tradesperson, for example, allows the cataloger to identify who should receive catalogs that specialize in work clothes and accessories. Identifying the household demographics may influence the age of the model mix in a catalog for that household. While a 60-year-old woman may appreciate the way a dress looks on a 25-year-old model, it is not realistic. A person closer to that age bracket modeling the clothes may make more sense. However, this is tricky because the person may want to appear youthful and resent a catalog containing older models.

7.6g Hotel and Travel

Two major customer segments—business travelers and consumer travelers—by nature of their stay at a hotel, provide substantial information. Name, address, phone number, e-mail address, credit card, purpose of travel, meal preferences, and entertainment preferences are a few data variables that can easily be captured. Knowing an individual's preferences enables the hotel to meet or exceed that person's expectations each time he or she visits by fulfilling or being prepared to fulfill his/her needs upon arrival. Length and number of stays coupled with expenditures on the property allow for an easy LTV calculation, which can be used to provide guidelines on how much to spend and what to spend it on.

7.6h Retail Grocery

Grocery stores receive an extremely large amount of transaction data each time a person shops. By providing price discounts via a customer preferred card, the retail grocer can easily identify shopping habits, days and hours of the visits, and total number of visits. An **algorithm** is a set of rules used to solve a problem or define an opportunity through a finite number of steps. Building algorithms to generate cost-saving coupons or "manager specials" raises the customer's switching costs and sustains customer relationships. This information can be analyzed to continually improve the algorithms than can be executed at POS when the customer is identified.

7.6i Small Businesses

Any small business can perform data mining. It does not need to be sophisticated; it may be as simple as remembering what a person purchased and when she purchased it, and then offering her a product or service based on her previous needs.

THEORY IN ACTION

Walmart[1]

Retail stores struggle to balance their inventory with consumer demand, and their suppliers are often unable to dispatch the right amounts of goods to warehouses. Walmart set up a massive DW in the 1990s to store information about sales and inventories. Its Retail Link program shares information with its suppliers such as Procter & Gamble, which has expertise in predicting consumer demand. The availability of real-time information enables suppliers to stock goods without waiting for orders to be placed. Based on past experiences, Walmart can predict, for example, that the demand for Strawberry Pop-Tarts will rise. A streamlined supply chain has enabled Walmart and Procter & Gamble to refocus their energies on category management and to use information for merchandising.

7.6j Fraud Detection and Other Nonfavorable Behaviors

An ancillary benefit to data collection and mining is the precipitation of unusual consumer activity, including fraud. Consumer activity patterns start to emerge. Consider the following examples:

- A person leveraged every opportunity presented by an infant formula company to use coupons, rebates, and free product offerings—the last one a result of complaints and misrepresentation of usage problems. She became an expert at creating multiple fake children's identities to support her effort; data mining revealed that she had 40 children who never aged. She had a good understanding of data integration and how to "use" the system against the organization. A data mining effort looking for unusual patterns at a general level identified this person.
- A group of customers was placed in a high-value customer segment based on their purchase activity. However, once a retailer included return merchandise transactions in the data mining effort, a percentage of perceived high-value customers were moved into a suppression segment. While the retailer could not prevent these people from purchasing and returning merchandise, it could minimize its costs by not marketing to them, thus saving money on the marketing effort and possibly reducing the knowledge base of these customers by not directly telling them about sales, product specials, and so on.
- A casino firm identified two players who several times a year betted the opposite on roulette, which resulted in one winner and one loser. The friends combined their wins and losses so that as a pair, they broke even on their gambling efforts. Additionally, the person who incurred

gambling losses received compensation from the casino in the form of several free guest nights. The casino determined what was happening through a random data mining exercise looking for patterns when referencing gambling activity with guest stay and nongambling activity. The pattern in this case was a break-even on gambling for two people staying in the same room and playing the same game.

- People will call manufacturers directly when they have a problem with a product. A soft drink manufacturer performed a data mining exercise that combined data from inbound complaint calls, inbound request calls, and Web coupon downloading activity. They also looked at this information relative to the same time period. A pattern emerged that indicated a certain percentage of customers were downloading coupons for the same product they were calling to complain about on the same day. So how dissatisfied were these customers? Were they taking advantage of a system that rewarded customers who complained?

Every industry has many examples of these types of patterns. As organizations become smarter in their efforts, the consumer also learns. Unfortunately, there are individuals who will use marketers' methods against them. Fortunately, these occurrences are uncommon, but they may lead to substantial cost or lost marketing opportunities if not known.

Chapter Summary

Improved data capture capabilities and the ability to generate more data have created both opportunities and challenges for the data-leveraging efforts of CRM practitioners. The opportunities include having more relevant data available for analysis in a timelier fashion. At last, marketers can analyze and leverage information in support of their CRM objectives. They have more resources and insights available to them as data mining solutions abound and are constantly improving. They have learned what data to capture, how to capture it, and how to make it accessible with the right tools. The challenges for CRM practitioners are not insurmountable but can neutralize or even be detrimental to their efforts if not considered. Determining which data to keep and which to discard is not an easy decision. Spending complete budgets on CRM efforts based on the interpretation of data demands that the data be transformed into information that, when appropriately analyzed, leads to knowledgeable decision making. Keeping abreast of noninvasive techniques is critical to sustaining profitable relationships with customers. The resources and knowledge are now available to the marketer; they require only that the right choices are made.

Key Terms

Algorithm is a set of rules used to solve a problem or define an opportunity through a finite number of steps.

Chi-squared automatic interaction detector (CHAID) is a technique used to build decision trees based upon a relationship between dependent variables and a series of predictor variables.

Classification and regression trees (CART) is a technique that creates a classification or regression tree based upon whether a dependent variable is numeric or category.

Cluster analysis is a process that segments a heterogeneous population into subgroups, or clusters, using no predefined classification.

Dashboard, similar to an automobile dashboard, is a graphical user interface–based software display of key information summarized to facilitate decision making via a series of charts, graphs, tables, and spreadsheets, often enabled with "drill-down" capability that allows one to see a high-level view of information with the ability to search for more detailed information.

Decision trees are a set of rules usually produced by techniques such as CART and CHAID.

Exogenous variables is a term used to define those variables that may have a positive, a negative, or no impact on an organization, such as government regulations, the availability of natural resources such as oil and water, technology trends, societal pressures, and population demographics.

Questions

1. What are the different types of data? Why is having less data sometimes better than having more data?
2. What is the difference between data and information?
3. What are the variables required to perform an RFM analysis?
4. Explain the differences in types of data across ODSs, DWs, and DMs.
5. A consumer buys a computer online from Dell.

    a. What types of data and information would Dell place in an ODS? How long would it be maintained in the ODS?
    b. What types of information would Dell place in a DW?
    c. What types of information would Dell put into a data mart? How would they be used?

Exercises

1. Give an example of how an organization may use household data and individual data as part of its CRM strategy.
2. Based on your own experience, identify the different touch points that an organization has created for you to interface with it.
3. Select an organization and attempt to identify aging rules for the data it may have captured on consumers.
4. Select an organization that you do business with frequently. Based on the data the organization has collected on you, explain what data mining opportunities are available to the organization. Explain how your transaction may flow through an ODS, a DW, and a DM.
5. Create 250 rows of data in Excel that represent the RFM variables. Randomize the variables. Run sorts per the RFM discussion and break the results into respective cells.
6. Create a decision tree scenario for an organization.

Appendix A

Data Mining Methods

- Analysis of variance (ANOVA)
- Artificial neural network
- Business intelligence (BI)
- CART
- CHAID
- Correlation
- Data stream mining
- Fisher's Least Significant Difference test
- Fuzzy logic
- Mann-Whitney U Test
- Nearest neighbor algorithm

- Pattern recognition
- Pearson product-moment correlation coefficient
- Principal components analysis
- A random forest
- R (free software often used in academia and research, as well as industrial applications)
- Recursion
- Regression analysis
- Relational data mining
- Rule based (if-then logic)
- Spearman's rank correlation coefficient
- Student's t-test
- Text mining

Section 3

Marketing Strategy

Chapter 8

Business-to-Business CRM

8.1 Introduction

Organizations invest heavily in research to determine what consumers think about their products and services and how they are perceived compared to their competition. In the business-to-business environment, however, more often than not, organizations are confident that they know to what degree their customers are satisfied and feel that they understand their customers' needs better than their customers understand them themselves. This becomes more even complicated when it is a business-to-business-to-consumer relationship. Unfortunately, many times an organization's business customer informs it of his or her dissatisfaction by not renewing a contract. Research demonstrates that the way to sustain relationships with current customers is to create a passionate customer-centric environment where everyone in the organization, including value delivery network partners, has a "buy-in" and demonstrates this attitude on a continuing basis. These efforts also need to be measured, reinforced, and continuously improved upon as everyone in the value chain adjusts to their respective environmental dynamics. This customer-centric approach must also be tempered by the fact that strong relationships are built on trust. Trust cannot be mandated but, instead, must be built over time. Therefore, either party may not readily see the results of this approach in the short term, which means that one must proceed knowing that, if done right, a trusting relationship will form over time. Thus, customer relationship management (CRM) and partner relationship management (PRM) strategies are key methodologies that, if adopted, can help a company not only sustain and grow profits with existing business customers but also serve as input to acquisition strategy formulation.

This chapter discusses some of the CRM-enabling methods and tools used in a business-to-business environment and the business-to-business CRM strategic complexity. The former is very dynamic, and a CRM strategist must consistently monitor changes in tools, methods, and best practices. We will also explore the critical need for value delivery network strategies via execution of PRM and other alliance strategies, as a business's CRM strategy is only as good as the weakest link in the value delivery network. Last, we must not forget that CRM and PRM are strategies enabled by technology, the optimal execution of which provides an organization with an opportunity to sustain and grow profitable relationships with customers. Technology is not the solution but is only a support function.

8.2 Business-to-Business Characteristics Relative to CRM

Relative to CRM, a business-to-business (B2B) environment shares similar characteristics to those in a business-to-consumer (B2C) environment. There are also unique B2B environmental components, however, that often require different CRM strategies solutions.

8.2a Similarities between B2B and B2C

Many technology solutions and basic CRM methods that we discuss in the context of a business practicing CRM with consumers can also be applied to businesses practicing CRM with other businesses as their customers. As was discussed in Chapter 4, the structure of an organization, along with its respective industry dynamics, has an impact on an organization's CRM and PRM strategy. We also saw that the size of an organization presented both advantages and disadvantages.

Data integration steps, database construction, utilization of data warehouses, operational data stores, and data marts are similarly constructed for both B2B and B2C and, in fact, can be constructed for use in both business and consumer market environments. The data resident in these entities may be different, but the structures can be similar, if not the same. Some B2B sources of purchased secondary data can be acquired in a similar method and from the same partners. Loyalty and customer equity (monetary value of the customer) measurement may use similar formulas, and retention strategies may use similar tactics. Fostering a customer-centric culture in the organization is similar just as the objectives are similar (i.e., customer retention and increased customer equity). Economies of scale can be leveraged when an organization has both business customers and consumers as customers.

8.2b Differences between B2B and B2C

Differences in database structures may be required based upon the software applications that utilize the databases. A sales management B2B application may require a separate data mart or data store to provide for optimal database access and storage environment. The data warehouse, however, may not need to be a separate entity for those organizations that have CRM strategies for both businesses and consumers.

Overall, there are fewer businesses than consumers. The B2B relationships tend to be more formal than with B2C relationships, most of which are established via a written legal document or contract. The expectations are clearer, and most of them are documented. There is generally a formal dialogue and even prescheduled meetings to discuss the ongoing relationship. Performance is continually assessed, and delivery expectations are usually specifically defined.

Additionally, business customers and prospects are less fragmented and easier to segment. While business customer needs are somewhat easier to define as a result of open dialogue, they are not necessarily easier to fulfill, which should hopefully provide an opportunity for definitive value propositions. It can be more difficult, however, to determine which person or area plays what role in the initial sales and relationship-building process. Business customers are people, and they have both personal and business objectives.

Rick Barlow, former CEO of Frequency Marketing, says, "The vast number of consumer programs is one reason loyalty programs are making inroads to B2B marketing. It is a manifestation of the broad acceptance within our culture of frequency–loyalty relationship marketing." Rick does acknowledge, however, that B2B programs are different from B2C programs. B2B programs are more complex and have higher costs. Rick goes on to say, "The most notable difference is what kind of recognition and rewards are appropriate for businesses versus consumers. In B2B, it is a huge challenge just identifying the right people. We need to have a program that is tailored to each type of business customer and their needs."[1]

Stephan A. Butscher, a senior consultant with Simon Kucher & Partners, states, "In B2B, very often the relationships between two companies are much better established and not as anonymous as those that sell to millions of consumers. There are often individual personal relationships established. If you use reps and account managers, then that relationship is present already. That relationship should be integrated with, not replaced by, the loyalty program."[2]

Business employees' behaviors may be influenced by, and their expectations may be framed by, their own personal experiences with CRM efforts targeting them as a consumer. With fewer customers and prospects than that in the consumer market, a successful relationship can be leveraged as goodwill in acquisition efforts, but failed relationships may have a very negative impact on those same efforts. A lost business customer has a larger impact on profitability than that of a lost consumer customer, due to both the potential longer-term relationship and transaction value. Investments in relationship-building efforts are higher in B2B situations because some of them may require customization in terms of products, services, infrastructure, and people. The sales cycle in B2B is usually much longer and complex, increasing costs and requiring more skilled employees. B2B salespeople tend to be more professional, knowledgeable, and customer-focused due to the nature of reward systems and personal psychological makeup, such as risk taking. There is usually much more interaction between the organization and its business customer than there is with its consumer customer. Privacy risks are better managed with a business customer, as most relationships include formal confidentiality agreements and other methods of data and knowledge protection.

Additionally, business customers are usually more involved in the conceptual design, implementation, and problem-resolution strategies associated with the organization's offerings. They also may see the relationship as strategic versus transactional, as the offering may be integral to the success of their product and service creation and subsequent marketing efforts (i.e., a strategic partnership). A personal computer manufacturer, for example, would most assuredly have close relationships with its computer component providers.

8.2c Other Unique Characteristics of a B2B Environment

8.2c.1 Formal Contracts

Formal contracts between firms can have an impact on relationship-building efforts. S. Seshadri and R. Mishra state that the ability to use contractual forms of **governance**, where possible, is crucial to the enhanced scope of relationship marketing management.[3] They argue that contracts and relationships are complementary and that contracts provide an evolving governance structure. They go on to say:

> Transaction costs arise due to the dynamic nature of economies. Incompleteness arises due to the costs associated with contracting in the presence of difficulties in (a) anticipation of contingencies and situations, (b) devising and agreeing on courses of action, (c) writing explicit causes and contingent agreements, and (d) monitoring and enforcement. Some transactions between organizations can be defined and thus easily formalized and viewed as a complete contract, while other transactions are incomplete transitionally speaking and rightfully so, as

some or all relevant information cannot be defined at the time of creating a contract. The inability to force contingencies in contracting itself would call for increased emphasis on relational contracting.

Relational contracting focuses on a long-term durable exchange particular to relationship marketing management.

8.2c.2 Internet-Based B2B

The dynamic environment of **Internet-based B2B exchanges** impacts a firm's relationship-building strategy. Also known as electronic marketplaces, these exchanges connect buyers and sellers efficiently and cost effectively. Organizations such as Covisint provide **cloud-based portals** for buyer and seller exchanges in multiple industries. These exchanges tend to move organizations to focus more on price than relationships. A major reason that buyers use these exchanges is to consolidate resources, which hopefully will lead to cost reduction. The costs reduced are production- and transaction-specific costs. Governance or control costs are costs associated with the planning, execution, and monitoring of performance. These costs are greatly reduced through use of the exchanges. This detracts from the opportunity to build relationships. So while costs may be reduced in the short term, transaction cost economies gained from more governance are lost in the long term. The challenge for organizations is to utilize their sales force to build the relationship while using the Internet as a means to manage transaction costs.

Another potentially negative impact on Internet-based B2B exchanges is the privacy issue. There are not only the risks inherent with purchasing via an exchange over the Internet, but there is also the risk of exposure to competitors who might be monitoring purchase activity.

8.2c.3 Market Orientation and Relationship Marketing

Market orientation and relationship marketing are two distinct marketing strategies that overlap. **Market orientation strategies** include activities related to the focus on delivering to the customer. These can be interpreted as more transaction-based strategies. While a **relationship management strategy** utilizes marketing orientation tactics, it is more about how the buyer and seller can attain a mutually profitable relationship with long-term strategic implications for both parties. There is much research being performed on these two approaches. To date, there have not been many definitive findings on how to close the gap between the two strategies. R. Deshpandé and J. U. Farley, however, used **social identity theory** research to frame hypotheses about market orientation and interorganizational relationships as viewed simultaneously from the point of view of suppliers and customers.[4] Their efforts led to insights regarding the existence of a "market orientation gap" between how customers think about suppliers and how suppliers think about themselves. In their study of B2B firms in five industrialized countries, they found a market orientation gap in which suppliers evaluated their own market orientation as being higher than that of their important customers in B2B relationships. There were indications that this gap is related to the change in the importance of a business relationship. The gap is smaller in highly collectivist cultures (Japan and France) that consider relationships to be more critical to their business orientation than do organizations in individualist cultures (United States and United Kingdom).

8.3 Value Delivery Networks

An organization's **value delivery network** must be taken into consideration, as organizations, in an effort to remain competitive, have a tendency to outsource many of their noncore competency activities. As a result, organizations have found themselves managing a portfolio of interorganizational relationships. This provides cost advantages and may increase efficiencies, but it also increases risks, as there is loss of control as well as potential issues with the quality of products, services, communication, and, ultimately, the strength or weakness of the customer relationship. Value delivery networks can be very complex and dynamic, and they can vary widely by industry. It is often said that in today's environment "companies do not compete; value chains compete." Assuming that the specific product or service quality is maintained with a value delivery network partner, the focus of our discussion is on the continuity of the CRM strategy throughout the value delivery network.

Value delivery networks can be as simple as a landscaping service or as complex as a multimanufacturer alliance utilizing a variety of channels, distribution networks, storage facilities, and manufacturer representatives, selling agents, retailers, and installers. Figure 8.1 depicts a simple example of what a value delivery network may look like. The Internet can be used by all members for the purpose of communication, transactions, and, in the case of digital assets (e.g., music, video, software), distribution. Within the last decade, value delivery network activity has also precipitated the formulation of a reverse value delivery network by nature of recycling by-products of the various processes. Each member of the value delivery network has its own unique opportunities and challenges with regard to creation and execution of a CRM strategy. Using a few different value delivery network entities as examples can help illustrate some of the opportunities and challenges the networks offers an organization as it attempts to create and execute a CRM strategy with its customers.

Scenario 1: A manufacturer in China sells products to retailers that, in turn, sell the manufacturer's products to the Chinese consumer. The manufacturer's customer is the retailer. The manufacturer solicits the assistance of an advertising agency to help it with its advertising, brand acceptance, and relationship-building efforts. The advertising agency uses CRM strategies with the manufacturer, as the manufacturer is the agency's customer. The agency, however, must also create a CRM strategy for the manufacturer's customers. In addition, the latter strategy requires the agency to define the optimal CRM strategies that the retailer should use with its customer, the consumer. The agency most likely partners with CRM technology-enabling firms, and possibly data mining and CRM consulting firms as well. The agency and its partners are also affected by macro-environmental forces such as the lack of data, undeveloped technology infrastructures, and less than extensive knowledge about this emerging market.

Scenario 2: A national chemical manufacturing company was losing its competitive advantage patent in two years. The patent was for a unique product that eradicates agricultural pest

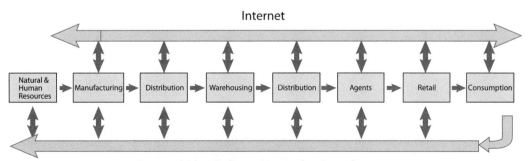

Figure 8.1 Product/Service Value Delivery Network

infestation. The farm manager's product purchasing is heavily influenced by intermediaries who purchase the product from the manufacturer and usually apply it to the farmer's crops as well. The manufacturer's competitors would enter the market with a similar product once this patent expires. In an effort to defend its market position, the manufacturer decided to implement a CRM strategy, with its primary focus being on the intermediaries. The manufacturer felt that if it built a stronger relationship with the intermediaries, it could minimize the competitor's impact on market share.

Scenario 3: A manufacturer of heating and air conditioning products reduced costs by importing cheaper internal components from offshore entities. Its business customers sold, installed, maintained, and serviced these units. Its growth was directly tied to word of mouth, which was extremely positive due to its attention to customer relationships. Clean trucks, professional staff attire, and friendly and competent service available 24/7 all contributed to a positive customer experience and long-term relationships. Its success was also attributed to delivering a reliable product. Inclusion of inferior components started to sharply reduce reliability, however, which led to deterioration in their relationships and eventually a sharp loss of business. It soon switched to a manufacturer that had more reliable products, albeit a little more expensive, and attempted to win back and rebuild its failed customer relationships. Unfortunately, this took many years due to the infrequent purchase cycle of this durable good.

Scenario 4: A famous movie studio's distribution partner was planning for a pre–holiday season release of what they envisioned to be a blockbuster hit. Part of their business plan depended on successful DVD sales of the movie in retail outlets. To help ensure optimal retailer orders of DVDs in advance for sale in the stores, they embarked on a relationship strategy that demonstrated how their movie-launch advertising and promotional strategies would increase the retailer's sales to existing customers, as well as attract new customers to the retail stores.

8.3a Ownership of Customers

Relative to CRM, conflicts can arise regarding ownership of the customer. The customer may be the person or entity that ultimately consumes the product, or it may be an organization in the network. One common problem is **disintermediation**. This is where one or more members in the network are bypassed. A manufacturer selling directly to consumers bypasses the traditional distribution, warehouse, and retail partners. They may also bypass traditional distribution and warehouse partners if shipping directly to the consumer.

8.3b Implementing and Maintaining a Cohesive CRM Strategy

Implementing and maintaining a cohesive CRM strategy across value delivery network partners requires coordination and cooperation in several areas. Primarily, the customer relationship strategy needs to be identified. This begins with some key questions that need to be answered:

- Who is the customer, and what are the expected relationship outcomes?
- Who owns the customer?
- What role does each member play in the relationship-building effort?
- What process is used to measure the effectiveness of the CRM strategy?
- What are the software requirements of each value network partner?
- What is the current software being used by each member, and what would constrain a member from being able to efficiently integrate its software with other members (e.g., original equipment manufacturer [OEM] software compatibility, version, licensing, rules of use, ability to process data)?

- What is the current hardware being used by each member? Is it compatible with other members' hardware? Are there licensing issues or data storage and recovery constraints?
- What are the network technology requirements? Constraints? Bottlenecks? Contingencies? Redundancies? Capacity and demand?
- Who owns what information?
- What are the data security requirements, and how are they satisfied across the value network?
- How are customer privacy expectations as well as regulatory requirements managed? Who manages the information and ensures privacy compliance?
- Are there conflicts of interest (e.g., partner's own use, which can detract from the effort or competitor access to information)?

A more serious question is, what are the exit strategies for a value network partner? If an organization invests heavily in a CRM strategy and relies upon key partners, what happens if that partner is no longer available for whatever reason?

8.4 Building the Relationship—Sales and CRM

Business relationships form over time. Traditionally, it has been the sales process that provides for the initial interactions with prospects, and that is still at the heart of any CRM strategy. While CRM initiatives have broadened beyond the sales function, the sales function is still the most critical component of any CRM strategy.

8.4a Customer Acquisition

Customer acquisition is an integral part of the CRM strategy. The acquisition process provides for the building of a set of expectations. Selecting the right business customer is key to a successful CRM initiative, as the selling process is where potential customers' perceptions of value are defined. Presenting a value proposition that can be delivered increases the chances for a successful relationship. Overpromising value results in a "no-win" situation that cannot be overcome by any CRM strategy.

Business selling can be very complex, and a lot is at stake for all parties involved. Long-term relationships are desirable because organizations rely on other organizations to supply them, and eventually the consumer, with quality products and services. It takes a much longer time for a business to build a relationship with a business than it does to build one with a consumer. There is usually more at stake for both parties, especially when the buyer includes the seller's product or service as part of its solution, as in the case of a strategic partner.

8.4b Sales Force Automation

Over the last decade, new technology solutions have provided organizations with the ability to automate those areas of the acquisition process that support the relationship-building process. Most of these tools have fallen into a category labeled **sales force automation (SFA)**. There is no doubt that the automation of certain processes and providing more accurate and timely information both within the organization and to the organization's partners are extremely beneficial. But how these technology solutions are used, as well as what expectations should be set on the outcomes of adoption, needs to be defined and assessed. The implications and consequences, both positive and negative, of their adoption as part of the organization's CRM strategy need to be considered. Once this is accomplished, a detailed examination of the specific functionality can be undertaken.

8.4b.1 Resistance to SFA

Many organizations' management teams report that their staff are reluctant to adopt SFA solutions for the following reasons:

- Concern over their confidential relationships with customers being compromised
- Risk of losing ownership of the customer relationship
- Reluctant to allow management to monitor their efforts at a very detailed level
- Perception that time away from their customer in order to use technology solutions hinders their relationship efforts and subsequent financial gains
- Propensity to avoid adoption of new methods when the current methods employed work for them
- Technology aversion and comfort level with their own methods
- Long learning curve

Some organizational perspectives also play a role in the conflict of whether or not, and to what extent, technology can help the customer relationship. Some people feel there may be a tendency to focus more on the technology and, therefore, lose sight of the customer relationships. There is also the perception that overutilization of metrics contributes to a depersonalizing of the customer relationship.

8.4b.2 Perceived Benefits of SFA

While organizational management struggles with the reluctance of their salespeople to adopt SFA technology, they clearly see how the organization will benefit. Some of the perceived benefits of a SFA solution include, but are not limited to, the following:

- Reduction of errors associated with manual processes
- Reduction in support costs
- Provision for more timely dissemination of key information to the organization
- Quicker flow of critical information to the salesperson, which can impact his or her relationship effort
- Ability to integrate information across strategic partners
- Provides a secure data repository with archiving
- Ability to leverage historical information quickly and with less effort
- Quicker and more inclusive assessment of current and potential increase in overall customer equity
- Ease of integration of sales-related information with other business functions such as customer service, order processing, warranty activity, and so on
- Quicker identification of potential customer acquisition issues
- Enhanced ability to preempt potential problems with customers
- Ease of detecting relationship-building trends, opportunities, and problems

8.4b.3 Knowledge Management Systems in SFA

An SFA system is perceived by some to include a **knowledge management (KM)** system, as SFA provides for an expedient flow of data. KM system solutions vary in their structure and usage, but all of them, in some way, provide an accurate, expedient, and cost-effective way to transfer knowledge to the person who needs it from the person who is considered the expert. The provider of information is called the seller, and the user of information is called the buyer. The transfer of knowledge from the seller to the buyer is accomplished by coding the information in such a way that it fulfills the specific needs of the buyers on demand. This is important to highlight when evaluating SFA because KM can leverage SFA functionality. In theory, one could say that an inexperienced salesperson or a low-performing experienced salesperson (we will call this person the buyer of knowledge) can have access to the experienced, high-performance salesperson's wealth of knowledge (we will call the experienced salesperson the seller). The key benefit here is that the experienced seller contributes knowledge (either one time or accrued) into a system that can be referenced continually by multiple people without taking the experienced person away from his or her respective selling efforts. A key assumption here is that the organization is able to overcome any reluctance by the experienced, high-performance salesperson to contribute to the KM and SFA system. One organization successfully overcame this hurdle by demonstrating potential value via access to other high performers' best practices.

Research performed on this concept of knowledge benefit from SFA systems by D-G. Ko and A. R. Dennis provides an interesting finding.[5] They examined the effect of using a KM-based SFA system on the sales performance of 1,340 sales representatives. They found that SFA system use was directly related to performance—the more knowledge documents sales representatives read, the more likely they were to exceed their quota. They also expected that, given the same level of use, sales representatives with greater experience would benefit less from the use of the knowledge in the SFA system than would an average sales representative because they had less to learn. Similarly, less knowledge in the SFA system would be new to expert sales representatives, and thus they would benefit less. Their research showed, however, that this was not the case. While the majority of sales representatives, on average, experienced the same benefit from the documents they read, the experienced, high-performance representatives benefited four times more than the average for the less experienced representative.

While not what they had originally anticipated, after further consideration, they determined that experienced representatives were better at assimilating vast amounts of knowledge quickly and more efficiently than less experienced representatives. This suggests that the ability to recognize the value of "new knowledge," assimilate it, and effectively apply it in a short period of time is critical to performance improvement. The less experienced representative may be "overloaded" with information and not be able to extract the value from the systems as a result of his lack of experience. This difference may also be a result of the ability of high-expertise sales representatives to effectively use new knowledge to boost current sales. Sales professionals tend to be very results oriented because their compensation is directly tied to their sales performance. Ko and Dennis believe it could be that the high-expertise sales representatives are particularly good at seeking relevant knowledge when there is an immediate potential to apply the knowledge and reap an immediate performance benefit.

8.4b.4 SFA Benefits

In their study of sales technology orientation, information effectiveness, and sales performance, researchers G. K. Hunter and W. D. Perreault Jr. identified another SFA benefit source. Their data source for the research was collected from the sales force of a major consumer packaged goods company. They focused on evaluating relationships that drive two key aspects of sales performance: performance with customers and internal role performance. Per their definitions, *performance with customers* is the extent to which the salesperson cultivates relationships with the customer's organization. *Internal role performance* refers to the salesperson's contributions on issues that are predominantly internal to the supplier's organization. This includes things like recommending improvements in company operations and procedures, acting as a special resource to cross-functional associates, knowing the company's products and services, and staying abreast of the company's production schedules and technological advances. They found that the total effect of sales technology orientation on internal role performance was greater than on performance with customers. Therefore, while there are sales technology orientation returns on both performance outcomes, Hunter and Perreault believe that the selling organization is realizing greater returns on its investments in sales technology from internal role performance outcomes, or efficiency gains in contrast to external effectiveness returns.[6]

One may ask if there is a diminishing point of return with regards to a salesperson's usage of a sales support system. Research by M. Ahearne, N. Srinvasan, and L. Weinstein produced results that show despite a positive payoff to SFA use in CRM initiatives, the enabling effect tapers off, and the relationship between technology usage and performance is curvilinear. Data from the SFA system studied was collected for a three-month period for all sales representatives in an operational CRM context. The total number of system hits (or total screens used in a three-month period) was used to measure salesperson technology utilization. The salespeople in this study produced 283 hits on average in this time period. The researchers found an ideal system usage of 488 hits, which was the point at which usage maximized job performance. They also found that about 20 percent of the salespeople in the study used the system above the ideal level of 488 hits. The researchers commented that one has to be cautious with using "hits" because it is possible, although not probable, that salespeople who had more "hits" were navigating a lot before they found what they were looking for (i.e., the number of hits could reflect a learning curve that has not stabilized). However, they did not expect this to be likely after more training was provided.[7]

8.4c SFA Solution Considerations

At a minimum, an organization must try to identify its SFA needs. SFA providers will usually help potential customers with their needs assessment, as they require inputs into their proposed solutions.

One must also remember that cloud-based, or **software as a service (SaaS)**, solutions eliminate the need for major investments, greatly reduce the amount of time it will take to become productive, require minimal IT resource allocations, and reduce overall ownership risk. It should also be noted, however, that sources of data, data definitions and relationships, and other data integration functions will still have to be performed, as well as possibly some customizations to specific user interfaces.

The following are some basic considerations when looking for an SFA solution:

- *Number of users (present and future):* How many people will be using the SFA system concurrently today and how many in the future? (**Concurrent users** means people accessing the system at the same time. It is also referred to as the "number of seats.") This may be relevant if the SFA provider prices and manages its offerings through seat licenses. The company only pays for the privilege of concurrent users. If there are 10 concurrent users but 20 total users, the company may create rules for access. Companies attempting to save money by limiting the number of concurrent users must take into account the potential negative impact on customer relationships.
- *Potential for integration with CRM and PRM:* SFA solutions by themselves are not the total CRM solution. Companies should define what the SFA system will interface with and identify integration requirements. A robust SFA system will lose its value if it is a stand-alone environment.
- *Modular:* Perhaps the company does not need all the SFA functions. Some SFA solution providers break down major functions into modules that can be purchased separately. This provides the company with the flexibility of purchasing what it needs today, but also allows for subsequent functionality to be added later when and if it is required.

- *Frequency of version updates:* Whether the SFA solution is to be implemented within the company's environment or if it is cloud-based, changes in the software interface usually require some type of training and potentially lost productivity. The paradox is that new versions allow for new features and problem resolution but at the same time can be disruptive. SFA solution providers attempt to minimize disruptions, while at the same time resolving problems and enhancing their solutions for existing customers. To do this and to attract new customers, updated versions will always be required. It is important to identify the frequency and to measure the impact of version updates in advance to allow for proper planning.
- *Dashboards:* Almost all SFA solutions provide easy-to-use desktop interfaces. A company must determine the extent of learning and training that will be required, ease of use, and compatibility (from a data interaction perspective) with other systems being used. For example, it must consider if there is easy integration with PowerPoint, Excel, and other commonly used office software tools.
- *Mobile device access and synchronization:* The company should determine how easy the SFA works with multiple devices (i.e., desktops, laptops, cell phones, tablets/iPads). The key is transportability and transparency. This is becoming more of a "must have" requirement as salespeople leverage the ease of transport and use while they travel and visit customers.
- *Offline access:* How easy is it to work offline when there is no Internet access or when the salesperson chooses to work offline? How does the loading and unloading process work, and how long does it take to synchronize?
- *Enterprise application integration:* Companies must determine which of their current and/or planned enterprise software and hardware systems the SFA will integrate with.
- *Ability to customize:* To what degree can the SFA solution be customized to better fit the needs of the company? If the solution is a "one-type-fits-all" solution, the price may be lower, but so will the flexibility.
- *Software developer toolkit:* What tools are available for the company to use as it develops applications using a core OEM software product as the base?
- *Scalability:* Growth projections may be difficult, but, assuming the company is successful, as it grows, it will need more data storage, the same or better speed of sending and retrieving information, and more concurrent usage. The SFA solution should allow for structured growth with minimal negative impact.
- *Technical training and support:* What training is offered by the SFA provider? Will it be at the company, or will the company have to send people to the SFA's site for training? What initial and ongoing technical support will be available? How helpful is the "Help" support function? Is all technical support provided by phone, chat, or e-mail?

A company searching for an SFA solution needs to determine which functions are needed immediately and which may be required in the future. Once it knows the required functionality, the company can then proceed to evaluate potential SFA providers.

SFA solutions vary in the functionality they provide. Typical SFA functions are detailed in the following sections. Some of these functions are completely integrated into an SFA solution, some are loosely connected via export and import functions, and some are stand-alone.

8.4c.1 Lead Management

Certain prospective customers are easily identifiable, but the majority are not. Consequently, salespeople utilize **lead management software** systems to help them identify viable prospects. These software solutions vary in function and feature, but all analyze, score, and route the lead internally. Variables analyzed include the prospect's budget, time-to-purchase, prospect authority, and specific needs today and in the future.

Here is an example of this methodology in use. A major high-technology manufacturer uses lead management software to differentiate between consumer and business Web inquiries. Its solution then scores the business lead as "hot," "warm," or "cold." All "hot" leads are routed to a salesperson. All "warm" leads are followed up by an inside salesperson as well as with a Web and direct marketing mailing (the content of which is based upon the nature of the inquiry). "Cold" leads are placed into a database for further analysis. Ancillary benefits to their use of lead management software include the ability to identify intent and need for personal or business use. For example, if a director of technology submitted an inquiry using her personal e-mail address, the software attempts to determine whether this inquiry was for personal use or for business use, with the latter presenting a potential opportunity. If it was for personal use, the CRM strategy is to satisfy and nurture the person as a consumer with the concept of growing the relationship to a point where this person may consider the manufacturer's products or services for her business. The lead management software also identifies the type of business (i.e., a small business or sole proprietor business).

8.4c.2 Opportunity Management

Some solution providers embed opportunity management into their lead management solutions, combine both and call it opportunity management, or make a distinction between the two. The functionality of opportunity management allows for expedient sharing of critical sales information, which includes sales lead status, issues, details on the specific sales process steps, ease of collaboration in team selling, integration with sales approach history, and the ability to modify the current approach.

8.4c.3 Sales Forecasting

Sales forecasting solutions provide for the ability to create accurate forecasts based on dynamic sales information. Users can create and assign sales quotas, analyze current activity in multidimensional views (across a business customer, industry, geographic area, teams, etc.), and modify quickly based upon the latest information. These solutions have now been or are soon to be enhanced with mobile device capability.

8.4c.4 Sales Analytics

Any sales analytics solution usually includes real-time access to the latest sales-related information via dashboard interfaces that have drill-down capabilities. The dashboard allows for preset data views but also allows the user to drill down and perform a variety of "what-if" scenarios as data is analyzed. These solutions generate current business intelligence that can be leveraged to preempt operational or customer issues, identify trends, gain insight into **key performance indicators (KPI)** on products and services, and import and export information to other CRM-based systems. Alerts notifications, the ability to customize, mobile interfaces, and standard security and data integrity management are other standard inclusions.

8.4c.5 Contact Management

Consolidation of all relevant customer or prospect information into a single customer-centric view, updated in real-time and available to anyone tied to the customer or prospect via a variety of communication software and hardware environments, including mobile access, is the core benefit of a contact management solution. These solutions have become very sophisticated. Many of the companies providing contact management systems ensure compatibility with other sales and CRM-based software solutions. This makes for easy, secure, data integrity import and export capabilities. Typical information present in these systems includes customer history, customer opportunities, customer issues, customer contact information identified in a variety of ways (e.g., decision maker, user, influencer, gatekeeper, etc.), prospect information (including sales attempts history), contact information (similar to customer contact information), revenue opportunity, and current and future need information.

8.4c.6 Quote Management

The quoting process for new or existing customers can be enhanced with relative ease as new market solutions provide all of the criteria for putting together consistent and accurate quotes. This enables businesses to respond quickly to their customers or prospects and is a very important component, since responsiveness is a key CRM enabler. Current solutions provide for ease of use when putting together a quote. These solutions integrate all necessary product and services information from different systems, including quote history. They provide for consistency in quote document content and pricing; allow for quote template creation, modification (e.g., by customer segment), and printing or e-mail integration; and reference tax and adjustment information. Some allow for customizing the finished document to match the customer's or prospect's specific requirements. These systems can update customer and prospect databases, which are referenced by a different CRM-based system, contributing to the customer-centric view.

8.4c.7 Order Management

The process of managing orders enhances the CRM effort. These systems provide efficiency, contain costs, and reduce response times to the customer. Some of the key features of these systems, which are related to enhancing CRM, include the ability to track orders from the desktop or mobile device, quick customization of purchase and sales order templates, simplified invoice creation, integration with value network partners, inventory management integration with alerts on "out of stock" in advance, monitoring orders in progress (including integration to dashboards for preempting customer order delivery problems), accurate shipping information and label creation to meet customer requirements (including special requests), and integration of accounts payable to customer accounts receivable systems.

8.4c.8 Contract Management

Efficient contract management systems, which allow for the use of templates that can be customized, make it possible for users to spend less time on writing and managing documents and more time on satisfying customers and building relationships. These systems also allow for the consistent and accurate creation of legal documents, which can be tailored to meet the specific customer requirements.

8.4c.9 Pipeline Management

Some CRM systems include the capability of monitoring potential sales and observing the activities in the sales process. This function can alert the user to trends as well as issues in the sales cycle. If not included in the other CRM system components, pipeline management is provided by many companies as a stand-alone software system.

8.4c.10 Territory Management

Sales managers use territory management systems to assist them in defining territories based on those dimensions that fit their objectives (e.g., size of territory, revenue and potential revenue, geography, product/service categories, or type of customer). An optimal territory structure inevitably contributes to improved customer service and management, as well as to the CRM effort.

8.4c.11 Activity Management

A system that helps users manage their customer-focused activities can enhance the CRM effort because it may eliminate redundancy, minimize or eliminate lost customer data, highlight areas that can be improved or used as an example of a best practice, and improve dissemination of customer information. Some solutions include project management within an activity management solution. Both are similar and can use, for example, typical project management methods such as Gantt charts and task management modules. Some of these solutions include the ability to streamline processes through the management of e-mails, meetings, schedules, calendars, and other activities. These efficiencies allow employees to focus more time on the customer.

8.4c.12 E-Mail Integration

Many e-mail integration solutions are available, and most have some or all of the typical e-mail management functions. Some solutions, however, provide the ability to extract data from an e-mail directly into a database or to update multiple CRM systems. This contributes to CRM by ensuring accuracy of data repository updates on a customer while reducing time to manage customer information. Other solutions also provide the ability to read and process messages from database records, text files, Web pages, and other feeds. Some of these solutions are easy to integrate with standard CRM systems, while others may require some level of customization. Additionally, e-mail template tools provide for the use of standardized e-mail document creation. They also allow for ease of integration with a salesperson's current e-mail provider so they do not have to use multiple e-mail systems.

8.4c.13 Shared Calendar

Consumer solutions, which allow multiaccess to one's calendar, have been widely adopted. There is nothing different here for business use other than that some of the major calendar systems have the ability to share or assign tasks and events within a secured, easily integrated system environment.

8.4c.14 Workflow Automation

Workflow process tools allow you to design and automate virtually any process, including product or service configurations, customer service, scripts for telesales, sales methods, quotes, sales, and contract processes. All of these workflows have either a direct or an indirect impact on the business customer. Some solutions have a predefined process or set of templates that allow for some modification, while others are completely customizable.

8.4c.15 Competitor Tracking

This is more of a service where organizations track the competition based upon its customers' requirements. The services could be generic, self-service, or highly customized. Information on the competition can be supplied via reports and/or available via search functions to their respective database. While competitor tracking is not unique to CRM, it should be considered as a viable option and used to monitor the competition's CRM efforts as well as industry trends.

8.4c.16 Ancillary Marketing Automation Tools

A wide array of software tools are available to make it possible for marketers to automate those functions that are predictable, require little decision making, and improve overall work process efficiency. The following entries are examples of some of these tools. This is a very dynamic area with software companies consistently upgrading or replacing current solutions.

- Document management tools allow for the facilitation of document movement, storage, and retrieval, along with secure archiving. Some SFA solutions include some form of document management, and some have an open connection to stand-alone document solutions, which may be more robust. A key benefit related to CRM is the mobility of information as new document management tools utilize cloud-based architecture.
- Product catalog management tools provide a company with easy-to-integrate interfaces to their e-commerce sites for the purpose of managing product offerings on the site via addition, changes, and delete functions. These systems can also provide for integration with other tools such as pricing and purchase analytics.
- Pricing management tools provide for demand measurement related to price changes (i.e., price elasticity) and help companies maximize revenue and profit by supporting product offering mix strategies with inventory and demand management capabilities.
- Campaign management tools provide for the integration of multichannel customer and prospect response data with customer and prospect databases. A marketer can easily analyze prospects or customers, segment them based on the results of analysis, and target select segments and subsegments for specific communications by respective optimal channels, usually tied into customer preference (e.g., e-mail, phone [voice or text], postal mail). The campaign management tool can automatically update the respective databases with information on control groups, the detail of each communication, channel(s) used, fulfillment pieces (if applicable), partners used (if applicable), mediums and media used, and all related costs. On the back end, responses are updated to databases that, in turn, update the campaign management software. This, then, automatically updates the same databases and, by default, identifies nonrespondents. History is updated, analyzed, and used as input to the next communication strategy. Return on investment, share of wallet, lifetime value, and other related measurement formulas can automatically be updated and recalculated with response data. Successful campaign execution can increase customer retention and acquisition rates.

8.5 Partner Relationship Management (PRM)

Forming relationships with members in the value delivery network is not new. Organizations, however, are now adopting structured approaches with specialized strategies and tools to build and sustain these relationships. **Partner relationship management (PRM)** is a newer methodology that attempts to optimize relationships with value delivery network partners as part of the overall CRM strategy.

CRM is increasingly reliant upon multichannel integration. Because companies concentrate on core competencies, they are relying more on their channel partners as extensions of their CRM strategy. This has become ever more important as the dynamics of the digital age offer great opportunities for new customer interactions but require even more capability, coordination, and cooperation from channel partners. An organization's CRM strategy is only as strong as the weakest CRM strategy link among its partners.

A PRM strategy is instrumental in managing channel conflicts, much of which can detract from a successful CRM effort. This requires partner role definitions, rules of behavior, suggested conflict resolution procedures, and possible solutions. Problems can arise when a partner attempts to rationalize its contribution by coming to some terms of what is an "equitable relationship" or, to put it more succinctly, "What do we get out of it?" PRM, if implemented and managed successfully, will resolve conflict and clarify the appropriate "quid pro quo" for its partners.

THEORY IN ACTION

PRM: Best Practices

Pitney Bowes Software leverages its partner network and channel as part of its sales strategy in marketing automation software. Since multichannel marketing automation software spans so many different areas of a marketing organization and its suppliers, it is critical to leverage external client resources such as agencies, marketing service providers, and systems integrators. These end-user vendor relationships help to implement, rather than hinder, the installation of customer engagement software and help get multiple disciplines on the same page inside and outside the enterprise.

Interview with T. Claytor, director of partner recruitment, Pitney Bowes Inc.

8.5a Value Delivery Networks and PRM

Value delivery network partners can be viewed as extensions of the organization, and, therefore, their business objectives should, in part, support and optimally be integrated with the organization's CRM strategy. Any PRM methodology and system has several key benefits, such as efficiency gains, optimal partner selection, partner retention, increased revenue and profitability, and customer satisfaction. They all, by nature of their capabilities, attempt to provide a platform that enables organizations to better recruit the right type of partners, build strong relationships, and grow those relationships.

Some PRM systems and methods are more formal than others. Depending on the PRM solution provider, these systems may be part of the CRM system, integrated with the CRM system, or stand-alone solutions. At the very least, a PRM system solution should include the ability to:

- Jointly manage marketing campaigns
- Provide an integrated capability for managing the path of turning a prospect into a customer
- Provide joint sales forecasting
- Manage and provide access to all partner discounts, commissions, and royalties
- Facilitate order tracking and sales tracking
- Allow for recruitment of new partners
- Provide for real-time access to all sales activity reports
- Provide for real-time interaction and feedback regarding all value-producing activity by all partners

Oracle Seibel provides PRM solutions and has identified key functions and benefits of partner relationship management. Oracle's website provides more insight into what it offers as solutions into a PRM strategy.

8.5b On-Demand PRM

On-demand PRM is becoming more of a requirement due, in part, to demand from mobile devices and system applications. Gartner has found that organizations investing in on-demand PRM benefit from more than a 25 percent increase in capturing new deals through registration processes and more than a 40 percent increase in visibility of leads managed by partners.[8] While there are multiple excellent on-demand PRM solution providers available, Salesforce.com, a leading provider of CRM and PRM B2B software solutions, has made it easy for organizations to adopt and get up and running quickly with its on-demand PRM solution. One of its advantages is the current installed base of its SFA solution users. Because one of the obstacles to creating a unified partner environment is the different software and hardware solutions currently in place, the odds that potential partners will have the same SFA solutions are greater with its solution due to the wide adoption of its SFA tools. The look and feel of its PRM solution is similar to its SFA solution, making it easier for organizations to use quickly. Salesforce.com promotes its PRM approach by identifying a PRM life cycle and clearly identifying how its product completes this cycle (Figure 8.2).

8.5c PRM Solution Considerations

Before selecting a PRM solution provider, an organization should decide if it wants to use a solution that is implemented in its organization environment, and subsequently across its channel members, or if an SaaS solution is the optimal solution.

Channel Revenue

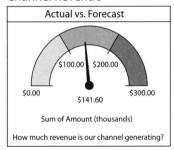

Channel Pipeline

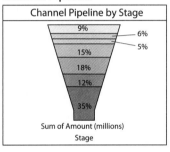

Partner Performance

Figure 8.2 **PRM Dashboard**

Source: http://www.salesforce.com/sales-cloud/partner-management.jsp. ©copyright Salesforce.com, Inc. Used with permission.

THEORY IN ACTION

Avanade[9] Point of View: Partner Relationship Management with Microsoft CRM

Securely sharing critical information with selected partners is helping businesses to be more responsive to customer needs and sales opportunities.

Grosvenor

This international property group with assets of more than £12 billion wanted to share more of its information with its partners as part of a general service transformation program. Previously, without a single view of business activity or the people involved—whether tenants, owners, employees, or contractors—this was impossible.

Using a customized version of Microsoft Dynamics CRM, Avanade provided Grosvenor with a system that worked the way it did and was customer-centric rather than asset-focused. Importantly, it also enabled selected partners to share—securely—the relevant information they needed via a Web-based portal.

Major European Electronics Company

The majority of this company's sales are through the channel, including various intermediaries, distributors, wholesalers, corporate dealers, and retailers. At the same time, the company manages a range of end-user campaigns and promotions to help stimulate demand for its products. Typically, however, partner management has been a disjointed process, carried out by different departments with varying levels of success.

With Avanade's CRM solution, it was able to create a centralized pool of sales and marketing information about its users that its channel partners could tap into. It enabled partners to easily get and manage the information they needed about customers and prospects and to follow up leads more efficiently. This will enable the company to improve repeat sales, up-selling, and loyalty by establishing a good relationship with its main profitable customers along the channel. According to Heidi Leroy-Short, "They (the consultants) really got to grips with the details. They really understood the requirements, which were complicated and detailed."[10]

8.6 Business Partner Associations

An organization will enter into different relationships with companies with regard to its respective position in the value chain and the specific opportunity or challenge. These relationships also provide for new opportunities, as new customer relationships may be generated as a result of these associations.

8.6a Value-Added Reseller

Value-added resellers (VARs) take an existing product or service from another organization, add value to the product or service, and then resell the new product or service. Here are some examples:

- The VAR may make an outright purchase of the product or service by paying the manufacturer and then providing the original product or service with its added value solution to its customers with a markup.
- There may be a financial arrangement between the VAR's customer, the VAR, and the manufacturer where the VAR is a "pass-through" on funds, and the VAR costs are either included as a markup on the product or service or the solution is unbundled and the VAR's customer views all separate costs.
- A company may purchase a product or service from a manufacturer and then select a VAR to work with it to enhance the purchased product or service.

Here are some examples of how a VAR may add value relative to CRM:

- The VAR may integrate a manufacturer's software CRM system for its customer within its customer environment.
- The VAR, in addition to integration, may act as a liaison between the manufacturer and the VAR's customer for initial training purposes and ongoing maintenance, including version updates.
- The VAR may create a packaged solution for its customer using a manufacturer's solution as part of its whole solution, thereby creating a packaged solution for the customer.
- The VAR may customize the manufacturer's solution for its customer and then be the main support structure for the customer for an ongoing period of time or as a one-time, stand-alone effort.
- The VAR may work with a combination of hardware and software manufacturers in putting together a completely integrated CRM system for its customer and then implement the solution and maintain the solution at the customer's site or host the new solution as a stand-alone solution at its own site. If hosted at its own site, the solution would be completely transportable to the customer's site based upon customer needs.
- VARs have a depth of CRM expertise, are usually certified in the products they use and sell, and can educate their customers on the different types of solution providers and what may best fit their needs.
- VARs may be more flexible in scheduling and customization than when dealing directly with an OEM.
- The VAR may purchase a combination of hardware and CRM-enabling software from respective manufacturers and host predefined environments. It can then provide these solutions to its customers with a time-share arrangement.
- The VAR may not be involved in the purchasing of any hardware or software for its customer, but it may only provide consulting services and use its own or the customer's CRM system.
- VARs have unique value in areas of data integration, data enhancement, data mining, and CRM best practices that are not available in most organizations.

THEORY IN ACTION

VAR as a "Staging Ground"

A major casino corporation with multiple properties was in the process of developing a new enterprise-wide CRM system but encountered several difficulties. Although the casino had a well-trained and professional IT staff, they were completely immersed in the day-to-day operations of the casino and did not have the time to evaluate a CRM design, build a strategy, and then implement the solution. They also had limited knowledge of CRM systems and CRM strategy. On top of that, the current system's structure was no longer efficient for the casino's current operations, nor would it be able to efficiently host a new on-demand CRM software environment. Also, because it was entering into new OEM and VAR relationships, the casino could not sign a new hardware lease and, in some cases, purchase agreements until the current lease expired. Another consideration was the comfort level with "turning on" a new CRM system when it had a CRM environment that worked but was not optimal. To overcome several of these challenges, the casino decided to enter into a four-phase relationship with a

VAR. The first three phases were short term—less than four years in total—while the fourth phase was a perpetual long-term relationship.

Phase one (two years) included the design and development of the CRM software solution, including data integration and data enhancement on hardware purchased by the VAR.

Phase two (one-half year) included running the new CRM environment at the VAR's site with live casino customer data as an initial test. Results were input to minor design changes and adjustments to data capture and other incidentals. Also, results of the new environment were compared to results of the existing environment on data quality, security, and the projected value lift with the new system versus the old system. During phase two, the casino purchased and installed new hardware (servers as well as desktops, laptops, and other supporting communications hardware).

Phase three was scheduled for the last half of the third year (i.e., the second half of the same year in which phase two commenced). By this time, the casino had all the new hardware and communications installed and tested. A copy of the new software solution was implemented on this new hardware. The casino IT staff ran the new system in the background, while the VAR ran the same system at its site as a six-month parallel test. After a thorough audit, the VAR's site was shut down. The casino's system went into production and replaced its old system.

Phase four was a long-term relationship with the VAR. The VAR provided data enhancement on a regular schedule and consulting on CRM strategies, data integration, and modifications to the CRM environment when needed.

8.6b Original Equipment Manufacturer

The term *original equipment manufacturer* (OEM) is used to describe the original maker, relative to CRM, of the hardware or software used in the creation of a CRM system environment. The term initially referred to the maker of equipment, but it has evolved into describing original software and unique protected methodologies. OEMs, such as Oracle, Microsoft, SAP, Salesforce.com, IBM, Cisco, and other various communication and hardware providers, maintain their brand presence when their products or services are embedded in the final solution. OEMs may work closely with VARs. Some OEMs work exclusively with VARs, as they remain focused on the creation of their solutions and not the installation and maintenance. Other OEMs provide the solution and can also provide installation and support. Large organizations planning on implementing enterprise-wide CRM solutions may work directly with OEMs for cost and service efficiencies, and they usually have a large enough IT infrastructure and staff to manage, under the guidance of the OEMs, the installation and maintenance of any CRM system. With these large investments, OEMs will have a concerted interest, due to the large revenue stream, and will provide services similar to a VAR. Small and medium-sized enterprises should be cautious, however, when dealing directly with OEMs, as they may not receive the same amount of "hand-holding" due to their lesser revenue potential.

8.6c Affiliate Partners

An organization's relationships with complementary companies may bring value to the organization's customers when the organization's customers have a need the organization cannot fulfill. An advertising agency, for example, may identify its customers' need for a CRM system and bring in a VAR who specializes in its customers' vertical market. The strength and trust of the relationship between the VAR and the advertising agency form the foundation for an affiliation partner relationship. In this example, the benefits to the advertising's client include a reduction in search time for organizations that can provide a CRM solution and economies of scale (related to time, knowledge transfer, and trust) due to the existing relationships between the advertising agency and the CRM solution provider. These benefits should ultimately lead to a reduction in total cost. Having affiliate partners adds value to an organization's total solution.

8.7 Other CRM Strategy Considerations

CRM strategies are discussed in more detail in other chapters. Some areas, however, require elaboration. Following are some key characteristics and trade-offs companies face when they create B2B CRM strategies.

CRM is a strategic methodology and not a technical solution. As we said before, technology is a CRM enabler. Unfortunately, some companies let technology drive their CRM strategy when it should be the other way around. CRM can be successfully executed with minimal technology. In fact, smaller businesses do not have the resources to purchase and maintain expensive technology-enabling software and hardware. Yet, many are successful in building and growing their customer relationships. This underlies the fact that while technology is a critical enabler for many organizations, successful CRM is all about building and growing relationships.

THEORY IN ACTION

P.F.A. Systems, Inc.—a Success Story

P.F.A. Systems, Inc. is a small Midwestern transportation business that specializes in the transport of chemicals, many of which are extremely hazardous. Its customers are extremely demanding, with very elastic service standard mindsets, and, by the nature of this industry, they do not enter into long-term contracts. Pat Anderson, founder of P.F.A., has instilled a sense of customer-centric urgency in his employees. Pat's approach to serving his customers is a classic example of what CRM epitomizes (i.e., the key to his success is based on relationships with his customers). This is evidenced by the fact that P.F.A. has lost only one customer in its lifetime, and that customer returned last year—a successful "win-back." P.F.A. has survived industry consolidation, and it is one of only two companies out of 20 that remain profitable and rapidly growing organizations.

Pat shared some of his key success factors while conducting a tour of his operations. "We answer the phone at the first ring and respond to customer e-mails within a few hours at the latest. All customer questions and issues are answered or resolved within the same day received, as myself and key personnel are on 24/7 for all customer communications. Our safety record is excellent; on-time delivery rate is 98 percent, even though most of our deliveries can be up to 400 miles away; and our drivers treat all customers with respect, present themselves professionally, and alert us days, nights, and weekends wherever we are to any customer issues immediately. All employees take advantage of an open-door policy." Continuing on, Pat says, "Reliability is critical to our business, and the people who have the biggest impact on the customer relationship are the drivers."

One key factor in sustaining reliability is Pat's choice of value chain partners. He is not so much concerned with price as he is with his supplier's reliability and knowledge. His customers view P.F.A. and its value proposition the same way, as Pat prices competitively but does not price low to attract customers. Pat has refrained from outsourcing maintenance on his tankers and praises the ability of his mechanics to ensure that his tankers meet all regulations, are safe, and provide for superior chemical quality transport. A new addition to Pat's staff, hired from a very large competitor, has found that Pat's approach is exactly what was missing in his former employer's strategy and, in fact, contributed to its recent decline in business. He feels it is the attention to detail, the employee morale, and the consistent and frequent customer interaction that create the customer intimacy and satisfaction that he found lacking at his former employer.

P.F.A. does not have any CRM technology, but it uses devices in its drivers' tractors for hands-free communications. With GPS technology, Pat or his staff, with one stroke on the keyboard, can tell where a driver is at any moment, the average speed, ETA, and other key service driver information. This enables Pat and his staff to anticipate and take appropriate action in advance to resolve potential issues before they may become a customer service problem.

P.F.A. Systems is so successful that its larger competitors pursue it as an acquisition target. One of its newly acquired customers exclaimed, "P.F.A. is one of the best-kept secrets out there in this industry." Existing customers continue to solicit P.F.A. to do more business with them, something P.F.A. turns down on occasion, as it would take the company out of its own core competency. As Pat states, "We have happy problems."

Interview with P. Anderson, owner of P.F.A. Systems, Inc. (December 1, 2011).

8.7a Employee Feedback Systems

Internal CRM is critical to external CRM. If employees are not engaging in productive relationships with one another, it is highly unlikely that they will foster positive outcomes with their business customers. One way of improving employee performance is with 360-degree feedback systems. With these tools, employees can receive feedback on their strengths and weaknesses from peers, subordinates, and managers. These efforts can tie into a discussion of employee appraisals and internal service-level agreements.

8.7b Core Selling Teams

Because the business customer often has varying needs and wants, customer needs–driven CRM strategies must be adaptable. Therefore, firms must search for ways to deliver value to their vast array of customers in an efficient, effective manner. A valuable CRM resource that enables firms to adapt to the needs of different customers is the core selling (CS) team. These teams are created around the needs of the customer. CS teams consist of selling organization members assigned to a particular customer. These members are actively involved in the development or implementation of the sales strategy for the customer. A study performed by D. B. Arnett and V. Badrinarayanan, which examined the CS team's ability to enhance the development of knowledge management competence and a relationship marketing competence, supports the growing need for a CS team approach. As the demands placed on selling organizations increase in the future, more firms will embrace customer needs–driven CRM strategies. Firms that understand the role that CS teams play in these strategies will have a competitive advantage over their rivals.[11]

8.7c Customer Contact Touch Points

Outsourcing customer contact touch points provides benefits but also comes with trade-offs. Noncore competency functions are normally outsourced because someone else can perform these functions better, faster, and cheaper. A CRM initiative creates an intimacy with the customer so areas of reliability, responsiveness, empathy, and assurance are highlighted. Outsourcing creates uncertainty with regards to these customer-sensitive areas. These areas, whether it be customer service, call centers, website management, order fulfillment, installation, maintenance, or billing, must be monitored, and quality measurement mechanics must be put in place. Using service-level agreements helps, but they do not ensure adherence to a CRM initiative.

8.7d Partner Selection

A B2B CRM strategy is only as strong as the weakest link in the organization's value chain. Organizations must assess what realistically can be expected of its partners in regards to their part in the execution of a CRM strategy. This places emphasis on partner selection. Partners must be included in CRM strategy formulation. Expectations of partners must be set and agreed upon. Formal agreement supported by contracts is optimal but not always possible.

8.7e Salespeople

A key component of any B2B CRM strategy is the salesperson. If the salespeople are successful, it increases the odds that the CRM initiative will be successful. According to E. Anderson and V. Onyemah,[12] strategy suffers and execution fails when companies don't help salespeople manage the tension between serving the customer and serving the company. They advocate that a holistic sales force control system can improve alignment and results. Their statistical study of more than 2,500 salespeople working in 38 countries for 50 companies suggests there are significant, often overlooked, differences between management systems that encourage salespeople to put the customer first and those that encourage sales reps to put their district or regional managers first. They advocate an evaluation of eight components across a continuum of outcome control at one end and behavior control at the other. The key is to be consistent across all of the following components:

1. Focus on performance criteria
2. Number of performance criteria
3. Degree of management intervention
4. Frequency of contact
5. Degree of management monitoring
6. Amount of coaching offered
7. Transparency of evaluation criteria
8. Compensation scheme

Outcome control is where the salesperson is critical to the sales process. Customers need information when the sale is open. Customers trust the salesperson, and there are many ways to complete the deal. Basically, the salesperson has autonomy. Behavior control, on the other hand, is where the sales manager is in control and there is a tendency to micromanage. This may be applicable in situations where the sales team has little experience, the company is trying to protect the brand, there are higher nonsale priorities, or it is hard to assign a sales credit. Either way, consistency across the components helps ensure successful strategy execution.

The realistic depth of the personal relationship that can or should be attained between a salesperson and a customer necessitates a priority scheme for key strategic areas. J. G. Tanner and colleagues feel that changes in resource allocation across customer-facing channels, and accompanying changes in relationship strategy, point to several issues at the strategic level that should be evaluated in light of the fact that the model of the one rep/one relationship no longer applies in a multichannel world.[13] The strategic issues they identified are account management issues, organizational structure, cultural and environmental issues, and enterprise-level knowledge management. They advocate more research in these areas in light of the multichannel effect.

When evaluating levels of trust between the salesperson and the customer versus the manufacturer and the customer, M. S. Kennedy, L. K. Ferrell, and D. T. LeClair found that the primary influences of customer satisfaction were, in order of importance, product quality, the ethical concern of the manufacturer (caring), the competence of the salesperson, and the use of low-pressure selling tactics. Familiarity with the product prior to purchase seemed to lower the customer's trust of the salesperson. Their research findings suggest that the trust of the salesperson must then be built on factors outside of the product itself and that buyers differentiate the roles of manufacturer (i.e., to create high-quality products) and sales agents (i.e., to match products with customer needs). This result may be common for business situations where the manufacturer does not technically employ the salesperson.[14]

8.7f Contractual Obligations versus Flexibility

Organizations must also evaluate the trade-offs between strict adherences to a contractual obligation versus being flexible. E. Roemer and M. Rese used a game-theory analysis to better understand this trade-off.[15] They found that the request for more flexibility in relationships is highly interrelated with the dynamics of the markets. In markets that potentially provide new business opportunities, relationship partners must retain a certain degree of flexibility to react to market changes, although this might result in less safeguarding of specific assets. Continuing on, they found that the management of the trade-off between the intention to safeguard a relationship against holdup by contractual commitments and the ability to respond to future changes is an important challenge in dynamic markets.

8.7g Customer Service, Satisfaction, and Retention

The degree of consistency in customer service has an impact on customer retention and satisfaction. M. Bruhn and A. Frommeyer examined relationship-marketing constructs over time in a B2B environment.[16] One of their findings identified core services and project management as two key areas that drive satisfaction. They also observed that rapid changes in customer service led to less of a dialogue between the customer service area and the customer. A reduction in dialogue led to lost up-sell and cross-sell opportunities and contributed to higher attrition. These are areas that should be addressed when evaluating the current CRM strategy.

8.7h Mobile Technology

Growth in mobile technology and applications requires companies to develop a dynamic 24/7, mobile CRM strategy. Choice of technology solutions, hardware, and software must be made, taking mobile requirements into consideration. This is easier to attain internally than it is externally with partners and other members of a value network. These mobile applications are becoming increasingly important to the CRM initiative.

Chapter Summary

CRM is very effective when integrated within the overall marketing strategy and can be a strategic advantage if the conditions are right and the CRM initiative is appropriately executed. Conditions are right if the marketing strategy is sound, measurable, and well executed. Attempting to build relationships when product quality is poor, service levels are subpar, marketing communications are confusing, price/quality perceptions are negative, or customer data is difficult to acquire or access, for example, will reduce or eliminate the effectiveness of any CRM strategy.

Implementing an expensive SFA system does not make sense if the salesperson avoids technology or adherence to dynamic information sharing. Additionally, not having specific measurable objectives can lead to poor or mismatched CRM design.

Maintaining relationships with uncooperative or weak value delivery network partners restricts any CRM initiative. Partner relationships are critical to success. Solution providers enter into a variety of partner relationships for different reasons. SaaS is a viable option, as it increases speed to market, reduces cost, and minimizes risk. The first step of any CRM strategy should be an audit of the current marketing and customer environment, including an assessment of the current value delivery network. The audit results should identify what needs to be changed and what limitations exist. Once the organization is comfortable with the audit results, it can then proceed to formulate a CRM strategy.

Key Terms

Cloud-based portals are entry points into a network from various locations using multiple devices and software for the purpose of accessing information that is stored in optimal locations on different hardware and electronic devices providing for access through the Internet or other electronic grid networks. An example would be the ability of having any update made to an Apple iPhone automatically sent to an Apple-supported server elsewhere (such as an iPad).

Concurrent users are people accessing the respective software simultaneously. Concurrent use usually results in an increase in computer processing capability and communication channel bandwidths.

Disintermediation is a CRM problem that occurs when one or more members in a network is bypassed.

Governance is a way of organizing transactions.

Internet-based B2B exchanges are electronic marketplaces that connect buyers and sellers efficiently and cost effectively.

Key performance indicators (KPI) are metrics that define and provide insight into a company's degree of financial and competitive success. Some examples of KPIs are cost per customer, customer retention rate, customer satisfaction rating, customer share of wallet, and customer lifetime value.

Knowledge management (KM) is a methodology that allows for the solicitation of knowledge from experts to be placed in a repository made accessible to people who need that knowledge.

Lead management software provides the salesperson with a method of managing all potential sales leads. It allows the flexibility for sharing of sales lead information among other salespeople as well as management.

Market orientation strategies include activities related to the focus on delivering to the customer.

Partner relationship management (PRM) is a business strategy for improving communication between companies and their respective value delivery network partners.

Relationship management strategy utilizes marketing orientation tactics. It is more about how the buyer and seller can attain a mutually profitable relationship with long-term strategic implications for both parties.

Sales force automation (SFA) is a methodology that leverages software and hardware to automate sales tasks of lead management, contact management, information sharing, inventory monitoring and control, order tracking, customer and prospect management, managing the sales cycle, providing sales forecast analysis, and salesperson rewards and performance management.

Social identity theory insinuates that a person perceives his or her social group to be the "in group," while those not in the group are considered to be in the "out group," implying that the in group is better and thus creates an "us versus them" conflict.

Software as a service (SaaS) is a method of delivering software over a network, usually the Internet. A software application company or reseller hosts the software applications, and the applications are made available for use for a fee. Software is not purchased.

Value delivery network (often referred to as value chain) is a group of organizations linked together in order to produce and market products and services for ultimate consumption.

Questions

1. What are major characteristics of a B2B environment relative to CRM efforts?
2. Why would relational contracts be adopted?
3. What is a value delivery network?
4. What is a reverse value delivery network?
5. What is sales force automation (SFA)? Define the major components of an SFA system.
6. What are some of the reasons why a salesperson would be reluctant to use an SFA system?
7. What are the advantages of using software as a service (SaaS)?
8. How does an affiliate partner differ from a value-added reseller (VAR)? Can they be the same?
9. What is a core selling (CS) team, and what are the advantages of using a CS team?
10. Within the context of sales force control, what is the difference between outcome control and behavior control? In what situation would outcome control be used? In what situation would behavior control be used?

Exercises

1. Identify members of a value delivery network that you purchase from as a consumer.
2. Identify two major SFA original equipment manufacturers (OEMs) and compare the differences in their offerings. Which would you choose and why?
3. Search the Internet for several SaaS providers and define their value propositions.
4. Define the major partner relationship management (PRM) solution providers. Compare how their offerings are similar and different.
5. Select a VAR and identify its relationships with OEMs.
6. Select a specific SFA, VAR, or CRM OEM and identify their affiliate partners. Define the synergies gained from the respective organization of choice, as well as what is gained from its affiliate partners.

Chapter 9

Understanding the Customer–Company Profit Chain: Satisfaction, Loyalty, Retention, and Profits

9.1 Key Constructs in the Customer–Company Profit Chain

CRM recognizes the importance of initiating, maintaining, and enhancing relationships with one's customers. The customer service delivery function revolves around CRM and is focused on satisfying customers, creating customer loyalty, and, whenever possible, creating commitment between company and customers. The hope is that satisfied customers will provide positive word of mouth, buy a greater variety of products and services, and trade up, which will in turn increase profits and improve company value (Figure 9.1). The marketing literature is rich in measures of **satisfaction** generated primarily by the services marketing field. All companies that have adopted the CRM orientation recognize the importance of providing quality service to maintain high levels of customer satisfaction. But will providing high levels of measurable satisfaction ensure that companies create a coterie of loyal customers, and will this in turn increase company profitability? Understanding the relationship between satisfaction, loyalty, and profits is critical to our development of CRM-generated marketing strategies.

If satisfaction is the key to creating, maintaining, and enhancing customer relationships, then measurements of CRM effectiveness can be based on the rich array of satisfaction measures that already exist, and marketing strategies can be developed that focus on increasing customer satisfaction. If satisfaction proves not to be intimately related to customer loyalty, then the reasons why must be established, and we must search for other CRM effectiveness measures and marketing strategies. This chapter discusses satisfaction, retention, and loyalty; their impact on profits; and how they can be influenced by marketing strategy.

Figure 9.1 The Customer–Company Profit Chain

9.2 Service Quality and Customer Satisfaction

Service quality and customer satisfaction are considered so important to U.S. businesses that each year the University of Michigan conducts a survey of customer satisfaction that examines customer perceptions of hundreds of companies in a variety of industries. The qualities of products and services are assessed by interviewing a total of 80,000 consumers on a quarterly basis regarding 200 companies and 40 government agencies.

While it is generally agreed that the concepts of service quality and service satisfaction are related, there is some confusion about exactly how the two variables relate to each other.[1] Some have suggested that customer satisfaction is transaction-specific, whereas a consumer's attitude toward an organization's service quality is an enduring attitude or global judgment.[2]

Overall or cumulative satisfaction is an evaluation based on the total purchase and consumption experience with a good or service over time, whereas transaction-specific customer satisfaction is an immediate postpurchase evaluation.[3] It is possible for a customer to experience low transaction-specific satisfaction but still have high cumulative satisfaction with a company. For example, a business traveler who has to wait a long time before checking into a hotel room and then finding out the hotel has no record of his reservation is bound to experience low satisfaction with the hotel for this particular transaction. He may have stayed at this particular hotel for a number of years without incidence, however, so the overall cumulative satisfaction with the hotel is still high. Transaction-specific satisfaction measures are more useful in determining the effectiveness of training or other quality improvement efforts. Cumulative satisfaction measures (measures of service quality) are more useful in determining the effectiveness of customer retention efforts.

Quality of service is what the customer, not the company, feels it is. A recent study showed that while 80 percent of the 362 companies surveyed felt they provide a superior service, only 8 percent of customers felt they received superior service from these companies.[4] Measures of service quality are discussed in Chapter 12.

9.3 Customer Satisfaction: Much Ado about Nothing?

> Customer research is a core discipline that should be embraced by CRM processes. Needless to say, I do not believe that the form this research should take is simply to manage "satisfaction." Satisfaction is only a very small part of the complex relationship (or lack of relationship) a customer or potential customer has with a brand.
>
> —J. Peel, *CRM: Redefining Customer Relationship Management*
> (Amsterdam: Digital Press, 2002).

Less than 30 years ago, service marketing was recognized as a unique branch of marketing with its own issues separate and distinct from tangible goods marketing. A separate stream of service marketing research was generated, resulting in contributions in the areas of service development, implementation, and assessment. Organizations needed to assess users' attitudes toward the quality of their service delivery, and the field of customer satisfaction measurement commenced. Restaurants, banks, airlines, hospitals, hotels, car rental agencies, insurance companies, and even universities and amusement parks queried their diners, account holders, passengers, patients, guests, customers, and students about the quality of service. This was the "Golden Age" of customer satisfaction studies. No effort was spared to ensure that customers were receiving the highest-quality service possible. The reasonable assumption was made that satisfaction does make a difference in maintaining and developing customer relationships and through better service would come higher profits.

One conclusion that seems to characterize the many diverse studies and contradictory findings with respect to customer satisfaction is that while satisfied customers may not remain loyal, dissatisfied customers certainly will not remain loyal if they have a choice. The vast majority of dissatisfied customers, reported to be as high as 90 percent in some studies, will not buy again from such companies.[5] Further, nearly all research studies have shown that dissatisfied customers tell more people about their bad experiences with a company than satisfied customers with good experiences. Satisfaction is, therefore, said to have an asymmetric impact on variables such as loyalty and profits. Thus, leaving a customer dissatisfied damages a company in two ways: loss of business from that customer and negative word of mouth leading to the loss of business from many others.

It behooves a company to strive to recognize dissatisfied customers and try to reverse a bad situation. Unfortunately, numerous studies have shown that only a small percentage of dissatisfied customers complain—usually less than 10 percent. T. Peters reported that 26 of 27 customers failed to report a bad experience.[6] Why? Perhaps because they felt that the time and effort involved was greater than the potential return they would accrue from the company satisfactorily handling their complaint.

THEORY IN ACTION

How a Bangkok Hotel Handles Customer Complaints to Increase Satisfaction and Loyalty

Handling customers' complaints satisfactorily is impossible if customers do not report them. Thus, companies must establish systems, procedures, and an underlying culture that views customer complaints as an opportunity rather than a threat. Tony Tuor, the late, Swiss-born executive manager of the Dusit Thani Hotel in Bangkok, could be seen every day talking with diners and hotel guests in one or more of the hotel's seven restaurants, soliciting their feedback regarding lapses in the hotel's service quality. Tuor once said, "I love when customers complain because that gives me the opportunity to solve their problem, provide a solution that exceeds their expectation, and cement the relationship. These previously dissatisfied customers will become more loyal to our hotel than if they didn't experience a lapse in quality service in the first place."

Now that we have seen the dire consequences that dissatisfied customers have for a company's business, let us turn our attention to the benefits that satisfied customers have. Here, the matter becomes less straightforward. The following are two definitions of what it means to be a satisfied customer:[7]

Satisfaction can be broadly characterized as a postpurchase evaluation of product quality given prepurchase expectations.[8]

Satisfaction is the consumer's response to and evaluation of the perceived discrepancy between prior expectations (or some other norm of performance) and the actual performance of the product as perceived after its consumption.[9]

Notice the similarity in these definitions of satisfaction: the comparison of prior service expectations with the actual service level received. This is referred to as the expectancy confirmation/disconfirmation model of satisfaction, wherein satisfaction is the difference between expectations and current experiences. If services rendered exceed what was expected, the consumer is satisfied. If services rendered are below what was expected, the consumer is dissatisfied. An important strategic outcome of this is that there are serious ramifications in store for those companies that promise more than they can deliver.

From the mid-1980s until 2000, service firms and academics worked diligently to establish the best ways to measure customer satisfaction. This focus on satisfaction was an attempt to fully comprehend the relationship between customer satisfaction and loyalty and how long-term relationships were more profitable than short-term relationships. As research results accumulated, however, some concluded that satisfied customers may not necessarily develop into loyal customers.

9.3a The Bond between Customer and Company

As a measure of the bond that exists between a customer and a company, satisfaction level was seen as appropriate and valid. However, B. B. Jackson identified three types of relationships—acquaintance, friend, and partner—that a company can have with its customers, and relationships based only on satisfaction were viewed as the weakest.[10]

1. An **acquaintance relationship** exists when a customer is satisfied with the product or service a company provides because it is on par with what he or she could get elsewhere. This implies that the satisfaction construct, in and of itself, cannot be expected to be a precursor to loyalty, since competitors' offerings are comparable with the selected offering, and any number of situation-specific variables could lead the consumer to switch to an alternate.
2. A **friendly relationship** exists when the customer trusts that a company provides differentiated value.
3. A **partner relationship** exists when the customer is committed to the company because it provides customized value. When there is commitment, both parties will do whatever is necessary to maintain the relationship. As such, partner relationships are more likely to occur in the business-to-business (B2B) sector, although they do occur in the business-to-consumer (B2C) sector as well.

Thus, the strength of a relationship, from weak to strong, moves from satisfaction to trust to commitment. Therefore, the satisfaction construct alone cannot be expected to lead to loyalty, since it indicates that only a weak bond exists between customer and company.

Organizations may want to determine what type of relationship—acquaintance, friend, or partner—characterizes ongoing customer–company bonds in their company or industry and then decide whether measures of satisfaction, trust, or commitment are most appropriate.

While satisfaction as a measure of a bond between customer and company may be a somewhat weaker construct than loyalty, research has shown a positive relationship between satisfaction and company financial performance. One study has shown that for every 1 percent, or 1 point, increase in satisfaction, a firm's market value increased from $240 million to $275 million.[11,12] Other research has shown that the satisfaction–profit link is asymmetric and nonlinear, with a 1 percent increase in satisfaction increasing return on investment (ROI) by 2.4 percent, but a 1 percent drop in satisfaction decreasing ROI by 5.1 percent.[13] The findings cannot be generalized, however, since the satisfaction–profit link varies by industry.

9.4 Customer Loyalty

THEORY IN ACTION

Behavioral versus Attitudinal Loyalty—The Case of Orange Juice

Whenever John Gordon goes to the store to buy orange juice, he buys Minute Maid. He buys a half-gallon per week and has purchased only Minute Maid brand for the past ten years, totaling 520 purchases. If one defines loyalty as the number of times a brand is purchased divided by the number of times the product category is purchased, John is 100 percent loyal to Minute Maid brand. His behavior never varies. He must really love the brand, right?

John lives in Nelma, Wisconsin, however, a town of less than 100, and he shops in the town's small grocery store. Minute Maid is the only brand of orange juice the store has room to carry. And actually, John does not really like Minute Maid brand orange juice. Does this change your perception of John's loyalty to the brand? John was loyal because of a situation-specific variable—availability—not because he preferred the brand.

Contrast John's behavior with that of a woman living in a major city who shops at a mega-market selling six different brands of orange juice and also buys Minute Maid 520 times without exception. She exemplifies the same behavior as John, and yet we ascertain a difference: she had a multitude of choices but chose Minute Maid every time. Certainly there is behavioral loyalty, but underlying this is a "preference" component. The woman could have selected five other brands but preferred to buy Minute Maid. In this situation, an attitudinal preference precedes behavior. For John, he either bought Minute Maid orange juice or went without. In both cases we see identical behavior, yet the underlying feeling toward Minute Maid orange juice could be extremely positive on the one hand and even somewhat negative on the other.

Researchers have still not developed a definition of *loyalty* on which everyone agrees, but there are four types of **loyalty**:

1. **Behavioral loyalty:** Simply look at the brand(s) purchased. John's loyalty can be referred to as "spurious," since he really doesn't like Minute Maid but buys it because he doesn't have a choice. His city counterpart also buys Minute Maid orange juice, but she buys it because she likes it more than the other brands. She therefore exhibits "affect loyalty": she buys it and likes it.

2. **Affect loyalty:** Affects are the feeling components of an attitude and include "liking" and "preference." Proponents of this approach state that loyalty is determined not simply by looking at what is purchased but also by looking at a person's "liking" and "preference" of the brand. Using this model, John Gordon would not be considered "loyal" to Minute Maid

brand orange juice, but his city counterpart would. Many feel that for true loyalty to exist, there must be affect loyalty—that is, a strong commitment to a brand. Many are committed to a brand because it represents the lifestyle they want to be associated with (Harley-Davidson, Jack Daniels, Starbucks), represents the values they identify with (National Geographic, John Deere), or represents prestige or quality (Rolex, Louis Vuitton, Bose). Affect loyalty really exists when someone has a brand such as Harley Owners Group (H.O.G.) tattooed on his or her arm. Affect loyalty means feeling strongly about the brand. This is true loyalty.

3. **Situation-specific loyalty:** Proponents of this approach state that the relationship between attitudes and behavior is moderated by other variables such as an individual's economic circumstances, personality, and the buying situation (on-the-shelf availability, low price, point-of-purchase displays, sales promotion). With this model, it is possible that a consumer may forgo purchasing a brand he likes and prefers because of another brand's promotion or availability.

4. **Latent loyalty:** John's favorite automobile is a Porsche. He is passionate about this brand, but he doesn't own one because he can't afford one. If one day his income increases so he can afford a Porsche, his latent loyalty will manifest itself, and he will then become the proud owner of a Porsche.

Figure 9.2 indicates four additional types of loyalty based on two dimensions: strength of the affect (liking and preference) toward the brand and likelihood of repeat purchase of the brand.

True loyalty is based on a strong positive "affect" toward the brand (i.e., liking and preference); therefore, it is the same as affect loyalty. Such positive feelings may lead to undivided loyalty or divided loyalty. Undivided loyalty exists when a customer purchases the same brand whenever purchasing an item in that product category—for example, the city orange juice purchaser. Divided loyalty is said to exist when consumers are loyal to two brands—for example, the beer drinker who only drinks Heineken or Beck's.

True loyalty can be temporarily interrupted when consumers occasionally seek novelty or a change of pace when buying items in a product category. They interrupt the purchase of their preferred brand(s) by substituting another. This has been called "novelty-seeking" behavior. For example, a teenager who loves Oreo cookies and buys that brand 90 percent of the time may occasionally purchase Chips Ahoy! and, thus, interrupt that loyalty. Such interruptions could occur not only because of novelty seeking but also because of the item being out of stock, special promotions, and so on.

When there is no feeling toward brands in a particular product category and the consumer purchases whichever brand the store sells (coffee filters, vegetable oil, sugar), there may be no loyalty

		Repeat Purchase	
		Strong	Weak
Strength of Affect	Strong	TRUE LOYALTY (Undivided or Divided)	SPURIOUS LOYALTY (Inertial Loyalty)
	Weak	LATENT LOYALTY	NO LOYALTY

Figure 9.2 Four Types of Loyalty

at all. "Convenience" goods are characterized by such brand indifference. Customers who exhibit spurious loyalty may purchase a brand due to situational constraints, a lack of viable alternatives (e.g., John's continual purchase of Minute Maid because it was the only brand sold), or out of convenience. Therefore, spurious loyalty is the same as situation-specific loyalty. Finally, latent loyalty characterizes a consumer who has positive feelings toward a brand but, for a variety of reasons, does not buy it—for example, someone who would like to buy a Porsche but cannot because she doesn't have the money.

THEORY IN ACTION

Put Down that Beer or Lose Your Job!

The day after Valentine's Day in 2005, an employee's picture was shown in the Racine, Wisconsin, morning newspaper. In it, he was celebrating the holiday with a bottle of Bud Light. When he arrived at work, he was called into his boss's office and fired. He worked for a Miller beer distributor and clearly was not exemplifying his company's brand values. If Miller beer had done a better internal marketing job, however, Miller would have become his "beer of choice."

Brands are not built by advertising and sales promotion alone. They are also built by customers' quality experiences with the brand. These experiences, to a large degree, are based on a customer's interaction with the company. When everyone in the company "lives" the brand, the brand's personality, attributes, and values are reinforced. Therein lies the major opportunity for CRM—the strengthening of the customer–company brand ties.

Employees at Inland Steel, a maker of cold-rolled steel for U.S. automobiles, were expected to drive autos produced in the United States as opposed to foreign cars not produced with U.S. steel. Anyone driving the latter and parking in the employee parking lot did so at the car's risk. One cannot imagine an executive at Lands' End wearing a Brooks Brothers sweater to work or a Nike executive wearing Reeboks. Employees can be expected to "live" the brand and convey their enthusiasm to customers.

A customer's feelings of liking and preference toward a brand may be based on one of four levels of the brand's meaning:

1. Liking and preference can be based on the benefits the brand provides. These benefits can be:

    a. Functional benefits (e.g., how the brand can provide a direct gain of security, health, or money)
    b. Emotional benefits (e.g., how the brand can provide a feeling of being "with it" or part of the in crowd)
    c. Internal benefits (e.g., how the brand can provide the feeling of self-satisfaction or having done the right thing)

2. The brand's personality conveys the type of personality the consumer would like to convey to others. Compare and contrast The North Face, Eddie Bauer, Patagonia, and Timberland brands with Barbie and Hello Kitty.

3. The brand's attributes have special meaning. BMW's "Ultimate Driving Machine" and Volvo's focus on safety are examples of ways companies make a key attribute part of the brand itself.
4. The brand conveys the company's values and the values of the company's host culture. For example, Japanese products in the 1950s were viewed as cheap and unreliable in the United States. By the 1990s, Japanese products were viewed as arguably the best in the world. This was due, in part, to the quality of major brands such as Sony, Lexus, Panasonic, Honda, and Toyota.

For decades, these four levels of brand meaning were conveyed primarily through mass-market advertising and sales promotion techniques. Today, the meaning of a brand can also be conveyed through CRM techniques based on one-to-one marketing. Robert Mondavi Winery projects an unobtrusive, refined, and personalized image to individual wine drinkers in its e-mail promotions. Its communications convey the beauty and serenity of the Napa Valley countryside, while providing the individual with high-quality wines. Lands' End's customer contact personnel strive to answer callers' questions regarding catalog items, even holding the items in their hand to convey the feel of the fabric. Amazon.com serves almost as a personal reference librarian in recommending books based on a reader's previous purchases.

9.5 Retention

F. F. Reichheld was one of the first to propose that companies needed to focus more on customer retention as opposed to acquisition. Along with W. E. Sasser Jr., he made a strong case that customer retention is a major driver of company profits. Reichheld and Sasser made the following points regarding the importance of retention:

- Customers defect at the alarming rate of 10 to 30 percent per year.
- A 5 percent increase in customer retention consistently resulted in 25 to 100 percent profit swings across all industries studied.
- Companies can boost profits by almost 100 percent by retaining just 5 percent more of their customers. For one auto service company, the expected profit from a fourth-year customer is more than triple the profit the same customer generates in the first year.
- Reducing defections by just 5 percent generated 85 percent more profits in one bank's branch system.
- Companies with loyal customers can financially outperform competitors with lower unit costs and high market share but high customer churn. For example, in the credit card business, a 10 percent reduction in unit costs is financially equivalent to a 2 percent decrease in defection rate.[14]

F. F. Reichheld, R. G. Markey Jr., and C. Hopton were not keen on measuring customer satisfaction, since they claimed that it is not related to customer retention. Instead, they stated that companies should carefully track repurchase loyalty as the "truer measure of how they stack up versus the competition." They stated that Lexus uses repurchase loyalty as its key satisfaction indicator.[15]

9.6 Satisfaction and Loyalty Factors

Loyalty measurement is the most fundamental and core CRM process. If we have no process for loyalty measurement, we cannot say with any degree of confidence how well the business (associated with the brand) is doing. . . . Loyalty is not about customer satisfaction or the measurement of it.

—J. Peel, *CRM: Redefining Customer Relationship Management*
(Amsterdam: Digital Press, 2002).

Loyal customers, high in repeat purchase behavior and strong in attitude, are, theoretically, the most desirable customers. . . . Loyalty indicates a commitment to the support of a relationship.
—W. G. Zikmund, R. McLeod Jr., and F. W. Gilbert,
Customer Relationship Management
(New York: Wiley & Sons, 2003).

Many factors influence a customer's level of loyalty with a company, product, or brand in addition to satisfaction. Following is a comprehensive view of such intervening factors that may negate or decrease the relationship between satisfaction and loyalty:

- The sheer numbers of competitive offerings that are on par with the company's offerings make it easy for satisfied customers to switch allegiance without any negative effects. Conversely, if few or no competitive offerings are available, a dissatisfied customer may, in fact, continue to purchase a product or frequent an enterprise he or she is unhappy with.
- The customer is looking for something new.
- The customer has no personal attachment to a brand with which he or she is satisfied.
- The product or service lacks consistency in performance.
- New competitors offer a better value.
- New competitors provide a greater variety of ancillary services that lead a satisfied customer to switch. Such ancillary services could include financing, guarantees, training, delivery, formulation, servicing, packaging, and so forth.
- With respect to customer retention, high expectations of future use may override low levels of satisfaction, and low expectations of future use may override high levels of satisfaction.[16]
- Customers may be very satisfied with a company's service and yet not want a long-term relationship with the firm. For example, some people cannot wait to stop doing business with major credit card companies even though their service is superb.
- Are consumers more likely to become emotionally attached to a brand of coffee filter, flashlight battery, or toothbrush on the one hand or a brand of watch (Rolex), luggage (Louis Vuitton), purse (Prada), or automobile (Mercedes-Benz) on the other? The former are convenience goods, and purchase depends more on availability than emotional attachment.
- Some market segments become so attached to certain brands that the brands become a central part of their lives—for example, Harley Owners Group (H.O.G.) members with their Harley-Davidson motorcycles.

Brands that provide consumers psychological and social benefits and brands that are highly visible are those through which strong relationships can be established. In such cases, convenience does not determine purchase; rather, satisfaction and loyalty drive the purchase decision.

McKinsey & Company recommends that companies develop a Loyalty Profile of their customer base that combines the elements of satisfaction, attitudes, and behavior. This results in three loyalist categories:

1. Emotive loyalists seldom, if ever, question the correctness of their brand selection.
2. Deliberative loyalists frequently compare their preferred brand against others and continue buying their preferred brand only if it merits selection.
3. Inertial loyalists are uninvolved and continue to select a brand because it is not worth the effort to switch.[17]

Different marketing strategies could be developed for each of the three loyalist segments. Further, companies might find it useful to compare the bond strength of their customers with the customer–company bond strength for their major competitors.

9.7 The Relationship between Satisfaction and Loyalty

The satisfaction/loyalty/repurchase model has a lot of academic and commercial support. Companies continue to invest in attitudinal satisfaction studies even though, as previously discussed, customers may have high satisfaction scores but defect anyway. Why do some researchers stress that satisfaction is intimately related to retention, but others caution that one should never relate satisfaction levels to retention?[18,19]

One can conclude that there are five reasons for such disagreement and that, upon further investigation, there may actually be no disagreement at all:

1. There is a relationship between satisfaction and loyalty, but it is not a simple linear relationship. V. Kumar and W. J. Reinartz state that the link between satisfaction and retention is asymmetric (dissatisfaction has a greater impact on retention than satisfaction) and nonlinear (the impact of satisfaction on retention is greater at the extremes, with the flat part of the curve in the middle called the zone of indifference) (Figure 9.3).[20]

2. One must make the distinction between spurious loyalty and true loyalty. The former can be generated in industries where competition is scarce, high-switching costs exist, or loyalty programs engender usage even when the service does not warrant it (Figure 9.4).

    Note, again, that there is no simple linear relationship between satisfaction and loyalty. With respect to autos, a concave relationship exists where even a slight drop from complete satisfaction causes a tremendous drop in loyalty. With local phone service, a convex relationship exists where customers are loyal (falsely loyal), even at high dissatisfaction levels. Thus, when it comes to measuring the effectiveness of CRM, a researcher must distinguish between true and false loyalty. As T. O. Jones and W. E. Sasser Jr. pointed out, to a much greater extent than previously thought, completely satisfied customers are more loyal than merely satisfied customers.[21]

3. Even though Reichheld, Markey, and Hopton provided findings that show that customers buy a lot more from companies with which they are completely satisfied, they merely hold to a more rigorous definition of "satisfaction" than most. To them, a customer is satisfied only if he or she is a "5" on a 5-point scale.[22]

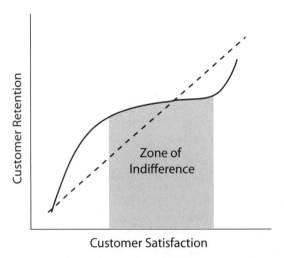

Figure 9.3 The Satisfaction-Retention Curve

Source: E. W. Anderson and V. Mittal, "Strengthening the Satisfaction Profit Chain and Journal of Science Research, 3, 2 (November 2000) 114. Reprinted by permission of Copyright Clearance Center.

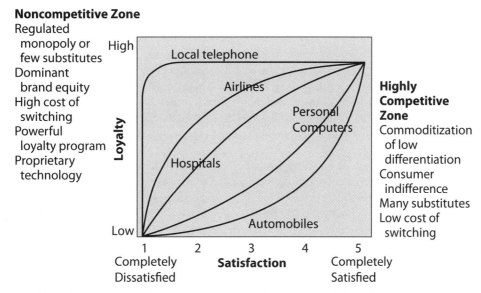

Noncompetitive Zone
Regulated
  monopoly or
  few substitutes
Dominant
  brand equity
High cost of
  switching
Powerful
  loyalty program
Proprietary
  technology

**Highly
Competitive
Zone**
Commoditization
  of low
  differentiation
Consumer
  indifference
Many substitutes
Low cost of
  switching

Figure 9.4 How the Competitive Environment Affects the Satisfaction–Loyalty Relationship

Source: Jones, T. O. & Sasser, W. E. (1995). Why Satisfied Customers Defect. Harvard Business Review, November-December, 88–99, p. 91. Copyright (c) 1995 by the Harvard Business School Publishing Corporation, all rights reserved. Reprinted by permission.

4. Many studies investigating the relationship between satisfaction measures (attitudinal measures) and other dependent variables (longevity, profits, providing positive recommendations, buying higher margin items) do not differentiate among first-time, short-term, and long-term customers. We posit that the relationships will be strongest for long-term customers with positive satisfaction scores and lowest for short-term customers with positive satisfaction scores. The former can be considered in a relationship, while many of the latter may turn out to be transactional buyers. This may result in their having high initial satisfaction scores but low scores on the dependent variables, such as retention.

5. Perhaps most important, your most loyal customers may also be your competitors' most loyal customers. Most loyal customers may not, in fact, be exclusively loyal. "Road Warriors" may actually be in the best customer segment for numerous airlines, many hotels, and several rental car agencies. This group may be highly satisfied with all company interactions, but one slight slip may cause them to defect, since there are so many high-quality alternatives. As G. R. Dowling and M. Uncles pointed out:

> There is reliable empirical evidence to suggest that many or most heavy users are multibrand loyal for a wide range of products and services. That is, a company's most profitable customers will probably be the competitors' most profitable customers as well.[23]

A. S. C. Ehrenberg found empirical proof for a logical corollary—namely, "100 percent of loyal buyers tend to be *light* buyers of the product or service" (emphasis added).[24] In other words, in many markets, the high-volume buyers split their purchases across companies, whereas the low-volume buyers are more likely to purchase from a single company. The implications for measuring the effectiveness of CRM efforts is that one must be careful in how loyalty is defined. Customers who are 100 percent loyal should be expected to be the most profitable. In actuality, those with divided loyalty may be a firm's most profitable segment.

9.8 The Relationship between Customer Loyalty and Company Profitability

Companies focus on developing a loyal customer base for profit. It seems intuitive that the longer loyal customers buy from a company, the more profitable the company is. Few would argue this in contractual situations—for example, between health clubs and their members or between phone companies and their subscribers. But these contractual settings should be contrasted with more transactional settings such as retail stores and their customers. Reichheld and Sasser's study showed that even a small increase in customer retention rates could have a major impact on profitability.[25] Reichheld and T. Teal showed that profits increase with the length of time a customer remains in a relationship with a company.[26] R. C. Blattberg and J. Deighton showed that it was much more cost effective for a company to retain its current customers than to acquire new ones.[27] R. J. Best said that retained long-life customers produce higher revenues and margin per customer than lost or newer customers and that total profits should increase over time.[28] These studies reinforced the benefits of what is called **defensive marketing** as opposed to **offensive marketing**.

The increased profits from loyal, long-term customers are said to accrue for a number of reasons:

- Increased number of purchases
- The tendency of long-term customers to "trade up" (i.e., to purchase more expensive items in a company's product lines)
- The tendency of long-term customers to lose their vigilance toward price and become less price sensitive. (The reasoning is that long-term customers, because they understand a company's procedures and product lines well, can extract more value in terms of convenience and purchase efficiencies and, therefore, are not as price sensitive as newer customers.)
- Word-of-mouth referrals among family and friends
- The supposed lower costs of servicing long-term customers, since greater knowledge of customer needs leads to greater efficiencies in meeting them

All of these factors have increased companies' efforts to retain current customers.

Recently, however, results of empirical studies have led to numerous qualifications regarding the preceding loyalty–profitability tenets. Uncles and Dowling cautioned, "In short, the contention that loyal customers are always more profitable is a gross oversimplification."[29] W. J. Reinartz and V. Kumar pointed out that if the cost of servicing customers is greater than the profit margin generated by customers, then profits will not increase over time, nor will the nature of the lifetime-profitability relationship be positive.[30]

Costs of servicing long-time customers can be high. Consider the catalog company that sends ten or more catalogs per year to a household that never buys. Consider the cost to a company that sends out millions of bills each month to customers with a $0 balance. Consider long-time customers who tie up the contact center personnel with constant complaints or consistently return merchandise. Finally, consider the significant costs associated with loyalty/rewards programs. Costs of servicing customers can actually exceed the profit margins they generate.

Does it truly cost less to service long-term customers than short-term customers? Those involved with B2B say "yes" because experience factors play a role in most of these relationships. When the transaction involves learning, long-term customers should cost less because the cost of educating them gradually decreases, while transaction efficiencies increase over time. For example, corporate tax accounting firms can service long-term clients more efficiently, since they have acquired a deeper knowledge of their business over time and trained the client in time-saving input routines. Those involved with B2C, however, point out that costs, such as mailing, are unaffected by a customer's tenure.

Reinartz and Kumar empirically tested the relationship between retention and profitability, and their findings contradicted many of the traditional tenets:

- In terms of profitability per month, short-lifetime but high-revenue customers were the most attractive.
- Profits for long-life customers did not increase over time.
- Short-life customers paid higher prices than long-life customers. This supported company managers, who said that long-term customers have a higher value consciousness (i.e., pay lower average prices).
- Some long-life customers may cost the firm more in the long run due to marketing expenses exceeding profits for this group.[31]

Their study illustrated the importance of weighing promotional costs against expected profits from varying tenured customer segments.

Additional empirical studies across industries will have to be conducted before the many tenets of the loyalty/profit relationship can be accepted or rejected. What can be recommended now, however, is that companies test these loyalty/profit tenets using their customer base. Transaction-based service companies, such as restaurants, hotels, and airlines, may have a significantly different loyalty/profit profile than health clubs, telephone companies, and insurers that have contractual service relationships with customers. In addition, companies producing highly identifiable products and services that are strong in psychological benefits and consumer involvement (university-degreed programs, professional sports teams) may have significantly different loyalty/profit profiles than companies producing products and services that are undifferentiated from their competitors (luxury hotels, airlines).

Based on a categorization of customers based on profitability (high-low) and Loyalty (high-low), here are the marketing strategies that researchers such as Reinhartz and Kumar would recommend:

> For high-profit/high-loyalty customers, use a CRP strategy: customize, reward, personalize.
> For high-profit/low-loyalty customers, try and OUTFOX the competition; in other words, this group probably divides their purchases among a number of competitors, so companies should try and increase their share by developing effective strategies and tactics. However, this must be done continuously because competitors will match the ones that prove successful.
> For low-profit/high-loyalty customers, X-RAY WALLETS—that is, separate the ones with the big wallets and market heavily to this group and not the other.
> For low-profit/low-loyalty customers, use the FAT strategy: "Forget about Them."

9.9 Loyalty/Rewards/Frequency Programs

THEORY IN ACTION

U.S. Mantra: Shop, Drop, Get Rewards

Financial adviser Ann Uno still talks about the dream vacation she took to New Zealand and Australia a few years ago, a trip largely financed by America's rewards economy. After cashing in her frequent flyer miles for that jaunt, Uno said she's now rapidly accumulating more mileage points through a rewards program that builds her account with every credit card charge.

She charged her daughter's college tuition to add 39,000 points and contemplated using a plan in which she could capitalize on mortgage payments. She used some of those miles to enable a friend to take a trip, and she holds some in reserve for emergency purposes.

Such behavior is not unusual. A passion for rewards that was born with Green Stamps has become a ubiquitous part of American consumerism for everything from buying a cup of coffee or loaf of bread to leveraging thousands spent to reap a trip or a plasma television in return.

The obsession for rewards has grown dramatically in recent years and so have corporate rewards programs aimed at attracting and retaining consumers. "Everybody wants something for nothing," said Uno, who nonetheless believes that the proliferation of rewards programs has hidden costs for society, her own rampant use of them notwithstanding.

As Americans pour into stores across the country on Black Friday, one of the busiest shopping days of the year, they will be able to take advantage of rewards programs in more ways than one—from points on credit cards to promotions such as two items for the price of one.

For almost every line of business, there is a rewards program available. Some aim to build brand loyalty, others simply to encourage spending. You can earn a free drink, a ticket to the Grand Ole Opry, a visit to the ski slopes, a ride in a hot-air balloon, rides at Disneyland and Disney World, and a free turkey—not to mention cold, hard cash—in return for credit card charges or debit card payments.

You can get bonus points for spending more than the average buyer at some stores or, in the case of one credit card, maintaining a good grade-point average in college. You can contribute to your college through these programs, and you can use them to save money.

Not Just for Credit Cards

Some credit cards provide rebates that can be applied toward college savings plans for children or grandchildren. The best credit card customers can call a special toll-free line where there is little waiting.

Rewards programs are expanding into every corner of the economy. "I think they are going to continue to grow in other industries beyond credit cards," said Gail Sneed, director of professional services for Maritz Inc.'s Loyalty Marketing Group in St. Louis. "We are starting to see them in more retail outlets. We may even start to see them in the pharmaceutical industry."

The explosion of rewards programs has become a distinct feature of America's consumer-driven culture and its inclination toward debt financing. It has given the impression that there is indeed a free lunch, although experts think these programs do have costs and lead people to make incentive-based choices.

Critics point out that sometimes there are catches—for example, the number of frequent flyer seats is limited on airlines, creating customer frustration. The choices have become as bewildering as they are creative, and some analysts said they are becoming too much of a good thing for some businesses. As these programs proliferate, they are losing their special character. Uno said many people find it hard to keep up with them, and it's difficult to maintain loyalty to one brand when there are so many programs.

Economists are undecided about the programs' real impact. They can help spur consumer spending, some say, or they simply might be a business cost. They are in essence price cuts, said Michael Drury, chief economist at McVean Trading and Investments, a Memphis futures company. If there were no such programs, he said, prices would be just as low because of competition.

Companies that adopt them often find they are involved in a "prisoner's dilemma," discovering that such programs often do not bring in the extra business they thought it would, said Scott Neslin, marketing professor at Dartmouth College's Tuck School of Business. He said they are easy to start, hard to end, and add up to a liability on the books of corporations.

"So many industries wish they could get out of their loyalty [rewards] programs," said Jack Aaronson, a New York consultant who writes an Internet column on marketing. "The airline industry spends millions of dollars a year just maintaining loyalty programs."

But there is a symbiotic relationship between airlines and credit card companies. When United Airlines went into bankruptcy in 2002, Bank One (since acquired by JPMorgan Chase) provided financing to help maintain United's MileagePlus frequent flyer program, said Chase spokesman Tom Kelly.

Experts on such programs say that if you don't have one, you are considered an outlier. "It has become a cost of doing business, almost a requirement," said Richard Metzner of Metzner Schneider Associates, a Dallas-based company that is itself a creation of the rewards economy. It advises clients on how to set up rewards programs that instill loyalty and increase returns.

Increasingly, corporations that adopt these programs are searching for ways to boost customer loyalty and build profits by offering creative new rewards, said Metzner and two of his associates, Howard Schneider and Kate Hogenson. Schneider said companies should move beyond the "mechanical" program of getting a point for every dollar spent. "You need to find more creative ways to get people involved with the brand," he said, such as offering special shopping nights for some customers and perhaps even a special service.

"There are too many dumb programs out there and not enough smart ones," added Hogenson, who is stationed in Chicago. Rewards programs that create an emotional attachment between company and customer are those that work best, she and her associates said.

Rewards programs also are catching on overseas, they said. Frequent flyer programs, now nearly a quarter-century old, are responsible for building the modern rewards programs, even though marketers had used gimmicks long before to try to attract and retain customers. The computer revolution lowered the cost of adding the programs. "We just have a huge list of credit cards," said Chase spokesman Kelly. "And the expansion has just been in the last five years or so."

Coffee, Colleges, and Causes

Like many other banks, Chase offers credit cards featuring rewards programs with businesses such as Starbucks and Sony, but it includes cards linked with organizations and colleges. You can contribute to Amnesty International or the Elks through its cards, for example.

Sneed of Maritz Inc. said awards are becoming more experience-based, such as going to a cooking school or learning to drive a race car. Universal Studios also auctions off movie props under its rewards program. When firms start rewards programs, they should expect that it will take a year to 18 months to break even. Retaining customers and building loyalty are key goals.

Washington political consultant Jim Duffy uses his corporate American Express card to build up frequent flyer miles, and recently he and his wife took a vacation to Scotland by using those miles to pay for the flight and two nights in a hotel. The reward was a powerful incentive. "When a bunch of us [consultants] take a client for dinner, you always get three guys going for their corporate Amex card so they can get the points. I go for the big bills. I let them take the small ones."

W. Neikirk, "U.S. Mantra: Shop, Drop, Get Rewards," *Chicago Tribune* (November 25, 2005).

Over the past few years, loyalty programs (LPs, or frequency programs) have become a key component of customer relationship management (CRM), serving a critical role in developing relationships, stimulating product and service usage, and retaining customers. Marketers have implemented such programs in a wide variety of industries, and more than half the U.S. (adult) population currently participates in at least one LP.

—R. Kivetz and I. Simonson, "The Idiosyncratic Fit Heuristic: Effort Advantage as a Determinant of Customer Response to Loyalty Programs," *Journal of Marketing Research*, *40*, 4 (November 2003): 454–467.

When one thinks of customer relationship management or relationship marketing, the most visible form is the loyalty/rewards/points/frequency program. **Loyalty programs**, frequently referred to as "points" or "rewards" programs, are offered by airlines, grocery stores, gas stations, hotels, car rental agencies, restaurants, coffee shops, book stores, and more.

We define rewarding as a customer's perception of the extent to which a retailer offers tangible benefits such as pricing or gift incentives to its regular customers in return for their loyalty. Frequent flyer programs, customer loyalty bonuses, free gifts, personalized cents-off coupons, and other point-for-benefit "Clubs" are examples of rewarding tactics.[32]

Frequent flyer programs that airlines offer are perhaps the most famous example of a customer loyalty program. Delta's SkyMiles, United's MileagePlus, and Continental's OnePass are all examples of frequent flyer programs. Typically, airline customers enrolled in these programs accumulate frequent flyer miles (kilometers, points, segments) corresponding to the distance flown on that airline or its partners. There are other ways to accumulate miles. In some recent programs, more miles are awarded for using co-branded credit and debit cards than for air travel. Acquired miles can be redeemed for free air travel, other goods or services, or increased benefits, such as travel class upgrades, airport lounge access, or priority bookings. Some airlines have programs that don't provide frequent flyers with anything extra other than the fact that they will not be charged for things that used to be free: extra leg room in economy class, first or second checked bag, and so on. The loyalty card in these programs is insurance protection against further declines in services.

Many companies offer loyalty programs for their elite customers. To earn a Platinum Preferred Guest status at Starwood Hotels and Resorts, you need to make 25 stays or spend 50 nights a year at Starwood properties. In return, you get free Internet access, access to the club lounge, and free suite upgrades. Lufthansa's HON Circle is reserved for customers who fly 600,000 miles over two consecutive years on Lufthansa or one of its partners. Singapore Airlines has a Priority Passenger Service plan for those who accumulate 500,000 miles under very tough admission standards: no partner flights count, and only seats in first and business class count. In return, these passengers get priority check-in, priority boarding, seat preference, special meal preference, waived or reduced fees, and personal escorts in and out of airports.

Many companies are getting innovative with their rewards programs. Hilton HHonors has partnered with General Electric Commercial Finance to offer loyalty points for investors in new Hilton Hotel developments. Those investing $10 million or more will get 2 million points—enough for 265 hotel nights. Jameson Inn provides repeat purchasers stock equal to 10 percent of their room rate after a three-night qualification stay.[33] AlleyCat Comics of Chicago has a very unique award that is probably not for everyone. People who accumulate 50 purchases are granted permission to punch a store employee in the stomach. The store owner expects to take all the hits.[34]

As you can see, types of loyalty programs are as prolific as an imagination allows, but they all have one thing in common: they provide cumulative economic incentives to those who buy the brand. In addition to loyalty programs, there are affinity programs and hybrid programs. With affinity programs, such as alumni associations, the purpose is to establish a dialogue between the organization and its constituency, not provide them with economic incentives. Hybrid programs offer characteristics of loyalty programs and affinity programs. College alumni can often get a MasterCard or Visa card sponsored by their college. The more the alumni use their cards, the greater the college's economic benefits from the sponsoring national charge card institution.

Many feel that loyalty programs don't build customer loyalty toward the company but rather build loyalty toward the loyalty program itself. Do United Airlines frequent flyers feel more loyalty toward United Airlines or the frequent flyer program it offers? Many would argue the latter. It is difficult for a company to develop a unique loyalty program, and, consequently, the programs themselves have taken on the look of commodities. The best loyalty programs differentiate among customers and are not simply mass-market oriented; further, the best loyalty programs acknowledge the importance of profitability and not simply purchase volume or frequency of usage. Are loyalty programs examples of CRM? They are, but only if the data obtained from participants is used to establish a dialogue instrumental in attracting, retaining, and developing them as customers, which is not always the case. As mentioned elsewhere in this book, a large grocery chain has millions of loyalty program participants but has never used this information to manage these customer relationships. Imagine the possibilities. The grocery chain has historical grocery purchases patterns and could easily develop cross-selling or up-selling promotional tactics. All loyalty programs are structured to collect participant information up front. If this information is used to customize offerings and communications vehicles for participants, the loyalty program becomes a CRM program.

9.9a Why Loyalty Programs Are Popular

The 2011 Colloquy Loyalty Census revealed that for the first time in history, the number of loyalty memberships in the United States exceeded 2 billion, netting out to more than 18 memberships per household. The census also provided counts for U.S. loyalty program membership by sector, shown in Figure 9.5. So what accounts for their popularity?

Sector	Value
Financial Services	428.8
Airlines	324.9
Specialty Retail	286.8
Hotel	176.8
Grocery	173.7
Gaming	133.0
Mass Merchant	129.7
Department Store	113.9
Drug Store	98.1
Fuel & Convenience	31.9
Car Rental & Cruise	17.8
Restaurant	9.7
Other	164.1

Figure 9.5 U.S. Loyalty Program Membership (in millions) by Sector, 2010

Source: Reprinted with permission from COLLOQUY (www.colloquy.com).

1. Because the consumer today faces so many undifferentiated, acceptable, and ever-changing alternatives, companies must continue to move ahead in order to stand still. Loyalty programs are in many respects defensive measures to maintain one's customer base and not lose it to a competitor. As such, a loyalty program may not attract many new customers to the firm, but it should prevent attrition from customers joining a competitor's program; as such, loyalty programs provide companies with barriers to exit.

2. A unique loyalty program may move a company from an awareness set in a consumer's mind to a consideration or choice set. For example, with all of the loyalty programs available in the hotel industry, a traveler may not even consider staying at one that does not offer a loyalty program.

3. Loyalty programs provide members with financial incentives. REI charges consumers $15 to become a rewards member. Once a member, consumers receive 10 percent off their purchases for one year. After a United Airlines frequent flyer club member flies 60,000 miles, he or she is entitled to a free round-trip ticket to Asia worth approximately $1,500.

4. Loyalty programs can be structured in such a way that they not only encourage positive word of mouth but also offer incentives for bringing friends and family into the program network.

5. Loyalty programs can be used to create a database. Companies today are asking for more and more customer information. In order to capture this information, which customers often view as an annoyance, companies have to give something in return. Very often that something is the incentive contained in a loyalty program.

6. Loyalty programs can be the nexus for a marketing alliance. The Star Alliance, consisting of United Airlines and its global partners, develops a sense of identity by all members sharing in the same rewards program.

7. Loyalty programs may enable companies to obtain a greater share of wallet, since members may consolidate their purchases with the company in order to earn greater rewards. In addition, customers may make additional purchases in order to reach a higher tier of rewards. For

example, a Premier Platinum member in United Airlines' MileagePlus frequent flyer program may take an unnecessary flight of 5,000 miles at the end of the calendar year to reach the Premier Gold level to receive more benefits for the upcoming year.

8. Loyalty programs can help a company earn a profit. American Airlines' AAdvantage frequent flyer program makes a substantial profit selling miles to other businesses to use as rewards for their customers.

9.9b How Well Do Loyalty Programs Work?

P. C. Verhoef studied the effects of relationship marketing instruments (RMIS) on customer retention and customer share development over time. RMIS consisted of loyalty programs and direct mailings and were of two types: those that provided economic incentives such as rewards and pricing discounts and those that provided a more personal touch by stressing social attributes. Verhoef found loyalty programs useful in two ways. First, they lengthened customer relationships, and second, they enhanced customer share. Loyalty programs with economic incentives led to greater customer retention. The positive impact of RMIS, however, was not large—less than 10 percent of the total explained variance in both customer retention and customer share development.[35]

It should be noted that Verhoef's study focused on insurance products. Such products are infrequently purchased, and the switching costs are high. Consequently, the results of this study should not be projected to other industries. The results, however, are useful as a cautionary note with respect to having unrealistically high expectations for a company's RMIS. Another study of loyalty programs suggests that members of loyalty programs are generally less sensitive to diminished quality ratings of the company and less sensitive to overall price advantages that competitors might have versus their company. Loyalty members perceive they are getting better quality and service for the price (i.e., good value).[36]

THEORY IN ACTION

Frequent Flyer Program

A businessperson flying from the United States to Thailand needs to select a carrier. She loves Singapore Airlines because of the great food, space, entertainment selection, and personalized service. There is really only one thing that she does not like about Singapore Airlines: Singapore Airlines' frequent flyer program requires many more flight miles to earn a free trip to Asia or Europe than United Airlines does. After some evaluation, she makes her decision—United Airlines.

This vignette exemplifies a number of things that we covered in this chapter. First, satisfaction does not necessarily lead to purchase. The businessperson loves Singapore Airlines but does not select it. Second, there is power attached to loyalty/frequent flyer programs. She rates Singapore Airlines higher on all attributes but one—its frequent flyer program—but that one attribute causes her to select United Airlines. Third, it could be said that her loyalty is directed toward United Airlines' frequent flyer program as opposed to United Airlines itself. Fourth, we have a situation in which the person exhibits behavioral loyalty but not attitudinal loyalty toward United Airlines. This is important because it means that this customer is not committed to United and may switch as soon as competitive offers are at par with United's.

Chapter Summary

This chapter investigates recent findings with regard to the relationships among variables in the "customer–company profit chain": service quality, customer satisfaction, retention, loyalty, customer profitability, company profitability, and value. Each variable is quite complex. For example, there is behavioral loyalty, affect loyalty, situation-specific loyalty, true loyalty, spurious loyalty, and latent loyalty. There are many diverse and contradictory findings with respect to customer satisfaction and loyalty, and customer retention and profitability. We saw the many factors that intervene between customer satisfaction and customer loyalty, making the relationship between the variables quite weak, and the effectiveness and success of loyalty/rewards/frequency programs.

Key Terms

Acquaintance relationship is a relationship where the customer is satisfied with the product or service a company provides because it is at parity with others.

Affect loyalty is an affective definition of loyalty based on a customer's liking and preference toward the brand. When a strong affect combines with consistent brand purchase, one has true loyalty.

Behavioral loyalty is a conative definition of loyalty based simply on what is purchased as opposed to why it is purchased.

Defensive marketing is marketing strategies and tactics aimed at current customers and focuses on retention, cultivation, development, and win-back.

Friendly relationship is a relationship in which the customer trusts that a company provides differentiated value.

Latent loyalty describes consumers who feel positively toward a brand but, for a variety of reasons, do not buy it.

Loyalty is a customer's attachment to a brand, store, manufacturer, service provider, or other entity based on favorable attitudes and behavioral responses such as repeat purchase. This definition implies a need for both behavioral (conative) and attitudinal (affective) elements.

Loyalty programs are often called frequency programs, points programs, or rewards programs. Loyalty programs serve a critical role in developing relationships, stimulating usage, and retaining customers. All loyalty programs provide cumulative economic incentives to those who buy the brand.

Offensive marketing is marketing strategies and tactics aimed at acquiring new customers and increasing the total number of customers for a firm.

Partner relationship is a relationship in which the customer is committed to the company because it provides customized value, often in the form of a structural component.

Satisfaction is a postpurchase evaluation of product or service quality given prepurchase expectations. When experience exceeds expectations, one is satisfied. When expectations exceed experience, one is dissatisfied.

Situation-specific loyalty is a type of loyalty in which the relationship between attitudes and behavior is moderated by other variables such as an individual's economic circumstances, personality, and the buying situation.

True loyalty is based on strong positive "affects" toward the brand that lead toward undivided loyalty (consistent brand purchase) or divided loyalty (primary purchase with an occasional deviation for novelty purposes).

Questions

1. Customer complaints are usually viewed as bad things companies should avoid. What are the benefits complaining customers can provide a company?
2. As a measure of the bond that exists between a customer and a company, satisfaction was previously seen as key. However, some view company–customer relationships based only on satisfaction as weak. What types of relationships can exist between customers and a company?
3. Researchers today have still not developed a definition of loyalty upon which everyone agrees. There are at least three different definitions of loyalty in use today. What are these three definitions of loyalty?
4. Explain what is meant by Figure 9.2 on page 222.
5. A customer's strong feelings of liking and preference toward a brand may be based on one of four levels of meaning the brand has for them. What are these levels of meaning?
6. What are some of the intervening variables that can exist between satisfaction and the creation of loyalty between a company and its customers?
7. One of the reasons that companies focus on developing loyal customers is that long-term customers are felt to be more profitable. Explain why many propose a strong correlation between loyalty and profits.
8. Why have loyalty programs—also referred to as frequency, points, or rewards programs—become so popular?

Exercises

1. Toward which companies, brands, or products do you have an acquaintance relationship? Friendly relationship? Partner relationship?
2. Which products, brands, or companies have you recommended to your friends? Toward which products, brands, or companies have you spread bad word of mouth? In both instances, explain why.
3. Describe any products, brands, or companies that you deal with that are best described in terms of behavioral loyalty, affect loyalty, and situation-specific loyalty.
4. Describe any products, brands, or companies that you deal with that are best described in terms of true loyalty, spurious loyalty, latent loyalty, and no loyalty.
5. Pick a brand or product that you feel strongly toward and describe the benefits that it provides you in functional, emotional, and internal benefit terms.
6. What brands can you think of that have a strong personality for infants, toddlers, preschool children, children ages 6 to 10, preteens, and teenagers?
7. What brands can you think of that have a strong personality for college students, young adults, adults in their 30s, and retired seniors?
8. Are there any products or brands that you are satisfied with and yet are not predisposed toward loyalty?

Chapter 10

The CRM Strategy Cycle: Acquisition, Retention, and Win-Back

TOPICS

10.1 The CRM Strategy Cycle   10.2 Is CRM for Everyone?

10.1 The CRM Strategy Cycle

Although CRM as a value proposition is a long-term strategy whereby an organization develops systems to manage its customer relationships, management often loses sight of short-term opportunities. McKinsey & Company reported that significant profitability can result in the short term through what it refers to as "tactical CRM." For tactical CRM to result in quick wins for an organization, it must first determine which stage of the **customer–business life cycle** it wants to focus on: acquisition, development, cross-selling, up-selling, retention, servicing, loyalty, or win-back. Next, tactical CRM uses existing information and processes to determine which profit opportunities exist in the identified stage. Finally, tactical actions are taken to capitalize on these insights.[1]

Companies selling contract services (telecommunications, magazines, health club memberships) traditionally focus on customer acquisition, retention, and win-back. Companies that have created high exit costs for customers (retail banks) focus on customer development. Fashion retailers focus on cross-selling and up-selling to elite market segments. Automobile manufacturers focus on up-selling. Some organizations, such as supermarkets, with their loyalty programs, and university alumni associations, with their affinity group programs, do far less than they are capable of in the areas of strategic and tactical CRM.

Quick wins create profit opportunities and counteract the contention that all CRM initiatives take too long to build and too long to produce profitable results. Most of the benefits that accrue through tactical CRM are due to manipulating current information within existing databases. This yields the customer segments that will be the focus of solicitations in the acquisition stage, cross-selling and up-selling in the development stage, targets in the retention stage, and so on.

10.1a Acquisition Strategies

Some may consider acquisition outside the scope of CRM systems. After all, acquisition strategies are aimed at prospects, not customers. Once prospects become customers then, the reasoning goes, retention strategies can develop the business, and win-back strategies can regain the business if lost. Since companies can lose 20 to 40 percent or more of their customers every year, however, acquisition strategies are necessary to feed the company's pipeline with prospects that hopefully will soon become customers. Companies need to mine their databases to identify the types of prospects who are likely to respond to acquisition efforts and become customers.

Mass media advertising is still the most widely used means of reaching the masses. Acquisition strategy continues through attempts to capture potential customers' identities and begin a dialogue. Creative approaches get prospects to identify themselves as interested in a product or service. BMW required viewers to provide their name, e-mail, and other information as a prerequisite for viewing online films. Leads can also be generated through partnerships with major portals, such as Yahoo! and AOL. Direct mail and sales promotion, such as games and sweepstakes, can also be used to develop a prospect list. Companies such as L. L. Bean and Chicago-based Plain-Spoken Furniture have used search engine optimization strategies to acquire new prospects by increasing the chances of generating their reference when typing in merchandise keywords. Keyword-rich copy can move a company up in the queue on search engines such as Google or Yahoo! Keywords should describe the products and services you offer. Include brand names if you offer them because many people search on the basis of brand names. Search engines pay even more attention to your keywords if they appear in bold type or in photo captions. Also, the more links your site has, the higher your rankings. Craig Klucina, owner of Plain-Spoken Furniture, has experienced a huge increase in traffic since he inundated his site with the keywords "Chicago Tansu" and "Chicago Shoji," which describe the furniture and Asian screens that he sells.

With respect to developing effective acquisition strategies, the following should be kept in mind:

1. **Reduce adverse selection.** Adverse selection involves targeting individuals who will have no interest in your offering or, if they do apply, will not qualify for your offering (e.g., charge cards and loans). Adverse selection hurts companies in two ways: wasted time and money in promotional efforts and negative word of mouth that inevitably results when applicants must be rejected. Alaska Airlines customizes advertising based on "cookies" (a small piece of code stored on a person's computer that contains personal information about the user). Alaska Airlines selects ads for each individual computer based on the information found in these cookies, such as whether the person has ever visited the company's website, where the person lives, the number of times the person has seen an Alaska Airlines ad, and so forth. People who have visited Alaska Airlines' site receive ads that are different from those who haven't visited the site. In addition, Alaska Airlines offers different flight prices to different people. (Airlines can offer special deals to particular individuals as long as those fares are not published.)[2]

2. **Develop the acquisition program/offer through qualitative and quantitative marketing research.** This helps determine the benefits and weaknesses of your proposed program versus competitors' programs. The last thing one of the authors wanted was another charge card. He has thrown out scores of direct mail that banks promoting their charge cards have sent over the past decade. However, he recently received an acquisition promotion piece that he kept. In fact, he applied for the Capital One® No Hassle Miles Ultra Visa® charge card. Why? Because as a frequent flyer, the card's acquisition program has none of the major deficiencies of the other frequent flyer cards: no blackout dates, hardly any airline selection restrictions, and no annual fee. In addition, the interest rate is low, balance transfers from other charge cards are free and done by the bank, and 5,000 bonus miles are awarded with the first purchase. What more could anyone want in a frequent flyer rewards program charge card?

3. **Switching costs should be eliminated.** As previously noted, Capital One® closes all of the applicant's other accounts, if desired, with no cost or effort required on the part of the applicant. This acquisition strategy sucked millions of customers away from more established companies.[3]

4. **Take advantage of acquisition timing.** Present your offer to the consumer at an appropriate time that coincides with life cycle or buying cycle changes. Allow enough lead time for your acquisition promotions to precede births; moves; retirement; children going to college; and contract renewals for insurance, telecommunications services, health care, and so on.

5. **Encourage word-of-mouth referrals** by paying for them (or offering discounts) or marketing to affinity groups that endorse your product to their members.

R. Kivetz and S. Itamar introduced the concept of **idiosyncratic fit heuristic**—the tendency for customers to be enticed by offers for which they enjoy a relative advantage. They reported on findings that men are significantly more attracted to a selectively hard-to-date woman (i.e., a woman likely to date the subject but unlikely to date all other men) than a uniformly hard-to-date woman or a uniformly easy-to-date woman. The authors proposed that increasing program requirements can enhance consumers' likelihood of joining the program if they feel they have an advantage over others.[4]

For example, the idiosyncratic-fit heuristic suggests that a person who flies regularly to the Middle East and Southeast Asia from the United States would be attracted more to a frequent flyer program featuring that as a requirement rather than a standard frequent flyer program. The trick is to make the recipient feel that they, but few others, can qualify while, at the same time, not appearing too deliberate in the program requirements.

The key to making the idiosyncratic-fit heuristic work for an organization is to balance customized requirements with a standardized program—in other words, promoting numerous idiosyncratic-fit requirement packages that all result in the same program rewards for different segments. Capital One® offers 6,000 different kinds of credit cards, each with slightly different requirements, benefits, terms, and type of monthly statement. Some pay nothing annually for the card, while others pay $29 or more. Some have a picture of a moose on their card, while others have a picture of Mt. Fuji. Some have $30,000 credit lines and others only $200. Capital One® presents itself a little differently to each potential cardholder, and each potential cardholder receives a "bundle" of card attributes that appear suitable for only a few people like themselves.[5]

10.1b Retention Strategies

While acquisition strategies are necessary to fill the pipeline with customers to counter inevitable attrition, it should be remembered that customer equity is more dependent on customer retention than customer acquisition.[6] For most firms, improving customer retention can lead to very significant increases in profitability. Retention strategies work best when industry retention levels are high and there is a significant steep skew in a company's customer base. In such situations, over time, a small 5 percent increase in retention can increase a company's profitability to over 85 percent. Retention strategies are profitable not only because of increased revenue from loyal customers but also, some say, because of reduced costs in serving long-time customers.

THEORY IN ACTION

The Harley-Davidson Posse Ride: A Successful Brand-Building Retention Strategy

A famous example of company–customer bond building is the annual Harley-Davidson Posse Ride in which Harley Owners Group (H.O.G.) members ride across major parts of the United States (e.g., from South Padre Island, Texas, to Minot, North Dakota) and spend a week to ten days with other H.O.G. members and executives from the Milwaukee-based company. It is an adventure that bonds riders to the company and brand for life. The prize for each participant is a shirt celebrating the achievement. Each shirt attracts attention from Harley riders who did not take the Posse Ride (less than 1,000 are taken) and non-Harley owners over the shirt's lifetime.

S. Fournier, "Building Brand Community on the Harley-Davidson Posse Ride," *Harvard Business Review* (August 23, 2000).

When developing retention strategies, it is important for companies to target only those customers whose retention will be profitable. Best Buy, for example, employed a "customer centricity" program that focused on identifying and targeting the most lucrative customers, while avoiding their "demon customers"—those who consistently tie up a salesperson but never buy anything, or buy only during big sales, or take advantage of the return policy by filing for a rebate and then returning the item. Fubon Financial Holding Company of Taiwan and Hong Kong, with over 5.8 million customers worldwide, implemented software that found that 2 percent of its customers contribute more than 90 percent of the bank's overall profit. With that knowledge, Fubon uses its database marketing programs to focus more on those valuable clients. Let us envision what a hypothetical wine seller could do to retain his customers.

A WINE SELLER'S CUSTOMER RETENTION STRATEGIES

- He could offer financial incentives to wine club members, such as offering every twelfth bottle free; a 10 percent per-purchase discount; a cumulative discount at year's end, the amount of which increases with the annual amount purchased; discounts for purchases of wine accessories; and so on. The frequent wine buyer incentives are analogous to frequent flyer incentives in that they are both rewards for purchase.
- She could communicate with customers regarding special sales and offerings via interactive technologies, such as 3G and 4G cell phones and social networking websites such as Facebook and Twitter. Using GPS technology, the wine merchant could even send these messages to those walking or driving in the area of the shop.
- He could offer in-shop wine-tasting parties, wine and cheese parties, personalized tours to wine regions in California and France, and in-home wine-tasting events (à la Tupperware parties). He could surprise wine club members with a gift of wine on their birthday or anniversary. Any of these activities help create a bond between the wine establishment and its customers. Over time, the proprietor may become more of a friend than a salesperson—a lifestyle guide as opposed to just a wine seller.
- The wine shop could provide wine collectors with a computer program geared toward helping them create a sophisticated global wine collection. The creation of such a collection would take years—in fact, it would be ongoing and never ending. The seller

would make regular recommendations with respect to great country vintages available for purchase. Variables entered into the program could be customers' preferred price levels, estimated amount of time the consumer wants to spend in completing the foundation of a good wine collection, and the purpose served by the wine collection (investment, consumption, or both). Once customers access the wine store's computer program and begin their collection based on store recommendations, switching wine stores becomes unlikely. The customer has too much time, effort, and information invested in the effort. Further, the service is mobile, allowing the wine store to keep customers regardless of their residence.

Which retention strategy is best: the rewarding, the bonding, or the service structure strategy? While industry, product type, and company objectives and costs affect the strategy emphasis, companies should try to implement all three.

It is important to retain customers through your CRM systems at each stage of the customer life cycle. The percentage of customers a company loses in a year, or other interval, is called "churn." Retention rate is 1-churn. Some churn is normal and cannot be prevented. For example, families will not buy diapers forever no matter how effective a company's marketing mix. Some churn can be prevented, however, especially churn due to dissatisfaction.

Retention strategy is based on two types of bonds: programmatic and humanistic. **Programmatic bonds** consist of rewards programs (priority treatment with regard to notices of sales and events, tickets, invitations, free merchandise, etc.) and procedures that make it difficult for customers to switch providers (termination penalties, lengthy forms to complete, lengthy time involved, etc.). **Humanistic bonds** refer to the treatment given to customers by highly trained personnel.

E-marketing (through e-mail and e-newsletters) and social networking have become two of the most cost-effective ways to retain customers and gain a greater share of wallet. Companies can also develop computerized systems that can personalize offerings by tailoring products and services to specific customers. Recommendations can be made based on the buyer's purchase history and the history of buyers similar to them. Amazon.com has a widely admired system of this type. TiVo automatically recommends television programs to users based on programs they have watched.

With regard to complaint handling and problem resolution, customer contact personnel can be trained to provide outcomes to customers based on their value to the company. After viewing a customer's value profile, they can choose to "accommodate" a high-value customer completely; compromise with a medium-value customer; and not accommodate the low-value customer, letting him or her terminate the relationship if so desired.

10.1b.1 CRM: Attaining Intimacy through Marketing

Conversational marketing, dialogue marketing, and event-based marketing techniques have made communication on a timely and informative basis possible. Conversational marketing is about building customer lifetime personalized dialogues across all marketing channels. It reflects the interactive nature of conversation that now exists between companies and their customers, whether outbound or inbound. As Capital One® has discovered, inbound customer contact is a much more conducive environment for cross-selling than outbound customer contact. Conversational marketing technology offered by companies such as Neolane enables a company to track and manage all marketing activity in order to generate targeted messages and the most relevant offers based on customer behavior and preferences.[7] Conversational marketing technology must provide a real-time single view of the customer, a catalog of marketing offers, and a recommendation engine that delivers personalized offers based on an individual's profile and behavior. The recommendation engine generates the best offers per contact based on context. For example, for a 3G or 4G phone it may be a personalized SMS message, whereas for a call center it may be a customized script.

Dialogue marketing is a more continuous, or "streaming," technology capable of generating a running dialogue with a customer based on every customer interaction with the business. Dialogue marketing is a fusion of personalization strategy and database technology and is very sensitive to the intervals between customer purchases, store visits, and contact. Based on customer events, the technology generates appropriate messages. For example, a change in the customer's life stage (e.g., birth of a child, retirement, marriage), change in purchase behavior (e.g., cross-category purchase, a purchase crossing a volume or profit threshold, change in CLV), or demographic change (e.g., address change) will trigger different types of messages across the appropriate channel. There are foundation dialogues that require only basic customer information; dialogues that are event centric; dialogues that are predictive of defection or purchase behavior; and dialogues that are on-site messages based on RFID cards or smart shopping carts.

Dialogue can be based on a wide variety of customer labels: inactive, new business, decliners, incliners, past due, due now, etc. The purpose of dialogue is to move customers from negative to positive status.[8]

Many firms are turning to technology to deliver the "high-touch" personal services that their elite clients expect. For example, Wachovia's Wealth Management division generates 15 contacts with new clients during the first four-month period. "Handwritten" notes can be generated via an online system that replicates them en masse. Regular contact by phone, mail, or e-mail is maintained by wealth advisors through 28 contacts during the year with elite clients.[9]

Event-based marketing (EBM) is based on the premise that consumers are more likely to respond positively to company offers at certain points in time; for example, immediately after they purchase a product, reach an age threshold, change address, enter a complaint, visit a website, etc. Instead of pushing products en masse, Fubon Financial Holding Company of Taiwan and Hong Kong wanted to become more customer focused and personalize their offerings. Using their data warehouse, Fubon has identified more than 400 events in a customer's life that enables them to target the right customer at the right time with the right offer through the right channel. Their system scans the database each night to identify customers needing attention. Thus, Fubon's offerings and contact with customers is need based. Fubon estimates an 850 percent return on investment from its enterprise data warehouse and related technology.[10]

10.1b.2 Moments of Truth

When emotions run high for customers, timely assistance or lack of assistance from a company will never be forgotten. Every day, there are countless "moments of truth" (instances of contact between a customer and a firm that gives the customer an opportunity to form an impression about the firm) that can have a dramatic impact on which customers stay and which ones defect. For example, after a customer complains or enters a warranty claim, there is a "moment of truth" in how a CSR responds. In that moment, a business can lose or retain the customer. It can create a loyal advocate or a vocal critic, or the customer may quietly disappear. Understanding these "moments of truth" and empowering and training employees to deal with them is a huge part of customer retention, as companies that can promptly assist customers in these "moments of truth" will create an emotional bond with the customer that will deepen the customer's trust and commitment with the company. McKinsey & Company states that one bank in North America experienced a 50 percent difference in share of wallet between its best and worst branches from their ability to service customers during their "moments of truth."[11]

10.1b.3 Preferential Treatment

Bear in mind that the effectiveness of retention strategies, such as preferential treatment, depends on customer, not company, evaluation. Preferential treatment is the customer's perception of how much better they are treated than the company's other customers.

THEORY IN ACTION

Were You Invited to Marshall Field's Glamorama?

Marshall Field's State Street store in Chicago (now Macy's), in an attempt to differentiate itself from other department stores, has focused on being a purveyor of trendy women's fashion designed by the world's best designers. To this end, it sponsors a highly promoted Glamorama fashion show that culminates in one of Chicago's fanciest private parties. Invitations to the party are impossible to get, unless, of course, you are one of its high-value customers. Your invitation, and the attention lavished on you during the party, identifies you as a preferred customer. It also serves as an emotional bond that lasts throughout the buying seasons—until the next Glamorama fashion show and party when bonds are reestablished.

Examples of retention strategies emphasizing preferential treatment are as numerous and varied as one's imagination. Some retailers provide their high-value customers with free coffee whenever they are in their store. Most high-end retail stores provide their regular customers with notices of sales before the general public is informed. Special days and hours are often set aside for regular clientele.

10.1b.4 Rewarding

Rewarding occurs when a manufacturer, wholesaler, or retailer offers tangible benefits such as pricing or gift incentives to its regular customers in return for loyalty. Frequent flyer programs, customer point programs, and free gifts are examples of rewarding tactics.

Frequent flyers with premier, executive premier, platinum, or 1K cards are allowed to board their plane, put their luggage in empty overhead racks, and get comfortable before general boarding. Numerous hotel chains provide their high-value and preferred customers with room upgrades and even free mini-bar usage.

THEORY IN ACTION

Would You Pick the Yacht Anchored off Monte Carlo or a Chance to Open the Mysterious Black Box?

Some claim that rewarding programs are more heavily used in trade transactions (manufacturer–distributor, manufacturer–dealer, and distributor–dealer) than in consumer

---

transactions. Take, for example, the agricultural chemicals industry. Characterized as an oligopoly (few major manufacturers competing against one another), the industry has been characterized by extremely high levels of rewarding programs aimed at agricultural chemical distributors. Manufacturers use cumulative buying rewards programs to leverage their positions with distributors, who then sell their products to agricultural chemical dealers, who in turn sell to farmers. Distributors accumulate points for every gallon of a manufacturer's product they purchase. At the end of the year, points are totaled and distributors exchange their points for rewards. The more points accumulated, the better the reward. If a distributor divides its purchases across a variety of manufacturers, they do not generally accumulate enough points with any one to achieve the highest level reward.

One year, Velsicol Chemical Corporation's top award was a two-week stay for two on a yacht anchored in the Mediterranean Sea off the coast of the French Riviera, with all expenses paid plus gambling money for the casinos in Monte Carlo! This type of award sold an awful lot of Velsicol chemicals, particularly toward the end of the year when many distributors realized they needed to buy more in order to earn enough points for the trip. During the same year, a competitor offered an Arctic Char fishing trip north of the Arctic Circle, another offered a caribou hunting trip in Alaska, and another provided a catalog of exclusive and expensive furniture distributors could get for exchanging their points. Perhaps the most unique prize was offered by Monsanto Company. It was a Black Box discount—money that distributors would get back based on an unknown percent of their dollar purchases. The Black Box percent that year turned out to be extremely high, making it an extremely lucrative selection for distributors.

One can certainly see that rewards programs aimed at the trade are ratcheted up several tiers in value when compared with rewards programs aimed at final consumers.

10.1b.5 Personalization

> It's one thing to train a sales staff to be warm and attentive; it's quite another to identify, track, and interact with an individual customer and then reconfigure your product or service to meet that customer's needs.
>
> —Peppers, Rogers, and Dorf, "Is Your Company Ready for
> One-to-One Marketing?" *Harvard Business Review*,
> *32* (January–February 1999), p. 152.

Personalization has separate meanings depending on whether one is referencing personalization over the Web or personalization during a more general service encounter. Over the Web, personalization refers to the ability of a customer to modify the website to suit his or her own purposes. Personalization during a more general service encounter is a consumer's perception about how personally they are treated.

Many websites, especially e-commerce sites, use cookies or personalization based on users' preferences. Users select their preferences by entering them in a Web form and submitting the form to the server. The server encodes the preferences in a cookie and sends the cookie back to the browser. This way, every time the user accesses a page, the server is also sent the cookie where the preferences are stored and can personalize the page according to the user preferences. For example, Google's search engine allows users (even non-registered ones) to decide how many search results per page they want to see. Amazon.com uses personalization to offer products based on your browsing and purchasing history.

UK-based retailing company Tesco sends out a monthly magazine to its millions of customers with promotional offers. However, it alters the content to suit the lifestyles of the individual customers. This results in over 150,000 variants of the magazine being published and circulated. Tesco also launched a loyalty card in 1995 which enabled the company to analyze over 8 million transactions that took place every week to figure out the preferences of individual customers and personalize the offers made to them based on the customers' updated profiles.[12]

Some companies have been built entirely around the concept of personalization. Take, for example, women's fashion. Enter the personalized, independently owned women's fashion business with women exhibiting and selling clothing from their own homes. A busy executive can arrange for a private showing during an entire morning or afternoon. Over time, the owner/buyer learns their preferences and buys accordingly. These owners/buyers restrict their clientele to between 100 and 200 women who love to shop in such a private, personalized setting. Their inventory changes according to two to four buying seasons every year. This is a personalized learning relationship that works.

10.1b.6 Customization

As is the case with personalization, customization has separate meanings depending on whether one is referencing customization over the Web or during a more general service encounter. With customization, the company modifies the website to suit the needs of the customer. Customization in a more general service encounter refers to the ability of an organization to adopt its 4 P's to the needs of a consumer or company.

The mechanics of implementing customization through CRM can be quite complex. Productive dialogues with customers remains one way companies can stay ahead of their competition. Companies can establish bonds with their customers through customization of their offerings (clothes, entertainment, and vacation packages) and evocation of a memorable experience.

10.1b.7 Cross-Selling

THEORY IN ACTION

Want a Tie with that Sport Coat?

Brooks Brothers clothiers searched their customer database to find men who had recently, within the past quarter, purchased a navy blue blazer without purchasing any clothing accessories. They then sent this segment a sales promotion piece for red ties and white shirts. The merchandise flew out the doors.

Bundling items together, such as the blue blazer with a white shirt and red tie, can be an effective way to cross-sell, with data mining procedures determining which items to bundle. The items to include in cross-selling initiatives are determined by customer habits on the one hand and clever "bundle" compositions on the other. Clever, creative, and ground-breaking super-bundles are the basis for the new "Lifestyle" stores that are cropping up across the United States. Restoration Hardware, Pottery Barn, and others select and combine seemingly incompatible product categories that somehow fit under the rubric of "Lifestyle." This approach can be taken when retaining and developing customers through cross-selling. A customer calling NRS to buy a kayak offers customer contact personnel the opportunity to cross-sell dry bags, hand and footwear, paddles, hydroskins, personal floatation devices, skirts, tents, and so on. However, creative cross-sells might include videos, books, a magazine subscription, and even a kayaking expedition to Greenland.

More recently, technology has provided a big assist in cross-selling. First Tech Credit Union of Beaverton, Oregon, has an automated advisor which suggests products and services that members might find useful based simply on the member's credit score and their relationship score that characterizes the depth and breadth of the member's current relationship with the credit union. If a member has a low relationship score but a high credit score, they are ripe for cross-selling initiatives. The automated advisor connects with qualifying members whether they are interacting with the credit union at the branch, by phone, or online. The design prevents members from hearing the same offer repeatedly, and their response is remembered on every delivery channel.[13]

Capital One® considers every customer interaction a buying opportunity. Its tests showed that people prefer to buy things when they call Capital One® rather than when Capital One® calls them; therefore, it started cross-selling items such as insurance, long-distance phone service, and club memberships. Inbound cross-selling begins when customers call an automated line to activate their card.[14]

Amazon.com has developed information-based techniques that allow it to cross-sell books to readers based on what other similar customers are reading. Expedia.com, an online travel agency, bundles hotels and rental cars with airline seats. Auto dealers offer numerous protection packages and extended warranties to new car buyers. Cruise lines offer onshore excursions as a supplement to those booking berths. Cross-selling is easily implemented by suggesting related purchases to buyers or utilizing a shopping cart platform, making it easy for users to buy additional items.

10.1b.8 Up-Selling

Of all the CRM strategies that can be implemented, up-selling is perhaps the most conversation oriented. Mass marketing has given way to target marketing; this, in turn, has given way to one-on-one or conversational marketing. Most companies engage customers in dialogue during the acquisition or selling stage and when handling a problem or complaint. Conversations are also held with former customers during win-back or regain management. Up-selling is different from cross-selling and, to be most effective, should be introduced after the relationship has progressed through the acquaintanceship and trust stages and entered the commitment stage.

THEORY IN ACTION

How Nordstrom Up-Sells

Nordstrom's "Personal Stylist" Shoppers Program is based on the development of a strong relationship between a fashion consultant and a customer. A customer profile and a purchase history database aid fashion consultants in selections; however, their fashion recommendations also rely on a personal touch. Balance theory suggests that over time, fashion consultants can be viewed so positively that their recommendations of a fashion ensemble that is slightly higher than a buyer's price range may be liked and purchased.

Once a person has stayed in a hotel suite, the regular room is not quite as good anymore. Or once a person gets used to drinking a $60 bottle of wine, the wine in the $12 bottle is not quite as tasty. This suggests that one way companies can get their customers to trade up is to expose them to higher-level rooms or better-quality wines, which can be done by occasionally providing them with complimentary "upgrades." It is amazing how quickly people get accustomed to the higher standard.

10.1b.9 Managing Migration

Companies spend so much time trying to retain customers and reduce attrition that they lose sight of a strategy that, according to McKinsey & Company, could provide them with two to four times more profit (some say ten times more value): reducing downward migration. Migration is the change in customer value over time, and downward migration characterizes customers who buy less. Customers downwardly migrate for three reasons:

1. Dissatisfaction
2. Attraction to a better attribute mix offered by alternative brands
3. Change in life stage or life cycle

Measuring customer satisfaction and conducting defection analysis are still valuable activities, but measuring downward migration, which is an easily measured construct given customers' purchase information available in company databases, can be much more valuable. Why? Because many more customers change their spending behavior than they defect.

When customers deal with multiple companies—as in the case of credit cards—managing migration is critical. To manage migration, companies must first determine their migration rate (which varies considerably by industry) and then the reasons for downward migration. Companies can then focus on the segment(s) offering greatest opportunity, selecting the best alternatives from a complete array of CRM and product strategies and tactics.

10.1b.10 Conversion of Transactional Buyers to Relational Buyers

Reinartz and Kumar, in an empirical study, found that the relationship between length of time as a customer and amount of profit for the company might be far from positive. They viewed many long-time customers not as treasures but as barnacles: "They are strongly attached to the firm but may cost the firm more in the long run."[15] Their message is that loyalty is vastly overrated and that short-term, transactional customers may, in fact, be more profitable. Companies should not avoid short-term customers interested in single or limited transactions; they simply should not spend too much money on them through expensive relationship programs. Such customers can be recognized through investigation of their buying patterns by data mining techniques.

The authors suggested that short-life customers might be converted to a more attractive segment through enrollment in a frequent shopper or rewards program. Rewards based on purchase frequency and dollar value may, in fact, elevate these short-term customers into longer-term profitable ones.

10.1b.11 Using "Profit Drivers" as Segmentation Variables

Data contained in CRM systems, such as data marts, enables companies to market to individuals or microsegments, increasing the effectiveness of their marketing campaigns. In addition, analyzing the information in data marts enables companies to make characterizations based on costs as opposed to just revenues.

Costs can be profit drivers as well as revenues. Some customers just cost too much to serve. They complain, they return merchandise, their accounts are riddled with credits and adjustments, they only buy on sale, they only use coupons, and their history shows an unrelenting trend of downward migration. Further, your company may have incurred bad debts with members of their family, and heaven forbid they recommend your company to friends and family members just like themselves. Companies should use both customer cost information and customer revenue information to determine which customers are driving profits up and which are driving profits down. CRM strategies can be developed and implemented for both groups, but most likely the marketing efforts will be completely different for positive and negative profit-driving customers and microsegments.

10.1b.12 CRM as a Brand-Building Tool

The meanings that brands convey can be organized into three categories: symbolizing, evoking, and creating. In other words, brands are symbols that convey meaning, evoke feelings, and create ties as detailed in the following table:

WHAT BRANDS DO

Symbolize: attributes, benefits, producer's values, culture of origin, brand personality and users' personalities.
Evoke: relationships, experiences, emotions, and life
Create: personal meaning, loyalty, friendship, and romance

P. Kotler, *Marketing Management*, 11th ed. (Upper Saddle River, NJ: Pearson Prentice-Hall, 2003); P. Temporal and M. Trott, *Romancing the Customer: Maximizing Brand Value through Powerful Relationship Management* (Singapore: John Wiley & Sons, 2001).

Will CRM become synonymous with brand building? Although it will have a prominent place in the building of brands, it will be one of many brand-building tools alongside public relations, event sponsorship, factory visits and trade shows, brand communities, and so on. Stephen Dull stated that marketers and brand executives must get more involved in customer contact center happenings by developing policies and even scripts detailing "Brand Manners" (i.e., everything the company says and does). Customer interactions over the phone, over the Internet, through direct marketing efforts, and at POS all create experiences with the brand for the consumer. These experiences should all be consistent and positive. Everything communicates, and brand manners impact the customer's experience, which, in turn, affects her relationship with the brand.[16]

10.1b.13 Online Customer Management

Online customer management consists of computing recency, size of last purchase, frequency of purchasing and margins attained on products purchased (**RSFM**) or customer lifetime value (**CLV**), studying visitors' and users' footprints, modifying the website to improve deficiencies, and measuring results.

Understanding customer segments is the first step in developing marketing strategy and tactics. CRM data marts make it relatively easy to measure customers' RSFM or CLV. Next, visitors' and users' footprints should be studied by conducting a Weblog analysis. This will reveal success or failure in attracting visitors, converting them to users and repeat customers, cross-selling and up-selling, and managing migration. Improving site registration, organization, and choreography can result in dramatic improvements throughout the customer–business life cycle, consisting of acquisition, retention, development, and, if necessary, win-back.

10.1c Win-Back Strategies

CRM orientation has focused heavily on the customer–company life cycle stage of retention as opposed to acquisition or win-back. Some marketers argue that win-back, or the process of firms' revitalizing relationships with customers who have defected, should play a more important role in a company's CRM strategies. They show the importance of the win-back strategy by citing results from Griffin and Lownstein's 2001 study:[17]

> **The Importance of the Win-Back Strategy**
>
> Research has shown that a firm has a 60 to 70 percent chance of successfully repeat-selling to an active customer, a 20 to 40 percent chance of successfully repeat-selling to a lost customer, and only a 15 to 20 percent chance of successfully closing the sale on a brand new customer.
> —J. S. Thomas, R. C. Blattberg, and E. J. Fox, "Recapturing Lost Customers,"
> *Journal of Marketing Research, 41,* 1 (February 2004): 31–45.

Findings such as this have led companies to concentrate more on retaining customers through CRM than attracting only new customers.

Win-back strategies, like most strategies, should be based on marketing research—in this case, defection analysis. **Defection analysis** seeks to identify the reasons why customers leave. These may be outside the organization's control (moving, life cycle changes, novelty seeking) or within the organization's control (poor service, price, better competitive offerings).

Defection analysis can also be extended to include customers who are migrating downward. Data mining techniques can reveal customer purchase or lack-of-purchase patterns that precede defection. Research with these customers is needed to determine the causes of downward migration. A variety of promotional tactics that address reasons for defection are then developed and tested, and the most cost-effective alternative is selected for use in the win-back strategy.

As experiences in the telecommunications industry revealed, reestablishing every relationship is not wise. If you have to give the store away to regain customers, the results will have extremely negative effects on the bottom line. Large market share at the expense of profitable but smaller market share usually proves to be a mistake.

What specific tactics can effectively be used to promote win-back among former customers? Marketers have found that the last price the customer paid in the prior relationship affects his or her price sensitivity and behavior in reacquisition and retention. Marketers have found that to reacquire lost customers, they must lower the reacquisition price. To maximize profits, increase these prices after the relationship has been reestablished. To maximize market share, both the reacquisition price and the retention price should be low to maximize duration of second tenure.[18]

The recommendations are useful if the business is subscription based. Lost health club members, telecommunications companies customers, and magazine subscribers can be won back more frequently than closing the sale on a new customer. The key is to manage the win-back strategy profitably. Some companies create win-back teams that are empowered to bring former customers back into the fold by accessing reactivation offers that they deem appropriate for the situation.

10.2 Is CRM for Everyone?

10.2a Steep and Shallow Skews

The iceberg, or **Pareto, principle** says that the top 20 percent of your customers account for 80 percent of your profits. When customers' value to the enterprise varies widely, the skew is said to be steep. When customers' value to the enterprise is similar, the skew is said to be shallow.[19] R. S. Kaplan reported on a European company selling electronic equipment. Twenty percent of its customers accounted for 220 percent of its profits. The "whale" curve in Figure 10.1 shows this relationship. Kaplan also showed that the last half of the company's customers destroyed value (Figure 10.2).[20]

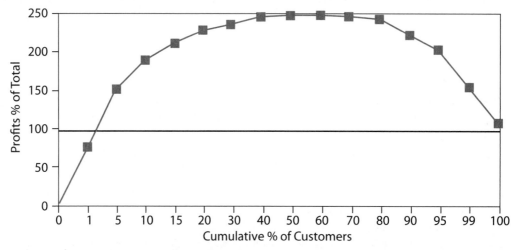

Figure 10.1 One Company's Customer–Profit Relationship

Source: Kanthal, HBS Case 9-190-002 as shown by Sunil Gupta, Columbia University, MSI Conference: Taking Stock of Customer Relationships, March 2, 2006. Copyright (c) 2006 by the Harvard Business School Publishing Corporation, all rights reserved. Reprinted by permission.

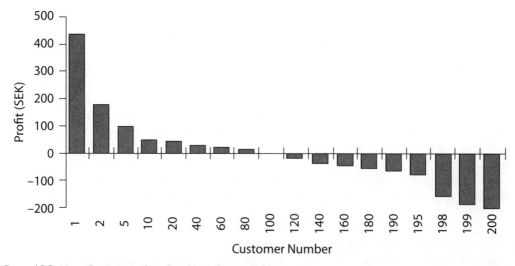

Figure 10.2 How Customers Can Cost Your Company Money

Source: Kanthal, HBS Case 9-190-002 as shown by Sunil Gupta, Columbia University, MSI Conference: Taking Stock of Customer Relationships, March 2, 2006. Copyright (c) 2006 by the Harvard Business School Publishing Corporation, all rights reserved. Reprinted by permission.

Tiered servicing is a method that allows companies to charge different amounts for different levels of servicing. For example, financial advisers provide service agreements that explain how often and by what methods clients will be serviced. Small-fee clients may only receive quarterly performance reviews over the phone, whereas larger-fee clients get quarterly in-person meetings. The trick for financial advisers is to find low-cost methods of servicing the 80 percent of their customers who are low profit in order to retain them but, at the same time, free up time to service the high-profit 20 percent.[21]

THEORY IN ACTION

The Steep Skew in Hong Kong Nightclubs

Trendy nightclubs in Hong Kong, such as Drop, Dragon-I, and FLY, have queues that are blocks long. Managing directors such as Colette Koo of Drop, however, have identified approximately 1,000 trendsetters who spell the difference between success and failure in Hong Kong's competitive nightclub environment.

These trendsetters visit two or three nightclubs during a night out and spend large sums of money. In addition, their influence as opinion leaders, affecting thousands of other night-clubgoers, has tremendous profit implications for the nightclubs that treat them "right." This group of trendsetters does not mind spending money as long as their status is recognized. Is it any wonder that they are immediately admitted to clubs, are seated in VIP lounges, and are frequently comped? Companies with a steep value-skewed customer base would be wise to identify and cultivate strong relationships with such highly profitable segments.

Occasionally, a very small potential customer base must be captured, since it makes the difference between success and failure. Companies with a shallow value-skewed customer base, where the profits generated by each customer are more or less the same, are better served by reducing costs across the board, perhaps through automation, in order to attract competitors' customers.

10.2b Multichannel or Single-Channel Value Propositions

Often, the highest-value customer segment uses multiple channels for shopping and purchasing through **"bricks"** (stores and kiosks) **and "clicks"** (ATMs and the Internet). Consequently, companies are moving toward brick-and-click distribution strategies to serve their customers (especially high-value customers). R. Verma, Z. Iqbal, and R. Baran found that business propositions in the e-brokerage industry that included both stores and online accounts were viewed much more favorably than business propositions including only one or the other.[22] To be effective, however, multichannel marketing must integrate field sales, store, telephone, and Internet sales and service approaches, and identify customer interactions with each touch point.

Companies today must actively manage the channels customers use to access their products and services. Customers quickly learn to use the channel that provides them the greatest reward. Consumers have learned that there is a substantial amount of money to be saved by booking over the Internet, from stays at hotels to buying automobiles. Occasionally, organizations have closed high-cost channels, forcing customers to use lower-cost channels. Try getting a campsite at any of the popular U.S. National Parks in person, for example. Campsites are reserved months in advance over the Internet.

The amount of information available on company websites, coupled with discounts, sales promotion, and special events, is a benefit customers rarely get over the phone. Managing the multichannel network can be a lucrative strategy for any company, but it takes time and experimentation to perfect. Rewards are worth it, however, since the high-value customer segment is a multichannel-user base.

10.2c "Always a Share" or "Lost for Good" Relationships

In the "always a share" model, customers can easily switch their patronage from one vendor to another. In the "lost for good" model, customers face high switching costs and change vendors reluctantly. Therefore, according to B. B. Jackson, companies should build switching costs to move customers closer to the "lost for good" model. Companies should create systems that link their customers closer to them (e.g., through ordering, delivery, or inventory systems). Companies should invest in building customer relationships with accounts that cannot easily switch patronage and are therefore likely to view the relationship with the vendor as long term.[23]

If a customer can easily switch vendors of some product category, then a company should realize it can easily win or lose that customer's business and focus on transaction marketing as opposed to relationship marketing. Such relationships are based on the type of product/service sold, not on the client/vendor interface. These relationships are short term and do not warrant heavy investments in CRM systems.

Chapter Summary

This chapter discusses and analyzes CRM in tactical terms (i.e., how it can result in "quick wins" for an organization). Tactical CRM uses existing information to determine which profit opportunities exist within the various customer business cycle stages. This approach counters the contention that all CRM initiatives take too long to build and produce profitable results. The chapter examines several CRM strategies based on the customer business cycle stages of acquisition, retention, and win-back. Retention strategies include many possibilities. Bonding can be both programmatic (rewards programs) and humanistic (preferential treatment). The use of the idiosyncratic-fit can make each strategy more effective. Personalization and customization are also effective retention strategies, whether implemented over the Web or during a general service encounter. Cross-selling and up-selling have direct profit implications, and the often-overlooked strategy of managing migration may be four times as effective as general retention strategies. Use of "profit drivers" as a segmentation variable focuses a company's attention on profitable market segments. We have also investigated the use of CRM as a brand-building tool and how it can be used to manage brands more effectively. The issue of whether it is possible for a company to attain intimacy with customers was also explored.

As we have seen previously, CRM is more important to some companies than others. The importance of CRM to a company is dependent on whether it has a steep or shallow skew, whether its market is characterized by "always a share" or "lost for good" relationships, and the number of multichannel users it has as customers.

Key Terms

"Bricks" and "clicks" refers to stores and kiosks (bricks) and ATMs and the Internet (clicks), which are two different company distribution strategies. Very often, the highest-value customer segments use multiple channels for shopping and purchasing; therefore, companies may need both bricks and clicks.

Customer–business life cycle consists of a number of stages, including acquisition, development, retention, and win-back.

Defection analysis is a highly useful marketing research technique whereby customers who are defecting are interviewed to understand their reasoning. The interview can occur naturally during the course of closing out the account. Reasons for dissatisfaction and defection are often very specific, and, therefore, they can easily be acted upon.

Humanistic bonds is a retention strategy based on superb treatment given customers by highly trained personnel.

Idiosyncratic-fit is the tendency for customers to be enticed and attracted to offers for which they feel they have a relative advantage.

Pareto principle is also called the iceberg principle. It says that the top 20 percent of your customers account for 80 percent of your profits.

Programmatic bonds is a retention strategy consisting of rewards programs and procedures that make it difficult for customers to switch providers.

RSFM is the customer's score based on recency and size of last purchase, frequency of purchasing, and margins attained on products purchased.

Win-back strategies are strategies to win back customers who have given notice to terminate or have ended the relationship.

Questions

1. Describe the CRM strategy cycle and the importance of each stage.
2. Why are more and more companies switching to brick-and-click or multichannel strategies?
3. List five retention strategies and give an example of each.

Exercises

1. Does the idiosyncratic-fit heuristic describe any loyalty programs of which you are a part?
2. Describe a buying situation in which you were successfully cross-sold. Traded up.
3. How can a high-fashion retailer use customization and personalization strategies?
4. What type of companies would benefit most from managing migration?
5. Have you had any dealings with a CCC staff that have either strengthened the bond between you and their brand/company or destroyed it?

Chapter 11

Privacy and Ethics Considerations

TOPICS

11.1 Introduction

The paradox: consumers complain about privacy issues, but, more often than not, they do not opt out, even when provided the choice. Typically, the age group between 18 and 34 only remotely think about privacy—as evidenced by their explosive use of social websites with little thought about the hazards of creating digital trails of themselves and family members. Organizations providing platforms for social interaction attempt to provide privacy protection in limited form and appear to become serious about implementing appropriate privacy containment measures only when pressured by society, government inquiry, or regulation.

This mindset should be taken into consideration when discussing privacy issues in a non-social media context. An organization compiles information on a prospect or customer in order to analyze and fulfill needs in a manner agreeable to the prospect or customer. If willing, the prospect or customer will take advantage of optimal need fulfillment by providing information to the organization. This appears to be a fairly straightforward agreement:

> I (customer or prospect) give something (information, behavior) to receive something (optimal exchange of products and services). I (organization) receive something (information, behavior) in order to give something (optimal provision of products or services).

Successful execution facilitates CRM. Unsuccessful execution will not only reduce CRM effectiveness but may also create a negative relationship out of a positive or neutral relationship. CRM efforts inherently create risks for both parties entering a relationship. The individual's risk is providing personal and behavioral information to an organization. The individual trusts the organization to adhere to his requests, whether explicit or implicit, to use the information to support the relationship. In many cases, the individual is unaware that information is being captured and thus cannot specify or imply adherence to a certain level of privacy. The organization, by taking this information, has a definitive or implied responsibility to adhere to the individual's request. Both parties take risks to achieve gains. CRM success is somewhat reliant upon the successful management of these risks. This chapter defines these risks, provides ideas on risk management, and demonstrates those exogenous variables that impact the relationship.

A different perspective is to view CRM as a partial solution to solving privacy problems. Part of CRM success is dependent on the ability to track and confirm consumer information. This process forces organizations to know consumer needs and expectations, including privacy. If they know consumer expectations, the organization need only comply with consumer wishes to technically comply with any law, while simultaneously building trust and sustaining relationships. A final note: *In all business dealings, being honest with the consumer is definitely the best policy.*

11.2 Consumer Privacy Concerns

The recent explosion in social media use, coupled with expanded use of the Internet not only for commerce but for many utility functions such as bill payment, has precipitated an increased awareness of how much information is being provided to organizations and, thus, potential risks of privacy.

An organization approaches consumers requesting that they furnish the organization with both their personal information and their family's. The organization also wants permission to monitor the consumers' buying behaviors, as well as their browsing activity on the Internet. In this example, you assume, correctly, that consumers will be unlikely to comply and actually be somewhat upset by the request. They may follow up with a consumer protection group or some regulatory body, either to file a complaint or to better understand what is going on and to ensure that their information will not be compromised. They are on alert. But if the same organization asks for just a few pieces of information, such as a phone number and automobile preference, and reciprocates with some product, service advice, or something else of value, customers will very likely comply. If multiple organizations ask for small pieces of information or monitor behaviors, then consumers perceive the multiple organizations as separate entities that do not share information, and they are even more likely to provide an organization with information.

Consider this quid pro quo over the course of several years. Consumers would probably be shocked at the amount of information they have provided over time. They would be further alarmed if they knew that some organizations have compiled information into one central repository, so it is entirely possible that one source comprises tens to hundreds of information variables on a person and his or her family. Customers would be livid if they discovered that these organizations sold this information indiscriminately to other organizations and provided a service for updating and maintaining that information.

THEORY IN ACTION

Are Organizations Capturing and Sharing Too Much Data?

Google's new overarching privacy policy will allow the company to share user data gathered from services such as YouTube, Gmail, Picasa, and the Google search engine, the company released in an updated privacy statement. Google explained that such information sharing will allow the company to learn more about its users and what marketing messages are most likely to appeal to them, thus better tailoring its advertising on more than 60 of its Web services.

> "You can bring in more data from across the different Web experiences, so you can build out that user persona more robustly," said Alex Funk, senior manager of paid media services at Covario, a search engine marketing agency. "As far as marketers go, this is a win. Before, you could build a campaign specific to YouTube or to the Google display network, but you were really working within the dataset within that one platform.... Now, if someone is searching for things online—maybe they're looking at pictures [or] having a conversation on Google Plus—you can better understand what types of products or services they're looking for."
>
> Google offered an example in its statement: When a user searches for a term like "jaguar," the company will be better able to determine if he or she was looking for the animal or luxury car.
>
> Alex Palmer, "Google's New Privacy Policy Will Share User Data across Products," *Direct Marketing News* (January 27, 2012).

Table 11.1 is a sample list of databases available for purchase. The information in the databases listed is compiled from directories, surveys, trade associations, government certification files, and other proprietary sources.

Looking at typical organization–consumer encounters can help demonstrate some of the consumer privacy and ethics concerns. The following is an example of a service contract solicitation timed to occur just before the original 12-month warranty expired.

Outbound telemarketer: Hello, may I please speak to John Roberts?
John Roberts: Speaking.
Outbound telemarketer: Mr. Roberts, I am calling to discuss an opportunity to . . .
John Roberts: Excuse me, but I am in the middle of dinner. Who did you say you were?
Outbound telemarketer: I am calling on behalf of ABC retail with an offer to extend your appliance service warranty. We wanted to . . .

Table 11.1 Databases Available for Purchase

– Accountants	– Ethnic Families	– New Movers
– Affluent Households	– Executives	– Nurses
– Ailments	– Farmers	– Pharmacists
– Airplane Owners	– Fire Departments	– Police Departments
– Attorneys	– Government	– Prenatal/Postnatal
– Auto Owners	– Health Care Professionals	– Professionals
– Bad Credit	– Hospitals	– Real Estate Agents
– Boat Owners	– Insurance Agents	– Schools
– Churches	– Libraries	– Students
– Clubs and Organizations	– Medical	– Teachers
– Colleges/Universities	– Mortgage	– Time Share
– Dental Hygienists	– Net Worth	– Voters
– Doctors at Home	– New Homeowners	– Women Executives

Source: www.mailing-lists-direct.com

John Roberts: I am sorry, but how did you get my phone number?

Outbound telemarketer: You gave us your number when you arranged delivery of your appliance ten months ago. Is this an inconvenient time to discuss this opportunity?

John Roberts: Yes, it is, and I am not interested. Please do not call me again.

There are several issues with this example. First, John Roberts forgot that he did in fact provide the company with information. He is a customer, and organizations can call customers with unsolicited offerings unless the customer has told them otherwise. The timing of the call was not optimal in this case and probably eliminated any chance of a service contract sales opportunity and may have left a negative impression. The situation would be worse if the call came over the consumer's cell phone, resulting in annoyance and possibly a bill for the incoming call. John Roberts's final comment not to be called again is very important. That telemarketer must now take steps to ensure the organization's compliance with John's request. This is where many organizations fail. We will address this issue later in this chapter.

Consumers have become proficient at sorting through postal mail. It is fairly easy to recognize what is often considered "junk mail," albeit the marketer would refer to this as direct mail or a targeted direct mail offer. Consumers have several concerns with unsolicited direct mail:

- Growing concern that personal information is embedded in the mail that may fall into the wrong hands and possibly be used illegally
- Wasted time sorting through the mail
- Clever mail that projects importance to make the consumer open the envelope
- Receipt of offensive or embarrassing mail as a result of a related activity (e.g., receiving a brochure for sexual enhancement drugs several weeks after performing a Web search for information related to incontinence)
- Failure to cease sending mail despite the consumer's request
- Inappropriate material sent to a child in the household
- Coincidentally receiving solicitations for products or services directly or indirectly related to any activity (e.g., purchases, travel, medical condition)
- Using personalization techniques within the contents of the mailing

Consumer activity leaves a trail of information. Organizations capture this information and make assumptions that lead to unsolicited targeted offerings.

11.2a Consumer Activity

11.2a.1 Unsolicited E-Mail

Unsolicited e-mails have created problems for consumers that go beyond those of direct mail. Some of the issues are:

- The amount of wasted time because often the consumer cannot readily determine whether to open the unsolicited e-mail based on cleverly written subject lines
- The amount of time and/or expense in using software to manage unsolicited e-mails from sources
- The threat of viruses that can lead to insurmountable damage by corrupting or losing data
- The use of spyware and other techniques (cookies, bugs) to monitor a consumer's activity
- The possibility that personal information in an e-mail, acquired from another source, can be captured by other parties in cyberspace
- The use of **phishing** (unsolicited e-mails disguised as reputable correspondence from banks, credit card companies, or companies of which the consumer is aware are vehicles to acquire the consumer's personal data, including bank account, credit card, and Social Security numbers) to trick people into divulging confidential information

11.2a.2 Solicitation via Cell Phone

Most of the preceding issues also apply with cell phone intrusions either via texting or actual calls made to the phone. Cell phone intrusions are, in fact, perceived to be much more invasive than direct mail or calls to a landline because a cell phone is perceived to be more personal.

11.2a.3 Unsolicited Fax Offerings

Receiving unsolicited fax offerings is considered by many to be very invasive, as well as it is actually using a machine in the person's private space, whether a home or business office. The latter has more implications; it is not only invasive but also may be uncontrolled and read by others if the machine is communal. Additionally, it may be against organization policy, so the recipient may be reprimanded.

11.2b Other Activity

Many types of organizations require the use of sensitive or private information to conduct business with the consumer and, in fact, require this information to protect the customer's privacy and the security of information that has been entrusted to them.

11.2b.1 Financial Services Organizations

Financial service organizations (e.g., banks, credit card issuers, savings and loan, brokerage firms, credit unions) are heavily transaction based. Sensitive personal information is usually required to do business. Bank account numbers, credit card numbers, taxpayer ID, Social Security number, age, source of income, assets owned, name, and address information for most, if not all, family members are usually required sensitive and private information for many transactions. Two major concerns are the organization's ability to secure the information and the assurance that the information will not be shared other than when necessary to complete the business transaction. The latter includes other areas of the organization conducting the transaction.

THEORY IN ACTION

"Trigger Lists" Spur Privacy Worries

If you have a mortgage, or have applied for one, beware: your personal and financial information could now be in the hands of hundreds of strangers. This growing trend is taking many homeowners and buyers by surprise, reports CBS News correspondent Mark Strassmann.

Mike and Beth Hayden told him they felt it firsthand when they applied to one mortgage company for money to build their 4,500-square-foot dream house in Orlando, Florida. Suddenly, they began getting calls from many other lenders seeking their business. The unsolicited solicitations seemed to come in nonstop, from early morning to late at night. The callers, Strassmann says, were relentless, with offers that sounded too good to be true. "Some told out-and-out lies," Beth Hayden says. The calls came even though the Haydens were on a "do-not-call" list and have a private phone number. The Haydens considered the calls nothing short of harassment, and they worry about identity theft, since their information is "out there."

And what happened to them, Strassmann stresses, could easily happen to anyone holding or seeking a mortgage. It's the result of what's referred to as a "trigger list." After a mortgage company checks credit, he explained, the credit bureau sells their personal financial information to other lenders hungry for their mortgage business. And overnight, your phone starts ringing. Trigger lists are legal, however, regulated by the Consumer Data and Industry Association.

Credit bureaus insist they sell the lists only to credentialed lenders, but critics say the practice is dangerous. "The real problem with this," contends National Association of Mortgage Brokers president Harry Dinham, "is that it's really open-ended. They are just selling it to anybody. They aren't vetting who they are selling to."

B. Dakss, "'Trigger Lists' Spur Privacy Worries," *CBS News* (February 11, 2009). Accessed at http://www.cbsnews.com/stories/2007/05/09/business/realestate/main2778651.shtml.

11.2b.2 Insurance Organizations

Insurance organizations are also heavily transaction based. They are in the risk business as well and, thus, require more information to conduct their transactions. Much of the data collected (e.g., Social Security number, medical information, age, income) can enable identify theft if compromised.

11.2b.3 Retail, Catalog, and Web-Based Organizations

Retail organizations frequently capture credit card information and, depending on the transaction type, name and address information, phone number, e-mail address, and alternate phone number. Over time, they accumulate purchase history. Using private credit cards and loyalty cards facilitates the capture of personal information. For example, most major grocery chain stores have implemented loyalty programs, and they carefully target their customers at point of sale by printing coupons based on their purchase activity on the back of their receipt.

Auto dealerships keep purchase and maintenance information for all of their customers. They also keep credit card information and certain financial information if the customer financed a purchase through the dealer.

Catalog and Web-based organizations are similar to retail. There is a privacy concern because of the distance nature of the transaction. Brand trust is also a factor and may be of concern. When filling out a catalog order form and including a credit card number, for example, there is the perceived risk of the mail being intercepted and the credit card number being stolen. Providing a Web-based storefront in some faraway location that the customer has never used heightens concern over what happens to the information being provided.

11.2b.4 Hotel, Entertainment, and Travel Organizations

Hotel, entertainment, and travel organizations routinely handle sensitive consumer information. This is obvious if you simply consider the information a consumer provides during the reservation process. Add to that the amount of purchase and behavioral data that can be gathered in one visit and you will find that an organization may have collected up to 30 different information variables on one consumer. They use this information to market to their guests, and, in many cases, they sell that information to other organizations.

Hotels require certain identification information from guests, including credit card information. Frequently, and this is usually stated in their privacy policy, much of the data that you provide, or data that is captured during your stay, is given or sold to the hotel's partners in an effort to facilitate the guests' travel plans or requests for information. Usually what these partners do with the data is not bound by the respective hotel's privacy policy, and these policies usually state this fact.

11.2b.5 Publication, Distribution, and Retail

Publishers gather **contact information** on subscribers in order to deliver their service. This may be Internet based or hard copy via mail. They may also gather subscribers' demographic information and sometimes via a survey ask for lifestyle information, such as hobbies or special interests. They may elect to supplement this information with secondary data. Publishers frequently sell this information to direct marketing list providers or resellers of secondary data. This can be quite invasive, depending on the publication.

Providers of video, audio, and book products or services also collect customer preferences and use them in their marketing efforts. Major organizations frequently employ **collaborative filtering**, which uses this information to present the customer with offerings. This information is personal in nature; consumers may not want anyone to know their tastes in movies, music, or literature.

11.2b.6 Government Organizations

Consumers provide governments with a tremendous amount of information. As recently as the early 1990s, state governments were selling some of the information they collected from citizens (e.g., driver, vehicle, and boat registration data) to supplement their revenue. Fortunately, this practice has stopped.

Governments also collect data on auto owners who use automatic toll transponder devices. Some have even experimented with sending speeding tickets in the mail after calculating average speed between two transponder readers at toll booths.

Continuing concerns over terrorism have resulted in a proliferation of monitoring devices in public places. Face recognition scans at sporting events or cameras monitoring city streets to reduce crime are digitized and placed in databases. Phone and Web activity monitoring for security reasons is another new method that governments and agencies have adopted. These government initiatives are not directly related to CRM, but they raise the consumer's consciousness about privacy.

11.2b.7 Pharmaceutical Companies

Pharmaceutical companies have collected various drug purchase information on consumers via pharmacies and certain health care providers. Extrapolating from the drug(s) used, they can guess, or in some cases determine, what health problem is being treated. This information can then be used to target the consumer for a variety of related products and services. Along with data captured from other health service areas and consumer over-the-counter purchases (obtained, for example, from a retailer's loyalty card), this information can migrate to other organizations that sell it to companies for marketing.

11.2c Other Consumer Privacy Concerns

With technology enablers for consumers becoming more affordable and easy to use, a growing area of concern is the privacy of children. Because of the various mobile devices that they use and the time they spend online, they are in a position where their activity can be monitored and information collected. Internet and wireless devices used for searching, inquiring, and, in some cases, purchasing are the main channels of data capture.

Analyzing data variables themselves, from a privacy perspective, raises concerns, regardless of the industry. Once an organization captures a person's age, they add one each year to keep the age on file accurate. Current income combined with occupation definition allows for a reasonable projection of income over time. Interestingly, age and income are two of the three most sought-after variables by organizations. Once captured, they can be maintained over time without future consumer input. There will be exceptions—people change occupations, lifestyles, and so on—but on a percentage basis, there is a good chance that this information can be preserved accurately.

Using the Internet for transactions or communication is definitely cost and time effective. There is increasing concern, however, over security of that information.

THEORY IN ACTION

Online Shopping Safety: The Avira Survey

In a survey, security firm Avira has found 70 percent of consumers choosing either not to shop online or being concerned about their safety while navigating the Internet. The July 2011 survey of Avira users found only 30 percent of respondents feeling secure enough to be worry free as they shop online.

The online shopping survey was presented to Avira's website visitors during July 2011 with the question "Do you feel secure while shopping online?" There were just under 3,000 respondents, of whom 28.62 percent shopped online but feared personal data getting into the wrong hands. Around 22.51 percent shopped only at known online retailers such as Amazon or iTunes, while 18.85 percent cited security concerns as a reason not to shop online. Just 15.65 percent believed in shopping online as long as the method of paying and the financial transactions are always secure, and 14.36 percent felt secure shopping online.

Sorin Mustaca, data security expert from Avira, said everyday reports of data breaches, phishing attacks, and security vulnerabilities left consumers feeling unsafe. He recommends checking for a secure connection to the online store, doing a reputation check on the website, and choosing payment methods that do not require upfront payments. "Always double check your bank accounts to make sure the amount you spent is the amount that was charged. If there is a discrepancy, contact the website where you made the purchase," he recommends.

Dhruv Tanwar, "Consumers Concerned about Online Shopping Safety—AVIRA Survey," *Computerworld* (June 24, 2005).

In general, consumers need to be more aware of what information they provide and to whom. There are many benefits to the consumer for providing personal and behavioral information to organizations. They should, however, question any request for information and ask for an explanation as to why it is required.

11.3 Organization Privacy Concerns

Successful CRM efforts depend on relative, accurate, and timely information on individuals, households, and businesses with which the organization wishes to sustain a relationship. A conflict has ensued due to the clash between organizations' quest for information and their obligation to observe privacy requests and use that information ethically. Organizations are further challenged by increases in regulation, fueled by social pressures as consumers become more aware of what information organizations have accumulated and their intended or unintended use of that information. The executive level position of chief privacy officer (CPO) has become even more important. This person usually has a legal background, and most are attorneys. The CPO has executive ownership of all privacy and ethical issues. This has provided some comfort for organizations, but ownership and titles do not guarantee successful execution. Their concerns can be categorized into several areas:

- What information is captured? How and where is the information captured? What was or was not said, implied, or agreed upon with the party the information represents?
- How is the information maintained within the organization? Who has access to the information? What security is in place to maintain the information? What mechanism is in place to modify the information?
- How is the information being used? By whom? For what purpose?
- Is the organization compliant with current, pending, and planned regulation for all of the previously mentioned areas?
- Are there global implications that may affect the organization's attempt to comply with legal requirements and acceptable privacy and ethical best practices?

Organizations vary in their ability or willingness to control and audit privacy practices related to data capture. Disparate organization efforts combined with disparate consumer touch points are fundamental to the best practice privacy control effort. The challenge is that, even though a consumer may have told a customer service representative he or she wants no further contact, the organization must ensure that future calls from within the organization and from outsourced telemarketing partners are stopped in a timely manner. This is not a simple effort, and it can be expensive. It gets more challenging when the consumer does not contact the organization directly, perhaps signing up with the National Do Not Call Registry instead. A consumer may also communicate through written letters, through a Web page entry form, or in person at a customer service desk. Organizations acknowledge all consumer privacy requests. The acknowledgment and agreement terms and wording should be the same across all channels. Standardizing these communications, however, is daunting in a dynamic environment, where employees change roles and different partners are used.

Audit and control procedures must ensure the secure receipt, transfer, and management of consumer privacy requests. For example, a written consumer request to cease all communications will require the organization to stop all communication across marketing mediums (e.g., telephone, postal mail, e-mail). The larger the organization, the more difficult the effort to ensure compliance across all areas will be, as compliance is required both internally as well as externally (e.g., partners).

The privacy legislation field is very dynamic lately due to increased consumer awareness of what information is being captured, concerns over who sees this information, and concerns over the information's intended use. Organizations must find the right people to monitor this growing force, and they are incurring rising expenses to support this monitoring effort. Small to medium-sized organizations are at a disadvantage. They lack the resources to monitor and act in this area of privacy. They must have some strategy in place to manage these forces, however, as their liability exposure and customer relationships depend directly on their ability to manage this growing concern. Large international organizations also have a disadvantage. Maintaining an awareness of privacy and ethical issues is difficult enough in an organization's country of origin. These concerns are multiplied when an organization is global.

THEORY IN ACTION

Regulators Sniff Around Mobile Privacy Issues

Regulators are starting to investigate what kinds of oversight are in place to make sure that mobile applications don't encroach on user privacy rights and have made some inquiries at Microsoft about the role the company plays in monitoring privacy policies of apps on Windows phones, said Mary Newcomer Williams, a lawyer in Microsoft's Windows Phone segment. "Suddenly, they're realizing this is something they should be concerned about, but they're not sure how to tackle it," she said. "Regulators are interested in looking to platform providers to play an enforcement role in this space." That's because there are so many mobile applications, it would be a major undertaking for regulators to oversee all of them.

But Microsoft doesn't particularly want to play that role, she said. "On the platform provider side, we aren't really equipped to do that kind of enforcement either." "We enable the download of a file to the phone. We don't know where it connects to and what data might come off the phone. So the idea that we might enforce a **privacy policy** that gets the right kind of **consent**, it's hard to imagine how you can do it."

Some operating system providers like Microsoft and Apple set privacy requirements for applications and approve applications before they can enter their respective app stores. Google, however, has a much more hands-off approach where it has defined some policies but doesn't serve as a gatekeeper. Developers can upload any application to the Android Market, but Google will remove applications that are found to run afoul of the policies. "Most operating system developers have privacy policies, but accountability isn't clear," said Chetan Sharma, principal at Chetan Sharma Consulting. If an application does encroach on a user's privacy, it's not clear who is to blame. Part of the problem is that clear regulations don't exist about what kinds of privacy rights mobile users have. "That's an indication of how new the market is," Sharma noted. "Until a few years ago, there wasn't a vibrant mobile application market, and laws that regulate that market don't exist yet."

Williams suggests that the best solution might be for a third-party organization to educate application developers on proper privacy practices and possibly run a certification program to demonstrate that apps comply with set requirements.

N. Gohring, "Regulators Sniff Around Mobile Privacy Issues," *Computerworld, Inc.* (November 14, 2011).

11.4 Current/Pending Privacy Legislation

Table 11.2 provides brief descriptions of some of the more relevant and "top-of-mind" areas of legislation. These legislations change over time, so sources of current information and where you can get information on other legislation are supplied at the end of this chapter. (Pending legislations were sourced from http://dmaaction.org.)

Table 11.2 Current and Pending Privacy Legislation

Legislation Name	Purpose/Description	Status (as of June 2012)
H.R. 2577: **Secure and Fortify Electronic Data (SAFE) Act** (introduced July 18, 2011)	To protect consumers by requiring reasonable security policies and procedures to protect data containing personal information, and to provide for nationwide notice in the event of a security breach	Pending
S. 1223: **Location Privacy Protection Act of 2011** (introduced June 16, 2011)	To address voluntary location tracking of electronic communications devices, and for other purposes	Pending
H.R. 2168: **Geolocational Privacy and Surveillance Act** (introduced June 14, 2011)	To amend title 18, United States Code, to specify the circumstances in which a person may acquire geolocation information, and for other purposes	Pending
H.R. 1895: **Do Not Track Kids Act of 2011** (introduced May 13, 2011)	To amend the Children's Online Privacy Protection Act of 1998 to extend, enhance, and revise the provisions relating to collection, use, and disclosure of personal information of children and to establish certain other protections for personal information of children and minors	Pending
S. 913: **Do-Not-Track Online Act of 2011** (introduced May 9, 2011)	To require the Federal Trade Commission to prescribe regulations regarding the collection and use of personal information obtained by tracking the online activity of an individual, and for other purposes	Pending
S. 1011: **Electronic Communications Privacy Act Amendments Act of 2011** (introduced May 7, 2011)	To improve the provisions relating to the privacy of electronic communications	Pending
S. 799: **Commercial Privacy Bill of Rights Act of 2011** (introduced April 13, 2011)	To establish a regulatory framework for the comprehensive protection of personal data for individuals under the aegis of the Federal Trade Commission, and for other purposes	Pending
H.R. 1528: **Consumer Privacy Protection Act of 2011** (introduced April 13, 2011)	To protect and enhance consumer privacy, and for other purposes	Pending
H.R. 611: **Best Practices Act** (introduced February 10, 2011)	To foster transparency about the commercial use of personal information; provide consumers with meaningful choices about the collection, use, and disclosure of such information; and for other purposes	Pending
H.R. 654: **Do Not Track Me Online Act** (introduced February 11, 2011)	To direct the Federal Trade Commission to prescribe regulations regarding the collection and use of information obtained by tracking the Internet activity of an individual, and for other purposes	Pending
Do-Not-Call Improvement Act of 2007	The National Do Not Call Registry is a list of phone numbers from consumers who have indicated their preference to limit the telemarketing calls they receive.	Current
H.R. 653: **Financial Information Privacy Act of 2011** (introduced February 11, 2011)	To amend the Gramm-Leach-Bliley Act to improve regulations dealing with the disclosure by financial institutions of nonpublic personal information, and for other purposes	Pending
Financial Services Modernization Act of 1999 (Gramm-Leach-Bliley Act)	Governs the collection and disclosure of customers' personal financial information by financial institutions and requires all financial institutions to design, implement, and maintain safeguards to protect customer information	Current

(Continued)

Table 11.2 (Continued)

Legislation Name	Purpose/Description	Status (as of June 2012)
The Children's Online Privacy Protection Act (COPPA) of 1998	Details what a website operator must include in a privacy policy; when and how to seek verifiable consent from a parent or guardian; and what responsibilities an operator has to protect children's privacy and safety online, including restrictions on the marketing to those under age 13	Current
Health Insurance Portability and Accountability Act of 1996	Addresses the privacy and security concerns associated with the electronic transmission of health information	Current
Telecommunications Act of 1996	Addresses widespread concern over telephone companies' misuse of personal records, and requires telephone companies to obtain the approval of customers before using information about users' calling patterns to market new services	Current
Communications Assistance for Law Enforcement Act of 1994	Governs government access to consumer electronic and wireless communications	Current
Driver's Privacy Protection Act of 1994	Restricts the public disclosure of personal information contained in state Department of Motor Vehicle (DMV) records	Current
Telephone Consumer Protection Act of 1991	Requires any person or entity engaged in telemarketing to maintain a list of consumers who request not to be called	Current
Video Privacy Protection Act of 1988	Prohibits videotape service providers from disclosing customer rental records without the informed, written consent of the consumer, and requires videotape service providers to destroy personally identifiable customer information within a year of the date it is no longer necessary for the purpose for which it was collected	Current
Cable Communications Policy Act of 1984	Prohibits cable operators from using the cable system to collect "personally identifiable information" concerning any subscriber without prior consent, unless the information is necessary to render service or detect unauthorized reception, and also prohibits operators from disclosing personally identifiable data to third parties without consent	Current
Privacy Protection Act of 1980	Prohibits government officials from searching or seizing any work product or documentary materials held by a "person reasonably believed to have a purpose to disseminate to the public a newspaper, book, broadcast, or other similar form of public communication," unless there is probable cause to believe the publisher has committed or is committing a criminal offense to which the materials relate	Current
Right to Financial Privacy Act of 1978	Protects the confidentiality of personal financial records by creating a statutory Fourth Amendment protection for bank records, prevents banks from requiring customers to authorize the release of financial records as a condition of doing business, and states that customers have a right to access a record of all disclosures	Current

(Continued)

Table 11.2 *(Continued)*

Legislation Name	Purpose/Description	Status (as of June 2012)
Privacy Act of 1974	Empowers individuals to control the federal government's collection, use, and dissemination of sensitive personal information, and prohibits agencies from disclosing records to third parties or other agencies without the consent of the individual to whom the record pertains	Current
Fair Credit Reporting Act of 1970	Protects consumers from the disclosure of inaccurate and arbitrary personal information held by consumer reporting agencies	Current

11.5 What Consumers Can Do

There are both formal and informal, and one-time and ongoing, actions that consumers can take to ensure that organizations recognize and, hopefully, adhere to their privacy needs. But the underlying theme is that the consumer must "get smart." No single organization, including the government, will be looking out for a specific individual. Social pressures have precipitated legislation that attempts to protect the populace at large in certain high-exposure areas. But consumers must take on the responsibility of ensuring their privacy is intact.

11.5a Mail Preference Service and Telephone Preference Service

Preference services provide the consumer with a way to help minimize unsolicited contact from organizations. Some consumers would like to receive less advertising mail at home. The Mail Preference Service (MPS) is designed to assist those consumers in decreasing the amount of national nonprofit or commercial mail they receive at home.[1] The MPS is a consumer service sponsored by the Direct Marketing Association (DMA), which is the oldest and largest national trade association serving the direct marketing field.

To receive fewer unsolicited telemarketing calls, consumers can also register for the DMA's Telephone Preference Service (TPS), which allows them to opt out of national telemarketing lists.[2]

11.5b National Do Not Call Registry

The National Do Not Call Registry is a list of phone numbers from consumers who have indicated their preference to limit the telemarketing calls they receive.[3] The Registry is managed by the Federal Trade Commission (FTC). Consumers can add themselves to the Registry by calling the FTC (1-888-382-1222) or filling out an online form on the FTC's website. Telephone numbers placed on this Registry will remain on it permanently as a result of the Do-Not-Call Improvement Act of 2007, which became law in February 2008. Organizations covered by this Registry must honor the requests of consumers who have placed their telephone numbers on the Registry and have up to 31 days to stop calling the respective consumer. Keep in mind that the Registry does not prevent calls from organizations:

- With which the consumer has established a business relationship
- For which the consumer has given prior written permission to call
- Which are not commercial or do not include unsolicited advertisements (i.e., survey companies)
- Which are tax-exempt nonprofit (i.e., charities)

In addition to complaints alleging violations of the National Do Not Call Registry, consumers may also file a complaint against a telemarketer who is calling for a commercial purpose (e.g., non-charitable organizations) if:

- The telemarketer calls before 8 a.m. or after 9 p.m.
- The telemarketer leaves a message but fails to leave a phone number that can be called to sign up for their company-specific do-not-call list
- A telemarketing call is received from a company, but the consumer has previously requested to be placed on that company's do-not-call list
- The telemarketing firm fails to identify itself
- The consumer receives a prerecorded commercial message from someone with whom he or she does not have an established business relationship and to whom he or she has not given permission to call

11.5c FTC Advice on Identity Theft

To help manage their personal information wisely and to help minimize its misuse, consumers may want to consider taking some of the following actions as advised by the FTC (from www.ftc.gov):

- Before revealing any personally identifying information, the consumer should find out how it will be used and whether it will be shared with others. They should ask about the company's privacy policy: Will there be a choice about the use of the information? Can the consumer choose to have it kept confidential?
- Consumers should read the privacy policy on any website directed to children. Websites directed to children or that knowingly collect information from kids under 13 must post a notice of their information collection practices.
- Put passwords on all accounts, including credit card accounts, bank accounts, and phone accounts. Avoid using easily available information—like a mother's maiden name, a birth date, the last four digits of a Social Security number, or a phone number—or obvious choices, like a series of consecutive numbers or a hometown football team.
- Minimize the identification information and the number of cards carried to what is actually needed. Don't put all identifying information in one holder or in a purse, briefcase, or backpack.
- Keep items with personal information in a safe place. When discarding receipts, copies of credit applications, insurance forms, physician statements, bank checks and statements, expired charge cards, credit offers received in the mail, and mailing labels from magazines, tear or shred them. That will help thwart any identity thief who may pick through the trash or recycling bins to capture personal information.
- Order a copy of your credit report. Make sure it's accurate and includes only those activities you've authorized. Each of the nationwide consumer reporting agencies—Equifax, Experion, and TransUnion—is required to provide you with a free copy of your credit report, at your request, every 12 months.
- Use a secure browser when shopping online to guard the security of transactions. When submitting purchase information, look for the "lock" icon on the browser's status bar to be sure the information is secure during transmission.

11.5d Unsolicited Sexually Oriented Advertising

Sometimes unsolicited sexually oriented advertising comes to a consumer's home mailbox. The U.S. Postal Service maintains a list of people who do not want to receive sexually oriented advertising mail and provides the list to companies that mail such promotions. Consumers can contact their local post office and ask for Form 2150 or Form 1500 to stop mail from a particular company.

11.5e Spam

Spam is unwanted electronic mail, also called "junk e-mail." Spam e-mail is a nuisance, cluttering up an inbox and leading to increased storage requirements and time spent verifying if it is legitimate before deletion. If embedded with a malicious code, spam can be a privacy threat if opened, as such spam e-mail places information on the consumer's computer or mobile device. Some companies creating spam often outsource the e-mail function to a company outside the consumer's home country, which makes it difficult for authorities to confront. Spam may also misrepresent legitimate companies whose information may be part of the spam e-mail. Send any spam received to the FTC at spam@uce.gov so it is available to appropriate law enforcement.

11.5f PayPal

PayPal is a service that lets consumers shop online without sharing their financial information with sellers. Since PayPal is considered a financial institution under the Gramm-Leach Bliley (GLB) Act, it cannot disclose its account holders' nonpublic personal information to third parties unless account holders opt in to those disclosures.

PayPal provides protection against unauthorized payments sent from the consumer's financial accounts. If an account is subject to fraud or unauthorized use, PayPal puts a "Limited Access" designation on the account. At this point, the account holder must:

- Log in
- Reset his or her password
- Develop a set of security questions based on the subjective and not fact (e.g., "What is your favorite ice cream?," *not* "What is your mother's maiden name?")
- Verify location by phone or by mail
- Provide a set of documents, including (but not limited to) a copy of the user's Social Security card and state ID, home utility bills, business licenses, and proof of original purchase of recently sold good[4]

11.6 What Organizations Can Do

For organizations, there are two key objectives that must be managed in parallel. First, organizations should ensure that they are, and will continue to be, in total compliance with all privacy laws and privacy legislation. This includes pending legislation at all levels of government and globally, where applicable. Second, organizations must determine their customer and prospect privacy and ethical expectations and meet or exceed those expectations. The second objective goes beyond the first objective; it assumes that the first objective has been met and then facilitates the effort to build a sustainable customer relationship that will provide a competitive advantage. The following example can help illustrate the difference between the two objectives.

A good ethical practice, and one that ensures compliance with legislation, is to ask the consumer for permission to share his or her information within the organization and with outside parties for the purpose of providing better products to customers. This is a common practice referred to as an opt-in and opt-out strategy. If consumers grant permission, they **opt in**, usually by checking a box near where the question is posed. By leaving the box empty, the consumer is denying permission.

Many organizations precheck the box, making it the responsibility of consumers to take action if they wish to **opt out**. The organization is betting, generally with success, that the consumer will not notice the box is checked. If the consumer later complains, the organization, if an audit and control procedure is in place, can prove that the box was checked and, therefore, did nothing wrong. This would fulfill the first objective. To build and sustain a relationship based on trust, however, organizations can instead ask customers the same question but leave the box unchecked. If a consumer checks the box, the organization can advise him or her of what was indicated and ask if the consumer is sure he/she wants to opt in. This is also known as a **double opt-in** procedure. Some organizations do not use this method because they feel some consumers, when specifically made aware of what they are agreeing to, will choose not to opt in. Therefore, the prechecked box may meet the legal requirements specified in the first objective, but the unchecked box can be envisioned as meeting and exceeding the consumer's expectations in the second objective.

11.6a Strategic Steps for Managing Privacy Issues

The following strategic steps are a good start to managing the privacy and ethics issues facing business today.

- Assign privacy strategy ownership at the executive level to maintain in-house knowledge of current legislation and best practices and to ensure appropriate resource allocation and continuous improvement. Executive ownership also demonstrates that the organization takes privacy issues seriously. As stated earlier in the chapter, many organizations today have chief privacy officers at the executive level who handle all privacy and ethical issues.
- Verify that the technical and business infrastructures support current privacy initiatives and can be quickly modified to support new initiatives. Monitor and change the respective infrastructure when needed for adherence to current laws, for rising and ever-changing consumer expectations, for overall efficiency, and to aid risk-reduction effort.
- Create internal awareness and support internal education on privacy and ethical standards, both hard (for strict adherence to specific privacy laws) and soft (to provide the employee with some flexibility when interacting with a consumer).
- Analyze each area that can be a source of consumer information. (This is discussed in Chapter 5.) Ensure that all data capture techniques support the organization's privacy initiative. Change where appropriate. If there is no easy solution, do without the information.
- Identify all locations of captured information in the organization, those employees who need access to this information, and for what purpose and how this information will be used. The same issues apply to external partners. Additionally, identify how and what information external partners are capturing on your behalf.
- Implement hardware and software that ensure data security and prevent fraudulent use of information. Some recently enacted strategies include **digital watermarking**, **data masking**, mobile location verification, application shielding (which detects intrusion), and context-aware analysis (which uses related information in algorithms to score data). Web management tools are also critical due to increased Web utilization. These tools manage and control authentication, handshakes, passwords, and so on. Security and event management tools log information and detect abnormal activity. Privacy and security measurement software and methodologies should also be implemented in an effort to ensure privacy compliance, best practices, and identification of weakness in infrastructure. These tools are separate from privacy control efforts, which are tools and decisions used to manage information.
- Create a formal privacy policy for internal use, for external partner use, and for the consumer. The policy should be simple and easy to understand. Communicate to all of these parties in

How does CRM giant Siebel advise its customers to craft privacy policies? Here are the guidelines it offers up:

An organization's privacy policy is a statement to its customers and sets out the way it will process the personal data it collects on its customers. It should state that any personal data collected by the organization is used in accordance with the relevant data protection legislation. The policy should be written in clear and comprehensive language and should avoid the use of legal jargon. As a guideline, organizations should include statements relating to the following areas:

- Introduction—what the privacy policy refers to
- The Data Protection—privacy legislation the organization must comply to
- The use that will be made of the customer's personal information
- Consent—whether the organization will operate an opt-in or opt-out policy
- Use of data from third parties
- Disclosure of data to third parties
- "How-to"—verifying, updating, and amending your personal information
- Security of customer data storage
- Notification of changes

Ensuring data protection and privacy compliance is not just a matter of operating within the law; it is also about the effective handling of personal information and respecting the interests of your customers.

Matt Hines, "Protect Privacy or Jeopardize CRM," SearchCRM.com August 12, 2002, http://searchcrm.techtar get.comoriginalContent/0,289142, sidell_gci843537,00.html (accessed October, 09, 2006).

Figure 11.1 Siebel's Guide to Building Effective Customer Privacy Policy

Source: http://searchcrm.techtarget.com/news/843537/Protect-privacy-or-jeopardize-CRM. Reprinted with permission of The YGS Group.

appropriate channels. Include the use of periodic formal audits of the policy by third parties to ensure compliance with current legislation, pending legislation, and consumer expectations. For example, there are new businesses that solely service organizations by auditing for compliance with the GLB Act. Passing an audit by some of these third-party auditing firms can be proof of compliance for industry or government monitoring purposes.

Figure 11.1[5] illustrates a privacy approach used by Siebel (part of Oracle Corporation), a leading CRM enabler.

11.6b Federal Compliance and Enforcement Activities

The U.S. Small Business Administration's national ombudsman and ten Small Business Regulatory Fairness boards collect comments from small businesses about federal compliance and enforcement activities and act as a liaison between them and federal agencies. Comments received from small businesses are forwarded to federal agencies for a high-level review, and federal agencies are requested to consider the fairness of their enforcement action. A copy of the agency's response is sent to the small business owner by the Office of the National Ombudsman. In some cases, fines have been lowered or eliminated and decisions changed in favor of the small business owner.[6]

11.6c Federal and State Regulations

The two easiest and most used channels of information exchange between consumer and organization are the telephone and the Web. Therefore, it may be prudent to start in these areas when analyzing current methods and procedures. Being that they are so popular, it is not surprising that ensuing social awareness and subsequent social pressure have resulted in a variety of legal activities surrounding these two channels.

It is important that sellers and other telemarketers recognize that both the FTC and the Federal Communications Commission (FCC) regulate telemarketing practices. Telemarketers should review regulations enacted by both agencies.

The government and private sector provide services to organizations in an effort to help the organization comply with consumer requests for privacy. These services are very dynamic in that new services are created and existing services may be eliminated or replaced periodically as a result of new best practices coupled with changes in technology interfaces between consumers and organizations. It is important for organizations to stay abreast of this rapidly changing environment.

11.6c.1 National Do Not Call Registry

Telemarketers and sellers are required to search the National Do Not Call Registry at least once every 31 days and drop from their call lists the phone numbers of consumers who have registered. Further information on how organizations can obtain the National Do Not Call Registry is available on the FTC's website at https://telemarketing.donotcall.gov. The best source of information about complying with the do-not-call provisions of the Telemarketing Sales Rule (TSR) is the FTC's website. TSR lists methods that can be used by consumers to better control unsolicited communications. The Do Not Call Registry is an example of one of these methods. The comprehensive guide "Complying with the Telemarketing Sales Rule" can be found at http://business.ftc.gov.

11.6c.2 Wireless Block Identifier and Wireless–Ported Numbers

Federal regulations restrict marketers when making unsolicited marketing calls to wireless numbers. To identify wireless numbers, telemarketers must use products like the DMA's Wireless Block Identifier and supplement it with new Wireless–Ported Number files. The Wireless Block Identifier file identifies those area codes and exchanges or blocks of numbers assigned to wireless carriers active within the North American Numbering Plan in the United States and Canada. The Ported Number files provide telemarketers with the information they need to identify:

- Numbers that appear to belong to wired landlines but are now assigned to wireless telephones. (Telemarketers must avoid making unsolicited sales calls to these numbers.)
- Numbers that appear to belong to wireless telephones but are now assigned to wired landlines. (If these numbers are not on the National Do Not Call Registry, telemarketers may call them.)[7]

11.6c.3 Telephone Preference Service

The TPS is a residential file of individuals throughout all 50 states and Puerto Rico who have contacted the DMA and registered with the TPS by providing their names, home addresses, and home phone numbers.[8] It is an easy and cost-effective way for organizations to purge their calling lists of consumers who do not want to receive telemarketing calls at home.

The TPS also includes the official state do-not-call lists for Pennsylvania and Wyoming. The DMA's State TPS Lookup Program works in conjunction with the Pennsylvania and Wyoming TPS files by assisting telemarketers in finding individuals on these states' do-not-call lists.[9]

11.6c.4 E-Mail Preference Service

Organizations must also respond to consumer requests for their choice in how much e-mail they receive. The DMA's E-Mail Preference Service offers two solutions to this:

- e-MPS Suppression File
- e-MPS Cleaning

The e-MPS Suppression File, which is only available to DMA members, consists of e-mail addresses from consumers who have contacted the DMA and registered with their E-Mail Preference Service in order to reduce the amount of unsolicited commercial e-mail they receive. These e-mail addresses are entered into the e-MPS Suppression File. All DMA members who wish to send unsolicited commercial e-mail are required to purge their prospect e-mail lists of the individuals who have registered with the E-Mail Preference Service. This is where the e-MPS Cleaning software comes into play. E-MPS Cleaning, which is available to all marketers, is a program where the DMA does most of the work for organizations. All the organization has to do is upload its prospect e-mail list to the DMA. The e-MPS Cleaning service then passes the organization's prospect list against the E-Mail Preference Service list of consumers who do not want to be contacted. The DMA then returns the "cleaned" list to the organization via e-mail within 24 hours.[10]

11.6c.5 CAN-SPAM

The Controlling the Assault of Non-Solicited Pornography and Marketing (CAN-SPAM) Act of 2003 applies to almost all businesses in the United States that use e-mail. It provides recipients of spam with the right to opt out of these spam messages and have their opt-out (or unsubscribe) request acted upon. Under the CAN-SPAM Act of 2003, permission of the e-mail recipient is not required prior to sending out the e-mails; however, if a recipient wants to unsubscribe or opt out of the mailings, then the business must stop sending the e-mails as per the opt-out request or face severe penalties.[11] More information on the CAN-SPAM Act can be found on the FTC's website at http://business.ftc.gov.

11.6c.6 Deceased Do Not Contact List

The DMA sometimes receives calls from family members, friends, or caretakers seeking to remove the names of deceased individuals from commercial marketing lists. To assist those who are managing this process, the DMA has created a Deceased Do Not Contact List, which is available to companies for the sole purpose of removing names and addresses of deceased people from their marketing lists. While the names of living individuals registered on the DMA's Telephone Preference Service and E-Mail Preference Service stay on the files for only five years, the names of the deceased individuals remain on the Deceased Do Not Contact List permanently.[12]

11.6d Other Considerations

Aside from specific government regulations, there are other resources that can help organizations to become more proactive in their approach to consumer privacy.

11.6d.1 TRUSTe and BBBOnline

Organizations can build trust with their customers by displaying acknowledgment of compliance with privacy and ethics as witnessed and monitored by organizations such as TRUSTe and BBBOnline.

TRUSTe is an online privacy seal program that certifies eligible websites, holding sites to baseline privacy standards. TRUSTe requires its licensees to implement certain fair information practices and to submit to various types of compliance monitoring in order to display a privacy seal on their websites.[13] **Trustmark** is the online seal awarded by TRUSTe to websites that agree to post their privacy practices openly via privacy statements, as well as adhere to enforcement procedures that ensure that those privacy promises are met. When you click on the TRUSTe trustmark, you're taken directly to the privacy statement of the licensed website.[14] Over 4,000 websites, including those from top companies like Apple, Disney, eBay, and Microsoft, rely on TRUSTe to ensure compliance with evolving and complex privacy requirements.[15]

BBBOnline is the Better Business Bureau's online privacy seal program. It certifies sites that meet baseline privacy standards. The program requires its licensees to implement certain fair information practices and to submit to various types of compliance monitoring in order to display a privacy seal on their websites.[16]

11.6d.2 Monitoring Industry Legal Activity

It may be prudent for the organization to monitor overall current legal activity and that specific to their industry. The FTC's website has a case list of current, pending, and past legal issues confronting specific organizations. The site reference to these cases does change on occasion. It is recommended that the search function be used at the FTC website using "pending cases" as the keyword search term.

11.6d.3 Information and Privacy Management Practices

There will be occasions when an agreement to protect a person's privacy will be breached. The Ponemon Institute is dedicated to advancing responsible information and privacy management practices in business and government. To achieve this objective, the Institute conducts independent research, educates leaders from the private and public sectors, and verifies the privacy and data protection practices of organizations in a variety of industries. Larry Ponemon, chairman and founder of the Ponemon Institute, offers a number of suggestions that companies should consider to maintain the trust and confidence of their customers or employees in the event of a data security breach:

- *Timeliness is important.* Companies should notify the victims as quickly as possible. A few days of delay can cause a significant drop in confidence in the organization.
- *Talk to customers, employees, and contractors.* Individuals are much more likely to view communication as truthful when a company representative contacts them by telephone. Written communication is viewed with a higher degree of skepticism and concern.
- *Document the issue.* Individuals want to know as much as possible about the incident. While companies may be unable to share all the details about a breach at the time of notification, it is important that the organization provides enough information so that an individual can take appropriate action.
- *Don't sugarcoat the message.* A spoonful of sugar won't make the bad news go down easily. People expect the notice to be truthful, clear, and concise.

- *Provide support.* People expect the organization to help them with problems created by the breach. Specifically, companies should have trained personnel to help if a data breach ultimately results in identity theft or other related crimes.
- *Show me the money.* Consumers expect to receive financial compensation in the event that they experience monetary or productivity losses as a result of the company's breach.
- *Personalization creates trust.* Companies should make sure the notification has accurate information about how the breach may affect the customer. Above all, the customer's name and address should be double-checked for accuracy on a notification.
- *Adjust the message to fit the severity of the breach.* Not all breaches are the same. Companies should make sure the notification communicates the necessary actions that are relevant to the type of breach that occurs. Again, organizations should make sure that individuals have help in resolving any problems created by the breach.
- *Notify all potential victims.* Some companies have made the mistake of not informing customers in states without a notification law. The media, government agencies, and lawmakers will not view such practices favorably.[17]

11.7 Global Issues

Keeping abreast of U.S. privacy legislation and society's privacy sensitivity trends is challenging enough, let alone monitoring privacy trends globally. Some privacy issues arise globally in addition to in specific countries. When countries agree to a regional policy, it is a little easier; an agreement at that level ensures that all countries comply.

THEORY IN ACTION

Global Dispatches: Tough Privacy Law Debuts in Japan

As of April 1, 2005, many companies throughout Japan, including foreign ones, have had to comply with a stringent data privacy law. The Personal Information Protection Law applies to any company that has offices in Japan and holds personal data on 5,000 or more individuals, including employees. Under the law, personal data includes a person's name, address, date of birth, sex, and home and cell phone numbers. E-mail addresses are also covered if they're recognizable as a person's name.

The law requires companies to designate a corporate privacy officer, take security measures to prevent data from being leaked or stolen, and obtain consent from individuals before using personal information for any purpose other than the ones originally stated when the data was collected.

The law also sets possible fines of up to 300,000 yen and jail sentences of up to six months for data managers who don't comply.

M. Betts, "Global Dispatches: Tough Privacy Law Debuts in Japan," *Computerworld* (April 4, 2005).

The European Union (EU) has been very progressive in this area. The European Commission's Directive on Data Protection went into effect in October 1998 and prohibits the transfer of personal data to non-EU nations that do not meet the European "adequacy" standard for privacy protection. While the United States and the EU share the goal of enhancing privacy protection for their citizens, the United States takes a different approach to privacy from that taken by the EU. The United States relies on a mix of legislation, regulation, and self-regulation. The EU, however, relies on comprehensive legislation that, for example, requires creation of government data protection agencies; registration of databases with those agencies; and, in some instances, prior approval before personal data processing may begin. As a result of these different privacy approaches, the Directive could have significantly hampered the ability of U.S. companies to engage in many trans-Atlantic transactions.

In order to bridge these different privacy approaches and provide a streamlined means for U.S. organizations to comply with the Directive, the U.S. Department of Commerce, in consultation with the European Commission, developed a "safe harbor" framework. The safe harbor—approved by the EU in 2000—is an important way for U.S. companies to avoid experiencing interruptions in their business dealings with the EU or facing prosecution by European authorities under European privacy laws. Certifying to the safe harbor ensures that EU organizations know that your company provides "adequate" privacy protection, as defined by the Directive.[18]

THEORY IN ACTION

Gartner Global Privacy Issues and Considerations

In discussing key privacy issues, Gartner has precipitated some interesting considerations with regards to global issues in general. Within the context of mobile Internet access, "Location information is not just GPD information. Linked with other information that identifies an individual, location information can be considered personal information. Location information connects the online world with the physical world, and for many individuals, this crosses a border. Many providers are still in the 'collect' stage rather than the 'use' stage. They compile vast amounts of information, often without a clear plan of what to do with it. This violates a fundamental privacy principle: Collect information only for the purpose for which you need it. Concerns about location data apply not only to providers but also to corporate environments. Especially in the EU, employers do not necessarily have the right to access location data from corporate-owned smart phones, for example. There are also personnel implications for the telematics systems used by fleet owners to monitor carrier and delivery vehicles. There are few rules about what is or is not allowed. Organizations that process location information should orient their behavior around privacy principles rather than concrete legal requirements. In most countries, existing privacy laws have to be interpreted for location information. Depending on the nature of the business, privacy officers will focus between 5 percent and 25 percent of their time on location-based services."

With respect to cloud computing, Gartner has summarized the issue of privacy as follows: Cloud computing and privacy are at odds by nature. Privacy laws always apply to *one* country; the public cloud, in its ideal form, is not related to *any* country. However, many organizations would already benefit from, and are actually looking into other forms of, cloud computing (private cloud, virtual private cloud, and jurisdictionally specific software as a service), which—from a privacy perspective—often resembles the traditional forms of outsourcing, hosting, and offshoring. Organizations should follow these guidelines:

- Don't accept "no" for an answer when asking whether the processing of personal information in the cloud or abroad is allowed. Most privacy laws have some flexibility, guidance is evolving slowly, and, in many cases, there are legally acceptable solutions.
- Focus on the location of the legal entity of the provider, not on the physical locations of its operation centers. Document all legal, technical, physical, and contractual controls on both ends—client and provider.
- Privacy, security, and compliance risks are overlapping, especially in cloud computing. Take an integrated approach. It will probably include the encryption of personal information in transit to/from the provider, and while stored in the provider's data centers; the physical, technical, or logical segmentation of personal information from different countries; and contractual guarantees that data is protected adequately, ideally coupled with the possibility to audit the data centers.
- Don't demand storage in a specific country for privacy purposes alone. There are other cases when sensitive company information should not leave the country (for example, if there are export control or national security concerns), but in most cases—and usually under conditions—in-country storage is not mandatory for privacy compliance. In some cases, it will be sufficient to ensure that personal data will *not* be stored in a specific country that is known for its privacy violations.

If privacy concerns from regulators, legal advisors, or the public persist, then mitigate residual risk in one of the following ways: Allow the viewing of personal information only from the country of origin; allow infrastructure management from abroad, but request domestic hosting of infrastructure; mask data in such a way that only deidentified or tokenized information leaves the country; and request complete physical and technical lockdown of the remote operation center.

Public and corporate opinions about privacy in the cloud vary greatly between "it's illegal" and "it's no big deal." Privacy officers—and enterprise decision makers—should aim for the "golden middle," supporting IT's cloud and offshore initiatives where possible, while achieving maximum privacy protection for the individual customer or employee. The complexity of the discussion will consume between 20 percent and 30 percent of the privacy officer's time."

Carsten Casper, "Top Five Issues and Research Agenda, 2011 to 2012: The Privacy Officer," Gartner (June 14, 2011).

The DMA provides another service for global marketers called the Foreign Mail Preference Service (FMPS). The FMPS is a way that organizations can purge international mailing lists of consumers who want to receive less advertising mail at home. It contains names and addresses of consumers from the United Kingdom, Belgium, and Germany who do not wish to receive promotional mail at home. Individuals register by sending their name and home address to the appropriate consumer organization in their country. Each country provides the DMA with their list of consumer names and addresses for distribution. These lists—the "Robinson Lists," as they are known in Europe—are updated by the DMA several times per year.[19]

11.8 New Technology Implications

New technologies are rapidly being developed and deployed as CRM enablers. Although technology can enhance the CRM effort, it also presents additional privacy-related challenges. While radio frequency identification (RFID), tollway transponders, and wireless applications provide the consumer with ready and quick access to products and services, they also allow real-time dynamic capture of information, including location and mobility patterns. A growing concern is that of placing RFID tags on medicine that is sold to consumers. This invariably gives someone the ability to track which consumers are using which medicines, leading to a potentially invasive action. Mobile applications, while convenient, open up the consumer and the organization to new security and privacy challenges. Cloud-based data management is relatively new and, as with mobile technology, presents new challenges. Privacy-enabling organizations are developing new hardware, software, and methodologies to manage privacy in these new areas, but it is currently evolving. Best practices are, therefore, yet to be determined.

11.9 Other Resources

Additional information about privacy is available online. While some resources may offer consumer-oriented information, others can provide background on the consumer privacy debate and how it can best be protected and strengthened. Each of the websites listed in Table 11.3 has areas that focus on privacy. This list is not all-inclusive, and although website addresses were live at the time this book went to press, some may change in the future. We hope that the list will give the reader insight into the growing activity surrounding privacy. Resources already mentioned in the chapter have not been reproduced in this table.

Table 11.3 **Additional Resources Concerning Privacy**

Resource	Web Address
AARP	http://www.aarp.org
American Civil Liberties Union	http://www.aclu.org
American Library Association	http://www.ala.org
Center for Democracy & Technology	http://www.cdt.org/issue/consumer-privacy
Common Cause	http://www.commoncause.org
Consumer Action	http://www.consumer-action.org
Electronic Privacy Information Center	http://www.epic.org
GetNetWise	http://www.getnetwise.org
National Consumers League	http://www.nclnet.org
Privacy International	https://www.privacyinternational.org
Privacy Rights Clearinghouse	http://www.privacyrights.org
Privacy Times (newsletter)	http://www.privacytimes.com
Privacy, Business and Law (newsletter)	http://www.pandab.org
U.S. PIRG (Public Interest Research Group)	http://www.uspirg.org
University of Denver's Strum College of Law's Privacy Foundation	http://www.privacyfoundation.org

Chapter Summary

Privacy issues should be an integral component of an organization's CRM strategy. To increase CRM effectiveness, organizations should be proactive with regard to consumer privacy concerns. Acknowledging concerns and communicating how the company is alleviating these concerns can actually solidify the relationship between the consumer and the company. Consumers understand that by giving personal information to organizations, they can expect something in return. However, increased company use of consumer information for marketing purposes, increased unsolicited communication, increased use of invasive technology techniques to gather and use information, increased occurrences of identity theft, failure to secure information, and more frequent selling of consumer information have contributed to growing consumer privacy concerns.

As companies become more aggressive and efficient in gathering information on consumers, they must take on more responsibility for the maintenance and usage of that information. Subsequently, there has been a proliferation of legislation to protect the consumer, driven primarily by social pressure. Technological advances have made it easier for consumers to take advantage of new legislation, as they can control how, when, and by whom they are marketed via the Internet. Recent legislation has "teeth," meaning organizations can receive bad press, be fined, and face criminal charges when they fail to comply with privacy legislation. Many resources exist to assist consumers and companies in efforts to monitor and control privacy issues. Organizations must determine optimal expenditures for hardware and software that will meet privacy objectives.

Additionally, an international privacy approach must be defined that includes selecting the appropriate partners who can grow globally. Management of cloud-based and mobile data should be a high priority as organizations migrate to this platform.

Key Terms

BBBOnline is the Better Business Bureau's online privacy seal program.

Collaborative filtering is making predictions automatically about a person's behavior by comparing the person's interests to others' interests. If a person purchases X, others who purchased X also purchased Y and Z. Therefore, the assumption is that this person may be interested in purchasing Y and Z.

Consent is explicit permission given to an organization by an individual to handle his or her personal information in specified ways. "Informed consent" implies that the organization fully discloses its information practices prior to obtaining personal data or permission to use it.

Contact information is information that allows an individual to be contacted or located in the physical world—such as a telephone number or an address.

Data masking is a quasi-encryption method by which organizations replace selected characters of consumer data with fictitious data such as "X," nonsense or different names, or similar-looking characters (i.e., numeric, alpha, special) but not the same characters, such as different credit card numbers.

Digital watermarking has the same effect as using a watermark in a Word or PDF document. It can be used for text (at the bit level), video, and audio. Technology allows one to hide identification information.

Double opt-in is a two-step process. In the first step it requires a person's explicit consent for the use and disclosure of his or her personal information beyond the original, primary purpose for which it was collected. If the person provides consent, usually by checking a box and then submitting, the second step is where the organization confirms the person's request with the person.

Opt-in is an option that requires a person's explicit consent for the use and disclosure of his or her personal information beyond the original, primary purpose for which it was collected.

Opt-out is an option that allows a person to prevent the use and disclosure of his or her personal information beyond the original, primary purpose for which it was collected.

Phishing is the art of tricking people into divulging confidential information by using unsolicited e-mails disguised as reputable correspondence from banks, credit card companies, or companies the consumer is familiar with.

Privacy policy is a description of a website's practices with respect to its collection and use of information.

Spam is unsolicited "junk" e-mail containing advertising or promotional messages sent to large numbers of people.

TRUSTe is an online privacy seal program that certifies eligible websites. To be certified, sites must meet baseline privacy standards.

Trustmark is an online seal awarded by TRUSTe to websites that agree to post their privacy practices openly via privacy statements. When a user clicks on the TRUSTe trustmark, he or she is taken directly to the privacy statement of the licensed website.

Questions

1. Why would a consumer knowingly give up extensive personal information?
2. What are the most sensitive and current privacy issues facing consumers?
3. What are some of the easiest things a consumer can and should do to protect his or her privacy?
4. Why do some organizations choose to use a double opt-in strategy?

Exercises

1. Provide several examples of phishing from your own personal experience.
2. Find a recent article on invasive CRM practices and discuss the privacy implications.
3. Find a website that has (a) a double opt-in strategy and (b) a prechecked opt-in component.
4. Find a children-oriented website. Discuss how it manages privacy issues related to children.
5. Create an outline for a generic policy.

Section 4

CRM Evaluation

Chapter 12

CRM Program Measurement and Tools

12.1 Introduction

When the proposal for a company-wide CRM system is first introduced, a chief executive officer (CEO) or chief financial officer (CFO) will inquire about the costs and benefits. Costs involve out-of-pocket CRM costs (relatively easy to measure but usually underestimated), in addition to management, employee development, training, and phasing-in costs (all more difficult to measure). Computing the benefits of CRM is not easy either. There are many effectiveness measures, and the appropriate ones need to be matched with the specific CRM goals and efforts at hand. In addition, it is sometimes difficult to relate certain effectiveness measures, such as satisfaction and loyalty, to the bottom line. Further, it is often necessary for company divisions to share customer transaction information and have a unified view of the customer before CRM efforts can be judged on their effectiveness. This can be a cumbersome undertaking if the divisions have legacy systems that do not mesh.

THEORY IN ACTION

Top Ten Mistakes Companies Make When Measuring CRM Effectiveness

Jesse Harriott, the former director of research at Monster.com, recognizes some significant areas of weakness in CRM implementation and measurement. Following is a list of what he considers the biggest problems.

Off in a Corner

All too often, a working group or committee in an organization will be tasked with creating a framework to measure a CRM deployment. This can often be a recipe for disaster. As the group works independently to create the best CRM measurement system the world has ever seen, the rest of the company marches on. The entire organization will be impacted by successful CRM implementation and measurement. Therefore, all key stakeholders must be actively involved in shifting the organizational processes to support the CRM effort.

Not Enough Leadership Support

Along with clear collaboration across the company, the importance of measuring and acting on the CRM information must be acknowledged as critical to the business. If the boardroom does not see CRM measurement as important, the rest of the organization will fail to support it over the long term.

Too Much Data

This is a huge challenge for organizations that set out to measure their CRM implementation. Given that there are so many different sources of information, there is an overwhelming amount of data. Separating the wheat from the chaff and turning what's left into insight are often more art than science for many organizations. The first step is starting with clear, measurable objectives regarding what the company wants to achieve with the CRM system.

No Clearly Defined Strategy

To create an effective CRM measurement system, there must be a clear strategy regarding what is to be achieved with the CRM deployment. This way, every metric tracked is helping to identify whether a specific objective is being achieved. Companies that fail to do this end up tracking more than is needed, with no clarity and agreement on whether the CRM implementation has been successful.

Knowing Is Not Enough

When creating a CRM measurement strategy, too often the primary focus is on how to capture and report all of the knowledge in the system. This is clearly important, but more critical is deciding how the information will be acted upon. For example, if an organization is tracking "cost to serve," what are the thresholds for acting on this information? Will it stop serving customers if its cost to serve is 30 percent higher than the average? Will it change its service model if the cost to serve drops below a certain level? These issues must be discussed and identified across the organization before a measurement plan is deployed.

Stale as Seven-Day-Old Bread

The business needs timely information to act upon. However, by the time information is circulated through the organization to the people that will actually do something, it is often old and outdated. It is important for each organization to clearly outline a process to collect and distribute information rapidly. Often, an organization is better served by looking at 70 percent complete information that is directionally accurate than waiting for 100 percent complete information that may be outdated.

Death by 1,000 Dashboards

Companies love "dashboards." Given this, every organization will eventually have a set of CRM dashboards when implementing a CRM strategy. In many organizations, everything that can possibly be measured is put in a dashboard, making everyone feel like they are part of a "metrics-driven organization." Meanwhile, some people don't know how to read the dashboard, and many others never even look at it. Companies must make sure that each dashboard has a purpose, has a review process, and is acted upon before effort is expended to create it.

Failure to Benchmark

The organization needs to benchmark against other companies when evaluating its CRM metrics. Many companies fail to do this and end up talking to themselves. For example, a company sees that the conversion rate for high-priority sales leads from its new scoring algorithm is 40 percent and is very pleased with what it feels is a good result. Because it did not check with others in its industry, it fails to realize that its competition is routinely getting 60 percent conversion just by leading with a different product during the sales cycle.

Failure to Recognize the Impact of Corporate Inertia

It's not enough just to have a good CRM measurement and action plan. The organization must be prepared to change processes to leverage the benefits of a CRM measurement program. For example, customer service must be prepared to adapt its service model if CRM monitoring consistently identifies an underserved customer segment. If departments are not adequately prepared, able, and willing to adapt, then corporate inertia will take over, and insight from CRM measurement will not impact the business.

Failure to Measure Outcomes

Spurring high-impact action across the organization is only the first step to successful CRM measurement. Companies must also remember to measure and monitor actions to see whether they have their desired impact. For example, a company notices that retention rates are slipping in the Phoenix metro area. After further analysis, it determines that the lack of a dedicated service representative with in-depth knowledge of the Phoenix market is the problem. The company takes action and changes the service staff. Because of the dynamic nature of the business, however, it moves on to other things and fails to measure its impact going forward. To avoid a situation like this, it is important that organizations keep a running list of actions, owners, and their intended impact, as well as progress toward that impact.

12.2 Areas Requiring Measurement

Where marketers once focused on measuring aggregate market share, they now focus on measuring their share of wallet, share of stomach, share of trips, and so on for distinct buying units such as individuals, couples, families, businesses, and organizations. Although aggregate measures of marketing success remain important, they have been supplemented by an increasing number of measures useful to those involved in CRM efforts. There are literally hundreds of CRM tools and effectiveness measures, and they vary in applicability and importance according to type of industry, type of firm, whether the relationship is contractual or noncontractual, whether the relationship is business-to-business (B2B) or business-to-consumer (B2C), and many other characteristics.

Company CRM efforts focusing on acquiring new customers require different measures than efforts focusing on cross-selling and up-selling to current customers. The unit or segment under review (i.e., individual, household, or organizational level) also impacts the types of effectiveness measures used. These factors help determine which CRM effectiveness measures are optimal. Bear in mind that some measures work well in more than one area of investigation.

The vast majority of CRM effectiveness measures can be grouped into four important and distinct areas:

1. The CRM customer cycle measures: acquisition, retention, and win-back
2. Company 3E measures: efficiency, effectiveness, and employee behavior
3. Customer value and customer equity measures
4. Customer knowledge measures

Before investigating the metrics in these four areas, let us first review the basic measures that comprise the very foundation of customer relationship management: service quality, customer satisfaction, loyalty, and retention.

12.3 Basic Measures

The customer–company profit model is presented in Chapter 9 and is reproduced as Figure 12.1. The variables in this model consist of both psychological and behavioral dimensions. In the long list of CRM metrics that are contained in this chapter, all can be characterized as psychological, behavioral, or hybrid. Variables such as satisfaction, trust, and emotional affinity are psychological components, whereas retention, profitability, defection, complaints, recommendations or referrals, products used, size, and frequency of orders are all behavioral components. As was discussed earlier in the book, loyalty can be considered a hybrid variable, for it can be "true" loyalty (psychological) or "behavioral" loyalty.

Figure 12.1 **The Customer–Company Profit Chain**

THEORY IN ACTION

How AT&T Uses CRM to Improve Customer Retention

To reduce high levels of customer churn, which are common characteristics of the communications sector, AT&T Wireless decided to focus on customer loyalty and retention. The company initiated and built a scalable data warehouse for planning and product implementation and used it to improve customer profiling. This feature of the data warehouse has enabled it to serve existing customers, as well as approaching prospects with more targeted information based on predictive modeling. Easy access to customer profiles enables AT&T staff to have a much better understanding of customer needs and how to meet them and analyze information to help continually improve customer satisfaction.

D. Sharp, *Customer Relationship Management Systems Handbook* (New York: Auerbach, 2002).

One of CRM's purposes is to improve customer perception of service quality (equally important in the sales of tangible and intangible goods) and increase customer satisfaction and loyalty. Consequently, these variables can serve as measures of the effectiveness of an organization's CRM initiatives. Some marketers feel that retention rate is the most important component of market share and that retention is driven by customer satisfaction.[1] R. T. Rust, A. J. Zahorik, and T. L. Keiningham state that customer satisfaction and service quality have a measurable impact on customer retention, market share, and profitability.[2] While we discussed these measures in Chapter 9 from a strategy perspective, let us now investigate them from a measurement perspective.

12.3a Service Quality

Companies measure customer satisfaction as an indicator of service quality. This enables them to improve the customer service experience when indicators of service quality go down. Another reason that companies measure service quality through customer satisfaction surveys is to establish links among service quality, customer satisfaction, retention, defection, and share of wallet.

A well-known measure of consumer perception of service quality is **SERVQUAL**. SERVQUAL is composed of two matched sets of 22 items (44 items in all), each describing expectations for a particular service category and then perceptions of a particular service provider. Both sets of items use a scale labeled "Strongly Agree" (7) to "Strongly Disagree" (1). Approximately half the items are worded negatively, which are denoted by a (–) at the end of the statement.[3] (See Appendix 1 for the complete SERVQUAL instrument.) SERVQUAL is based on five factors that customers use in assessing service quality:[4]

1. *Tangibility:* Physical facilities, equipment, and appearance of personnel
2. *Reliability:* Ability to perform the promised service dependably and accurately
3. *Responsiveness:* Willingness to help customers and provide prompt service
4. *Assurance:* Knowledge and courtesy of employees and their ability to inspire trust and confidence
5. *Empathy:* Caring, individualized attention the firm provides its customers

Note that, while the above items are common and relevant to all service firms, the SERVQUAL measure does not contain items relevant to specific firms or services. Thus, SERVQUAL must be adapted to suit one's specific service or industry.

How can SERVQUAL be used? First, it should be used periodically to measure changes in service quality. Second, an overall score can be computed to assess an organization's standing across all five variables, or individual scores can assess each service dimension individually. Third, although reliability has been found to be the most important, an organization may want to study the relative importance of each of the dimensions in determining customer perceptions of service quality. Fourth, customers can be grouped into segments based on their SERVQUAL scores and strategies developed accordingly. Finally, SERVQUAL can be used to determine service quality among stores in a chain and a company's scores vis-à-vis its competition.[5]

12.3b Satisfaction and Loyalty

Since CRM focuses on improving service to an organization's desirable customers, one of the underlying measures of CRM effectiveness is customer satisfaction. Companies, when conducting satisfaction studies, must be careful to differentiate among first-time buyers, short-term buyers, long-term buyers, those about to defect, and desirable versus undesirable customers. Much of the "disconnect" between customer satisfaction and customer loyalty—for instance, totally satisfied customers not remaining loyal—may be attributed to company researchers not differentiating their customer base when conducting such studies. Feedback from a company's desirable customers deserves emphasis as opposed to feedback from customers the company has little or no interest in keeping. Something else to keep in mind is that as a company continues to lose customers, its customer satisfaction scores may rise. Why? Because the customers who remain really like the company.

12.3b.1 Customer Satisfaction

Satisfaction can be broadly characterized as a postpurchase evaluation of product quality given prepurchase expectations.[6] According to R. L. Oliver, satisfaction judgments are a function of the baseline effect of expectations plus a perceived disconfirmation of expectations.[7] Expectations provide the baseline measure for satisfaction. If disconfirmation occurs, then customer satisfaction may be high (service received is higher than expectations) or low (service received is lower than expectations). Discussion regarding how disconfirmation should be measured has resulted in two approaches:

1. *Service quality gap measure:* On a series of attributes such as "visual appeal of physical facilities," "prompt service," "convenient operating hours," and so on, respondents rate their perception of the organization's service. Next, they rate their expectations regarding each service dimension. Finally, the disconfirmation score is computed.
2. *Direct measure:* Respondents' answers on each dimension regarding whether or not the service was "much better than expected," "about what was expected," or "much worse than expected" are computed.

Recent research has indicated that the second approach is preferred, since the difference score computed in the first approach is not as reliable as the two components from which it is computed. The direct measure avoids this problem.

It should be kept in mind that satisfaction can be measured at a global level (e.g., "How satisfied are you with InterContinental Hotels & Resorts?") or at the attribute level (e.g., "How satisfied are you with InterContinental Hotels & Resorts on the following attributes: check-in, room service, quality of food, ambiance, loyalty club, etc.?"). The global measure is useful in monitoring overall satisfaction over time and as a comparison with other hotel scores. If the global score is low, however, it does not provide management with a focal point warranting change. The attribute scores are more helpful in addressing deficiencies because of their specificity.

Today, product and service parity among rival brands leads consumers to believe they can switch brands without experiencing any loss of quality even if they are totally satisfied with yours. When all competitive brands are viewed as excellent (some say this is true for brands of luxury cars), your brand has to achieve the highest satisfaction ratings even to be considered for repurchase. Achieving the highest customer satisfaction ratings of 5 on a 5-point scale is necessary to be considered for repurchase; a 4 simply isn't good enough. There are too many competitors operating at the 5 level for a company to be satisfied with anything less. A company is better off investing in moving customers from a 4 to a 5 than in moving them from a 1, 2, or 3 to a 4. Xerox found that its "totally satisfied" customers were six times more likely to repurchase Xerox products over the next 18 months than its customers who were merely "satisfied."[8]

Research has shown that customers who participate in satisfaction surveys subsequently increase their purchasing behavior at both the brand and product category levels and are less likely to switch to a competitor for up to a year after their participation. It is hypothesized that survey participation fosters positive feelings about the firm and motivates customers to become more loyal. This holds even for those who initially expressed dissatisfaction with the firm.[9]

12.3b.2 Customer Loyalty

Several different metrics can be used to measure customer loyalty. Three of the most popular are **past customer value**; the recency, frequency, monetary value (RFM) approach; and share of wallet.

Past customer value extrapolates the value of a customer's past transactions into the future. The problem with this approach is that a high-value customer in the past may have been merely "transactional," and projecting high past value may seriously overestimate future value. Furthermore, companies are likely to spend significant amounts of money maintaining this type of relationship that never amounts to anything. Conversely, mislabeling customers as "transactional" based on past purchases may underestimate their future value if they develop into "true friends."

The recency, frequency, monetary value (RFM) approach was extensively discussed in Chapter 7. Recency is the date of the most recent customer transaction. Frequency is the number of customer transactions with the organization within a specific period of time. Monetary is the amount spent within the same specific time period used. Customers are ranked on a scale from 1 to 5 on each parameter. The best customers have a ranking of 555, and the worst customers have a ranking of 111. High RFM customers are felt to have high future revenue potential because those who purchased recently, frequently, and spent the most money are more likely to buy again. RFM scores can be used to direct different types of messages and strategies, and thus even 111 customers should not be abandoned; rather, different appeals should be directed at them. RFM is widely used even though the measure ignores purchase "pacing"—that is, the amount of time that elapses between each purchase.

Share of wallet refers to the proportion of category value the customer spends with the company.[10] Share of wallet measures the amount a customer spends with your company compared with what he or she spends in the entire category—for example, the amount a person spends with United Airlines compared with the total he or she spends on all airlines. The difficulty with this measure is obtaining the total amount spent in the entire category. For a rough approximation, surveys can be done with various customer segments to gather this information and then apply it to other customers who are similar.

12.3c Retention

Repeat customers are important because they may generate more income than new customers, marketing expenditures may be less for repeat versus new customers, and they may positively influence many others. First purchases by new customers may be of the "trial" variety and therefore of lesser value than repeat purchases. Measures of retention or defection are therefore key in evaluating the success of one's CRM efforts. Since retention and defection rates are easily measurable, they become key measures of CRM effectiveness.

Defection curves can show how responsive profits are to changes in defection rates (Figure 12.2). As a credit card company cut its defection rate from 20 percent to 10 percent, the average life span of its relationship with a customer doubles from 5 to 10 years, and the value of that customer more than doubles from $134 to $300. As the defection rate drops another 5 percent, the average life span doubles again and profits rise 75 percent from $300 to $525.[11]

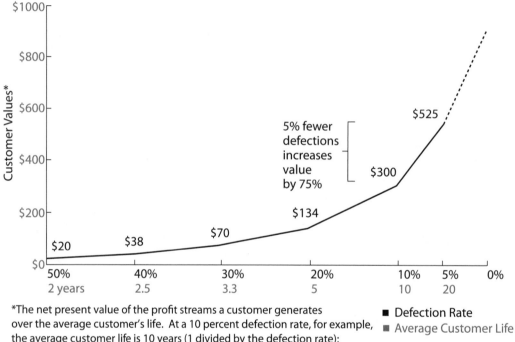

*The net present value of the profit streams a customer generates over the average customer's life. At a 10 percent defection rate, for example, the average customer life is 10 years (1 divided by the defection rate); the customer value is the net present value of the profit stream for ten years.

■ Defection Rate
■ Average Customer Life

Figure 12.2 A Credit Card Company's Defection Curve

THEORY IN ACTION

The Importance of Customer Retention

Retention rates in financial services vary dramatically by product and channel. In general insurance, with annual contracts, the rates range from 30 to 90 percent or even more. In

investment products with fixed terms, the rate can be well under 10 percent. Where retention rates are very low, acquisition rates need to be very high for the customer base even
to stand still.

E. Aspinall, C. Nancarrow, and M. Stone, in B. Foss and M. Stone, eds., *CRM in Financial Services: A Practical Guide to Making Customer Relationship Management Work* (London: Kogan Page, 2002).

12.4 CRM Customer Cycle Measures

Keeping in mind that the CRM customer cycle consists of customer acquisition, retention, and, when necessary, win-back, a company can choose from a wide range of CRM metrics to measure its performance. In addition, keep in mind that customer retention can take many forms—developing closer bonds, changing behavior, and avoiding defection—so different metrics may be used depending on the form of retention being addressed by a company's marketing programs. Table 12.1 details some of the more commonly used CRM metrics applicable in each of the various phases of the CRM customer cycle.

Table 12.1 CRM Customer Cycle Measures

CRM Customer Cycle	Measures	Notes
Customer Acquisition	Acquisition rate/yield rate/ capture rate	Ratio of new customers versus the number of proposals to win them
	Conversion rate	Number of B2B prospects converted to company customers
	Conversion efficiency	Number of new customers per dollar investment
	Average customer acquisition cost	
	Acquisition campaign cycle time	Amount of time needed to develop and implement an acquisition campaign
	Communication and administrative costs directly attributable to acquisition activities	
	Acquisition campaign results versus expectations	
	Percent growth in customer acquisition	

(Continued)

Table 12.1 (*Continued*)

CRM Customer Cycle	Measures	Notes
	Ratio of sales wins to losses	An important measure of the effectiveness of new business initiatives, proposals, and sales presentations
Retention: Developing Closer Bonds	Share of wallet	Percentage of the total expenditures in a category that an individual store or brand satisfies
	Share of category	Similar to share of wallet, except it is based on volume or frequency of purchase as opposed to value
	Purchase cycle time	
	Net promoter score	
	Maintenance ratio	Number of current customers retained versus number of customers defected
	Defection rate	Number of customers defected versus total number of customers
	Continuity of most profitable customers	
	Customer satisfaction	One of the key measures in CRM
	Customer loyalty	Another one of the key measures in CRM
	Sales generated by long-term customers versus short-term customers	Remember to compare identical customer cohort groups (e.g., sales to two-year customers)
	Emotional affinity	
	Service/transaction satisfaction	A particular type of customer satisfaction measure relevant to determining the effectiveness of employee training techniques
	Measures of service quality	Tangibility, reliability, responsiveness, assurance, and empathy
	Perceptions of value	Benefits/costs
	Number of customer complaints	
	Number of recommendations or referrals	

(*Continued*)

Table 12.1 (Continued)

CRM Customer Cycle	Measures	Notes
	Mean time between winning a customer and losing that customer	
Retention: Behavior Changes Reflected by Customer Growth and Development	ROR (return on relationship)	
	Size of wallet	
	Share of wallet	
	Share of category	
	Number of company products held per customer	
	Profitability	
	Depth of relationship (share of customer)	As measured by share of customer wallet, stomach, travel, salty snacks, etc.
	Number of referrals	
	Type of channel usage	For example, more efficient website and e-mail usage versus phone or in-person contacts
	Number of customer service representative interactions	
	Self-entry of consumer data, product purchases, etc.	
	More repeat business	
	Shorter purchase cycle time	
	Brand switching and brand switching warnings	
	Number of complaints	
	Increased sales	
	Customer revenues	By segment, by top 20 percent, etc.
	RFM	Recency of purchase, frequency of purchase, amount of purchase
	Event history models	
	Customer response rate	The number of customer-initiated contacts versus company-initiated contacts
Retention: Defector Indicators		
	Acceleration or deceleration in customer purchases	
	Average retention rate	

(Continued)

Table 12.1 (Continued)

CRM Customer Cycle	Measures	Notes
	Average lifetime duration	
	Change in number of product categories purchased	
	Change in number of cancelled orders, returns, exchanges, or complaints	
	Change in purchase of ancillaries, such as service contracts, extended warranties, installation, training, etc.	
	Change in order size	
	Change in order frequency	
	Change in number of references or referrals	
	Change in number of contacts and types of contacts	
	Change in use of touch points	
	Change in customer revenue	
	Customer retention	
	Days since last purchase	
	Share of wallet changes	
	Survival rate	
Win-Back	Average cost per customer reactivated	
	Percent of customers reactivated per campaign	
	Percent of "saved relationships"	
	Second CLV (i.e., lifetime value of reactivated customers)	Generally lower than the original CLV

12.4a Acquisition

While CRM recognizes that customer retention is critical to a company's growth and profits, it also recognizes that it is necessary to acquire new customers to feed a pipeline that is losing customers through attrition and defection. Through data mining efforts, companies can determine the characteristics of profitable customers. Once they have these profiles, they can create effective acquisition techniques directed at prospects that match the characteristics of their profitable customers.

Particularly relevant measures in assessing the effectiveness of acquisition efforts are acquisition rate, conversion rate, and acquisition cost.

12.4a.1 Acquisition Rate, Yield Rate, or Capture Rate

This value reflects the number of prospects acquired divided by the total number targeted. In B2B situations, this measure is referred to as the conversion rate. An example is a credit card company that sent 500,000 promotional pieces to an affinity group consisting of alumni from a Big Ten university, which resulted in 15,000 new cardholders. Thus, the acquisition rate is 3 percent (15,000/500,000).

12.4a.2 Conversion Rate

The conversion rate is the number of B2B prospects converted to company customers by a salesperson, sales territory, and so on. The conversion rate is calculated as:

$$t/(t-1)$$

where
t =   Number of customers in the time period
$t-1$ =   Number of prospects in the time period

12.4a.3 Acquisition Cost or Conversion Efficiency

The acquisition cost or conversion efficiency is the cost of the acquisition campaign divided by the number of prospects acquired. An example would be the credit card company acquisition campaign that cost $400,000 and resulted in 15,000 new accounts. Thus, the cost of acquiring a customer was $26.67 ($400,000/15,000).

12.4a.4 Other Acquisition Effectiveness Measures

Other measures frequently used to determine CRM acquisition effectiveness include percent growth in customer acquisition, computing acquisition campaign cycle time (the amount of time needed to develop and implement an acquisition campaign), and ratio of sales wins to losses (an important measure of the effectiveness of new business initiatives, proposals, and sales presentations). Naturally, communication and administrative costs need to be determined. It is also valuable to quantify expectations against which acquisition campaign results can be compared.

12.4b Retention

It has been shown that if a company wants to increase customer lifetime value (CLV), retention measures have a greater effect than customer acquisition.[12] Given the high levels of customer defection in many industries, simply retaining customers is a difficult endeavor. Strategies developed to retain and increase the value of a customer by increasing the breadth and worth of their purchases are difficult to develop and assess. The most prominent CRM effectiveness measures in this area are share of wallet, share of category, and purchase cycle time. However, measuring the size of wallet is necessary before share of wallet can be meaningfully measured.

The data needed to compute these measures is gathered from a variety of sources such as individual company marketing research studies, panel-based data, scanner data, and/or syndicated marketing research studies done for specific industries. For example, Nielsen audits for supermarkets, drugstores, and mass merchandisers, while Technomic, Inc., studies the food industry.

Another customer retention measure that is used is the net promoter score (NPS). The NPS was introduced by F. F. Reichheld. To determine this score, a company asks its customers only one question: "How likely is it that you would recommend us to a friend or colleague?" The results are scored on a scale of 0 to 10, with 10 meaning "extremely likely." Those with a 9 or 10 rating are "promoters," and those with a score between 0 and 6 are "detractors."[13] Then, the company's NPS is computed by subtracting its percentage of "detractors" from its percentage of "promoters."

Here are some other useful measures:

- Maintenance ratio (the number of customers from a cohort retained versus the number of customers defected)
- Defection rate (the number of customers defected versus the total number of customers)
- Continuity of most profitable customers
- Measures of overall customer satisfaction, loyalty, and commitment
- Emotional affinity
- Service/transaction satisfaction
- Measures of service quality (tangibility, reliability, responsiveness, assurance, and empathy)
- Perceptions of value
- Number of customer complaints
- Number of recommendations or referrals
- Mean time between winning a customer and losing that customer

12.4c Effecting Behavior Change

Cross-selling (getting customers to purchase a wider variety of goods and services) and up-selling (getting customers to purchase higher-priced offerings) are very effective ways to increase sales and profits. Measures of success include share of wallet and share of category, among others.

12.4c.1 Size of Wallet

Size of wallet is the total amount of a buyer's spending in a category. The following example is the total weekly amount a family spent at supermarkets:

Jewel-Osco	$ 90
Dominick's	45
Whole Foods	30
Size of family wallet	**$165**

12.4c.2 Share of Wallet

Share of wallet is the percentage of the total expenditures in a category that an individual store or brand satisfies. For example, Jewel-Osco has a 55 percent share of the above family's supermarket wallet ($90/$165).

To calculate share of wallet, a company must gather information on a customer's purchases from competitors, which can be done on an aggregate basis through a clearinghouse. For example, the eight major "Loop" (central business district) banks in Chicago provided information on new accounts opened and closed by value and account type to a clearinghouse. The clearinghouse then provided each bank with its market share on these and other variables without disclosing competitor information.

Companies can also collect share of wallet information through clever promotional campaigns. For example, United Airlines conducted a campaign by awarding 2,000 frequent flyer miles for each frequent flyer statement (up to three) a member sent in from other non-Star Alliance airlines. These enabled United to determine its major competitors and gather information on its share of flying miles. Most importantly, United gathered valuable information about its most profitable customers, which helped determine whom to target with special offers in order to counteract competitors' sales promotions aimed at their most profitable frequent flyer members. For one of the newest techniques used to measure share of wallet, refer to the Theory in Action feature "Wallet Allocation Rule."

THEORY IN ACTION

Wallet Allocation Rule

Keiningham, Aksoy, Buoye, and Cooil developed the Wallet Allocation Rule, which enables computation of share of wallet by simply knowing two things: the rank consumers assign to a store or brand relative to other stores or brands, and the number of brands or stores in the category the consumer uses. For example, when ranking commercial airlines, John ranks Cathay Pacific a 1, United a 2, and American Airlines a 3. To arrive at each brand's share of wallet, use the following formula:

Share of wallet = [(1 − (Rank/# of brands + 1)] × (2/# of brands)

John's share of wallet is:

50% for Cathay Pacific: $[1 − (\frac{1}{4})] \times \frac{2}{3} = \frac{3}{4} \times \frac{2}{3} = \frac{1}{2}$

33% for United: $[1 − (\frac{2}{4})] \times \frac{2}{3} = \frac{1}{2} \times \frac{2}{3} = \frac{1}{3}$

17% for American: $[1 − (\frac{3}{4})] \times \frac{2}{3} = \frac{1}{4} \times \frac{2}{3} = \frac{1}{6}$

The formula is based on data from 17,000 consumers in 9 countries across more than 12 industries. The authors claim there is a 0.9 correlation between a brand's Wallet Allocation Rule score and its actual share of wallet.

"Customer Loyalty Isn't Enough. Grow Your Share of Wallet," in *Harvard Business Review* (October 2011): 35–37.

12.4c.3 Share of Category

Share of category is similar to the computation for share of wallet, except share of category is based on volume or frequency of purchase as opposed to value. An example is when in an average month, a family visits Jewel-Osco six times, Dominick's four times, and Whole Foods twice. Thus, Jewel-Osco's share of category for this family is 6/12, or 50 percent.

According to V. Kumar and W. Reinartz, share of category may be the better measure when the amounts customers spend are similar (groceries) rather than different (furniture, cars). They also pointed out that a buyer's attractiveness depends not only on the company's share of the buyer's wallet but also the size of that person's wallet (i.e., would you rather have a 70 percent share of a $1,000 wallet or a 30 percent share of a $4,000 wallet?).[14]

THEORY IN ACTION

Enterprise Incentive Management Software

Enterprise incentive management (EIM) software, offered by companies like IBM and Callidus, promote employee cross-selling and up-selling behavior by monitoring their successes in each area and providing prompt bonuses and compensation for achieving company objectives. Companies often reward employees for bringing in new customers but neglect compensating employees for the more time-consuming customer retention activities like cross-selling and up-selling. This is due in part to the ease of awarding bonuses for new accounts that are easy to measure and the difficulty of tracking successes in the retention areas. EIM makes the latter easy and contributes to company success in the area of implementing retention strategies. Employees are much more likely to implement cross-selling, up-selling, personalization, customization, and other retention strategies when they know their efforts will be rewarded on a prompt and accurate basis.

12.4c.4 Other Effectiveness Measures

There are many other measures of effectiveness. At the macro level there are measures of customer equity (the sum of all customer lifetime values for a company) and return on relationships (the long-term net financial outcome caused by the establishment and maintenance of an organization's network of relationships).[15] Depth of relationship can be measured in a variety of ways, including number of referrals, repeat business, number of company touch point interfaces, shorter purchase cycle time, number of company products purchased, RFM, and event history measures (discussed later in the chapter).

12.4d Retention and Defection Indicators

Now that companies are at or nearing parity levels in product and service areas, one of CRM's major goals is the retention of customers by anticipating needs and providing better service. Various measures are relevant here: retention, defection, lifetime duration, and survival rate.

12.4d.1 Average Retention Rate

The average retention rate is the number of active customers in cohort in time t who were active in time $t-1$ divided by the number of active customers in cohort in time $t-1$. A cohort is a batch of customers acquired or active within a specified time period. An example would be if out of 50,000 Stew Leonard's customers who were active in 2012, 45,000 were still active in 2013, then the average retention rate would be 90 percent.

12.4d.2 Average Defection Rate

The average defection rate is the opposite of the average retention rate. It is calculated as 1 – Average retention rate. An example would be if Stew Leonard's has an average retention rate of 90 percent, that means 10 percent of its customers are defecting each year (1 – .90).

12.4d.3 Average Lifetime Duration

The average lifetime duration is calculated as $1/(1 -$ Average retention rate). An example would be if Stew Leonard's has an average retention rate of 90 percent, then the store's average lifetime duration is $1/(1 - .9)$, or 10 years. Thus, the average lifetime duration for a Stew Leonard's customer is 10 years.

12.4d.4 Survival Rate

The survival rate is equal to how many customers remain between the formation of a cohort and any point in time afterward. Survival rate in time t equals the survival rate in time $t - 1$ times the retention rate in time t. An example would be if Stew Leonard's acquired 2,500 new customers in 2011, how many will survive to 2014?

Year	Retention Rate	Survival Rate	# of Survivors
2012	.90	.90	2,250
2013	.93	.837	2,093
2014	.95	.795	1,988

Although Stew Leonard's has an average retention rate of 90 percent, this does not mean that retention rates will be 90 percent in every year. The reason is that over time, proportionately fewer customers leave. Retention rates tend to increase at a decreasing rate. Managerial judgment is used in estimating retention rates in the future. (See Kumar and Reinartz for some useful formulas.)[16] The survival rate in year 2013 is computed by taking 0.90, the survival rate in time $t - 1$ (year 2012) times 0.93, the retention rate in time t (year 2013). This is calculated as .90 × .93 = .837.

12.4d.5 Preventing Defection and Downward Migration

Customers often change their buying behavior before defecting. While it is less expensive to win back lost customers than to attract new customers, it is better to avoid losing them in the first place. Consequently, many companies have developed leading indicators of customer defection. Measures of individual downward migration are very relevant here.

A base formula is:

Customer revenue in time period $t/$Customer revenue in time period $t - 1$

If an American Express customer averaged $3,000 in charges per month in 2011 but only $800 per month in 2012, the difference could be due to retirement or the customer switching activity to a different card. If the customer database indicates the former is unlikely, then American Express might assume the customer's decreased activity is due to their increased use of another company's card. This could presage defection, and American Express may want to be proactive and increase the cardholder's American Express activity through an incentive offer.

12.4d.6 Other Defector Indicators

Other indicators of defection include days since last purchase; buying cycle sales changes; share of wallet changes; change in number of product categories purchased; change in number of cancelled orders, returns, exchanges, or complaints; change in purchase of ancillaries, such as service contracts, extended warranties, installation, and training; change in order size; change in number of contacts; and change in use of touch points.

12.4e Win-Back

Although companies do their best to retain customers, it is inevitable that some customers will defect. Rather than assume these customers are permanently lost, CRM-oriented companies realize that it will cost far less to win back these customers than to attract new customers. Numerous win-back or regain measures are available to assess CRM performance in this area. J. S. Thomas, R. C. Blattberg, and E. J. Fox suggested computing CLV for customers who defect but are won back and call the measure *second customer lifetime value* (SCLV).[17] Of course, it is important to factor in the costs of winning back lost customers. Sometimes their SCLV is less than what it cost to win them back. The lifetime value of reactivated customers is generally lower than the original CLV. Other measures include average cost per customer reactivated, percent of customers reactivated per campaign, and percent of "saved" relationships.

12.5 Company 3E Measures

12.5a Increasing the Efficiency and Effectiveness of Marketing Programs

More effective marketing campaigns, better campaign management, and report generation time efficiencies are all important measures of efficiency and effectiveness. Other effectiveness measures include the following:

- First contact resolution of problems by customer contact personnel
- Successful resolution of problems by customer contact personnel
- Time to resolution by customer contact personnel in terms of clock time and human hours
- Reduced customer attrition
- Revenue per CRM dollar (total revenue versus total expenditures on managing CRM)
- Improved customer response rates across touch points
- Time spent in generating targeted promotions, sales reports, and marketing research information
- Reduced sales cycle, campaign development cycle, and product development

THEORY IN ACTION

Google Adds Software Designed to Track Success of Customers' Ads

Google Inc. introduced free software that gives customers more information on the effectiveness of their online advertising. Google Analytics will let customers track how often Web surfers click on ads next to Internet search results and whether they purchase a product or generate a sales lead, said Richard Holden, a product management director.

The new features heighten competition for companies, including WebSideStory Inc. (which was acquired by Omniture in 2008), that offer rival software. Google's move also highlights the company's ability to use its surging ad business to offer for free a product it once priced at hundreds of dollars. The changes may mean that Mountain View, California–based Google will sell more ads. "We think this will make advertisers more effective," Holden said in an interview. "It will drive our business faster."

Using Google Analytics software, website owners will be able to track how many people click on their ads and then follow their movement through the site to determine how many request a brochure or buy a product, Holden said.

Bloomberg News, "Google Adds Software Designed to Track Success of Customers' Ads," *Chicago Tribune* (November 15, 2005): 3.

12.5b Cost Reduction Measures

Cost reduction measures go hand in hand with efficiency and effectiveness measures but are also important measures of CRM effectiveness alone. Such measures include reduced transaction costs, cost savings through improved customer selection, more cost-effective campaign management, and staff efficiency gains.

12.5c Employee Changes

Often forgotten beneficiaries, CRM efforts can positively affect employees by making their jobs more rewarding, leading to greater loyalty and fewer turnovers among the employee base. Research indicates that there is a clear relationship between employee satisfaction and customer satisfaction. Satisfied employees provide better customer service that, in turn, leads to less customer turnover, greater loyalty, and higher profits for the company.[18] Consequently, many feel that companies should measure employee satisfaction regularly. Relevant effectiveness measures include employee general job satisfaction, employee satisfaction toward specific aspects of the job, employee turnover, employee referrals, percentage of calls or contacts leading to cross-sell or up-sell, and staff efficiency gains.

In their book *Customer Relationship Management: The Bottom Line to Optimizing Your ROI*, J. Anton and N. L. Petouhoff discuss specific efficiency metrics such as number of calls handled per shift, number of calls handled per hour per customer contact personnel (CCP), percentage of calls abandoned, average talk time, cost per call, percentage of calls handled by self-serve, and annual turnover (percent).[19]

Note that scores on these specific efficiency metrics can be interpreted as good or bad only with respect to specific strategies and objectives, and with respect to specific customer segments. For example, companies may look favorably upon an increase in average talk time with their high-value customer segments but unfavorably upon an increase with their low-value customers. Recall also that customers, upon contacting a company, are often asked to enter their account number. This enables a company to respond quickly to high-value customers, while keeping low-value customers waiting. An increase in abandoned calls among low-value customers may be viewed favorably, whereas a company would immediately address an increase in abandoned calls among their high-value customers.

12.6 Customer Value and Customer Equity Measures

> The focus on relationship management makes it extremely important to understand CLV because CLV models are a systematic way to understand and evaluate a firm's relationship with its customers.
>
> —D. Jain and S. S. Singh, "Customer Lifetime Value Research in Marketing:
> A Review and Future Directions," *Journal of Interactive Marketing*,
> *16*, 2 (Spring 2002): 34–46.

The nature of CRM is to differentiate between high-value and low-value customers and provide varied service. A neighborhood restaurant owner may find it easy to determine who the big spenders are and give them exceptionally warm service and complimentary courses. A company with millions of global customers, however, has a more difficult time determining who its most valuable customers are. Consequently, a quantitative measure is needed to rank customers in terms of value to an organization. The measures are customer lifetime value (CLV) and customer equity.

12.6a Customer Lifetime Value

CLV is a measure of the future financial value of the customer's purchases with an organization. It takes into account the following aspects:

- How much the customer spends on each purchase with the firm and the resulting profit
- How often the customer purchases from the firm
- How likely the customer is to remain a customer in the future
- How much it costs to serve the customer
- The organization's discount rate (for calculating the net present value of the future purchases)[20]

What is so special about CLV? V. Kumar points to five certain characteristics:

1. CLV looks forward and not backward regarding a customer's value.
2. CLV includes all of the elements of revenue, expense, and customer behavior that drive profitability.
3. CLV focuses on the customer as the driver of profitability and not the product.
4. CLV can be used to include the value of prospects.
5. CLV helps marketers adopt the appropriate marketing activities today to increase profits in the future.[21]

Improvements in technology, database management, and development of marketing models led companies to compute the economic worth or CLV of each of their customers. Computing each customer's CLV allows a company to rank customers by their profitability and, therefore, enables companies to provide differential treatment. The difficulty in computing CLV is determining whether or not the customer is going to be active in the future. Computing CLV enables a company to better establish expenditure estimates for its CRM efforts. R. C. Blattberg and J. Deighton give an example of how this can be done:

> The magazine subscription divisions of publishers adopted the lifetime value concept early. Time-Life offers significant price discounts to prospects, sometimes in the form of premiums, to become subscribers. The company may break even or lose money on the initial subscription,

but by tracking renewal rates and additional purchases, it can determine the profitability of the acquisition offer over the lifetime of the subscriber's association with the firm. It can test different offers and determine which has the greatest long-run profitability.[22]

There are simple ways such as this to calculate CLV as well as more realistic, but more complicated, ways. More realistic, but more complicated, CLV calculations take into consideration "other benefits" such as referrals and customer development. Satisfied customers provide referrals and positive word-of-mouth advertising to their friends and associates. Some referrals will become profitable customers of the firm. Consequently, a customer's CLV for a company is not only the profits he or she contributes but also the profits resulting from people the customer influences.

Developing a CLV measure for a company can be complex, and there are numerous issues that must be considered. One of the major issues is whether costs should be considered or simply revenues when computing a customer's lifetime value. If costs are considered, which specific costs of serving the customer should be included? Should acquisition costs, retention costs, or both be included? Should only the "directed" costs (e.g., costs associated with reaching specific individuals such as direct mail and sales calls), only general nondirected costs (e.g., mass-media advertising), or both be included?

Another issue is that there is no single simple CLV formula that can be used in all cases to calculate a customers' economic worth to the company. For example, different models apply if customers buy once a year (e.g., insurance policies), more than once a year (e.g., semiannual or quarterly contracts for products or services), or less than once a year (e.g., automobile purchases). Further, different models are needed if it is assumed that gross margins and promotional costs may vary, not remain static, over the life of the customer. Different models are needed if it is assumed that there are continuous cash flows as opposed to discrete cash flows.

The importance of CLV as a construct cannot be underestimated, for it not only enables managers to make decisions regarding the budget levels for marketing programs, but it has been linked to the value of the firm itself. In fact, for many firms, CLV may be the only way to get a good estimate of a firm's worth.

12.6b Customer Equity

Customer equity can be defined as the sum of CLVs of all the company's individual customers minus company expenditures discounted to a net present value. Customer equity is a similar concept to return on relationships (ROR), which includes accounting and measurement approaches pertinent to a company's marketing efforts to customers, suppliers, and channel members. Thus it considers a company's entire network of relationships instead of just the company–customer relationship.

Customer equity puts customer value at the core of the company. Further, it is a measure that can be used to assess the effectiveness of alternative marketing strategies. Marketers are finally able to quantify bottom-line returns on their marketing investments, whether it is an expansion in the number of sales reps or customer contact personnel, an increase in the advertising or sales promotion budget, or the introduction of a rewards program.

R. T. Rust, K. N. Lemon, and D. Narayandas view customer equity as being driven by three components: value equity, brand equity, and **relationship equity**.[23] They broke each of these three components into specific parts:

- **Value equity** is the customer's objective evaluation of the firm's offerings based on price, quality, and convenience. Value is relative, which means that consumers determine the value of your product or brand offerings in comparison with competitive product and brand offerings. As such, value equity is best determined by using comparative rating scales.

- **Brand equity** is the customer's subjective view of the firm and its offerings. Brands create, evoke, and symbolize meaning for their users. The key drivers of brand equity are liking and preference—the affective or "feeling" components of an attitude.
- **Relationship equity** is feelings of loyalty and affinity toward the firm—often engendered by loyalty/point/rewards/affinity programs.

Each organization must determine which of these three drivers plays the most prominent role in creating customer equity. That determines relative expenditures on the three equity-building components. Rust, V. A. Zeithaml, and Lemon feel that companies should first build value equity, then enhance the relationship with brand equity, and then cement the relationship with relationship equity.[24]

12.6c CLV versus Customer Equity

CLV and customer equity are two of the most important new concepts to be introduced in the field of marketing within the past 20 years, although CLV has been used in direct marketing for many years. While some have also equated CLV with customer equity, we take the position that there is a significant difference between the two terms. Customer equity calculations take nondirected acquisition costs into account (for example, expenditures on mass-media advertising and sales promotion that cannot be identified with specific prospects), whereas calculations of CLV may or may not do so. To determine customer profitability, we feel that measures that include acquisition costs are preferred to measures that do not.

The following definition of customer equity explains the relationship between measures of CLV and customer equity:

> Customer equity equals the profit from first-time customers (which is the number of prospects contacted times the acquisition probability times the margin) minus the cost of acquiring the customers (which is the number of prospects times the acquisition cost per prospect) plus profits from future sales to these newly acquired customers (which is the retention rate in each future period times the profit obtained from the customer in that period summed across all future periods) divided by the discount rate, which transforms the future profits into current dollars (or any currency), summed across all customer segments.[25]

Why should a firm calculate CLV and customer equity? It should do so to focus resources on high-value customers and reduce resources aimed at low-value customers. In addition, when used as a dependent variable, CLV and customer equity can measure effectiveness among various marketing strategies.

12.7 Marketing Research

THEORY IN ACTION

How Wells Fargo Gathers and Uses Metrics to Improve Customer Service

Wells Fargo has 9,000 "stores" (i.e., retail branches) and monitors the productivity of each. However, just looking at total branch performance may mask problems. By looking at individual customer data, Wells Fargo management can see if a branch is doing a good job or not. Consequently, metrics are used to evaluate individual branch performance and to make comparisons across all branches.

To do this, Wells Fargo supplements customer behavior information gathered through its CRM systems with traditional marketing research survey results. Wells Fargo calls 40,000 customers per month and asks about their banking experiences, their intentions regarding the use of Wells Fargo services in the future, and whether or not they would recommend Wells Fargo to a friend. In addition, Wells Fargo correlates survey results regarding channel usage with customer retention and profitability. Metrics allow Wells Fargo to keep customer service personnel informed regarding changes in their customers' attitudes, intentions, and behaviors.

Presentation by D. Holvey, senior vice president of consumer banking, Wells Fargo & Company, at the MSI conference "Taking Stock of Customer Relationships" (March 2, 2006).

Customer knowledge is the final measurement area critical in assessing CRM effectiveness. Knowledge of the customer is vital to developing effective CRM activities. Marketing research should play the pivotal role in accumulating customer knowledge and establishing CRM effectiveness metrics. Traditionally, marketing research departments have been responsible for measuring consumer behavior through well-defined and proven techniques such as qualitative research (e.g., one-on-one in-depth interviews and focus groups) and quantitative research (e.g., surveys, observations, and experiments). Although marketing researchers will continue to use the tried and proven qualitative and quantitative techniques of focus group interviews and survey methodology, CRM requires that marketing researchers use new techniques and methods to better understand consumers and measure the effectiveness of CRM efforts. With its emphasis on continuous customer relationships, CRM means that marketing researchers must do the following:

- They must expand their cross-sectional methodological focus to include greater emphasis on longitudinal studies.
- They must employ techniques that enable them to understand consumers' total involvement with the brand as opposed to the limited information provided by brand awareness, recognition, and satisfaction scores.
- They must quantify the drivers of loyalty and commitment.
- They must develop ways to convey a company's rating across the customer's experience cycle (i.e., a customer's satisfaction with a company's field sales staff, website, public relations programs, marketing communications, service, call center, point-of-sales activities, channel members, quality of staff members, and so on).[26]

Before a company can be said to truly understand its customer base and its relationship with the company, its products, and its brands, it must have processes in place to collect the following types of data continuously:

- Longitudinal data
- Ethnological data
- Observational data

- Customer buying cycle data
- Customer experience cycle data
- Customer–company interaction scores
- Critical incident scores
- Acquisition/defection data
- Customer–brand relationship data
- Customer–website relationship data
- Customer response rates

By focusing on the 11 types of customer knowledge measures discussed in this section, marketing researchers will become customer specialists. By supplementing their traditional techniques with these, they may be able to attain the chief customer specialist role that each organization needs.

12.7a Customer Behavior Over Time—Longitudinal Research

Since CRM focuses on relationships instead of transactions, marketing researchers must develop longitudinal profiles of consumer behavior as opposed to merely cross-sectional information. Continuous connecting is now the norm, and companies need to find ways to collect customer information continuously without annoying customers. A more measured approach to building customer profiles may be preferred to gathering all of the information at once. Pulte Homes tracks customers over a long period of time to determine how well it is doing. The first survey takes place immediately after home buyers move into their home, and several years later, Pulte gathers additional satisfaction measures. Such longitudinal surveys have helped Pulte Homes grow its repeat and referral business from 20 percent in 2001 to 45 percent in 2006.[27]

12.7b Ethnological Research

Researching the characteristics of cultures and subcultures can often lead to invaluable marketing insights not easily uncovered through more quantitative research approaches. Before marketing in England, Hallmark Cards employed ethnologists to visit families in their homes to get a better idea of how the English lived. They noticed that greeting, congratulations, and holiday cards had an important place in many homes, being displayed on shelves and tables. Further, many of the cards had been displayed for decades (and had consequently become rather weathered). Hallmark learned two things: its line of cards would be readily accepted in England, since cards had an important role in family life, and a line of cards coated in plastic might prove successful because they would not weather. Hallmark was right on both counts and successfully penetrated the English market. It is doubtful that this same sort of insight would have been gained from a paper-and-pencil or telephone survey.

12.7c Observational Data

The gains from transaction-based knowledge cannot be underestimated. However, companies that engender a deep interaction between employees and customers are able to generate another type of customer information: that derived from human interaction. For example, a prestigious hotel chain has customer information boxes on every floor so service personnel can record any customer insights gained while servicing patrons.

There are many ways in which companies gain knowledge beyond the typical survey research route. McDonald's, for example, regularly requires its top executives to work in its restaurants to experience firsthand what its franchisees and customers experience. Harley-Davidson sponsors the ingenious annual Posse Ride, which sees hundreds of Harley-Davidson owners travel the United States or Europe for nearly two weeks on their cycles. They visit dealers, tour the country, and tell stories about their cycling experiences every evening. Harley-Davidson managers accompany the riders during the ride. They observe behavior, listen to new ideas, hear about problems, and really experience the product and brand alongside their customers. Deep human insights are gained regarding the Harley-Davidson experience and the community.

Similarly, Jeep hires professors to observe and interpret customer behavior at rallies and discuss their observations and findings with marketing executives.[28] Also, General Electric and Apple require R&D personnel to review customer hotline calls to assess the depth and nature of the problem and perhaps develop new product ideas.

In another example, a nightclub owner in Los Angeles that catered to the mainland Chinese student segment could not understand why these students stopped frequenting his club for one down the street. They were on par in terms of decor, prices, and food and drink quality. He finally visited the competitive club and talked with its customers. He found that this club was getting karaoke songs and videos from the mainland's hottest singers long before he was. It gave his competitor the panache that his club lacked. (The fact that his competitor was pirating the karaoke songs and videos instead of paying the steep price required for them is another matter.)

12.7d Customer Buying Cycle Data

Insights gained in the area of customer buying cycles are basic to the success of a company's brand or product. Answers to the following questions are critical:

*   Why does a customer first purchase your offering?
*   In what situation does a customer first purchase your offering?
*   What is the progression of product/service orders for the typical customer? For the high-profit customer?
*   How do changes in a customer's life cycle or life stage affect his or her relationship with your organization?

It should be noted that the insights gained through customer buying cycle analysis might enable a company to differentiate those customers gone for good from those who merely are at a standstill until another life stage. In such cases, promotional costs can be cut to the bone until a predicted future life stage makes the customer more receptive.

12.7e Customer Experience Cycle Data

M. Nykamp recommends that companies evaluate their performance along what she calls the "**customer experience cycle**." In other words, have your customers evaluate your performance in the following areas: field sales, point of sale, service, customer contact center, Web, marketing communications and corporate communications, public relations, and advertising. Her point is that since it is the customer's experience with your organization in all of the eight areas that drives satisfaction and, ultimately, loyalty, these customer interaction points need to be assessed.[29]

12.7f Customer–Company Interaction Scores

Customer–company interaction scores represent the customer's assessment of the quality of interaction in each of the eight experience cycle areas. Scores should be analyzed for inconsistencies.

Inconsistencies in performance in customer interaction points may be quite harmful to the relationship above and beyond what a single low score may indicate. For example, one of the authors of this book is a member of a hotel rewards program that is terribly mismanaged. After numerous phone calls, faxes, and e-mail correspondence, the rewards program manager still has not responded or granted credit for three long-term stays (averaging three weeks each) in its Hong Kong and Bahrain hotels. This impacts the hotel's credibility. The author now questions the true concern and customer orientation of the receptionists, the room service and housekeeping staff, and the restaurant staff. Even though their service has been stellar, the author keeps waiting for the other shoe to drop. Companies must work to ensure that there are no inconsistencies between what is promised in their advertising, marketing communications, customer relations, customer reactivation, and public relations and what is actually delivered.

12.7g Critical Incident Scores

When developing critical incident items upon which customers will evaluate the organization, it is important that the items be specific, not global. Do not ask how good the service is at a restaurant because such an item is too general, and the score, if low, provides no clue as to what should be improved. Rather, have the customer rate the following specific aspects of service: receptionist, server, restaurant ambiance, bar ambiance, salad bar, main course, dessert, and so forth. Further, the critical incident describes the service provider in behavioral terms (e.g., brought our entire party's items as ordered) or describes the service/product with specific adjectives (e.g., fun, relaxing, romantic).

12.7h Acquisition/Defection Data

While it is instructional for organizations to know their acquisition and defection rates, it is perhaps even more operationally important for them to know to whom they are losing their customers or from whom they are gaining them. The creation of an **acquisition/defection matrix** is ideal for conveying such an understanding.

The following partially completed acquisition/defection matrix indicates a number of important characteristics about the customers of Continental Illinois National Bank (CINB). First, those who leave CINB are more likely to migrate to 1st National as opposed to Harris or LaSalle, whereas former Harris customers are the best source of new accounts for CINB. Such information can be easily gathered when the customer is closing or opening an account. Such matrices are helpful when designing win-back campaigns. For example, if a high-CLV customer is closing his or her account and defecting to 1st National, special offers could be extended to prevent defection.

			TO						
			CINB		1st National		Harris		LaSalle
		CINB	.7		.25		.03		.02
FROM		1st National	.02		×		×		×
		Harris	.25		×		×		×
		LaSalle	.03		×		×		×

12.7i Customer–Brand Relationship Data

The study of brand equity is increasingly popular, as some marketing researchers have concluded that brands are one of the most valuable assets a company has. R. McKenna was one of the first to point out that when companies start to have dialogues with their customers about products and brands, these customers have a say in modifying the brand to their liking, whether it be the size and color of a pair of jeans or the features in a CRM system.[30] Once this begins to happen on a large scale, the brand is no longer a static monolith. Rather, the dialogue becomes part of the customer's brand or brand experience.

There are many models that provide information on the customer–brand relationship. One particular model is Millward Brown's BrandDynamics™ model. As shown in Figure 12.3, the BrandDynamics™ model is based on a hierarchal methodology designed to measure consumer attitudes, opinions, and beliefs about the brand. Consumers or prospects are surveyed and asked such questions as "Do you know about the brand?" and "Does it offer you something?" This approach defines five levels of relationship with the brand, each believed to depict a stronger connection between the consumer and the brand: Presence, Relevance, Performance, Advantage, and Bonding, with Bonding being the most powerful relationship of all.[31]

By measuring consumer attitudes over time with the BrandDynamics™ methodology, the marketer can see changes in the relationship between the customer and the brand, and it can trace those changes to various marketing and communication activities.[32]

Young & Rubicam, a marketing communications agency, has developed the Brand Asset Valuator, a tool to diagnose the power and value of a brand. In using it, the agency surveys consumers' perspectives along four dimensions:

1. *Differentiation* (the defining characteristics of the brand and its distinctiveness relative to competitors)

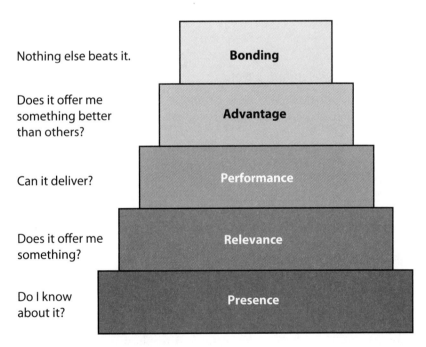

Figure 12.3 Brand Dynamics Methodology

Source: Millward Brown 2012; reprinted with permission.

2.   *Relevance* (the appropriateness and connection of the brand to a given consumer)
3.   *Esteem* (consumers' respect for and attraction to the brand)
4.   *Knowledge* (consumers' awareness of the brand and understanding of what it represents)[33]

The **hierarchy of effects model** contains a useful heuristic for measuring a customer's relationship with a brand once the items contained within are fine-tuned.[34] The model proposes that before consumers purchase a product or brand, they must go through a series of stages consisting of awareness, knowledge, liking, preference, intent to purchase, and actual purchase.

With respect to measuring awareness, three metrics have traditionally been used:

1.   Top-of-mind awareness ("What brands have you seen or heard advertised lately?")
2.   Aided recall ("What brands of beer have you seen or heard advertised lately?")
3.   Recognition ("Which of the following brands of beer have you seen or heard of before?")

With respect to liking, attitudinal rating scales have traditionally been used: "Please rate each of the following fast-food restaurants on the following attributes: speed of service, quality of food, quality of decor, friendliness of staff, and so on." With respect to preference, ranking or paired-comparison techniques have traditionally been used: "Please rank the following five fast-food outlets from your first choice to your last choice for lunch." Intentions are notoriously poor predictors of behavior but are often operationalized by asking a question such as "Which fast-food outlet do you plan to have lunch at the next time you go out for lunch?"

There is face validity to the BrandDynamics™ and hierarchy of effects models, and the levels/stages are certainly ones that we can all relate to when selecting among competitive products, brands, and services. Nonetheless, will any rating or ranking scale really provide Sears or JCPenney with the information it needs to determine how its stores fit into a person's life and what it needs to do to establish a meaningful bond with its customers? Probably not. It is not quick or easy for a company to determine its brand's place in a person's life, yet it is necessary.

12.7j Customer–Website Relationship Data

Customer/prospect online engagement with a company's website is important and companies should encourage active participation. As measures of online engagement, companies are using:

• Reach (aggregate number of interactions on site versus competitors' sites)
• Engagement measures (based on time on site, pages viewed on site, etc.)
• Activation of leads or sales
• Interactions leading to bookmarking, rating, or sharing of content[35]

Many companies are using tools such as Google Analytics and Clicky to measure customer–website engagement. As reported by S. Ganapathy, C. Ranganathan, and B. Sankaranarayanan, however, measuring online interactions can be difficult because of data overload. They suggest using visualization tools to analyze the increasing amount of customer interaction data. The National Institute of Standards and Technology (NIST) offers two tools—Web Variable Instrumenter Program (WebVIP) and Visual Variable Instrumenter Program (VisVIP)—for assessing the usage levels and usage patterns of websites. The former captures surfing parameters such as use of buttons, time on page, page transitions, and so on. Routes through websites can also be determined and shopping patterns specified by market segment. Especially important is the identification of where customers are being lost. These visual tools are a tremendous aid to managers in understanding customer online behavior.[36]

12.7k Event History Model versus RFM

Fred made four purchases from L. L. Bean this year—the first one in January and the last one in July. How likely is he to still be an active customer the next year?

JoAnne made two purchases from L. L. Bean this year—the first one in January and the last one in July. How likely is she to still be an active customer the next year?

To whom would you send the expensive L. L. Bean promotional Christmas catalogs?

As previously mentioned, RFM stands for a customer's recency, frequency, and monetary value of purchases. Customers are given points based on recency of purchases, how frequently they have purchased, and the dollar amount spent. The higher their point score, the more likely they are to receive promotional pieces from the organization. This is a seemingly logical approach to categorizing customers based on their probable value to the company. It is an approach that companies have used for decades and is still being used by many.

Recently, however, the RFM approach has come under attack. Researchers such as Kumar and Reinartz[37] pointed out that using such a point-scoring system results in a significant overinvestment in lapsed customers, primarily because it ignores the "pacing" of a customer's interactions, or the time between each purchase.

Consequently, Kumar and Reinartz developed a model to take "pacing" into account. They called it the **event history model**, and it merely consists of taking t to the nth power, where:

n = The number of purchases made in the time period
t = The fraction of the period between the first and last purchases

The formula predicts the probability that a particular customer is still active or will remain active at a particular point in the future. Their formula prevents a company from overinvesting in customers who will no longer be active because it is particularly sensitive in predicting the speed with which a customer's purchasing activity will end. The model depends on knowing the answers to three questions:

1. When did the customer begin buying?
2. When was the last time he or she bought?
3. How many purchases did he or she have in between?

Applying the formula to the data from our example at the beginning of this section, the company should invest more in JoAnne than in Fred because, as the calculations below show, the likelihood that she will still be an active customer in December is 0.34. The likelihood for Fred is only 0.116. Therefore, JoAnne is three times more likely to remain an active customer than Fred.

$$\text{Fred:} \left(\frac{7}{12}\right)^4 = (.583)^4 = .116$$

$$\text{JoAnne:} \left(\frac{7}{12}\right)^2 = (.583)^2 = .34$$

12.8 CRM Scorecards and the CRM Measurement Hierarchy

Over the past decade, companies have developed a "balanced scorecard" approach to set and track performance goals for everything from product and campaign development to sales to CRM. R. S. Kaplan and D. P. Norton[38] introduced the balanced scorecard in 1992 because they were concerned that managers only concentrated on financial measures of performance and were neglecting three equally important measures: customer outcomes, internal business processes, and future growth orientation.

What should be the focus of these CRM scorecards? Kaplan and Norton suggested that companies create scorecards to reflect customer outcomes, internal business processes, financial objectives, and learning and growth. This is almost identical to our four categories of measures of CRM effectiveness: CRM customer cycle, company 3E measures (effectiveness, efficiency, and employee satisfaction), customer and company worth, and customer knowledge.

Given the plethora of existing CRM effectiveness measures, it is perhaps beneficial to develop a schema or hierarchy of existing measures. Focusing on the measure of customer equity and its drivers, the schema in Appendix 2 attempts to organize the measures presented in this chapter.

THEORY IN ACTION

Collecting "REAP" Measures

Measuring the effects of CRM efforts is not enough. Although it is important to measure campaign effectiveness, customer service, channel effectiveness, and customer survival, these measures must be disseminated to all customer contact personnel and reviewed and acted upon by management to manage the CRM effort effectively. To get the most out of these CRM effectiveness measures, companies should do the following:

- Ensure that all marketing campaigns have a formal review phase and clearly defined key performance indicators so campaign performance can be compared.
- Have a clear top-level set of measures that define customer management performance in terms of the REAP (retention, efficiency, acquisition, and penetration) measures and cascade these down to customer-facing people, and ensure they understand and accept the performance criteria on which they are measured.
- Understand the relative cost of serving customers through the various channels, measure the proportion of their business in terms of volume and margin managed by each channel, and seek and store on the customer database the reasons for customer loss.

B. Foss and M. Stone, *CRM in Financial Services: A Practical Guide to Making Customer Relationship Management Work* (London: Kogan Page, 2002).

Chapter Summary

There are an enormous number of ways to measure the effectiveness of CRM efforts. In this chapter, we grouped these measures into four important and distinct categories. The first category is CRM customer cycle measures, which presents effectiveness measures based on the distinct stages in strategic CRM. These stages include customer acquisition, development of closer bonds, behavior changes, customer retention, prevention of downward migration, and win-back. The second is company 3E measures, which are ways to measure CRM's impact on company efficiency, effectiveness, and employee behavior. The third category is customer and company worth measures, or how to compute CLV and customer equity. Finally, customer knowledge measures constitute a variety of marketing research approaches used to better understand a firm's customers. Methods include critical incident score analysis, acquisition/defection matrix, and customer–brand relationship data, among others.

This chapter also discusses ways in which customer satisfaction and service quality have been measured, as well as loyalty, retention, and defection. Well-known acquisition measures are discussed, with examples given for computations of acquisition/yield/capture rate, conversion rate, and conversion efficiency/acquisition cost. Share of category, size of wallet, and share of wallet measures are discussed with respect to determining effectiveness of cross-selling and up-selling strategies. With regards to retention strategies, measures such as average retention rate, average defection rate, average lifetime duration, net promoter score, and survival rate are discussed and examples provided. Components of value equity, brand equity, and relationship equity are discussed in the important area of computing CLV and customer equity.

Key Terms

Acquisition/defection matrix is a matrix indicating to whom a company is losing its customers and from whom it is gaining them.

Brand equity is the customer's subjective view of the firm and its offerings. The main drivers are cognitive and affective components: awareness, knowledge, liking, and preference.

Customer equity is the sum of CLVs of all the company's individual customers minus company expenditures (including nondirected acquisition costs) discounted to a net present value. It is driven by value, brand, and relationship equity.

Customer's experience cycle is a customer's satisfaction with a company's field sales staff, website, public relations programs, marketing campaigns and communications programs, service, call center, channel members, and so on.

Defection curve is a graph that depicts how responsive a company's profits are to changes in customer defection rates.

Event history model is a formula that predicts the probability that a particular customer is still active or will remain active at a particular point in the future. It is based on the number of purchases the customer made in the time period and the fraction of the period between the first and last purchase. Because it takes the customer's purchase pacing into account, it is said to reduce overinvestment in lapsed customers—a deficiency in the RFM model.

Hierarchy of effects model is a useful heuristic for measuring a customer's relationship with a brand. It consists of cognitive components (awareness and knowledge), affective components (liking and preference), and conative or action tendency components (intention to purchase and purchase behavior).

Past customer value extrapolates the value of a customer's past transactions into the future. The problem with this approach is that a high-value customer in the past may have been merely "transactional," and projecting high past value may seriously overestimate future value.

Relationship equity is the bond that exists between customers and the firm and its offerings. Drivers of relationship equity are loyalty and commitment.

SERVQUAL is a 22-item instrument for assessing customer perceptions of service quality.

Value equity is the customer's objective evaluation of the firm's offerings. The main drivers are price, quality, and convenience.

Questions

1. Numerous CRM tools and effectiveness measures are available to companies today. How can these tools and measures be grouped into separate and distinct categories that companies can measure their existing tools and metrics against?

2. What are some specific CRM effectiveness measures useable for each CRM function?
3. Define "satisfaction" and how it can be measured, indicating the preferred way to measure it.
4. Why is customer retention so important?
5. Through CRM, companies attempt to develop closer bonds with their customers. In addition to the measures of retention, defection, and survival, what are some other useful measures?
6. Quantitative measures are needed to rank customers in terms of their value to an organization. The measures that have been developed to do this are CLV and customer equity. What are the similarities and differences between these two measures?
7. Customer equity is driven by three components: value equity, brand equity, and relationship equity. Explain what these three components mean.
8. In order to truly understand its customers, companies must collect information on the customer buying cycle. What type of information would this be?
9. When a company collects customer experience cycle data, what type of data is it collecting?
10. What are critical incident scores, and how do they differ from more general marketing research questions?

Exercises

1. A company is spending significant sums trying to create closer bonds with its customers. They ask you to measure the effectiveness of their efforts. What measures would you suggest, and how would you go about collecting this information?
2. CRM systems affect employees as well as customers. A company wants to know how its CRM systems are affecting its employees. What measures would you suggest, and how would you go about collecting this information?
3. Compute your CLV at McDonald's, indicating all components and considerations.
4. Select a product, company, or brand with which you are familiar. Describe what it would find in measuring your value equity, brand equity, and relationship equity.
5. Develop a series of attributes regarding three fast-food franchises. Then compute your own service-quality gap measures on each component for each franchise.

Appendix I The SERVQUAL Instrument

Expectations

DIRECTIONS: This survey deals with your opinions of _____ services. Please show the extent to which you think firms offering _____ services should possess the features described by each statement. Do this by picking one of the seven numbers next to each statement. If you strongly agree that these firms should possess a feature, circle the number 7. If you strongly disagree that these firms should possess a feature, circle 1. If your feelings are not strong, circle one of the numbers in the middle. There are no right or wrong answers. All we are interested in is a number that best shows your expectations about firms offering _____ services.

Strongly Disagree   **Strongly Agree**

E1.   They should have up-to-date equipment.

        1   2   3   4   5   6   7

Strongly Disagree   **Strongly Agree**

E2.   Their physical facilities should be visually appealing.

1   2   3   4   5   6   7

E3.   Their employees should be well dressed and appear neat.

1   2   3   4   5   6   7

E4.   The appearance of the physical facilities of these firms should be in keeping with the type of services provided.

1   2   3   4   5   6   7

E5.   When these firms promise to do something by a certain time, they should do so.

1   2   3   4   5   6   7

E6.   When customers have problems, these firms should be sympathetic and reassuring.

1   2   3   4   5   6   7

E7.   These firms should be dependable.

1   2   3   4   5   6   7

E8.   They should provide their services at the time they promise to do so.

1   2   3   4   5   6   7

E9.   They should keep their records accurately.

1   2   3   4   5   6   7

E10. They shouldn't be expected to tell customers exactly when services will be performed. (−)

1   2   3   4   5   6   7

E11. It is not realistic for customers to expect prompt service from employees of these firms. (−)

1   2   3   4   5   6   7

E12. Their employees don't always have to be willing to help customers. (−)

1   2   3   4   5   6   7

E13. It is okay if they are too busy to respond to customer requests promptly. (−)

1   2   3   4   5   6   7

E14. Customers should be able to trust these firms' employees.

1   2   3   4   5   6   7

E15. Customers should be able to feel safe in their transactions with these firms' employees.

1   2   3   4   5   6   7

E16. Their employees should be polite.

1   2   3   4   5   6   7

Strongly Disagree   **Strongly Agree**

E17. Their employees should get adequate support from these firms to do their jobs well.

1   2   3   4   5   6   7

E18. These firms should not be expected to give customers individual attention. (−)

1   2   3   4   5   6   7

E19. Employees of these firms cannot be expected to give customers personal attention. (−)

1   2   3   4   5   6   7

E20. It is unrealistic to expect employees to know what the needs of their customers are. (−)

1   2   3   4   5   6   7

E21. It is unrealistic to expect these firms to have their customers' best interests at heart. (−)

1   2   3   4   5   6   7

E22. They shouldn't be expected to have operating hours convenient to all their customers. (−)

*The items are distributed among the five dimensions of tangibility (items E1 to E4), reliability (items E5 to E9), responsiveness (items E10 to E13), assurance (items E14 to E17), and empathy (items E18 to E22). (−) denotes reverse-coded items.

Perceptions

DIRECTIONS: The following set of statements relate to your feelings about XYZ. For each statement, please show the extent to which you believe XYZ has the feature described by the statement. Once again, circling a 7 means that you strongly agree that XYZ has that feature, and circling a 1 means that you strongly disagree. You may circle any of the numbers in the middle that show how strong your feelings are. There are no right or wrong answers. All we are interested in is a number that best shows your perceptions about XYZ.

Strongly Disagree   **Strongly Agree**

P1.   XYZ has up-to-date equipment.

1   2   3   4   5   6   7

P2.   XYZ's physical facilities are visually appealing.

1   2   3   4   5   6   7

P3.   XYZ's employees are well dressed and appear neat.

1   2   3   4   5   6   7

P4.   The appearance of the physical facilities of XYZ is in keeping with the type of services provided.

1   2   3   4   5   6   7

P5.   When XYZ promises to do something by a certain time, it does so.

1   2   3   4   5   6   7

Strongly Disagree   **Strongly Agree**

P6.   When you have problems, XYZ is sympathetic and reassuring.

   1   2   3   4   5   6   7

P7.   XYZ is dependable.

   1   2   3   4   5   6   7

P8.   XYZ provides its services at the time it promises to do so.

   1   2   3   4   5   6   7

P9.   XYZ keeps its records accurately.

   1   2   3   4   5   6   7

P10. XYZ does not tell customers exactly when services will be performed. (−)

   1   2   3   4   5   6   7

P11. You do not receive prompt service from XYZ's employees. (−)

   1   2   3   4   5   6   7

P12. Employees of XYZ are not always willing to help customers. (−)

   1   2   3   4   5   6   7

P13. Employees of XYZ are too busy to respond to customer requests promptly. (−)

   1   2   3   4   5   6   7

P14. You can trust employees of XYZ.

   1   2   3   4   5   6   7

P15. You feel safe in your transactions with XYZ's employees.

   1   2   3   4   5   6   7

P16. Employees of XYZ are polite.

   1   2   3   4   5   6   7

P17. Employees get adequate support from XYZ to do their jobs well.

   1   2   3   4   5   6   7

P18. XYZ does not give you individual attention. (−)

   1   2   3   4   5   6   7

P19. Employees of XYZ do not give you personal attention. (−)

   1   2   3   4   5   6   7

P20. Employees of XYZ do not know what your needs are. (−)

   1   2   3   4   5   6   7

P21. XYZ does not have your best interests at heart. (−)

   1   2   3   4   5   6   7

P22. XYZ does not have operating hours convenient to all its customers. (−)

   1   2   3   4   5   6   7

*The items are distributed among the five dimensions of tangibility (items P1 to P4), reliability (items P5 to P9), responsiveness (items P10 to P13), assurance (items P14 to P17), and empathy (items P18 to P22). (–) denotes reverse-coded items.

A seven-point scale ranging from "Strongly Agree" (7) to "Strongly Disagree" (1), with no verbal labels for the intermediate scale points (i.e., 2 through 6), accompanied each statement. Also, the statements were in random order in the instrument. A complete listing of the 34-item instrument used in the second stage of data collection can be obtained from the first author.

Appendix 2 CRM Measurement Hierarchy

Customer Equity

Profits from Newly Acquired Customers	Future Profits from Existing Customers	Win-Back Profits from Defectors Who Return
(Number of prospects contacted × Probability of acquisition × Margin) – Cost of acquisition **Cost of Acquisition** (Number of prospects × Acquisition cost per prospect) **Acquisition Cost per Prospect** [(Directed cost + Mass promotion cost) ÷ Number of prospects acquired] **Acquisition Cost and Effectiveness Measures** Yield rate or capture ratio Conversion efficiency Average customer acquisition cost Acquisition campaign cycle time Acquisition communication and administrative costs Acquisition campaign results versus expectations Percent growth in customer acquisition	(Sum of retention rate × Profit in each future period) **Measures of the Efficiency and Cost Effectiveness of CRM Programs Directed at Existing Customers** Cost to serve Operating costs More efficient campaign management Speed of developing targeted campaigns Ability to cross-sell products Ability to up-sell products Staff efficiency gains First contact resolution by CCP Successful resolution by CCP Time to resolution by CCP Percent of sales representatives meeting quotas Reduction in sales cycle time Reduction in time between orders Reduction in time to market Percentage of total accounts closed Time to distribute sales reports across divisions Reduced transaction costs Reduced customer attrition Cost savings through improved customer selection Revenue per CRM dollar Improved customer response rates across touch points	(Sum of retention rate × Profit in each future period for number of defectors contacted × Probability of win-back) **Effectiveness of Win Back Strategies Measured by:** SCLV Average cost per customer reactivated Percent of customers reactivated per campaign

Drivers of Customer Equity

VALUE EQUITY		
(Primary Driver of Acquisition)	*BEHAVIOR CHANGES: CUSTOMER GROWTH, DEVELOPMENT, RETENTION*	
Price	*(Measured by)*	More repeat business
Quality	Return on relationship	Shorter purchase cycle time
Convenience	Number of products held per	Brand switching warnings
Value equity	customer	Number of complaints
(measured by linear	Customer retention	Number of returns
compensatory or attitude–	Survival rate	Sales volume
belief models)	Profitability	Revenues
	Share of wallet	RFM
	Depth of relationship	Customer response rates
	Number of referrals	Days since last purchase
	Type of channel usage	Changes in order size
	Number of customer service	Buying cycle sales changes
	representative interactions	Defection rate
	Greater customer self-entry of data	Ratio of sales wins to losses
	Share of wallet changes	
	Change in order frequency	
	Maintenance ratio	
	Continuity of key customers	
	Number of recommendations and referrals	
	Percent of sales generated by key customers	
	Acceleration or deceleration in purchases	
	Increase or decrease in the number of product categories purchased	
	Change in the number of cancelled orders, returns, exchanges, or complaints	
	Change in the purchase of ancillaries (e.g., service contracts and extended warranties)	
	Change in the number of references or referrals	
	Change in the number of contacts and types of contacts	
	Mean time between winning and losing a customer	
	DEVELOPING CLOSER BONDS (Primary Driver of Behavior Change)	
	(Measured by)	
	Customer satisfaction	
	Customer loyalty	
	Service/transaction satisfaction	
	Measures of service quality (i.e., tangibility, reliability, responsiveness, assurance, and empathy)	
	Emotional affinity with the company	
	Emotional affinity with the brand	

Relationship Equity and Brand Equity

(Primary drivers of closer bonds between customers and a company and its products/brands)

BRAND EQUITY	RELATIONSHIP EQUITY
(Measured by)	*(Measured by)*
Hierarchy of effects variables:	Program success levels of:
Awareness of the brand	Loyalty programs
Knowledge/relationship with the brand	Affinity programs
Attitude toward the brand versus competitors	Community building
Preference level toward the brand	Knowledge building
Strength of intention to purchase the brand	Special recognition and treatment
Feelings toward the company and its ethics	

CRM New Horizons

Chapter 13

Social Networking and CRM

TOPICS

13.1 Introduction

13.2 Social Networking Sites

13.3 Company Social Media Campaigns

13.4 Why Social Media Works

13.5 Social Networking in China and the United States

13.6 How and Why Marketers Should Use Social Networks

13.1 Introduction

Social media can be defined as "an online mass collaboration environment where content is created, posted, enhanced, discovered, consumed and shared, participant to participant, without a direct intermediary."[1] Companies that engage customers via social media are, in effect, practicing social CRM, for it provides a new channel perfectly attuned to increasing customer retention, as well as acquiring new customers and winning them back should they defect. According to Gartner, the starting point for most social media initiatives is in the marketing, communications, or public relations (PR) departments—with customer service adopting soon after.[2]

Social media today is impacting all aspects of people's lives worldwide. As just a few examples, consider the following:

- The Arab Spring uprisings in 2011 were due, in part, to people banding together through social media.
- The Illinois Supreme Court published rules instructing jurors not to post their thoughts about the trial on any social networking site.[3]
- Lady Gaga has nearly 10 million "little monsters" following her on Twitter.[4]
- Social networking sites exist for caregivers so they can better coordinate care for older family members.[5]
- Sarah Palin used Facebook to communicate with voters and had approximately 1 million "friends."[6]

At the core of social networks are people and their connections, where people can be categorized as opinion leaders/influencers, advocates, detractors, or merely observers. It is generally agreed that companies need to establish a presence in this social media environment because it generates brand awareness, is a vehicle for unleashing the various retention strategies, aids in customer service, and supports advocacy. Companies in the vanguard of social CRM are already reaping the benefits of co-creating value with contributors whether it be in the creation of new product functions and features, product/service delivery, pricing, or new applications.

Interacting with and within social networks has become one of the most important new ways marketers can acquire customers and maintain relationships with current ones. The definition of CRM has, therefore, expanded to include social media as a new channel. CRM can be extended through the social networking channel because it provides new ways of acquiring and retaining customers. Social networking unleashes a whole new domain of customer engagement opportunities and requires a new paradigm for marketing activities. Unlike traditional marketing activities that connect marketers with customers, social networks enable customers and prospects to interact with each other. Mass collaboration is enabled and conducted through social media. The issue for marketers concerns what position they should play in these interactions.

In the age of social media, traditional customer relationship management techniques require modification, since once company material is online and in the hands of millions of users, those users are free to manipulate the material in any way they choose and transform it into messages and images contrary to what the company originally intended. One of the issues regarding a company's use of social media is whether to become active or passive participants in conversations, with most opting to become active when misinformation is apparent or when customers need help. Some worry about managing such sites, fearing that conversations may become detrimental to their brands. The reality is that negative comments will appear regardless of whether a company has its own social media site or not, and it is better to be a part of the conversation instead of a speechless observer. It is true that social media enables disgruntled customers, competitors, and special interest groups to generate scathing remarks about a company and its brands. Companies need to have procedures and standards in place so they know how to react quickly and consistently when issues arise regarding their brands. If companies participate and emphasize commercial aspects in their message, users may discount it as being nothing more than traditional advertising and sales—best done through traditional channels. On the other hand, if there is no commercial tie-in, benefits may not accrue to the bottom line.

Marketers have always tried to influence consumers throughout the stages in their decision-making process: initiating, information search, evaluation, decision making, purchase, and usage. Today, marketers must stay involved in another stage: advocacy. Social media is the outlet through which buyers publicly promote the advantages of the brand or assail it for its shortcomings—real or imagined. Buyers seem to enjoy disseminating information during the advocacy stage; they talk, tweet, post, and blog about their purchases and experiences. Companies need to stay involved during the advocacy stage to better understand their customers' experiences with their products or services, correct misconceptions, and engage in the conversation with their customers and others.[7]

Relatively few companies have developed formal social CRM strategies, and even fewer have developed metrics to measure effectiveness. Social media monitoring accounts for three-fourths of the social CRM market, and its use is fragmented by departmental usage in marketing, customer service, sales, and public relations. All are concerned about capturing the voice of the customer. But monitoring conversations over social media is only the first step. With this information, companies can gain insights into how customers think about and use their products and services. Most, however, are still wrestling with systems and procedures that allow such findings to be shared across organizational departments. Monitoring conversations and collecting information are relatively simple operations. The trick for companies is to convert this into social intelligence and then to disseminate it to the appropriate departments and divisions worldwide.

THEORY IN ACTION

Best Buy Believes in Social Networking

Brian Dunn, former CEO of Best Buy, had this to say about marketing over social networks:

Ultimately, I believe that Best Buy's message has to be where people are. Today, that means being on social networks. . . . If a company, or even its chief executive, doesn't have a presence on social networks today, that company risks not being in the conversation at all. Over time, I believe, that can be fatal to a business. . . . I tend to focus on the positive aspects of social networking. The right question is "How am I going to deepen my relationship with customers and employees and deepen the conversation that goes on where they are?" Right now, social networks are an important part of the answer.

B. J. Dunn, "How I Did It: Best Buy's CEO on Learning to Love Social Media," *Harvard Business Review, 88*, 12 (December 2010): 43–48.

13.2 Social Networking Sites

Social networking sites generally offer the following basic features:

- Member profiles (including searchable variable fields such as age, education, marital status, gender, geography, interests, significant brands, and so on)
- Network of friends
- Discussion forums
- Blogging facilities
- Ratings of companies, products, brands, services, and so on
- E-mail facilities
- Reputation ratings of connectedness (referred to as "clout"), business referrals, member desirability, time spent online, and so on

The numbers of worldwide users of social networking make mass-marketing techniques possible. (It is said that Facebook, with 1 billion members worldwide, would be the third largest country in the world.) Data available in membership profiles and the ability to market to networks of "friends," however, make segmentation efforts even more attractive. Social networking enables social interactions among users sharing activities, social status, occupational status, life stage, interests, opinions, avocations, brand usage, academic disciplines, and mutual friends. For example, Friendster is an online community that connects people through networks of friends; Flickr enables people to share photos; MeetUp organizes local interest groups for gatherings about anything, anywhere in 612 cities across 51 countries; Ryze is a network that helps users grow their business and careers; LinkedIn is a professional network of friends and colleagues who can put you in touch with others; and Referent is a business networking tool to help entrepreneurs acquire new business and customers.[8] Segmentation is consequently possible using the networks themselves as well as social groups within the networks.

13.2a Social Networking for Companies

Companies interface with social media for a variety of reasons: to listen, to participate, to generate buzz, and so on. Social media such as Facebook, Twitter, and LinkedIn enable companies to engage and bond with customers and prospects. Reflecting this, smart phones have become social aggregators connecting social tools such as e-mail, text messages, Facebook, and Twitter.

Social networks are as equally applicable in B2B as in B2C marketing endeavors, although usage is not as great in the former. Twenty-six percent of companies used Twitter and Facebook in 2009.[9] In 2011, four out of five U.S. businesses with 100 or more employees were using social media marketing—up from 42 percent in 2008—and seven out of ten companies on the 2010 Inc. 500 list said they have Facebook pages, with half saying they use blogs to communicate with customers.[10] Twitter is used by 59 percent of these companies. Two-thirds of B2B marketers have established group pages on social networking sites.[11] Seventy percent of these companies monitor their brands on social networks, and more than half said they recruit and evaluate potential employees on search engines or social networks.[12]

13.2b Size of Market

Spending on CRM applications grew over 8 percent in 2010, but spending on "social CRM" grew by more than 50 percent, even though this represented only 5 percent of all CRM spending. In absolute terms, social CRM spending is small; however, its growth and interest in it exceed spending in other CRM areas. **Operational CRM**, the automation of processes such as campaign management, grew about 4 percent but represents over 70 percent of all CRM spending. **Analytical CRM**, which includes predictive analytics and segmentation applications, grew about 9 percent and represents nearly 25 percent of all CRM spending.[13] Advertising spending through social media channels is currently small but growing. In 2010, the online advertising industry was worth $23 billion,[14] and advertising spending on social networks worldwide was estimated at $2.5 billion—just a fraction of online spending but one of the fastest-growing segments.[15] Social media spending is estimated to grow at a compound annual rate of 34 percent. The Veronis Suhler Stevenson investment bank projected that in 2011 the Internet would surpass newspapers to become the largest advertising medium. Forrester forecasts spending on interactive marketing of $55 billion by 2014—driven by social media spending and mobile marketing. As an example of the significance of this prediction, Sony, as of November 2011, began allocating 30 percent of its advertising budget into social sites for its PlayStation console.[16] More recently, application companies, looking for new revenue channels, have begun selling advertising on applications they are building for social networking sites. They feel they can customize campaigns for their clients across the social networks where their apps are installed.[17]

Facebook, a social media site that lets people create online profiles or personal Web pages allowing interaction with others, is the largest social media site in the United States. There were 157 million Facebook users in the United States in 2012, with 70 percent logging in daily. The average Facebook user is on Facebook 55 minutes per day, has 130 friends on the site, and creates 90 pieces of content each month.[18] Facebook has become so pervasive in the United States that the federal government began issuing terror alerts through the system in 2011.[19] Gadget makers are also adding it to their products—from cameras to video game consoles—so that people can easily log into the service with any device. Sony's Handycam camcorders and Bloggie cameras, for example, allow users to upload photos and video directly to Facebook.[20]

Today, electronic engagement is a major part of people's lives. A 2010 study by the Kaiser Family Foundation found that students ages 8 to 18 spend more than 7.5 hours per day engaged with computers, cell phones, TV, music, or video games. Forty percent of those in middle school and high school say that when on the computer they're also plugged into other media. Kids 11 to 14 years of age spend an average of 73 minutes per day texting, and older teens spend close to 2 hours.

Over 50 percent of U.S. teens log on to a social networking site more than once a day, and nearly 25 percent do so more than 10 times a day.[21] It appears that preteens and teens in the United States today prefer texting to talking.

13.3 Company Social Media Campaigns

According to W. Wong, social media marketing is built on the premise that conversing about brands is a natural part of how consumers interact. People who love a product or service will recommend it to their friends and family, creating a word-of-mouth chain that's more trustworthy than any message conveyed on a billboard or TV commercial. With much of that conversation moving online to social networking sites, marketers are looking to jump in and connect with consumers.[22]

There is another side of the coin, however. P. Guenzi and O. Pelloni's research points out the dangers of social networks for a company:

> As for the customer-to-customer relationships, our study suggests that it may be risky for a firm to have close interpersonal friendship bonds among its customers. In fact, customer-to-customer relationship closeness increases the risk of switching behaviors in case a "friend" customer changes the service provider, and at the same time it apparently does not contribute to customer satisfaction or to customer loyalty. The risk of losing a customer due to switching behaviors of friend customers is mitigated only by the existence of customer-to-employee relationship closeness but not by the overall customer satisfaction with the service provider.[23]

J. A. Deighton and L. Kornfeld point out that consumers use digital media to communicate with one another beyond the control of marketers and respond to company promotions and information by disseminating counterarguments, rebuttals, reproaches, parodies, and occasionally compliments and support. Social networking provides for better interaction among consumers and to a lesser degree between companies and consumers. As Deighton and Kornfeld point out, marketers can no longer expect to dominate; rather, perhaps the most they can expect is to simply "fit in." Companies cannot control everything that appears about them in digital media. Perhaps the best they can do is get involved in the digital conversation—trying to handle complaints and criticisms that are bound to appear.[24]

Word-of-mouth advertising has always been more influential than traditional advertising because consumers are more trusting of information they receive from peers than of information they receive from commercial sources. In addition, today's younger consumers view traditional marketing campaigns differently than older consumers: they often ignore them. Further, anything companies do online also needs to be done on mobile devices. This does not mean that companies should not exert digital influence. However, companies need to be careful how they do so. They need to be honest, authentic, and transparent in their messages and avoid the appearance of "sploging"—creating a message solely as a sponsored promotion. Often, they need to react quickly to unfavorable situations (e.g., health scares, environmental disasters, flight disruptions, product deficiencies, stock-outs, etc.). For example, when Facebook introduced an advertising program called Beacon, 50,000 people signed a petition calling for Facebook to allow users to completely opt out of the service. The problem revolved around the issue of privacy. Beacon shared information about users' purchases and other activities outside Facebook and consumers revolted. Facebook agreed to shutter Beacon in 2009.[25]

Rather than fearing confrontation, companies need to interact. Companies need to communicate on a personal level and not "bureauspeak." It should be comforting for companies to know that the top reason consumers want to establish social relationships is to learn about specials and sales. Second, they want to learn about new products, services, and features.[26] Dell earned $6.5 million in revenue directly through Twitter between 2008 and 2010 when it started posting coupons and word of new products on its microblogging site.[27] McKinsey & Company claims that while it is difficult to relate ROI to a company's use of social media, companies that do use it enjoy greater market share and higher margins than those that don't. Social media should be used to interact not only with customers but also business partners and employees.[28]

13.4 Why Social Media Works

Using C. Figello's literature on virtual communities, H. H. Bauer and M. Grether state that virtual communities have relationship-building potential that can lead to long-term relationships between the provider of a virtual community and its members. According to Figello, virtual communities are characterized by the following:

- Members feel part of a larger social whole.
- There is an interwoven web of relationships among members.
- There is an ongoing exchange among members of commonly valued things.
- Relationships among members last through time.[29]

Based on these characteristics, Bauer and Grether feel that virtual communities can lead to customer retention. Their argument is based on the concept of social capital—a resource that individuals can draw upon in their personal and professional lives and that is similar to the Western concept of networking and the Chinese concept of guanxi. Social capital is built by interpersonal interaction in social networks and the exchanging of information. This information is available to everyone in the community whether they contribute or not. Sharing information increases a contributor's self-esteem and status, and people contribute because of expected future reciprocation from others. This reciprocity strengthens community bonds and builds trust and commitment among members, leading to mutual willingness to help one another and provide information. It is said that social trust—expectations that people have of one another—is the most important factor determining social capital. The feeling of social trust is projected onto the supplier, with trust being defined as a willingness to rely on an exchange partner in whom one has confidence.[30]

13.5 Social Networking in China and the United States

The impact of social networking is not restricted to the United States. Over twice as many Chinese use social media as do U.S. residents. While 46 percent of the U.S. population uses social networking versus 23 percent in China, China has 1.35 billion residents versus 320 million in the United States. Thus, over 310 million Chinese are using social media versus 147 million in the United States. The impact of social media in China is just as great as in the United States; however, due to government restrictions, business regulations, and culture, the Chinese use social media differently than those in the United States.

Chinese usage of social networking sites (SNS) also varies by size of city. There are three tiers of cities in China based on population, economic scale, and importance. Tier 1 cities consist of Shanghai, Beijing, Guangzhou, and some include Shenzhen. There are over 20 tier 2 cities—mainly provincial capitals. Tier 3 cities tend to be prefecture or county-level city capitals. Differences consist of the specific SNS used. Let us now take a look at social networking sites and usage in the United States and China.

13.5a The Leading Social Networking Sites in the United States

The leading social networking sites in the United States by category are:

- Social networks: Facebook, MySpace, Tagged, LinkedIn
- Microblogging: Twitter

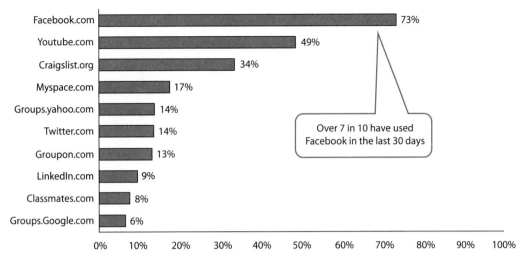

Figure 13.1 **Comparing the Top 10 Social Networking Sites in the United States**

Source: Social Media Use: Has the U.S. Lost its Edge to China?" April 18, 2011. Reprinted with permission of www.netpop research.com

- Location-based social networks: foursquare, Yelp, Gowalla
- Blogging platforms: BlogSpot (Google), Wordpress
- Video/photo sharing platforms: YouTube (video sharing by Google with 86 percent of U.S. online video watchers), Flickr (photo sharing by Yahoo!)[31]

The top 10 social sites in the United States are shown in Figure 13.1. Contrary to popular belief, social networking is not restricted to the young. The average age of social networking site users in the United States is 37 years old. The average MySpace user is 32 years old; LinkedIn, 40 years old; Facebook, 38 years old; and Twitter, 33 years old.[32] An examination of Facebook and Twitter users provides examples of how prolific social networks can be and how intensive users interact with them.

13.5b Leading Social Networking Sites in China

Facebook, YouTube, and Twitter are blocked in China, but social networking in China is happening through other networks. The China equivalents are Qzone and Renren for Facebook, SinaWeibo for Twitter (*Weibo* is the Mandarin word for "microblog"), Tudou and YouKu for YouTube, and Jiepang for foursquare. The SNS 51.com is popular in second- and third-tier cities. According to Nielsen, 51.com was the biggest social networking site in china in 2008 but has since fallen to fourth place with 10.1 percent market share. The largest are Renren (25.1%), Kaixin (19.4%) and Pengyou (18.1%).[33] The most important Internet company in China, and the third largest in the world after Google and Microsoft, is Tencent, with nearly a half billion active users. According to M. Colaizzi,[34] their membership bases are Qzone (Tencent's social network), with 310 million users; 51.com, with 160 million users; Renren, with 117 million users; and Kaixin001, with 75 million users.

When ranked by page views, Renren (whose name means "everyone") is said to be China's largest social networking website. Local social media platforms as opposed to their international equivalents are often preferred throughout Asian countries due to the former's ability to adapt to local language, culture, and economic development. The top 10 social sites in China are shown in Figure 13.2.

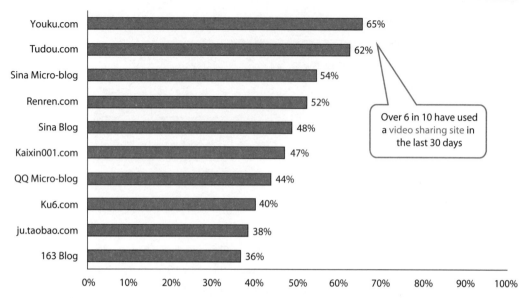

Figure 13.2 Comparing the Top 10 Social Networking Sites in China

Source: Netpop Research, 2011. Reprinted with permission of www.netpopresearch.com

As in the United States, social networks themselves provide marketers with segmentation opportunities. Renren attracts university students and is organized by schools and graduation class. (Renren users do not have the option to display their relationship status unless they build a couple's page. Also, users cannot post their political views or religious beliefs like they can on Facebook.) QZone attracts teens through people in their midtwenties, often from smaller cities as well as migrant workers. Kaixin001 attracts young, professional, white-collar workers from tier 1 cities. Douban attracts students who are interested in the fine arts.[35]

A study conducted in June 2010 found that 100 million Chinese microblogged Twitter style. The leading microblogging platform in China is SinaWeibo, with more than 50 million users.[36] SinaWeibo is censored, and if sensitive information is posted, a pop-up message announces that managers are checking the content. While Twitter is the only major microblog in the United States, Chinese regularly use Fanfou, QQ Microblog, and SouhuMicroblog. Launched in 2009 (three years after Twitter), SinaWeibo allows users to post 140-character messages (the same as Twitter) and to follow friends; however, unlike Twitter, users can post videos and photos, comment on others' updates, and add comments when reposting a friend's message.[37] Also, on Twitter each character is only a letter, but in Chinese each character is a word. Therefore, Chinese users can write much more.

13.5c Internet and Social Networking Usage in the United States and China

The number of Internet users in China grew from 23 million in 2000 to 384 million in 2009—a compound annual growth rate (CAGR) of 37 percent. The number of Internet users in the United States during the same period grew from 124 million to 228 million—a CAGR of 7 percent. As can be seen in Table 13.1, the number of Internet users in China is greater than in the United States, but the percentage having access to the Internet is significantly lower. The use of **bulletin board systems (BBSs)** in China is prolific. It was the first social networking site available and is still widely used throughout the country.

Table 13.1 Comparison of China versus the United States on the Internet

	China	U.S.
Internet users (June 2010) (in millions)	420	239
No Internet (% of population 2010)	68%	23%
No Internet (% of population 2011)	53%	18%
Internet growth 2000–2010	1,700%	150%
% of population using social networking sites (2011)	23%	46%
Number of social media sites used (average)	11	3
Population (Netpop Research)	1.35 billion	320 million
BBS accounts (2009)	3 billion	NA

Source: L. Evans, "China v America: How Do the Two Countries Compare," *The Guardian* (April 20, 2011). Accessed at http://www.guardian.co.uk/news/datablog/2011/jan/19/china-social-media; L. Lam, "Chinese Social Media Sites No Mere Clones," *South China Morning Post* (February 27, 2011). Accessed at http://topics.scmp.com/news/china-news-watch/article/Chinese-social-media-sites-no-mere-clones; Pew Research Center.

The evolution of China's Internet architecture from BBS to social networking proceeded as follows:[38]

1994–1999	Bulletin board system
1999–2002	Instant messaging
2002–2004	Blogs
2004–2006	Video sharing
2006–2008	Microblogging/Wiki/online gaming
2008–2010	Social networking sites

BBSs are anonymous interactive online message boards and have been at the center of social media usage in China since the beginning. A BBS allows users to exchange information through e-mail or public message boards. It is through BBSs that users find product-, brand-, service-, and interest-based communities and connect with others for group purchasing at discounts. Users can use the BBS to evaluate products and services in an anonymous manner. Today, BBS is used to refer to any Internet forum or message board. Started in 1978, BBS reached its peak usage in the 1990s. Ninety-eight percent of China Internet users have used BBS, and it is still extremely popular in China compared to many other countries.

In 2011, Netpop Research sampled 1,253 U.S. broadband users and 1,221 Chinese broadband users and found the Chinese to be more involved in every social media activity. As can be seen in Figure 13.3, the percent of Internet users posting to social networking sites is almost identical in the United States and China; however, Chinese Internet users are more likely to participate in every other social media activity.[39]

Chinese Internet users not only participate in a greater number of social networking activities than users in the United States, but they also are more active in each. As seen in Figure 13.4, 40 percent of Chinese Internet users are heavy contributors to social networking sites compared to just 11 percent in the United States.

As seen in Figure 13.5, while usage of social networking sites is similar in China (90%) and the United States (81%), the Chinese are far more likely to use other types of social media, especially blogs, forums, and location-based service sites.

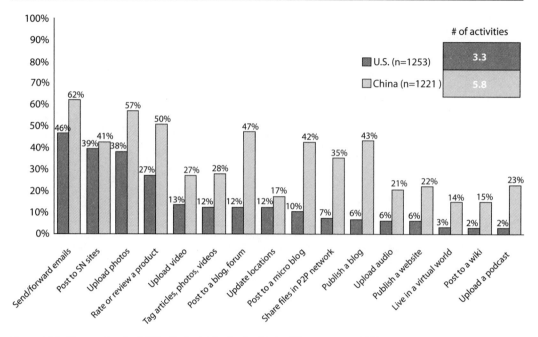

Figure 13.3 Comparing Social Media Activities in the United States versus China

Source: Netpop Research, 2011. Reprinted with permission of www.netpopresearch.com

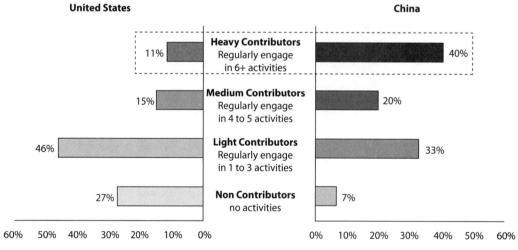

Figure 13.4 Engagement with Social Media: United States versus China

Source: Netpop Research, 2011. Reprinted with permission of www.netpopresearch.com

The Chinese Internet and social networking habits by number of users include:

- 420 million Internet users (Pingdom statistic)
- 321 million music downloaders
- 272 million instant message users
- 265 million online gamers
- 222 million creators of online videos

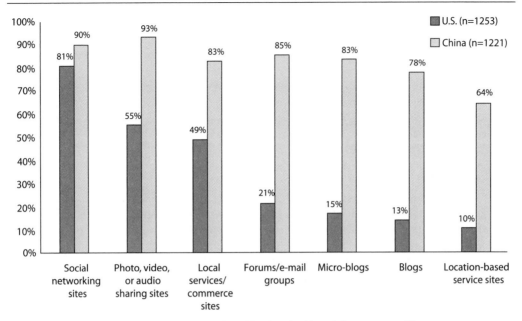

Figure 13.5 Comparing Types of Social Media Sites Used in the United States versus China

Source: Netpop Research, 2011. Reprinted with permission of www.netpopresearch.com

- 221 million bloggers
- 176 million users of social networking systems
- 117 million users of BBSs
- 108 million online shoppers

While these numbers are large, over half of China's population is not yet online (versus less than 20 percent in the United States). Those who are online average 2.7 hours per day[40]—on par with usage in the United States and Japan.

Reasons put forth for the heavy Chinese use of social media include:[41]

- Rural to urban migration that has separated families
- Loneliness of the one-child generation
- Distrust of information from government-controlled media

13.5d Internet and Social Media Usage in China

One might think that the number one online activity in China would be communicating with friends, but the Frands Report from OgilvyOne Worldwide indicates that this is number two.[42] The number one activity is seeking information before buying. Many experts feel that compared to their Western counterparts, Chinese consumers are much heavier users of the Internet, and social media in particular, to research, discuss, evaluate, and make purchasing decisions regarding brands, products, and services. This makes it imperative for companies to participate in the discussion and evaluate the buzz surrounding their offerings. Chinese consumers pay particular attention to the price tag when making their purchase decisions; however, many feel the concept of brand is becoming increasingly important given the many quality deficiency incidents in the news in China and the importance of country of origin for many products. Many of the social media discussions center around the concept of "value": price versus performance in numerous product categories.

According to Roland Berger,[43] these are the main reasons Chinese consumers participate in online communities:

- Share knowledge and personal experiences
- Defend or expose the truth about products
- Seek and give advice about purchases or product use
- Make a name for themselves within the community
- Communicate with customers online

In China, brand awareness and purchasing decisions are the stages most influenced by Internet word of mouth (IWOM), with 56 percent of consumers first learning about a brand through IWOM and 59 percent deciding to purchase based on IWOM. Communication Intelligent Corporation collects over 46 million comments each month related to brands, products, and services from 16 industries and uses proprietary Chinese-language text-mining software to monitor online buzz. Roland Berger[44] found that nearly 60 percent of Chinese consumers review rating sites, discussion boards, blogs, and other online sources before making a purchase decision versus about 20 percent of their U.S. counterparts. Nearly two-thirds of Chinese consumers said they want companies to be more involved online, and nearly half want to see them actively participate in online communities. Two-thirds prefer to interact with companies on third-party BBS sites as opposed to official company pages or blogs because they feel they will read more objective content that hasn't been edited by companies that delete negative content about them.

For many in China, particularly those who use the Internet only for social media reasons, there is no distinction between the Internet itself and social media. Unlike in Germany, where users tend to be private online, Chinese users freely share personal information. Chinese users actively chat, blog, and microblog, saying things online that they normally wouldn't say offline.

13.5e Social Networks and Customer Relationship Management

While social networks began as a way to connect individuals with one another, they are now being used by businesses in their B2C and B2B efforts, with the former being much more developed than the latter. Effective CRM management involves identifying prospects, selecting and acquiring the right ones, and developing the relationship in order to maximize the profitable lifetime of the customer. Successful CRM communication is founded on the ability to engage customers in a dialogue that results in greater satisfaction with the brand and/or the organization. CRM can enhance brand value by providing customers with information they require, providing offers that add value, and transparently facilitating the acquisition of information to improve future CRM efforts.

CRM usage in Asia has lagged behind that in the United States in all areas: software, call centers, process redesign, customer data, customer strategy, and so forth. A number of reasons have been put forth to explain this:

- The Chinese focus on technical education at the university level and not management strategy.
- Price, rather than customer service, has been the primary competitive weapon in China.
- Brand management in China is weak, and CRM, being a primary way to create bonds between customer and brand, is not stressed.
- Customer contact personnel in Asian companies are not empowered to make "first-person" resolution decisions and must defer to those at the "top."

- Infrastructure for CRM in the form of databases, database management, and call centers is still relatively undeveloped in Asia.
- In Asia's fast-growing economies, companies are inclined to focus on customer acquisition and not customer retention.
- Subject matter experts (SMEs) in China are cost conscious and will defer CRM software and hardware spending.
- In Asian companies, labor receives resources at the expense of information technology.
- CRM systems may not result in quick payback—a key for Asian companies.[45]

Some of Asia's larger companies have successful CRM systems in place, and CRM adoption has begun among Asian CRM SMEs. The spread of CRM throughout Asian companies will be accelerated through CRM software as a service (SaaS) solutions. Excluding Japan, SaaS accounts for nearly half of CRM software implementation in the Asian region. SaaS sales in Asia are expected to hit $570 million (USD) by 2012.[46]

Monitoring social networks enables companies to gather information from online conversations and get a 360-degree view of customers so they can better manage the CRM strategy cycle. Is social networking a new channel within CRM, or are traditional CRM strategies merely enhanced through social networking? Are CRM and social networking strategies complements or opposites? A 2010 Gartner report calls social networking a "disruptive influence" on the CRM market. Is this correct, or is social networking an enhancement?[47]

Companies already use CRM approaches to interact and communicate with their customers, so using CRM tools in these efforts through SNS makes sense. Social networking provides new ways for companies to manage, engage, and service their customers. CRM tools are already used to analyze information and to listen and respond in meaningful ways to customers. However, social networking brings a dimension to the fore that CRM up to this point has not had to deal with: customers, prospects, and the general public talking among themselves about companies, products, and brands. The issue is a new one for companies. Should they enter into the social networking conversations and, if so, how?

Case studies in both the United States and China have shown that companies attempting to "manage" social networking are inclined to fail badly. The very nature of social interaction requires give-and-take and not one party "managing" another. There are many examples of poorly managed social media efforts in China. Here are a few of them:

- KFC released ads in China that implied that those who eat KFC would be admitted into universities and those who did not would be rejected. The company did not participate effectively in the subsequent negative viral conversation.
- SK-II, a Japanese cosmetics brand, left China when online discussion spread the news that they were using forbidden ingredients in some products.
- One purchaser in China complained about a Dell computer in an online forum, and the forum administrator invited others to complain about Dell. This led to a class-action lawsuit, creating "Dell Hell" for the company. This is a good example of why companies should have SNS monitoring centers and quell small problems before they become big problems.[48]

Here are some examples of well-managed social media efforts in China:

- By using Kaixin Garden, a virtual community game, Lohas Juice gained 3,676,464 participants.
- Carlsberg's (beer) viral videos for Chinese football fans "Dreams of Winning the World Cup" were very favorably received given the unique delivery of the sports' competition.

- Six hundred China Eastern Airline crew members signed up with Sinamicroblog to better communicate with their customers.
- Mercedes-Benz sold 200 smart cars in 3.5 hours by using Taobao—a Chinese-language website for online shopping similar to eBay and Amazon.

The point is that companies need to listen to what consumers are saying about them. There are a number of products on the market that enable companies to monitor what is being said about them on social networks. For Microsoft Dynamics® CRM users, there is the Social Networking Accelerator, which enables users to do the following:

- Identify key influencers in each product area
- Track public online conversations
- Quickly spot negative public relations, misperceptions, and product/brand complaints
- Launch online marketing efforts to social customers' preferred platforms
- Identify prospects by their conversational topics relevant to products or services
- Engage in conversation with prospects and customers online
- Help customers en masse via social networking sites as opposed to individually[49]

Tools such as BuzzGain, Radian6, Tackurt, PeopleBrowsr, and SocialRadar help brands monitor, steer dialogue, and maintain their reputation on Twitter. FriendFeed.com enables companies to view comments about brands from various social networks aggregated into one stream. BackType will reveal what users are saying in the comments section of blog posts. Google Blog Search will provide your company with relevant blog posts. Companies should also view Ning, Google, Yahoo!, and Facebook groups to see communities built around the company or a specific product.[50]

13.5e.1 Acquisition and Win-Back

CRM strategies must include acquisition of prospects, since companies lose between 2 and 40 percent of their customers every year. Some, like newspapers, lose a lot more: 66 percent. L. L. Bean uses search engine optimization strategies to acquire new prospects. This increases the chances of prospects and customers generating a reference to the L. L. Bean website when typing in merchandise keywords. Since Facebook users provide demographic and personal information, companies can engage them at appropriate times coinciding with life stage and life cycle events such as birthdays, retirement, graduations, and so on. Companies can also acquire new customers by marketing to those in affinity groups—particularly using endorsements from other members. A review of the literature provided no examples of companies implementing unique win-back strategies through social networking, but there are many ways this can be done.[51]

13.5e.2 Retention

Retention strategies can be based on three techniques: rewarding, bonding, and service structure. The bonds that companies create with their customers can be programmatic (loyalty/frequency/rewards programs) or humanistic (personalized treatment). Retaining customers has become the major focus of many companies, since the cost of acquiring customers is much higher—some say five times higher or more. Consequently, companies have developed many tactics useful in making sure customers don't leave or downwardly migrate in terms of purchasing or usage. Social networking opens up a new venue for the complete array of retention tactics, such as the following:[52]

Preferential treatment: Notices of sales, new products, and special promotions are sent to valued customers before the general public is informed via traditional marketing methods.

Rewarding: Notices of specials are sent to regular customers that can be extended to their "friends." McDonald's did this successfully in China, giving free food items to a target and their friends if they dined as a group.

Idiosyncratic-fit: This is the tendency for customers to be enticed by offers for which they enjoy a relative advantage. Such is the nature of location-based offers, where free or heavily reduced items are offered to only those in the vicinity.

Personalization: Efforts connoting individual attention are possible by matching your offers to customer demographics, life stage, and interests, all of which are available through social networking site membership information.

Customization: Based on productive dialogues, companies can customize their offerings to meet a customer's needs with respect to product, delivery, promotional, channel, and payment terms.

Cross-selling and up-selling: Companies can make recommendations to customers based on what their friends are buying. Marketers know that up-selling can more easily be introduced once the relationship with the customer has progressed through the acquaintanceship and trust stages and entered the commitment stage. Social networking enables companies to more quickly move the relationship through these various stages.

Managing downward migration: As good customers begin to visit less frequently, buy fewer and less expensive items, and buy fewer high-profit items, companies realize the relationship is in danger and the customers may soon defect. Through social networking, companies can regenerate the relationship through all of the previously mentioned tactics.

Converting transactional buyers into relational buyers: Some short-life customers are merely purchasing from a company because of price and aren't interested in a long-term relationship no matter what is offered. Other short-life customers can be converted into long-term customers if the company provides something of value. Brand community groups, company-sponsored brand informational pages, and fan pages can be useful in creating bonds with the short-life customer.

Brand building: Customer interactions over the phone and Internet, through direct marketing efforts, and through point-of-sale activities all help create a brand experience for the customer. Social networking efforts, it could be argued, offer an even better way to provide a brand experience given the opportunity for group influence and interaction among group members and the company/brand.

Providing and attaining intimacy: Consumers for whom the product/brand is important reveal higher tendencies to engage in long-term relationships. Members of social networks discuss products and brands on a regular basis, offering opportunities for companies to ratchet up the prestige of their products and brands.

Retention strategies through social networking are as feasible in the B2B environment as they are in the B2C environment; however, the former will see greater use of structural solutions in creating bonds and the latter greater use of humanistic bonding. More meaningful and deeper customer–brand relationships are possible via social networking than through traditional CRM methods given the greater frequency of contact that is possible. As seen in the intensity of usage of social networking by members, social networking has become a prominent activity in everyday life, and brands can and do play a prominent role in social networking activities. Consequently, brands now have the means to embed themselves deeper into their customers' lives.

13.5f Conclusions

U.S. and Chinese consumers are heavy users of the Internet and social media in particular to research, discuss, evaluate, and make purchase decisions regarding brands, products, and services. This makes it imperative for companies to participate in the discussion and evaluate the buzz surrounding their offerings. Participation can include sending messages to defined target markets, building customer engagement with the company or brands, and creating awareness and buzz. Companies must be cautious, however, in that the viral nature of social networking can spread negative company publicity faster than positive publicity.[53]

13.6 How and Why Marketers Should Use Social Networks

Many feel that social networking is where companies will see the return on investment in their CRM business model for the foreseeable future. For one thing, it is a new channel within the CRM network. For another, it will enable companies to get a true 360-degree view of their customers. It is a way to reach customers and prospects fast. Finally, it is a proven way for companies to get attention, educate consumers, increase sales, increase customer satisfaction, assist buyers through better customer service, and retain customers through the development of new and meaningful relationship strategies. Social networking enables companies to develop scale economies in peer-to-peer word-of-mouth advertising. See Table 13.2 for a complete array of social networking benefits. The following sections discuss how companies have used social networking to achieve success in many of the areas listed in Table 13.2.

Table 13.2 **Why Companies Should Use Social Networking**

Company-Specific Reasons	To get attention
	To increase awareness
	To increase knowledge
	To increase revenue
	To help deal with detractors and message hijackers
	To correct small issues before they become major
	To discuss the company
	To educate
	To turn fans into customers
	To shorten the sales cycle by speeding up introduction and adoption stages
	To improve company's ranking on Internet search engines
	To enable employees to communicate across company divisions
	To stay in touch with channel members and partners such as franchisees
Customer-Oriented Reasons	To develop meaningful relationships
	To engage with customers in new ways
	To increase customer satisfaction
	To develop a community of users providing peer-to-peer support
	To increase customer service and complaint handling and provide speedier help
	To keep customers from "failing" (medication/diet regimens)
	To reach segments such as "influencers," opinion leaders, and high "clout" scorers

(Continued)

Table 13.2 (*Continued*)

Tactical Reasons	To introduce new products
	To send messages to specifically defined targets
	To target customers in competitors' stores
	To implement location-based promotions and loyalty programs
	To buy ads on social networking sites based on user characteristics
	To raise money or contributions ("crowdfunding") or to generate new ideas ("crowdsourcing")
	To promote a point of view/generate publicity/public relations
	To conduct marketing research
	To predict "hits"
	To seek out shoppers through developing an online retail store on social networking sites
	To lower costs
	To experience word-of-mouth peer-to-peer advertising to scale

13.6a Company-Specific Reasons for Using Social Media

13.6a.1 To Get Attention, Increase Awareness, and Create Buzz

According to the Yaffe Center, almost one-fourth of daily youth social networking users said that they learned about new products on social networking sites.[54] Buzz marketing involves sending out an initial marketing message that is then spread virally for free. Elements of buzz marketing often include offbeat videos, games, contests, sweepstakes, and free products. Companies must carefully review the commercial orientation of such marketing efforts. If the commercialism is too blatant, users react negatively; however, users don't like to be fooled either. An online video that appeared in China called "Beijing Arm-Swinging Man" showed a man with a phone on a subway, and it went viral to great acclaim. When it was learned that it was a Sony Ericsson–produced video for its F305c mobile phone, the viral buzz turned negative because viewers felt it was commercial manipulation.

Facebook fan pages are associated with a company, brand, artist, or anything else users might want to have an affiliation with. These are essentially replacing company brand home pages. To engage users, content should be informational or entertaining, with the brand-specific messages secondary. According to a recent study by Vitrue, a fan base of 1 million translates into at least $3.6 million in equivalent media in a year—each fan being worth $3.60.[55]

An example of brand-specific messaging at work can be found with Sprinkles Cupcakes. They have a Facebook page, and more than 70,000 people have declared themselves fans. Each day Sprinkles announces a secret word, and the first 25 or 50 customers who show up at any of its five stores in the Chicago area and whisper the secret word get a free cupcake. Sprinkles acts like any person on Facebook, posting updates and staying up to date with what its fans are doing. Other companies employ MySpace, Twitter, LinkedIn, and other social sites to gain attention, create awareness, and establish buzz.[56]

Jeweler Janet Rothstein suggests companies use their expertise to promote their business. Her posts about the dangers of unsanitary ear piercing or the price of gold and its effects on jewelry sales invariably increase traffic to her sites and her store.[57]

JetBlue Airways rolled out an "All You Can Jet" monthly pass for $599 on Twitter the second week of August 2009. Within 36 hours, officials were worried about having to curtail the promotion because it was so successful the airline was running out of seats. JetBlue has about 1 million followers on Twitter, and the promotion led to multiple mentions of the company every second on Twitter.[58]

13.6a.2 To Increase Revenue

Free Spirit Yacht Cruises increased business by 30 percent in one year to 300 charters through a social media push. The company tweets regularly on Twitter and recently launched group and fan pages on Facebook. This is quite a change from a company that had previously relied on the Yellow Pages as its main source of new business. The owner decided to market over Facebook after she noticed picture postings of Free Spirit Cruises on Facebook pages.[59]

The general manager for Coffee Groundz set up profiles for his café on Twitter and Facebook. He simultaneously posts blog entries on Twitter, Facebook, and a company website three times a day, devoting no more than 30 minutes managing the company's social media. In response, customers started tweeting orders and special requests. Additionally, in-store events promoted on the sites drew crowds three times larger than promotions generated through traditional means.[60]

To fully appreciate the potential to generate revenue, companies must consider that users of social networking sites are into their accounts several times per day and view an enormous amount of Internet content. For marketers to stand out, their message must add value in a unique and compelling way, be updated frequently, and be easily shared so that the social network community can add value to the message. The owner of Berry Chill frozen yogurt of Chicago created a Facebook page before even opening the business and then quickly added Twitter, Tumblr (an SNS), and foursquare. The store now has over 10,000 Facebook fans and 3,000 Twitter followers. The store has more than 1,000 customers per day, many generated through discounts and specials offered through social media.[61]

13.6a.3 To Help Deal with Detractors and Message Hijackers

A company's message on the Internet can be affected in more subtle ways than merely being trashed. The very fact that a company's information is being shared by others means it will be tarnished, abbreviated, altered, made ineffectual, and subjected to what can be agonizing parody. Politicians learn to speak in "sound bites" so that the intent of their message can still get through even after media reduce a one-hour talk to 10 seconds. Developing "sound bites" for the Internet is more difficult because the audience can participate in message deterioration and, further, send the altered message to countless others. It is extremely difficult for companies to maintain the integrity of their brands and brand messages across social media. Digital magazines offer a solution in that once a company's message is in digital magazine format, the entire message can be passed on to all social sites through a simple link.[62]

The viral nature of social media is a blessing if rave reviews about your brand get passed on, but it is a curse if the reviews are negative. Companies must, therefore, develop policies to deal with negative comments. Walmart developed a Facebook profile aimed at students and did not expect to have its wall filled with criticism regarding low wages, aversion to trade unions, and negative effects on small-town-America Main Streets. Nestlé attempted to deal with a problem when it removed negative comments regarding its use of palm oil in its products. This, however, created an uproar greater than the initial comments by Greenpeace. In this instance, Nestlé missed an opportunity to educate the market.

The viral nature of social networking can also spread negative company publicity overnight. For example, a professional musician, Dave Carroll, saw his guitar get severely damaged by United Airlines baggage personnel on the tarmac in full view of other passengers. When United refused to compensate him for the damage, he wrote a song for YouTube that has been viewed nearly 10 million times and, if you total all media references, hundreds of millions of times. The *London Times* estimates the first song caused United stock to plunge 10 percent, costing shareholders $180 million. When he was totally exacerbated by United's bureaucracy in trying to collect money for the damaged guitar, he wrote a second song. After he received thousands of communications from others regarding United's poor service, he wrote a third song. All went viral, and all became nightmares for United Airlines' management.[63]

Another example of social media becoming a nightmare for management started when two employees of Domino's filmed themselves spitting mucus on a Domino's sandwich and putting pizza cheese up their noses. The videos went viral and were viewed by millions of people. Two-thirds of respondents said they were less likely to visit or order from Domino's after viewing the YouTube video. It took Domino's management far too long to pull the videos down from YouTube and two days to respond via a YouTube apology. Experts say Domino's should receive an "F" for its handling of the crisis.[64]

Environmental activists took Nestlé to task over purchasing Indonesian palm oil for use in Kit Kat candy bars and other products. They produced a very negative and highly agitating video of an office worker taking a Kit Kat break at his desk and biting not into a chocolate-wafer candy bar but rather into the finger of a severed orangutan's hand. The fact that the supplier produced just a little over 1 percent of the palm oil used by Nestlé the previous year did not matter. What did matter was Nestlé telling Facebook users it would delete their negative comments from its Facebook page. This merely made the matter worse.[65]

Even McDonald's has had major claims of deficiencies go viral. A patron spent eight months calling attention to dirty conditions at indoor fast-food playgrounds—including McDonald's. She referred to the playgrounds as "pinkeye factories." She appeared on Anderson Cooper's daytime show but did not mention specific restaurants. She was banned from McDonald's restaurants, although a local director of operations agreed to work with her regarding her concerns. When she posted on Facebook that she was banned, she heard from thousands of outraged parents countrywide.[66]

These videos were so devastating to these companies' image that crisis-intervention teams are now permanent fixtures in corporate America. B. Solis suggests companies use tools such as BuzzGain, Radian6, Trackur, PeopleBrowsr, SocialRadar, and others to monitor and contribute to dialogues that help protect a company's reputation online. He suggests that the first step to building a company's sCRM (social customer relationship management) is simply to listen. He also suggests using:

- FriendFeed.com to see comments about your brand from various social networks aggregated into one stream
- Search.Twitter.com for related tweets or Advanced Twitter Search to measure conversations by time frame, sentiment, location, or individuals
- Google Blog Search to view relevant blog posts
- BackType to see what is said about you in the comments section of blog posts
- Groups on Facebook, Google, Yahoo!, and Ning to see what others have built around your company or product[67]

As discussed by Leslie Gaines-Ross, your company adversaries have a social network arsenal consisting of blogs, tweets, text messages, online petitions, Facebook protest sites, and digital videos that can be used to ruin your reputation. She suggests the following strategies for counteracting these reputation busters:

- Do not hit back with a disproportionate show of force. Act humane. Nobody will support a Goliath.
- Respond quickly.

- Empower frontline teams to meet unfair/incorrect messages with countermessages.
- Respond using the same social media your adversaries used.
- Recruit your advocates to rise to your defense.
- Stockpile your company and brand credentials and be ready to display them at the first sign of trouble.[68]

13.6a.4 To Discuss the Company

Very often a company will develop its own social networking site, sometimes referred to as a corporate blog. This enables a company to have better control over its marketing efforts. For example, Procter & Gamble's Pampers Village online community allows users to connect with one another, participate in discussion forums, and receive Procter & Gamble commercial and noncommercial information. Also, Bank of America has created a B2B community on its "Small Business Online Community" site, allowing businesses to communicate with both one another and the bank.

13.6a.5 To Educate

Social media can be used to educate consumers about a particular company and its product or about an industry in general. One example is the farmers and ranchers who are turning to social media to connect with consumers, educators, and others about agriculture. The AgChat Foundation teaches farmers how to use online social media to tell their stories to the general public. Of course, large agribusiness firms are also using social media to portray their products in a favorable light. Together they address the public's concern about food safety, food quality, food labeling, antibiotics and hormones, government subsidies, and prices. They also focus on reaching bloggers and other influencers. They are attempting to have honest dialogues with the public and educate them regarding food production and food safety.[69]

13.6a.6 To Enable Employees to Communicate Across Company Divisions

Communication within a company has always been a crucial element in a company's success. Social media provides another avenue for this communication. As reported by Z. Karabell:

> Countless corporations have created internal Facebook pages and Yammer accounts for employees to communicate across divisions and regions. Industry groups for engineers, doctors, and human resources professionals have done the same to share new ideas and solutions on a constant basis rather than episodically at conferences.[70]

13.6b Customer-Oriented Reasons for Using Social Media

13.6b.1 To Build Customer Engagement and Establish Meaningful Relationships

Companies can set up profiles for their brands that members of the community can then join or "friend." Many users add their favorite brands to their personal profile. The Marketing Evolution study found that more than 70 percent of the marketing value created by social network marketing campaigns resulted from the "momentum effect" of these viral pass-along elements.[71] Following are some examples of customers becoming engaged by social media.

A Dove video, *Evolution*, and a television commercial available on video, *A Girl's Self-Esteem*, have been seen millions of times and fostered television programs devoted to the topics raised in the videos. These videos went viral overnight, spawning hundreds of viewer parodies that were supportive of Dove's point of view.

In November 2009, Burberry launched a program called *Art of the Trench*, along with an accompanying website, and invited customers to upload images of themselves wearing the brand's trench coat to the website. Within the first week, 400,000 people from 191 countries had sent in pictures; within 9 months, the site had been visited 9 million times. Burberry developed a Facebook page and now has 5 million followers. Burberry streams its runway shows live over its website to millions who can immediately click on the products they like and receive product delivery in a few days.[72]

Chefs have begun sending tweets to their "inner circle" of customers, informing them of specials and restaurant special events. One chef tweets to almost 10,000 followers. Twitter seems to create a sense of loyalty between chef and customers. Customers are often seen sending photos of their dishes to their friends.[73]

13.6b.2 To Engage with Customers in New Ways

The ever-changing landscape of social media and the Internet, as well as individuals' innovative ways of using it, provides countless possibilities for companies to interact with their customers. Spot Dessert Bar in New York's East Village, for example, didn't let a blizzard that dumped two feet of snow keep away customers. It offered half-price hot drinks on Facebook, Twitter, and its company blog, convincing customers to get to the store. Through social media, Spot Dessert Bar also holds contests and offers discounts to people who "like" the store. It offers laptops and iPads for customers to use so they can add the shop to their social media profiles. It has experienced a 15 to 20 percent increase in sales since starting the social media blitz.[74]

Another example can be found with Burger King, which ran the "Whopper Sacrifice" campaign in 2009, in which a customer received a free Whopper coupon for dropping ten friends from their social networking sites. Their friends then received the message that they were dropped for a sandwich.[75]

While many companies engage with customers on Twitter and Facebook, some are successfully joining conversations on YouTube with video blogging (also known as vlogging). Some vloggers, in turn, become opinion leaders and influencers regarding the products by recommending them in forums. Benchmade Knife Company, for example, contributes to conversations on YouTube but won't start them. Benchmade will answer questions posted about its knives and discuss anything that has to do with the company—including commenting on vlog reviews. On YouTube, there are currently about 4,000 videos reviewing Benchmade knives, with new comments being made all the time. By interacting with vloggers, the company claims to have generated significant sales increases, while at the same time giving vloggers a sense that it is listening to what they have to say.[76]

13.6b.3 To Better Handle Customer Service and Complaints

Using social media to address customer issues and complaints is one way to improve customer satisfaction. AT&T is trying to improve its image with customers by being responsive through social media. AT&T gets pummeled mercilessly on Twitter, Facebook, and other social media sites. Management realizes it cannot turn around its image overnight but, over time, hopes that its social media efforts to help customers with problems will favorably reshape its image. On a normal day, AT&T has 10,000 mentions on social networks and a social media staff of 19 devoted to responding to customer dissatisfaction expressed over social media. A program scrapes Twitter for mentions during off hours so staff can respond the next day. AT&T also responds to customers on its Facebook wall.[77]

13.6b.4 To Develop Peer-to-Peer Support

Consumers today trust one another more than they do commercial third parties. This is true in the United States and even more so in China, where the tremendous usage of message boards supports consumers' faith in one another more than in the government or companies. Consumers like to discuss products and brands and contribute answers to questions. This adds to their self-esteem and builds social capital. Companies have recognized this tendency and created forums and brand communities. Consumers turn to these sites in addition to blogs, message boards, Facebook, Twitter, wikis, and so forth, to contribute and gather helpful information. Customer contact center (CCC) personnel, as well as others, need to have easy access to these online communities to enable them to monitor conversations and, perhaps, offer assistance. Involvement in these sites is important to companies even though inquiry calls will decrease due to customers helping one another. Some feel CCC personnel will take on the role of brand community managers in addition to responding to problems. Thus, their role will become central to increasing customer satisfaction as opposed to merely handling one-off problems.[78]

Social media allows users to connect with one another, offer advice and support, and solve problems. It is felt that brand communities will provide the support previously provided by customer contact centers. Companies such as Hewlett-Packard (HP) are embracing the opportunities provided by social media. HP launched a consumer support forum in seven languages in over 20 countries, with more than 4.6 million customers resolving issues through the forum—a function previously provided by company CCCs.[79]

13.6b.5 To Increase and Expedite Customer Service

Recognizing and addressing issues that customers are reporting on social media sites can be critical in some industries. Hotels and resorts have social networking sleuths who monitor what is being said about them online. They search networking sites like Facebook and Twitter to detect unhappy guests and to address complaints as quickly as possible. Sometimes using social media to lodge a complaint or request can be more effective than calling the front desk. Hotels and resorts know that since so many travelers turn to reviews and blogs on the Web before deciding where to stay, negative comments can seriously erode business. Guests reaching out to hotels through social media often find themselves getting freebies and better service. Even hoteliers state they go out of their way a little bit for those who comment on Twitter and Facebook.[80]

Another example is Delta Air Lines, which has a headquarters control room containing monitors that stream social media mentions of the airlines. Delta continuously peruses the monitors to hunt for traveler complaints and to try to solve problems using a computer program that searches for key Delta mentions. When tweets fly about flight delays and missed connections, agents respond with specific information about the causes of delays. Many airlines, like Delta, have social media teams dedicated to finding and resolving online complaints. Workers in the social media headquarters are empowered to offer customers quick fixes. Several airlines check passenger clout scores when resolving issues.[81]

13.6b.6 To Keep Customers from Failing

Customers today are viewed as coproducers of products and services, since they are often involved in their design, delivery, usage, and recommendations to others. However, research indicates that about a third of all service problems are caused by customers.[82] For example, the World Health Organization found that half of all patients in the United States do not follow their medication regimen for high blood pressure, and 92 percent of those patients have lost control over their blood pressure. Failure to properly take medications results in one-fourth of all nursing home admissions.[83]

Companies have a very difficult time managing customer failures. Of course, when outcomes are bad, customers have a difficult time blaming themselves, and complaints are directed instead toward the company. Thus, both the consumer and the company are hurt by customer failure.[84] Following are some examples of companies that are attempting to prevent customer failure.

Fair Isaac Company has developed what it calls "The Medication Adherence Score," which indicates the likelihood that a person will take his prescribed medications. Fair Isaac hopes health care providers will use the score to target e-mails and other reminders at people who are less likely to take their medications.[85]

Weight Watchers certainly wants members' weight loss programs to be successful. It benefits the consumer as well as the company. It has found that the key to members' weight loss is maintaining users' motivation. What better way to maintain motivation than social networking with others in the weight loss program? Similarly, health clubs and health-oriented magazines often create a community consisting of those who want to lose weight. Members blog about their daily successes and failures, motivating others to stay with the program.

13.6b.7 To Reach Influencers, Opinion Leaders, and High Clout Scorers

Companies are monitoring videos on YouTube and reaching out to vloggers who demonstrate their brands online. They realize vloggers can turn into effective influencers who promote their brand. One Benchmade vlogger called Nutnfancy produces detailed 10- to 20-minute videos for each product Benchmade produces—a promotional endeavor the company could not itself afford.[86] Recently, Benchmade even hired a few vloggers to help its YouTube efforts by doing in-store demonstrations. Benchmade offers vloggers loaner knives for review as well as discounts on current products and previews of future product offerings.

13.6c Tactical Reasons for Using Social Media

13.6c.1 To Introduce New Products

Social media can provide new and innovative ways to introduce a company's new products. Ford Motor Company provides a perfect example. Ford wanted to drive awareness and sales in a new and interesting way when it was introducing its new Ford Fiesta automobile. It used social media in launching a program that consisted of lending its car to 100 people—out of 4,000 applicants. These 100 drivers were asked to make and send in videos of their experiences with the new economy car. Ford posted the videos on its corporate site as well as on social media sites such as YouTube. Nearly 5 million people viewed the drivers' YouTube videos, and millions more tweeted their impressions.[87]

13.6c.2 To Send Messages to Specifically Defined Target Markets

Most social networking sites collect information from users, enabling marketers to target segments based on country, state, city or town, age, gender, marital status, religion, interests, activities, and so on. Sites such as YouTube, Facebook, and MySpace have systems in place that let marketers create and bid on ads through a self-service website similar to the way they buy ads on search engines. They do not, however, buy ads tied to search terms. Instead, the ads are linked to information users provide about themselves: age, gender, hobbies, personal interests, and other personal information. Of course, search engine advertising is still popular with companies bidding on keywords in a continuous auction. For example, if a consumer searches using the word "pizza," it is likely a Pizza Hut or Domino's ad will appear, since those companies buy ads on the major search engines tied to pizza-related search terms. Lately, Pizza Hut has begun buying ads through Facebook as well.[88]

Gatorade is one of PepsiCo's most profitable brands, but imagewise it is on the decline. In an attempt to breathe new life into the brand, PepsiCo is trying to reconnect with teen athletes who have switched to other sports drinks because they view Gatorade as having lost its street credibility. The company set up what is called "Gatorade Mission Control," which consists of four full-time employees who monitor blogs and track mentions of the product on Twitter, Facebook, or other social media. Trying to be part of the social circle, these employees correct misconceptions about Gatorade or provide information about the product.[89]

13.6c.3 To Target Customers in Competitors' Stores

Using mobile phone technology, retailers can target customers while they are in competitors' stores—in effect, stealing a sale. Consumers regularly shop for the lowest price for big-ticket items. Many consumers are starting to compare prices they see in a retail store with competitors' prices available online using one of dozens of price-comparison apps—such as theFind or RedLaser on their smart phones. Through a partnership with theFind, Best Buy can direct ads to shoppers when they are in a competitor's store. For example, if shoppers use theFind's free app to price TVs in a Walmart store, the phone gleans particulars from their search and Best Buy then shows them ads of similar electronics for sale at the Best Buy outlet. The offers are only sent to customers who opt to allow the program to use their phone's global positioning system to track their location. In addition, if a customer inside a Best Buy compares prices through theFind and discovers a better deal elsewhere, Best Buy can then show them ads for other deals in their store before they leave. In addition, online sellers can steal customers from any store once customers enter a store product bar code.[90]

13.6c.4 To Implement Location-Based Promotions and Loyalty Programs

Foursquare has made location-based service (LBS) a user favorite on Internet and mobile devices. Users "check in" online at real-world locations and receive virtual badges that earn awards, such as Starbucks coffee. Brands are building relationships through LBS websites.

In 2010, Facebook added location "check-ins" for mobile users and the ability for merchants to post discounts or coupons for shoppers who virtually "check in" or click online to show they are in the store. In addition, loyalty perks can be awarded to smart phone users who are near stores sponsoring the loyalty program.

In an experiment, Gap gave away 10,000 pairs of jeans to people who "checked in" at stores using Facebook. During the 2010 Christmas shopping season, JCPenney offered 20 percent discounts to those who checked in with Facebook, foursquare, and BrightKite.

A mobile app called ShopKick has signed up Target, Best Buy, Macy's, and other large American retailers for its loyalty program, which gives points just for users walking in their doors. The points can be converted into gift cards and other rewards. ShopKick occasionally holds sweepstakes where shoppers win prizes just for turning on the app in the store.[91]

13.6c.5 To Raise Money or to Generate New Ideas

Open source marketing ("crowdsourcing" and "crowdfunding") occurs when users participate in contributing to a firm's marketing efforts in creating brand names, designs, slogans, ads, and so on, or generating funds. Crowdfunding relies on two forces: social media and the need for people to feel part of the social whole. Hearing about a cause from a friend is much more potent than hearing about it from the charitable organization. Crowdfunding sites make money by charging the organization a small fee.[92] Following are some examples of open source marketing that worked:

- Crowdfunding worked superbly for Barack Obama in his 2008 presidential campaign.
- Kiva, which channels money to entrepreneurs in developing countries, has processed more than $200 million in loans.
- Chicago-based GiveForward raises money for out-of-pocket medical expenses.

The business plan of Threadless, an online T-shirt company, centers on crowdsourcing. The company has attracted more than 1 million buyers and designers for its T-shirts without using any traditional advertising. It finds that Facebook is effective because it has detailed knowledge of its fan base. It is also experimenting with Twitter, even though Twitter doesn't provide as much information about its users.[93]

THEORY IN ACTION

Crowdsourcing

This is what Brian Dunn, former CEO of Best Buy, had to say about his company's use of crowdsourcing:

> Today, when people buy a new device, they often "crowdsource" advice by asking for recommendations on Twitter or Facebook. That practice will become more and more influential over time. . . . On Twitter, we have a feed called Twelpforce. Customers can post about their tech problems, and Best Buy associates—or other Twitter users—can post solutions. By monitoring the feed, we're able to learn a lot about what our customers are doing and to help them with problems in real time.

B. J. Dunn, "How I Did It: Best Buy's CEO on Learning to Love Social Media," *Harvard Business Review*, 88, 12 (December 2010): 43–48.

13.6c.6 To Conduct Marketing Research

While ethnographic research is instrumental in better understanding the place of your brands and products in people's lives, monitoring social networks provides an unobtrusive and nonreactive way to really see firsthand the value consumers attach to your offerings. For example, does your brand deliver on its promise? Are consumers committed to it? What additional functions or features are they seeking? Conversations over social media are an invaluable addition to discovering such things via traditional surveys and feedback from the customer contact centers. Some feel that the number one use of social media by companies lies in gathering insights to drive continual incremental improvements to products and services.[94]

13.6c.7 To Predict Hits

Advertisers are monitoring social media buzz to evaluate TV shows. Researchers monitor conversations across social networks to predict which shows will be hits. Mentions of programs on Facebook and Twitter and other sites increasingly encourage people to watch them.[95]

13.6c.8 To Experience Word-of-Mouth Advertising to Scale

Companies are advertising on Facebook because it allows consumers to have discussions about brands with their friends. The ads themselves can be shared, enabling companies to reap the benefits of digital word-of-mouth advertising. Since the 1940s, it has been well known that people are more influenced by friends than by commercial sources. Taking advantage of this, Facebook has launched a service for advertisers called "sponsored stories" that enables advertisers to buy and republish messages on Facebook that users voluntarily post about brands. These stories copy the likes, comments, and location check-ins that users post on their walls and show up on their friends' home pages. With "sponsored stories," these get posted again on the top right-hand column of the home page next to other ads. The user's name and photo appear in the ad, providing companies for the first time with what can be referred to as "word-of-mouth" at scale.[96] Tactically, social media provides a vehicle companies can use to collect customer feedback on new products and services before and after launch.

Chapter Summary

Interacting with and within social networks has become one of the most important new ways marketers can acquire new customers and maintain a relationship with current customers. Social networking, however, requires a new paradigm for marketing activities. Unlike traditional marketing activities that connect marketers with customers, social networks enable customers and prospects to interact with each other. Word-of-mouth peer-to-peer advertising has always been more powerful than commercial advertising because consumers trust their friends' opinions more than those of a commercial third party. Consequently, companies must engage in these peer-to-peer conversations because of their impact on future sales.

Social networking provides companies with new opportunities to interact with customers as opposed to just "managing" them. The numbers of worldwide users of social networking make mass-marketing techniques possible; however, data available in membership profiles and the ability to market to networks of "friends" make segmentation efforts even more attractive. While the CRM cycle of acquisition–retention–win-back can be implemented through social networks, companies should be cognizant of the fact that participation is expected of them, and this participation should not be blatantly commercial but rather interesting, informative, and potentially novel enough for the viral aspects of social networks to provide them with positive mass exposure.

More meaningful and deeper customer–brand relationships are possible via social networking than through traditional CRM methods given the greater frequency of contact that is possible. As seen in the intensity of usage of social networking by members, social networking has become a prominent activity in everyday life, and brands can, and do, play a prominent role in social networking activities. Consequently, brands now have the means to embed themselves more deeply into their customers' lives. As a result, consumers become advocates or detractors, voicing their opinions over social media. Companies need to stay involved during the advocacy stage to better understand customer experiences with their products or services, to correct misconceptions, and to stay engaged with the conversations. Of course, a company's social media strategy cannot be completely standardized, since there are modifications that need to be made based on cultural usage in foreign markets, as seen by comparisons of the United States and China.

Companies must use the new CRM channel of social media to effectively and efficiently carry out CRM strategies dealing with the company and brand, the customers, and the marketing mix. While the issue of how companies should deal with detractors and message hijackers over the social media is important, company usage of social media must go way beyond that. Social media can be used to influence consumers throughout every stage in the hierarchy of effects (creating awareness, knowledge, liking, preference, intention to purchase, purchase behavior, and advocacy). Social media can be used to increase customer satisfaction, develop communities of users, increase customer service, and handle complaints.

Finally, social media can be used to impact tactics centered around the marketing mix and other activities, including new product introduction, advertising to key target segments, influencing retail store patronage, marketing research, raising money, generating new ideas, and generating scale in word-of-mouth recommendations.

Key Terms

Analytical CRM includes predictive analysis, data mining, segmentation applications, and so on. Virtual communities are a social network of individuals interacting and focusing around a particular interest (e.g., companies and brands) and sharing information through SNS, BBSs, and chat rooms.

Bulletin board systems (BBSs) are anonymous interactive online message boards that allow users to exchange information. It is through BBSs that users find product-, brand-, service-, and interest-based communities and connect with others for group purchasing at discounts. Today, "BBS" is used to refer to any Internet forum or message board.

Operational CRM consists of the automation of processes such as sales force automation, campaign management, and so on.

Social Media can be defined as an online mass collaboration environment where content is created, posted, enhanced, discovered, consumed, and shared, participant to participant, without a direct intermediary.

Questions

1. What is social media?
2. How can social media be used as a channel for CRM?
3. Why must companies be involved with social media in their CRM efforts?
4. What are the basic features of most social networking sites?
5. How can companies dominate social media channels?
6. What are the characteristics of virtual communities?
7. What are BBSs?
8. What explains the heavy use of social media in China?
9. Why has CRM usage in Asia lagged behind that in the United States?

Exercises

1. Dove's campaign for natural beauty included the "Dove Evolution" Internet commercial. It was met with numerous parodies, including "Slob Evolution." View both to gain an understanding of what companies can expect when they place their messages online.
2. Musician Dave Carroll's guitar was damaged by United Airlines baggage personnel. He was not satisfied with United Airlines' response to compensate him for damages. He wrote and

recorded three songs, each going viral, which have been viewed over 10 million times. View his songs titled "United Breaks Guitars" to understand how a single person can hold a company hostage.

3. Have you ever used social media to learn about a company's products or brands? If so, what was your experience?

4. Do you belong to any brand communities? Have they proven valuable?

5. What companies, if any, engage you through social media? Do they do a good job, or can their CRM efforts be improved?

6. View the Burberry.com website to see how it generates buzz regarding its cutting-edge fashion line Prorsum and how it engages viewers with runway shows and British music groups.

Chapter 14

CRM Trends, Challenges, and Opportunities

TOPICS

14.1 Introduction

14.2 Organizational Environment and CRM

14.3 Trends in Current Technology

14.4 Emerging Technologies

14.5 Dynamic CRM: Transitioning
for the Future

14.1 Introduction

In this text, we attempted to define the key inputs, components, strategies, and best practices of the CRM methodology. Some of the findings include:

- Organization structure and management can enable or hinder a CRM effort.
- Data transformed into information and, subsequently, knowledge is the cornerstone of CRM.
- Improved and cost-effective computer hardware has made it easier to build the backbone—simple or complex—architecture of a CRM system.
- Communication within the organization, across the value chain, and between customers and organizations has become increasingly efficient and reliable.
- CRM software options are more readily available, efficient, and easier to manage.
- CRM measurement approaches have proven to be effective and are becoming more integral to an organization's marketing strategy.
- Rapid technology adoption by customers and prospects has provided efficient communication mediums between them and organizations.
- Social media activity has generated an abundance of data that, when transformed into knowledge, provides for a more optimal CRM effort.
- Rising consumer concerns over privacy have precipitated the need for proactive measures with regards to managing customer information. Many organizations have assigned executive ownership by creating the chief privacy officer position.

Industry experts provide insights into the current trends in an attempt to help organizations position themselves to manage future challenges as well as opportunities. While it is difficult to predict which direction customers and organizations will take, it is important that organizations make an attempt to formulate a CRM strategy that can generate the optimal environment to maximize customer equity. In this chapter, we provide a summary of the current trends as well as possible challenges and opportunities that these trends may precipitate. Note that this summary is not all inclusive due to the ever-changing market dynamics, but it should give you a good starting point when considering the trends that are active at the time of your reading.

14.2 Organizational Environment and CRM

Traditionally, CRM technology solutions have been extremely expensive and have required lengthy implementations (so long that most utilized a phased approach), large numbers of highly skilled human resources, and a cash investment with a long time to the targeted return on investment (ROI). While large organizations are continuing with their CRM implementation efforts, major CRM technology–enabling organizations see future growth in the small to medium-sized business market. Microsoft, for example, is leveraging its current customer base and providing CRM capabilities to its customers in a way that minimizes changes as well as reduces the learning curve by integrating CRM applications into its current Office suite. Increased acceptance of service-based applications, such as those provided by Salesforce.com, while still requiring organizational input to data definitions and design, have, by their business model, eliminated the need for organizations to rely upon a large IT resource base (whether internal or outsourced). This trend is very attractive to large, medium-sized, and small organizations alike because it reduces costs and increases speed to "CRM-ready" environments.

Organizations, in an attempt to reduce costs and enhance their competitive position, are improving their front-end and back-end software applications, which are designed to perform specific business functions. They are now realizing that silos formed around these functions must be broken down so as to allow a fully integrated flow of customer information.

As organizations adopt new CRM-based and related applications, they will need to staff or have access to human resources that can use and extract value from these applications. This will be required not only at customer touch points, but also in "back-end" analytical exercises. As a result, there is now increased pressure on the HR functions, since current human resources must be trained and, in some cases, new human resources must be acquired.

All of the economic and technological forces driving CRM allow companies to better focus on customers as opposed to brands, products, and regions. This will impact organizational structure in many ways. All departments will become customer centric, leading to even greater decentralization of marketing. There will be more cross-functional teams, with marketing working more closely with research and development, engineering, manufacturing, and finance to ensure that the voice of the customer is heard in product development. This focus on customers will lead to stronger relationships among partners because of the necessity of sharing customer and product information. In addition, more functional areas will interact with customers and external partners, ensuring that key and correct information is disseminated. There will be a shift from product/brand-focused to customer-focused strategic business units, and key account managers will assume a more important role in B2B because of their focus on the customer.[1] Quick response teams will be increasingly important in dealing with company and product emergencies and derogatory messages gone viral. Customer contact centers will not only handle customer complaints and problems but will also become more involved in increasing customer satisfaction through the use of social media.

In addition, we will see the continuation of new positions being created in organizations, given the ability to capture information through new technology. Likely positions include:

- Social media manager
- Online communities manager
- Manager of multichannel marketing
- Touch point manager

These new positions require expertise with social networking sites, as well as with company products, brands, and strategies. They and their staffs will be responsible for creating buzz, trolling for problems and complaints, and scanning social media sites for any mentions of company products and brands. They will also be involved in integrating social media into more traditional advertising and sales promotion campaigns. These are important positions, since they create a "face" for the brand.[2]

In addition, existing jobs will change. Many companies currently have chief data officers who are responsible for analyzing and interpreting internal data mart information in conjunction with data from outside sources. They are responsible for building mathematical models and spotting patterns, such as the correlation between diaper and beer purchases in convenience stores. In the future, data available through social media will become part of their domain. This data will need to be integrated with internal data mart and other outside source data in order for them to be able to present a complete picture of consumer behavior. Consequently, data accessible through the analysis of social media conversations will be a major addition to their job responsibilities. Recently, universities have seen an increase in CRM-enabling organizations expressing interest in funding specialized university programs in an attempt to produce highly trained and qualified people who can then be hired by the businesses' customers. Without these qualified people, these organizations are reluctant to purchase CRM-enabling applications. There will not only be a need for the sophisticated, well-trained statistical analysts, but also a greater need for people to formulate customer strategy based upon the analytical results. As organizations move to a more dynamic "real-time" CRM environment, fostered in part by increased Web activity, there is a growing need for well-trained network specialists, Web software engineers, and database architects, as well as people who understand consumer behavior.

14.3 Trends in Current Technology

CRM technology solutions are extremely dynamic. Advances in processing power have enabled new solutions to be developed. Increased communication bandwidths have enabled new methods of data capture, analysis, storage, and retrieval to be designed and implemented. Competitive forces are driving new solutions so quickly that organizations must decide when to adopt these solutions, knowing very well that they may be less than optimal within a shortened period of time. Rapid adoption of social media tolls by consumers is a new challenge to companies, as they must implement newer solutions for the purpose of capturing and integrating consumer information. The following discussions highlight some of this growth phenomenon.

14.3a Database Environment

Data marts are growing in popularity as CRM applications become more specific and needs vary. While this places pressure on data loading and data security, the trade-offs exceed the risk, as marketers have access to only relevant data, the size of which is usually smaller. This results in quicker access for analytics and increases the speed-to-market for functions such as campaign management; conversely, customer contact center and Web interaction activity times are shortened.

Most data warehouses are still being developed, maintained, and managed internally. However, there is a trend to outsourcing the data warehouse as well as a desire to determine new approaches to managing data. Even when outsourcing construction and maintenance of a data warehouse, it may still need to be resident within the organization. A risk of outsourcing is loss of intellectual capital as providers learn about an organization's method and can carry that knowledge, indirectly, to another organization via design and management approaches.

Some databases are being constructed in a way that places all relevant data into memory. While this drastically increases the speed of processing and reduces reliance of input and output processing, it is high risk, as memory backup and data redundancy processes are not yet reliable. Once these challenges are overcome, there should be a trend to more widespread adoption of placing relevant data in memory.

14.3b Sales Force Automation

Sales force automation (SFA) continues to grow in importance. As a technology-enabling methodology, it is well positioned to fill the gap created by an increasing dependence on the need for information integration in a mobile environment. Providers of these technology solutions have and will continue to modify their infrastructures to be compatible with and support a wide variety of mobile devices such as smart phones, iPads, and tablets. Salesforce.com, Microsoft, and Oracle are major providers of SFA.

14.3c Customer Contact Technologies

There has been a gradual consolidation in customer contact center software and hardware providers used by organizations to manage phone interactions with their customers. Management of both inbound and outbound customer phone calls for a variety of services in various industries involves different software and hardware technologies. These include interactive voice response (IVR), call queuing, "screen pops," surveys, order processing, customer account management, and others. These different areas appear to be falling under the umbrella of contact center workforce optimization solutions. These all-encompassing approaches provide economies of scale with regards to labor, software, hardware, and other costs and also provide a one-stop-shop opportunity for businesses requiring these different services.

14.3d Customer Contact Channel Management

CRM strategies usually include some type of campaign management technology. This software is evolving into a true multichannel customer management solution. New solutions not only manage the segmentation, targeting, and value proposition offers to customers, but they can also integrate these efforts across multiple channels simultaneously, including the rapid collection and dissemination of data customers provide to the organization. These solutions also allow organizations to better capture current behavioral, lifestyle, and personality data on customers versus traditional demographic and historical information. It provides for an optimal, multichannel, customer interaction management environment. This has been accomplished via a consolidation in the industry where large CRM technology providers have purchased niche solution providers and enabled new solutions to be created via an influx of cash and expertise. The acquisitions of Unica by IBM, Aprimo by Teradata, and Siebel by Oracle are examples of this consolidation activity.

14.3e Customer Service

The solutions provided to enable better customer service are fragmented. These areas involve self-service (which requires a base of knowledge that customers interact with to assist them in their transaction), chat session capability, e-mail management and response handling, and mobile service (e.g., SMS).

14.3f Enterprise Resource Planning

Installing an enterprise resource planning (ERP) system is costly, requires anywhere from nine months to several years to implement, and requires an organization to adhere to the respective

ERP method of managing the business process. Several Focus experts[3] have defined the following ERP trends:

- Companies are becoming less accepting of expensive, never-ending projects.
- Projects will start with smaller, more targeted implementations.
- Companies will reduce support and maintenance costs.
- Packaged, or productized, services offerings will gain traction.
- Software as a service (SaaS) and cloud computing will make more of an impact on the ERP space.
- Enterprise mobility features are becoming must-have tools.
- Collaboration tools will gain momentum in ERP offerings.

14.3g Marketing Application Life Cycles

Marketing applications follow a life cycle curve. Gartner's Hype Cycle[4] is a tool that places marketing application vendors on a life cycle curve and is a good first step in a marketing application vendor evaluation. The Gartner Hype Cycle illustrates how these vendors emerge, peak, and decline and rise. It also shows a steady slope of increased productivity with proven reliability and economies of scale. They partition their Hype Cycle curve into four areas. A *Technology Trigger* connotes a vendor emerging and passing through entry barriers. This is a steep growth curve that includes a growing Hype of expectations. Most of the technologies provided at this point are emerging technologies that contain a certain level of risk, so risk-taking companies or companies with the experience necessary to manage risk are better suited for adopting vendor applications on this part of the curve. Today, most of these applications focus on social media measurement and management, marketing integration across business disciplines, and on-demand applications.

As the Hype of these applications diminishes, the steep curve reaches a peak, which Gartner calls the *Peak of Inflated Expectations*. As expectations are met and applications become harder to differentiate, the Hype of these applications declines in a steep downward curve, which Gartner calls the *Trough of Disillusionment*. These applications represent loyalty and personalization capabilities, financial planning and management, and other predictive type methodologies. Some of these applications prove to be more applicable and successful than others, so a "shakeout" occurs, with survivors becoming more widely adopted. Applications start to become "off-the-shelf" types, are easily implemented, and increase the adopter's productivity. Thus, a new, steadily rising slope emanates from the bottom of the trough, which Gartner calls the *Slope of Enlightenment*.

14.4 Emerging Technologies

14.4a Cloud Computing

The use of cloud computing is growing quickly. A key reason for adopting cloud computing is that it allows for relatively unrestricted scalability in storage and processing. This solves a major problem for organizations, as the pressure of hardware acquisition and planning is greatly reduced. It also reduces the reliance on the use of cookies on a customer PC and places the organization in a better position to manage data captured in a mobile environment. The former is a growing concern, not only for reasons of management activity but also because of the challenges faced with a rise in cookie disabling by customers concerned about privacy.

Cloud computing is also attractive because organizations, in the short term, do not have to worry about storage capacity management when there are sudden surges in customer data capture activity, such as from a website or in response to an organization's CRM effort. Cloud computing also supports the relationship effort, as all relevant customer data can be easily captured and managed by the organization as well as the customer. Ease of access for both parties is a benefit to both.

As CRM efforts encourage the capture and usage of more customer information in the mobile environment, the use of cloud computing minimizes data storage issues for both parties. It also provides the customer with access to his or her data from a variety of technology platforms in a secured reliable environment.

Hi-tech organizations are rapidly adopting cloud computing services, and newly developed technology solutions rely heavily on this methodology. The Norris Group, a Riverside, California–based real estate company, switched to Microsoft Dynamics CRM after its in-house system led to salespeople duplicating efforts, and a corrupt database nearly cost it a decade's worth of information. By switching to Microsoft Dynamics CRM, it slimmed its prospect list from 40,000 to 8,000 and also found that events didn't generate as many leads as its executives thought:

> "We've done lots of live speaking engagements, and we thought they were a big part of our leads. When we looked at the analytics, we saw that wasn't the case at all," says Aaron Norris, marketing director at The Norris Group. "The year before we started using the Microsoft service, we spoke 26 weekends out of the year. The next year, we cut that in half, and our sales increased."[5]

According to International Data Corporation (IDC), cloud computing will continue to reshape the IT landscape over the next five years. Spending on public IT cloud services continues to expand at a compound annual growth rate (CAGR) of 27.6 percent, from $21.5 billion in 2010 to $72.9 billion in 2015.[6]

Not all companies, however, are jumping on the cloud computing bandwagon just yet. Concerns about security are the most prominent reasons that organizations cite for not adopting cloud services. Industry experts also say that cloud computing can present customization hurdles for marketers. Chris Hubble, vice president of brand strategy at market research company Dogs Bollocks 5 (DB5), which switched to in-the-cloud service InfoStreet three years ago, says it can also be more challenging to make simple changes like switching font styles. "If it's something other [companies] aren't asking for, it goes to the bottom of the list, or else we have to pay a fee to get that change made," he says, adding that these are minor concerns overall.[7]

14.4b Radio Frequency Identification

As discussed in Chapter 6, radio frequency identification (RFID) is a widely accepted technology used predominately to track items. It has been heavily adopted in numerous industrial settings as well as municipality and government areas. Since the tags can hold an infinite amount of information; be scanned at a distance; and write to themselves, other tags, and other systems, it has proven to be more efficient and flexible than the bar code. So how can this technology benefit CRM?

There is a division of thought on RFID CRM applications, but evidence seems to be growing that shows that this technology will soon be an integral part of the CRM strategy. Channel management, campaign effectiveness, and customer service are just a few of the areas where organizations might be able to leverage information from RFID. Christine Spivey Overby, senior analyst with Cambridge, Massachusetts–based Forrester Research, states, "Consumer goods and pharmaceuticals are the main private-sector industries that are taking a long look at RFID right now." Other experts believe that by leveraging RFID to improve inventory control, they are indirectly providing customer service and, therefore, are indirectly contributing to the CRM effort.

Some researchers have proven that there is now an opportunity to leverage RFID at the retail level[8]:

- E. W. T. Ngai and fellow colleagues at the Hong Kong Polytechnic University performed research and development of an RFID-based personal shopping assistant (PSA) system for retail stores. RFID technology was employed as the key enabler to build a PSA system to optimize operational efficiency and deliver a superior customer shopping experience in retail stores. They show that an RFID-based PSA system can deliver significant results to improve the customer shopping experience and retail store operational efficiency by increasing customer convenience, providing flexibility in service delivery, enhancing promotional campaign efficiency, and increasing product cross-selling and up-selling through a CRM system.[9]
- By using an Apple iPad, Global Bay's mobile platform for retail is a "real-life" application of RFID in a retail setting. The top 10 percent (i.e., most loyal) of retail customers receive an RFID-enabled loyalty card. When they enter the store, scanners relay the entrance with customer identification to a retail salesperson's iPad. The retailer has instant access to all customer information and can then proceed to provide that customer with a personal shopping experience. Additionally, the customer can remain at home and the salesperson, using the customer information, can add items to a shopping cart for the customer and the customer can pay from home. The salesperson has a credit card reader, and while the customer is in the store, the salesperson can print the receipt for the customer, e-mail the receipt to the customer, or both. These features enhance the customer's experience and build a stronger relationship.[10]

There have been other similar applications tested in grocery stores, where the consumer's RFID-enabled loyalty card is tracked as he shops. This test provided the store managers with shopping patterns. Other attempts went further and included a tablet affixed to the cart, where manufacturers could position ads as the consumer walked past their product category area.

Once consumers have a uniform device with standard software, we may see RFID tags embedded in clothing. When a consumer purchases the clothing at point of sale, the specific clothing article, via the RFID tag, will be scanned and linked to the database alongside the customer's identification information. When that consumer is wearing the clothing in public, another consumer may use a universal device and scan the article. Once scanned, the manufacturer's website will pop up on the device and point that new customer to the site, where she can purchase the same article. If purchased, the first customer is credited and receives a commission at the end of the month for all purchases made as a result of the clothing being scanned. This seems far-fetched, but companies are experimenting with this as well as many other areas.

14.4c Field Service Management

A critical component of CRM is the interaction between the organization and customers in their homes or at their jobs. In B2B situations, organizations have relied upon laptops to assist them when servicing a customer and, in some cases, a smart phone. In a consumer's home, where, for example, a serviceperson is installing an appliance or a salesperson is explaining the benefits of his company's furnaces, a laptop is an expensive and unnecessary enabler. New applications are being developed for iPads and tablets that enable the field serviceperson or salesperson to interact directly with the appliance, to connect with his home office, or to demonstrate an appliance for the customer in his home.

14.4d Knowledge Management

Customer knowledge is becoming the new competitive asset in e-business that enables companies to serve each customer in his or her preferred way and to nurture profitable and durable customer relationships. As companies grow and interact with more and more customers through increasingly diverse media and channels, having a systematic approach to customer knowledge management (KM) becomes critical. While KM methodologies have been used for decades, current advances in technology have created an opportunity to integrate that knowledge into the customer interaction. This may be done at a website or within a variety of mobile applications.

14.4e Artificial Intelligence

New intelligence software systems are being tested in an effort to integrate loyalty programs, database information, and consumer behavioral data. The objective of these efforts is to identify information-based relationships that would normally not be seen by existing systems. A good example of this is the use of intelligent agent technology. M. Woodridge and N. R. Jennings define an intelligent agent as "an encapsulated computer system that is situated in some environment and that is capable of flexible and autonomous action in that environment in order to meet its design objectives."[11]

Building on Woodridge and Jennings's research, S. Daskou and E. E. Mangina have found that customer needs can be monitored from a multiagent software system. By using specialized software agents, they show how to simulate the procedure of data analysis to extract useful information for the customer's benefit. These findings are then integrated with decision-making functions for data interpretation. The following are some other implications from their research:

- There is an increased level of dependency between a manufacturer and a retailer. The manufacturer depends on the data collected by retailer intelligence (i.e., databases of loyalty programs) to improve product development, communication practices targeted to both intermediaries and consumers, and brand positioning.
- Trust levels will automatically increase as both members of the channel have confidence in each other's capabilities in the exchange.
- The processed data can provide ongoing information about consumers.
- Both parties should gain better cooperation, and the resulting optimal marketing initiatives should enhance value to the customer, thereby increasing customer equity.[12]

While intelligent virtual agents have not yet become a commonly used term in the field of CRM, they have great potential to make a major impact on the customer experience in an online or mobile environment. Intelligent virtual agents (IVAs) can be defined as artificial intelligence programs that translate to autonomous graphically embodied agents that appear in an online environment. Graphic design for each individual virtual agent may vary from video animation to a photo or an avatar, in an interactive 2D or 3D environment, in order to fit with a company's brand image. IVAs are increasingly being sourced by companies to bring more personalized interaction to their CRM effort. IVAs can provide the consumer with help and advice as he or she navigates a website and assist with sales functions, customer support, or sales follow-up.

14.4f Real-Time Data Analysis and Streaming

Customer data stored in company data banks often goes stagnant. If and when the data is analyzed, reports based on such are often no longer timely at the time of release. Today, innovative organizations are using technologies that deliver data between devices as the data is being generated, called **real-time data analysis**. For example, retailers using GPSs on customers' smart phones can send coupons or messages related to the product lines customers are near in the store. A quick scan of the customer's historic data in the data bank would allow the store to customize the offer based on the customer's purchase history or demographics. Combining streaming of data as it is happening with historical data, advanced data analytic techniques enable companies to implement customized and timely CRM tactics.[13]

14.4g Augmented Reality

A new and powerful technological innovation bound to affect future CRM strategies is "augmented reality." **Augmented reality**, relying on smart phones with an electronic compass and GPS chip, enables people to point the device at anything and receive layers of information about what they are looking at. Currently, an application called Yelp allows you to point your phone down any street and find restaurant reviews where applicable. Anheuser-Busch InBev's Stella Artois has an app allowing customers to find bars selling its brand. IKEA and Pier 1 Imports use an app called SnapShop that puts their furniture at a spot in your home pointed to by your smart phone camera.[14] Techniques are also available that allow shoppers to see how they look in new clothes without actually trying them on.

14.5 Dynamic CRM: Transitioning for the Future

The economic and technological forces driving and permitting marketers to become customer-centric—with a focus on relationships with individuals as opposed to mass markets—will continue unabated for many reasons. The ability to gather both internal and external data regarding customers and prospects is increasing in depth and ease. Smart phones and social media, in particular, are facilitating this effort. The rewards from maintaining, bonding with, enhancing, and retaining current customers will continue to grow. The ability of companies to differentiate between high-profit potential customers and low-profit potential customers will continue to dramatically affect the bottom line, and the profit implications of reducing downward migration and churn have the attention of CEOs.

CRM tactics will significantly change in the short term for the following reasons:

- Social media
- Smart phones
- New CRM metrics
- New developments in marketing research
- New developments in mass customization

In turn, these effects will result in major changes to the implementation of strategy and tactics in the CRM strategy cycle (acquisition, retention, and win-back) as well as to the organization itself.

14.5a Social Media: A Driving Force in the Future of CRM

Social media provides a new channel for customer engagement, leading to what is called **social CRM.** Interacting with and within social networks has become one of the most important new ways marketers can acquire customers and maintain relationships with current ones. Social networking provides a new domain for customer engagement opportunities and requires a new paradigm for marketing activities. Facebook fan pages are essentially replacing company brand home pages. They enable companies to reach customers and prospects fast and to get a true

360-degree view of customer behavior. By monitoring social media conversations, companies can capture the voice of the customer and use this information to measure potential success of new products and services, to suggest modifications to features and functions, or to offer new product uses and applications.

In addition, many feel that virtual brand communities can lead to customer retention through the interpersonal interaction and exchanging of information that builds up social capital. If companies effectively participate in these social media discussions, they may build up social trust and increase consumer confidence in dealing with them. As we learned in Chapter 13, research indicates that social media are used differently throughout the world. In China, more so than in the West, the number one reason people use social media is to seek information before buying products. Many of the discussions center around the concept of price versus performance (value) in numerous product categories. Consequently, companies may need to localize their social media strategies as opposed to standardizing them across the globe.

Further, we can expect to see companies developing structural ties with customers via social media. For example, regimens and schedules developed to keep customers from failing on their diet, medication programs, automobile maintenance, home repair, financial planning, and so on, can be easily implemented through social media channels. In addition, influencers and advocates can be encouraged to contribute their thoughts, which will increase the motivation of users of company products and services.

We can expect to see companies developing more "offbeat" videos and messages in the hopes that they will go viral. There is a fine line, however, between what is viewed as a successful offbeat message and crass commercialism. Positive buzz can quickly turn negative, and that is why we will see increasing company emphasis on departments and policies formed to deal with detractors, message hijackers, and those developing parodies focusing on company brands and products. When company messages are unique, compelling, and easily shared, however, they can be very effective profit drivers for companies. At the very least, customer contact centers will be increasingly involved in the new social media channel to increase customer service and handle customer complaints.

As we have discussed, data mining is an integral part of CRM and is now being broadened to include analysis of social networks. There are more than 100 programs available for **network analysis**.[15] By conducting network analysis, companies can categorize customers and prospects into opinion leaders/influencers, advocates, detractors, and merely observers. They can then develop different strategies for each group. For example, influencers and advocates can be encouraged to publicly promote the advantages of the brand and their positive postpurchase experiences with it.

14.5b Smart Phones: Reshaping the Retail Environment

Smart phones are affecting organizations to the same extent that personal computers reshaped organizations. Once every desk had a PC, company divisions could analyze their own customer data, develop their own marketing programs, assess program effectiveness, and then make adjustments where needed. No longer was it necessary to rely on corporate headquarters or the marketing department. Similarly, smart phones are changing the way retailers do business: how they price, advertise, promote, compete, staff, create store ambiance, and even provide their services. Following are some of the reasons why and how this is happening:

- *Price comparison apps have introduced a new era of price transparency.* Consumers can use their smart phones to check on store "specials" by referring to price comparison apps such as "the-Find." Nearly half of all smart phone users perform pricing due diligence through their phones. Other apps such as RedLaser allow shoppers to use their mobile phone cameras to scan bar codes and check for lowest prices.[16]

- *Brick-and-mortar retailers' historic advantages are eroding.* Companies such as Best Buy are fearful of becoming mere "showcases" where consumers enter to view, test, and learn about products, only to purchase them at cheaper prices from online retailers.

- *Consumers prefer phones to retail clerks for basic assistance, lowering cross-selling and trading-up opportunities (unless they are implemented over the phone).* In 2010, Accenture found that nearly three-quarters of all mobile phone shoppers preferred phones to retail clerks for basic assistance.

- *Customers can be "stolen" when in competitors' stores via phone messaging.* For example, theFind app enables Best Buy to send a message regarding similar items to customers in Walmart when they use the theFind price comparison app for items in that store. Also, Amazon.com has a price comparison app that allows customers to compare its prices to a scanned bar code on in-store items.[17]

- *Location-based marketing/geofencing is a new way to promote in real time.* We are just seeing the beginning of location-based strategies (LBSs) by applications such as foursquare, Gowalla, and Loopt. As of 2010, only 4 percent of Americans had tried LBSs, but the usage is growing given the built-in advantages for both merchant and customer.[18]

- *Geofencing is a strategy used by companies when they draw perimeters around their outlets and use GPS to send a text message offer to customers in the vicinity.* Papa Murphy's reads consumers' computer IP addresses and sends coupons only to those in its area. This allows for local as opposed to national or regional campaigns.[19]

- *Rewards programs can be developed that kick in once a consumer enters your store.*

- *Deals available during retail "downtimes" via applications such as Groupon will enable retailers to better manage demand.* Groupon Now is a real-time deals program aimed at consumers' smart phones with the ability to smooth out demand for retailers by bringing in customers during slow periods or "downtimes." The Groupon app delivers offers to consumers with a 24-hour purchase window based on their location.[20]

- *Phones are becoming digital wallets, able to pay for anything.*

Privacy issues will be increasingly prominent in the future. A *Wall Street Journal* study of smart phone applications found that over half transmitted the phone's unique ID to other companies, and nearly half transmitted the phone's location. Five percent sent personal details to outsiders. It is almost impossible to delete cookies from smart phones, and, with only a few exceptions, users cannot opt out. When smart phone users let an application see their location, it is possible that this information is forwarded to advertising companies.[21] Currently, there is a lack of transparency regarding exactly what information is being collected through smart phones and how it is being used.

14.5b.1 Social Networking and Smart Phone Technology

Implementation of the CRM strategy cycle will require warp-speed development and delivery given competitors' abilities to unveil tactics quickly and communicate with consumers one on one via smart phones. The importance of companies bonding with customers is inherent in CRM, but will the strength of company bonds be as strong if delivered by smart phone as by humans? Bonding with customers via humanistic strategies may still work effectively in the future with some segments, but new ways must be developed to maintain the humanistic bond in the age of the smart phone. Staying in touch with your customers on a regular basis is the key to attaining intimacy; however, sending countless messages makes each message nothing but a commodity. The issue for organizations will be balancing the exchange of pertinent information without being repetitive, leading to loss of impact. Technology can be used to deliver "high-touch" personal services that can be replicated en masse, but whether this is a sufficient substitute for human contact remains to be seen.

- Personalization and customization strategies can be effectively implemented via smart phones, but competition will be fierce in this area.
- Cross-selling and up-selling, two of the most conversation-dependent retention strategies, are going to require very new techniques using smart phones, just as recruiting a high school athlete requires a different technique via text messaging versus going to the athlete's home to meet his or her parents. Customer information contained in data marts, however, will enable companies to more effectively pinpoint items that are good candidates for cross-selling or trading up. In addition, data marts will be accessed in order to "time" such offerings in conjunction with changes in consumer life stages.

14.5c Reducing Expenses and Increasing Profits

Just as recency, frequency, monetary value (RFM) is being replaced by CLV as the metric to use to measure a customer's future potential, there will be refinements in how CLV is measured. As V. Kumar and W. J. Reinartz pointed out, the RFM approach results in significant overspending on lapsed customers because it ignores the pacing of a customer's interactions—the time between each purchase.[22] The event history model takes pacing into account, giving a better prediction of whether a customer will still be active at a particular point in the future. This will reduce company costs in that money can be directed at those having true future profit potential as opposed to those exhibiting high one-transaction profits but offering no real future profit potential. This gets to the very nature of CRM and its focus of differentiating high- and low-value customers. Further refinements can be expected, particularly with the development of company-specific models.

14.5d New Developments in Marketing Research

Marketing research is making a quantum leap into the future due to:

- Neurometric and biometric technologies
- Network analysis/link analysis/predictive analysis
- Crowdsensing
- Increasing emphasis on longitudinal research
- Crowdsourcing

14.5d.1 Neurometric and Biometric Technologies

Functional magnetic resonance imaging (MRI), medical scanners, and electroencephalography (EEG) brain wave monitors are being used by **neuromarketers** to study brain wave responses to ads, brand names, and car designs.[23] They can also be used to evaluate among and select the best loyalty programs and retention strategies. The belief is that while voiced opinions can be misleading, brain waves provide a more valid indicator of what people really feel. Over $8 billion was spent in 2006 on neuromarketing research, and it is expected that this new technique will become a routine part of company marketing plans in the future.[24] The Advertising Research Foundation advises, however, that neurological studies are still experimental and there is not enough data to support the value of the neuromarketing efforts[25] at this time.

In addition to neuroresearch, companies are using biometric research technologies to study consumer behavior. For example, companies are using biometric tracking sensors to determine how a consumer's emotional state affects spending and how stress differs between in-store and online shopping. And by monitoring electrodermal activity, it is possible to determine what sparks a reaction in shoppers and what does not.[26]

14.5d.2 Network Analysis

One doesn't have to resort to physical and mental measures to predict people's feelings. Analytics can now handle unstructured as well as structured data. Research has found that through analyzing Twitter messages, known as "**network analysis,**" one can capture the mood swings of a nation and predict changes in the Dow Jones Industrial Average with 88 percent accuracy.[27] SAS Institute Inc. has software capable of analyzing the sentiment of chatter on social media, including Facebook and Twitter.[28]

14.5d.3 Crowdsensing

It is said that today nearly three-quarters of the world's population carry a mobile phone.[29] In addition, calling records in some countries are now available for research. Consequently, there is an immense database of calling records available for the study of dissemination of ideas, opinions, innovations, and so on. Studies are being conducted on how behavior and ideas spread through social networks and how companies can use this relationship network to influence the marketing of products.[30] iPhones and Google keep databases on phones' locations, and there are tens of thousands of applications that enable the forecasting of traffic congestion based on users' phone locations. TomTom uses connection data from mobile networks to update directions in case of delays—a form of "**crowdsensing.**"[31]

14.5d.4 Longitudinal Research

Cross-sectional research will give way to longitudinal data collection in the future simply because it is now easier to collect information from consumers on a continuous real-time basis. This will lead to greater understanding of customer buying cycles, enabling companies to understand what causes a customer to purchase a product in the first place, what the progression of purchases looks like over time, how changes in life stage affect purchase behavior, and other relationships not so apparent through traditional cross-sectional methods.

14.5e Crowdsourcing

We will see much greater use of crowdsourcing by companies in the areas of brand name selection, product designs, slogans, product usage, and so on. Recall from Chapter 13 that crowdsourcing occurs when users participate online in contributing to a firm's marketing efforts.

Crowdsourcing works on the elements that go into campaigns, not the campaign itself. Amazon.com's "Mechanical Turk" can be used for generating creative input from people on the Internet. Everyone gets a small amount of money for their contribution. However, crowdsourcing contributors are not motivated by the money, but rather, they contribute because they are trying to hone their skills. Some even do it for the competition itself or to prove themselves.

Most crowdsourcing projects cost less than $1,000. Companies cannot only test new product ideas and brand names but can also ask a number of questions in survey form. One company received 650 designs in three days and considered 200 of them great designs. The cost was $1,000.[32]

Companies realize that when people buy new products today, they often crowdsource advice over social media. Consequently, the company needs to be "wired" into these conversations. Thus, crowdsourcing will become an approach increasingly used by companies to generate new ideas, select among them, and evaluate success.

14.5f Mass Customization as a CRM Strategy

Mass customization, enabling customers to design everything from coats to chocolates to computers to cars, will increase due to more advanced Web technologies, such as 3D printing, leading to mass customization of products. In the future, we will see mass customization of clothes, entertainment, vacation packages, electronics, and many consumer goods. Customization will make further inroads in the areas of promotion and loyalty programs. Data marts enable companies to understand the lifestyles of their customers. Combined with transaction data, this will enable them to customize promotional messages, newsletters, and offers that will prove appealing to recipients.

A current example of this customization can be found in British luxury fashion house Burberry's "Burberry Bespoke" program, which allows online customers to design their own trench coats in 12 million different ways by selecting fabric, cut, color, sleeves, cuff-straps, lining, collars, and so forth.[33]

Another example can be found in Nestlé, which has developed a personalized chocolate business through its Maison Cailler brand. Customers order chocolate samples and complete a questionnaire about their preferences, resulting in a chocolate profile. Nestlé hopes, of course, that they will post their profile on Facebook. The personal profile is used by Nestlé to create personalized boxes of chocolates for customers. The program isn't rocket science, but it does create some customer engagement, and that is the whole purpose of this mass-customization effort.[34]

Chapter Summary

In this chapter, we identify certain trends in adoption and use of the CRM methodology as a sustainable marketing strategy. These trends actually support the adoption of CRM since not doing so will expose the organization to the possibility of a less than optimal competitive position in its respective market space.

CRM enablers—that is, organizations providing the hardware and software necessary to support a CRM strategy—are producing solutions that are easier to implement, maintain, and upgrade, which reduces the barriers to CRM adoption as a strategy. The ease of implementation and use has reduced the time necessary for employee training, which leads to quicker utilization and hopefully quicker positive returns on investment.

Emerging technologies have accelerated the attractiveness of CRM adoption. Cloud computing is reducing data latency, which is a key CRM inhibitor. While businesses have used RFID for utility processes in the past, advances in consumer mobile devices and consumers' rapid acceptance of these devices have placed companies in a position where real-time customer interaction is becoming the norm. Real-time interaction presents opportunities for more efficient, accurate, and timely capture of consumer information, which is an enhancement to any CRM strategy. However, this real-time activity also raises consumers' expectations. As a result, consumers may start to choose companies based upon their abilities both to interact and to provide optimal products and services. Field service management systems employ similar benefits and opportunities as mobile devices enhance the ability of business to serve the customer in a face-to-face situation. Knowledge management methodologies empower the employee, which provides an environment for enhancing the customer experience. Advances in the ability of artificial intelligence systems to uncover customer insights not observed through traditional CRM technology may provide a "lift" to the organization's CRM efforts.

Social media usage has created a new area for organizations to observe and engage with customers. New Web-based technologies not only allow for social interaction between consumers, but they provide an opportunity for organizations to give control to the consumer for purposes of assisting in the creation of their own products or services via a mass-customization approach. Consumers may soon be able to not only create their own solutions but also precipitate the formulation of new products and services.

This is an exciting era for both organizations and consumers. These environment dynamics make adoption of a CRM strategy by organizations almost a necessity in order to maintain and hopefully improve their competitive position.

Key Terms

Augmented reality relies on smart phones with an electronic compass and GPS chip, enabling people to point the device at anything and receive layers of information about what they are looking at. This can be used by companies to help consumers find establishment locations or provide information.

Crowdsensing is the use of calling records to determine the dissemination of information across a country or subsection or the use of phone locations to discern traffic and population patterns.

Geofencing occurs when a company draws a perimeter around its outlets and uses GPS to send a text message offer to customers in the vicinity.

Intelligent agent technology is an encapsulated computer system that is situated in some environment and that is capable of flexible and autonomous action in that environment in order to meet its design objectives.

Intelligent virtual agents (IVAs) are artificial intelligence programs that translate to autonomous graphically embodied agents that appear in an online environment.

Network analysis consists of analyzing the sentiments of chatter on social media sites such as Facebook and Twitter. Some claim a nation's mood can be discerned through network analysis.

Neuromarketers study brain wave activity to determine consumers' feelings toward marketing stimuli such as brand names, package designs, and so on. Neuromarketing researchers study brain wave activity because they feel it may be a better indicator of what consumers really feel as opposed to their self-reports.

Real-time data analysis is the capture of consumer data as it is occurring—for example, a consumer scanning a product code in a store. Real-time data is often combined with the consumer's historical data residing in a data bank. The combination of real-time and historic data can often be effectively used to generate point-of-sale offers.

Social CRM, sometimes referred to as sCRM, is a way that companies can implement their CRM strategies and stay in touch with consumers through social media such as Facebook and Twitter.

Questions

1. How are evolving technologies impacting CRM strategies?
2. Which applications provide the best competitive advantage quickly?

3. Which application types are currently maturing and need to be reevaluated for continued use in an organization's suite of tools?
4. What specific steps can an organization take now with regards to emerging technology adoption?
5. How will social media impact the ways companies practice CRM?
6. How will smart phones impact the ways retailers operate?
7. How can crowdsourcing aid companies in their marketing efforts?
8. How can LBSs be used in CRM?
9. Can companies establish humanistic bonds through social CRM?

Exercises

1. Call several organizations you currently do business with, using their 800 number. Identify which technologies are being used by each and explain why one approach is better than another. Make recommendations for improvement for each of the organizations identified.
2. Select an organization that you shop with frequently and discuss which of the emerging technologies this company is using.
3. Identify how organizations can use intelligent virtual agents to strengthen their CRM effort. List examples of organizations using IVAs today.
4. Give an example of how a company could use real-time data analysis and streaming in conjunction with historic customer information residing in a data bank.

Notes

1 Introduction to Customer Relationship Management

1 Frederick Newell, *Why CRM Doesn't Work: How to Win by Letting Customers Manage the Relationship* (Hoboken, NJ: Bloomberg Press, 2003).
2 A. Payne and P. Frow, "A Strategic Framework for Customer Relationship Management," *Journal of Marketing, 69* (October 2005): 167–176.
3 Ibid.
4 D. Gefen and C. M. Ridings, "Implementation Team Responsiveness and User Evaluation of Customer Relationship Management: A Quasi-Experimental Design Study of Social Exchange Theory," *Journal of Management Information Systems, 19,* 10 (2002): 47–70.
5 W. G. Zikmund, R. McLeod, and F. W. Gilbert, *Customer Relationship Management: Integrating Marketing Strategy and Information Technology* (New York: Wiley & Sons, 2003).
6 D. P. Hamilton, "In Translation," *Wall Street Journal* (May 21, 2001): R6.
7 J. Anton and N. L. Petouhoff, *Customer Relationship Management: The Bottom Line to Optimizing Your ROI* (Upper Saddle River, NJ: Prentice-Hall, 2002).
8 R. S. Swift, *Accelerating Customer Relationships: Using CRM and Relationship Technologies* (Upper Saddle River, NJ: Prentice-Hall, 2001).
9 A. R. Zablah, D. N. Bellenger, and W. J. Johnston, "Customer Relationship Management Implementation Gaps," *Journal of Personal Selling & Sales Management, 24,* 4 (2004): 279–295.
10 B. Bergeron, *Essentials of CRM: A Guide to Customer Relationship Management* (New York: John Wiley & Sons, 2002).
11 T. M. Bodenberg, *Customer Relationship Management: New Ways of Keeping the Customer Satisfied* (New York: The Conference Board, 2001).
12 The Gartner Group.
13 J. Peel, *CRM: Redefining Customer Relationship Management* (Amsterdam: Digital Press, 2002).
14 M. Meyer and L. Kolbe, "Integration of Customer Relationship Management: Status Quo and Implications for Research and Practice," *Journal of Strategic Marketing, 13* (2005): 175–198.
15 See note 8.
16 M. Rogers, "Customer Strategy: Observations from the Trenches," *Journal of Marketing, 69* (October 2005): 262–263.
17 J. Galbreath, "Relationship Management Environments," *Credit World, 87,* 2 (1998): 14–21.
18 L. L. Berry, "Relationship Marketing," in L. L. Berry, G. L. Shostack, and G. D. Upah, eds. *Emerging Perspectives on Service Marketing* (Chicago, IL: American Marketing Association, 1983).
19 S. Kutner and J. Cripps, "Managing the Customer Portfolio of Healthcare Enterprises," *The Healthcare Forum Journal, 4,* 5 (1997): 52–54.
20 L. Ryals and A. Payne, "Customer Relationship Management in Financial Services: Towards Information-Enabled Relationship Marketing," *Journal of Strategic Marketing, 9* (2001): 3–27.
21 M. D. Johnson and F. Seines, "Customer Portfolio Management: Toward a Dynamic Theory of Exchange Relationships," *Journal of Marketing, 68,* 2 (April 2004): 1–17.
22 R. McKenna, "Real-Time Marketing," *Harvard Business Review, 73,* 4 (July 1995): 87–95.
23 Ibid.
24 M. Georgiadis, R. Seshadri, and C. Yulinsy, "Tactical CRM: Three Steps to Mining Profits, Not Data," *McKinsey Marketing Solutions* (August 2001).

25 D. Peppers, M. Rogers, and B. Dorf, "Is Your Company Ready for One-to-One Marketing?" *Harvard Business Review*, *77*, 1 (January 1999): 151–160.

26 B. J. Pine II, D. Peppers, and M. Rogers, "Do You Want to Keep Your Customers Forever?" *Harvard Business Review*, *73*, 2 (March 1995): 103–113.

27 L. Alcorn and A. Wiryawan, "Banking on CRM: Customer Relationship Management (CRM) Initiatives Can Help Sustain the Benefits of the Fading Refinancing Wave," *Mortgage Banking* (February 2004): 74–78.

28 D. K. Rigby and D. Ledingham, "CRM Done Right," *Harvard Business Review*, *82*, 11 (November 2004): 118–129.

29 See note 5.

30 J. Griffin and M. W. Lowenstein, *Customer Winback: How to Recapture Lost Customers—and Keep Them Loyal* (San Francisco, CA: Jossey-Bass, 2001).

31 F. F. Reichheld and W. E. Sasser Jr., "Zero Defections: Quality Comes to Services," *Harvard Business Review*, *68*, 5 (September–October 1990): 105–111.

32 C. Yulinsky, "Multi-Channel Marketing: Making 'Bricks and Clicks' Stick," *McKinsey Marketing Solutions* (August 2000).

33 M. Georgiadis, D. Harding, M. Singer, and K. Lane, "Online Customer Management: Five Killer Actions to Drive Your E-Business," *McKinsey Marketing Solutions* (November 2000).

34 S. A. Neslin, Presentation at the MSI Conference: Taking Stock of Customer Relationships (March 1, 2006).

35 V. Kumar, "A Customer Lifetime Value-Based Approach to Marketing in the Multichannel, Multimedia Retailing Environment," *Journal of Interactive Marketing*, *24*, 2 (May 2010): 71–85.

36 www.Clickatell.co.UK, April 23, 2010.

37 J. Williams, "Worldwide SaaS Sales to Grow 21% in 2011 Driven by CRM Purchases, Says Gartner," *ComputerWeekly.com* (July 7, 2011). Accessed at http://www.computerweekly.com/Articles/2011/07/07/247209/Worldwide-SaaS-sales-to-grow-21-in-2011-driven-by-CRM-purchases-says.htm.

38 www.Tyntec.com, Tyntec White Paper: SMS & Airlines.

39 Ibid.

40 A. Tugend, "Far from Always Being Right, the Customer is On Hold," *New York Times* (May 24, 2008): 5.

41 S. Zimmerman, "High-Tech Call Center Knows How Angry You Are," *Chicago Sun-Times* (December 19, 2005), 4.

42 K. C. Cooper, *The Relational Enterprise: Moving Beyond CRM to Maximize All Your Business Relationships* (New York: AMACOM, 2002).

43 E. Krell, "A Gamble No More," *Baylor Business Review* (Spring 2006): 21–23.

44 S. Gupta and D. Lehmann, *Managing Customers as Investments: The Strategic Value of Customers in the Long Run* (Upper Saddle River, NJ: Wharton School Publishing, 2005).

45 P. Temporal and M. Trott, *Romancing the Customer: Maximizing Brand Value Through Powerful Relationship Management* (Singapore: John Wiley & Sons, 2001).

46 J. S. Thomas, R. C. Blattberg, and E. Fox, "Recapturing Lost Customers," *Journal of Marketing Research*, *41*, 1 (February 2004): 31–45.

47 J. Deighton, "Privacy and Customer Management" in *Customer Management* (MSI Conference Summary), (Cambridge, MA: Marketing Science Institute, 2005).

48 See note 11.

49 J. Dyché, *The CRM Handbook: A Business Guide to Customer Relationship Management* (Boston, MA: Addison-Wesley, 2002).

50 K. Vermond, "The CRM Scrum," *CRM Management*, *78*, 2 (April 2004): 24–27.

51 C. Costanzo, "The Tech Scene: Surprise—CRM at ATM Has Users Clicking," *American Banker*, *169*, 2 (March 17, 2004): 1–2.

52 Ibid.

53 See note 25.

54 B. B. Jackson, "Build Customer Relationships That Last," *Harvard Business Review*, *63*, 6 (November 1985): 120–128.

55 F. R. Dwyer, "Customer Lifetime Valuation for Marketing Decision Making," *Journal of Direct Marketing*, *11*, 4 (1997): 6–13.

56 See note 21.

57 R. Richmond, "Needs of Nonprofits Provide a Growing Market," *Wall Street Journal* (March 30, 2004): B2.

58 *USA TODAY* (October 23, 2008).
59 J. Tsai, "Helping Hands," *Customer Relationship Management* (February 2010): 22–28.

2 The History and Development of CRM

1 L. O'Malley and D. Mitussis, "Relationships and Technology: Strategic Implications," *Journal of Strategic Marketing*, 10, 3 (2002): 225–238.
2 J. G. Freeland, *The Ultimate CRM Handbook: Strategies and Concepts for Building Enduring Customer Loyalty and Profitability* (New York: McGraw-Hill, 2003).
3 J. Dyché, *The CRM Handbook: A Business Guide to Customer Relationship Management* (Boston, MA: Addison-Wesley, 2002).
4 J. Peel, *CRM: Redefining Customer Relationship Management* (Amsterdam: Digital Press, 2002).
5 L. A. Petrison, R. C. Blattberg, and P. Wang, "Database Marketing: Past, Present, and Future," *Journal of Direct Marketing*, 11, 4 (1997): 109–125.
6 P. Kotler in D. Peppers and M. Rogers, *Managing Customer Relationships: A Strategic Framework* (Hoboken, NJ: John Wiley & Sons, 2004).
7 R. S. Winer, "A Framework for Customer Relationship Management," *California Management Review*, 43, 4 (2001): 89–105.
8 R. McKenna, "Real-Time Marketing," *Harvard Business Review*, 73, 4 (July 1995): 87–95.
9 C. K. Prahalad and V. Ramaswamy, "Co-opting Customer Competence," *Harvard Business Review*, 78, 1 (January 2000): 79–87.
10 See note 3.
11 R. Verma, Z. Iqbal, and R. Baran, "Understanding Consumer Choices and Preferences in Transaction-Based e-Services," *Journal of Service Research*, 6, 1 (August 2003): 51–65.
12 See note 9.
13 See note 4.
14 R. Dodes and G. A. Fowler, "Retailers Feed Holiday Demand for Free Shipping," *Online Wall Street Journal* (October 21, 2009).
15 S. A. Brown and M. Gulycz, *Performance-Driven CRM: How to Make Your Customer Relationship Management Vision a Reality* (Mississauga, ON: John Wiley & Sons Canada, 2002).
16 See note 4.
17 See note 15.
18 J. Compton, "Finding Happiness with CRM Software Difficult for Some," *Chicago Tribune* (April 2, 2001): 4.
19 See note 18.
20 J. Anton and N. L. Petouhoff, *Customer Relationship Management: The Bottom Line to Optimizing Your ROI* (Upper Saddle River, NJ: Prentice-Hall, 2002).
21 See note 3.
22 M. Georgiadis, R. Seshadri, and C. Yulinsky, "Tactical CRM: Three Steps to Mining Profits, Not Data," *McKinsey Marketing Solutions* (August 2001).
23 K. Mukerjee and K. Singh, "CRM: A Strategic Approach," *The ICFAI Journal of Management Research*, 8, 2 (2009): 65–82.
24 McKinsey & Co., "The Financial Impact of Customer Relationship Management," *InfoWorld*, 26, 7 (February 16, 2004): 17–25.
25 B. Bold, "Teachers Agency Invests 10 Million Pounds in CRM," *Marketing (UK)* (2004): 8.
26 M. Georgiadis and K. Lane, "Customer Marketing Organization: The Key to Turbocharging Customer Marketing Performance," *McKinsey Marketing Practice* (2001).
27 See note 23.
28 See note 18.
29 See note 1.
30 K. Thompson, L. Ryals, S. Knox, and S. Maklan, "Developing Relationship Marketing through the Implementation of Customer Relationship Management Technology," *Proceedings of the 16th Annual IMP Group Conference* (2000).
31 K. El Emam and A. G. Koru, "A Replicated Survey of IT Software Project Failures," *IEEE Software*, 25, 5 (September/October 2008): 84–90.
32 See note 18.
33 Ibid.
34 See note 3.

35 T. W. Morris, "Customer Relationship Management Overkill?" *The CPA Journal*, *73*, 5 (May 2003): 12–13.
36 S. L. Botwinik, "Organizing to Get CRM Right," *Forrester Research* (May 30, 2001).
37 D. Tynan, "CRM on the Cheap," *Sales & Marketing Management*, *156*, 6 (June 2004): 37–40.
38 See note 18.
39 Ibid.
40 See note 3.

3 Relationship Marketing and CRM

1 P. R. Timm and C. G. Jones, *Technology and Customer Service: Profitable Relationship Building* (Upper Saddle River, NJ: Prentice Hall, 2005).
2 L. A. Petrison, R. C. Blattberg, and P. Wang, "Database Marketing: Past, Present, and Future," *Journal of Direct Marketing*, *11*, 4 (Fall 1997): 109–125.
3 L. L. Berry, "Relationship Marketing" in L. L. Berry, G. L. Shostack, and G. D. Upah, eds., *Emerging Perspectives on Services Marketing* (Chicago, IL: American Marketing Association, 1983).
4 L. L. Berry, "Relationship Marketing of Services—Growing Interest, Emerging Perspectives," *Journal of the Academy of Marketing Science*, *23*, 4 (Fall 1995): 236–245.
5 F. F. Reichheld, R. G. Markey Jr., and C. Hopton, "The Loyalty Effect—The Relationship between Loyalty and Profits," *European Business Journal*, *12*, 3 (2000): 134–139.
6 T. Gokey and H. Yin, "The New Physics of Customer Loyalty: Manage Customer Migration Based on the Loyalty Profile of Your Customer Base," *McKinsey Marketing Practice* (May 2000).
7 J. N. Sheth and A. Parvatiyar, "Relationship Marketing in Consumer Markets: Antecedents and Consequences," *Journal of the Academy of Marketing Science*, *23*, 4 (1995): 255–271.
8 L. O'Malley, M. Patterson, and M. J. Evans, "Intimacy or Intrusion? The Privacy Dilemma for Relationship Marketing in Consumer Markets," *Journal of Marketing Management*, *13*, 6 (1997): 541–560.
9 J. N. Sheth and A. Parvatiyar, "Evolving Relationship Marketing into a Discipline," *Journal of Relationship Marketing*, *1*, 1 (2002): 3–16.
10 M. J. Harker, "Relationship Marketing Defined? An Examination of Current Relationship Marketing Definitions," *Marketing Intelligence & Planning*, *17*, 1 (1999): 13–20.
11 J. N. Sheth and A. Parvatiyar, eds., *Handbook of Relationship Marketing* (Thousand Oaks, CA: Sage, 1999).
12 Ibid.
13 P. F. Drucker, *Managing for Results: Economic Tasks and Risk-Taking Decisions*, 1st ed. (New York: Harper & Row, 1964).
14 A. R. Zablah, D. N. Bellenger, and W. J. Johnston, "An Evaluation of Divergent Perspectives on Customer Relationship Management: Towards a Common Understanding of an Emerging Phenomenon," *Industrial Marketing Management*, *33*, 6 (2004): 475–489.
15 L. L. Berry, "Relationship Marketing of Services—Perspectives from 1983 and 2000," *Journal of Relationship Marketing*, *1*, 1 (2002): 59–77.
16 N. Bendapudi and L. L. Berry, "Customers' Motivations for Maintaining for Relationships with Service Providers," *Journal of Retailing*, *73*, 1 (1997): 15; P. Kotler, *Marketing Management*, 1st ed. (Upper Saddle River, NJ: Prentice Hall, 1991); J. N. Sheth and A. Parvatiyar, "Relationship Marketing in Consumer Markets: Antecedents and Consequences," *Journal of the Academy of Marketing Science*, *23*, 4 (1995): 255–271; C. Grönroos, "From Marketing Mix to Relationship Marketing: Towards a Paradigm Shift in Marketing," *Management Decision*, *32*, 2 (1994): 4–20.
17 F. E. Webster Jr., "The Changing Role of Marketing in the Corporation," *Journal of Marketing*, *56*, 4 (1992): 1–17.
18 See note 7.
19 Ibid.
20 P. Guenzi and O. Pelloni, "The Impact of Interpersonal Relationships on Customer Satisfaction and Loyalty to the Service Provider," *International Journal of Service Industry Management*, *15*, 4 (2004): 365–384.
21 M. A. Jolson, "Broadening the Scope of Relationship Selling," *Journal of Personal Selling & Sales Management*, *17*, 4 (Fall 1997): 75–88.
22 S. E. Beatty, M. Mayer, J. E. Coleman, K. E. Reynolds, and J. K. Lee, "Customer Sales Associate Retail Relationships," *Journal of Retailing*, *72*, 3 (1996): 223–247.

23 E. Gummesson, "The New Marketing–Developing Long-Term Interactive Relationships," *Long Range Planning*, *20*, 4 (August 1987): 10–20.

24 Richard P. Bagozzi, "Reflections on Relationship Marketing in Consumer Markets," *Journal of the Academy of Marketing Science*, *23*, 4, 272–277.

25 R. A. Peterson, "Relationship Marketing and the Consumer," *Journal of the Academy of Marketing Science*, *23*, 4 (Fall 1995): 278–281.

26 See note 7.

27 R. C. Blattberg and J. Deighton, "Manage Marketing by the Customer Equity Test," *Harvard Business Review*, *74*, 4 (July 1996): 136–144; W. J. Reinartz and V. Kumar, "The Impact of Customer Relationship Characteristics on Profitable Lifetime Duration," *Journal of Marketing*, *67*, 1 (January 2003): 77–99; W. J. Reinartz and V. Kumar, "The Mismanagement of Customer Loyalty," *Harvard Business Review*, *80*, 7 (July 2002): 86–94.

28 K. Mukerjee, and Kundan Singh, "CRM: A Strategic Approach," *The Icfaian Journal of Management Research*, *8*, 2 (2009): 65–82.

29 See note 4.

30 W. J. Reinartz and V. Kumar, "The Mismanagement of Customer Loyalty," *Harvard Business Review*, *80*, 7 (July 2002): 80–94.

31 T. O. Jones and W. E. Sasser Jr., "Why Satisfied Customers Defect," *Harvard Business Review*, *73*, 6 (November 1995): 88–99.

32 D. Peppers and M. Rogers, *Managing Customer Relationships: A Strategic Framework* (Hoboken, NJ: John Wiley & Sons, 2004).

33 See note 16.

34 See note 7.

35 R. T. Rust, K. N. Lemon, and D. Narayandas, *Customer Equity Management* (Upper Saddle River, NJ: Prentice Hall, 2005).

36 P. O'Connell, "Taking the Measure of Mood," *Harvard Business Review*, *84*, 3 (March 2006): 25–26.

37 B. J. Pine II, D. Peppers, and M. Rogers, "Do You Want to Keep Your Customers Forever?" *Harvard Business Review*, *73*, 2 (March 1995): 103–114.

38 J. Peel, *CRM: Redefining Customer Relationship Management* (Amsterdam: Digital Press, 2002).

39 P. Temporal and M. Trott, *Romancing the Customer: Maximizing Brand Value Through Powerful Relationship Management* (Singapore: John Wiley & Sons, 2001).

40 See note 6.

41 See note 38.

42 See note 36.

43 T. Osenton, *Customer Share Marketing: How the World's Great Marketers Unlock Profits from Customer Loyalty* (Upper Saddle River, NJ: Prentice Hall, 2002).

44 See note 6.

45 M. Nycamp, *The Customer Differential: The Complete Guide to Implementing Customer Relationship Management* (New York: AMACOM, 2001).

46 C. Moorman and R. T. Rust, "The Role of Marketing," *Journal of Marketing*, *63*, 4 (1999): 180–189.

4 Organization and CRM

1 D. K. Rigby, F. F. Reichheld, and P. Schefter, "Avoid the Four Perils of CRM," *Harvard Business Review*, *80*, 2 (February 2002): 101–109.

2 Thomas H. Davenport, *Mission Critical* (Cambridge, MA: Harvard Business School Press, 2000).

3 H. W. Kim and S. L. Pan, "Towards a Process Model of Information Systems Implementation: The Case of Customer Relationship Management (CRM)," *Database for Advances in Information Systems*, *37*, 1 (Winter 2006): 59–76.

4 M. D. Hartline and D. Bejou, *Internal Relationship Management: Linking Human Resources to Marketing Performance* (Binghamton, NY: Haworth Press, 2004).

5 E. Thompson and M. Goldman, "Ten Best Practices to Make CRM Project Change Management More Effective," Gartner Research Note (July 23, 2009).

6 A. Agarwal, W. E. Pietraszek, and M. Singer, "Connecting CRM Systems for Better Customer Service," *McKinsey Quarterly* (August 2006).

7 L. H. Ho and C.-C. Chuang, "The Application of Knowledge Management and Customer Relationship Management of ROC Government," *Journal of American Academy of Business, Cambridge*, *9*, 2 (September 2006): 63–71.

5 CRM and Data Management

1 The example for this subsection was taken from Experian Corporation.
2 Information taken from the USPS's website at http://www.usps.com/business/move-update.htm (accessed August 1, 2011).
3 Stephen D. Sieloff, Senior Systems Architect for The Allant Group, Inc., in Naperville, Illinois.
4 Ibid.

6 Technology and Data Platforms

1 Adapted from C. Carden, *Understanding Computer Telephony: How to Voice Enable Databases from PCs to LANs to Mainframes* (New York: Flatiron Publishing, 1997).
2 Adapted from *The McKinsey Quarterly, Web exclusive, March 2006*, Wayne E. Pietraszek and Adesh Ramchandran. (This article was first published in the Spring 2006 issue of *McKinsey on IT*.)

7 Database and Customer Data Development

1 C. L. Hayes, "What Wal-Mart Knows About Customers' Habits," *New York Times* (November 14, 2004): 8.

8 Business-to-Business CRM

1 L. Loro, "Loyalty Programs Paying Off for B-to-B," *Business Marketing*, *83*, 9 (September 1998): 1–3.
2 Ibid.
3 S. Seshadri and R. Mishra, "Relationship Marketing and Contract Theory," *Industrial Marketing Management*, *33*, 6 (2004): 513–526.
4 R. Deshpandé and J. U. Farley, "Looking at Your World Through Your Customer's Eyes: Cross-National Differences in Buyer–Seller Alliances," *Journal of Relationship Marketing*, *1*, 3/4 (2002): 3–22.
5 D-G. Ko and A. R. Dennis, "Sales Force Automation and Sales Performance: Do Experience and Expertise Matter?" *Journal of Personal Selling & Sales Management*, *24*, 4 (Fall 2004): 311–322.
6 G. K. Hunter and W. D. Perreault Jr., "Sales Technology Orientation, Information Effectiveness, and Sales Performance," *Journal of Personal Selling & Sales Management*, *26*, 2 (Spring 2006): 95–113.
7 M. Ahearne, N. Srinvasan, and L. Weinstein, "Effect of Technology on Sales Performance: Progressing from Technology Acceptance to Technology Usage and Consequence," *Journal of Personal Selling & Sales Management*, *24*, 4 (Fall 2004): 297–310.
8 Gartner, Hype Cycle for CRM Sales, 2009. Adapted from http://www.avanade.com/Documents/Resources/POV-2011q3-Sharing_information_through_CRM-Partners_in_business_success.pdf.
9 Avanade Point of View: Partner Relationship Management with Microsoft CRM.
10 Heidi Leroy-Short, Head of Projects and Process, Grosvenor.
11 D. B. Arnett and V. Badrinarayanan, "Enhancing Customer-Needs-Driven CRM Strategies: Core Selling Teams, Knowledge Management Competence, and Relationship Marketing Competence," *Journal of Personal Selling & Sales Management*, *25*, 4 (Fall 2005): 329–343.
12 E. Anderson and V. Onyemah, "How Right Should the Customer Be?" *Harvard Business Review*, *84*, 7/8 (July–August 2006): 59–67.
13 J. G. Tanner, M. Ahearne, T. Leigh, C. Mason, and W. Moncrief, "CRM in Sales-Intensive Organizations: A Review and Future Directions," *Journal of Personal Selling & Sales Management*, *25*, 2 (Spring 2005): 169–180.
14 M. S. Kennedy, L. K. Ferrell, and D. T. LeClair, "Consumers' Trust of Salesperson and Manufacturer: An Empirical Study," *Journal of Business Research*, *51*, 1 (2001): 73–86.

15 E. Roemer and M. Rese, "Managing Commitments and Flexibility by Real Options," *Industrial Marketing Management*, *33*, 6 (2009): 501–512.
16 M. Bruhn and A. Frommeyer, "Development of Relationship Marketing Constructs Over Time: Antecedents and Consequences of Customer Satisfaction in Business-to-Business Environment," *Journal of Relationship Marketing*, *3*, 4 (2004): 61–76.

9 Understanding the Customer–Company Profit Chain: Satisfaction, Loyalty, Retention, and Profits

1 S. W. Brown, R. P. Fisk, and M. J. Bitner, "The Development and Emergence of Services Marketing Thought," *International Journal of Service Industry Management*, *5*, 1 (1994): 21–48.
2 R. L. Oliver, "Measurement and Evaluation of Satisfaction Processes in Retail Settings," *Journal of Retailing*, *57* (Fall 1981): 25–48.
3 R. Evans, "Make Time to Build Customer Relationships," *Western Mail* (April 11, 2011): 29.
4 E. W. Anderson, C. Fornell, and D. Lehmann, "Customer Satisfaction, Market Share, and Profitability: Findings from Sweden," *Journal of Marketing*, *58*, 3 (July 1994): 53–67.
5 V. Knauer, "Increasing Customer Satisfaction," U.S. Office of Consumer Affairs. (1992). Pueblo, Colorado.
6 T. Peters, *Thriving on Chaos: Handbook for a Management Revolution* (New York: Alfred A. Knopf, Inc., 1987).
7 K. N. Lemon, T. B. White, and R. S. Winer, "Dynamic Customer Relationship Management: Incorporating Future Considerations into the Service Retention Decision," *Journal of Marketing*, *66*, 1 (2002): 1–14.
8 E. W. Anderson and M. W. Sullivan, "The Antecedents and Consequences of Customer Satisfaction for Firms," *Marketing Science*, *12*, 2 (Spring 1993): 125–143.
9 D. K. Tse and P. C. Wilton, "Models of Consumer Satisfaction Formation: An Extension," *Journal of Marketing Research*, *25*, 2 (1988): 204–212.
10 B. B. Jackson, "Build Customer Relationships That Last," *Harvard Business Review*, *63*, 6 (November 1985): 120–128.
11 E. W. Anderson, C. Fornell, and S. K. Mazvancheryl, "Customer Satisfaction and Shareholder Value," *Journal of Marketing*, *68*, 4 (October 2004): 172–185.
12 C. Ittner and D. Larcker, "Non-Financial Performance Measures: What Works and What Doesn't," *Knowledge @ Wharton* (December 6, 2000). Accessed at http://knowledge.wharton.upenn.edu/article.cfm?articleid=279.
13 Presentation by S. Gupta at MSI Conference: Taking Stock of Customer Relationships (March 2, 2006).
14 F. F. Reichheld and W. E. Sasser Jr., "Zero Defections: Quality Comes to Services," *Harvard Business Review*, *68*, 5 (September–October 1990): 105–111.
15 F. F. Reichheld, R. G. Markey Jr., and C. Hopton, "The Loyalty Effect—The Relationship Between Loyalty and Profits," *European Business Journal*, *12*, 3 (2000): 134–139.
16 See note 7.
17 T. Gokey and H. Yin, "The New Physics of Customer Loyalty: Manage Customer Migration Based on the Loyalty Profile of Your Customer Base," *McKinsey Marketing Solutions* (May 2000).
18 R. T. Rust and A. J. Zahorik, "Customer Satisfaction, Customer Retention, and Market Share," *Journal of Retailing*, *69*, 2 (Summer 1993): 193–215.
19 F. F. Reichheld, "Loyalty-Based Management," *Harvard Business Review*, *71*, 2 (March–April 1993): 64–73.
20 V. Kumar and W. J. Reinartz, *Customer Relationship Management: A Databased Approach* (Hoboken, NJ: Wiley, 2005).
21 T. O. Jones and W. E. Sasser Jr., "Why Satisfied Customers Defect," *Harvard Business Review*, *73*, 6 (November–December 1995): 88–99.
22 See note 15.
23 G. R. Dowling and M. Uncles, "Do Customer Loyalty Programs Really Work?" *Sloan Management Review*, *38*, 4 (Summer 1997): 71–82.
24 A. S. C. Ehrenberg, *Repeat-Buying: Facts, Theory and Applications* (New York: Oxford University Press, 1988).
25 See note 14.

26 F. F. Reichheld and T. Teal, *The Loyalty Effect: The Hidden Force Behind Growth, Profits, and Lasting Value* (Cambridge, MA: Harvard Business School Press, 1996).

27 R. C. Blattberg and J. Deighton, "Manage Marketing by the Customer Equity Test," *Harvard Business Review*, *74*, 4 (July–August 1996): 136–144.

28 R. J. Best, *Market-Based Management: Strategies for Growing Customer Value and Profitability*, 2nd ed. (Upper Saddle River, NJ: Prentice Hall, 2000).

29 See note 23.

30 W. J. Reinartz and V. Kumar, "On the Profitability of Long-Life Customers in a Noncontractual Setting: An Empirical Investigation and Implications for Marketing," *Journal of Marketing*, *64*, 4 (October 2000): 17–36.

31 Ibid.

32 G. Odekerken-Schroder, K. DeWulf, and P. Schumacher, "Strengthening Outcomes of Retailer–Consumer Relationships: The Dual Impact of Relationship Marketing Tactics and Consumer Personality," *Journal of Business Research*, *56*, 3 (March 2003): 177–190.

33 C. Elliott, "Frequent-Guest Perks Grow More Generous," *New York Times* (August 7, 2005): 6.

34 W. Wong, "Loyalty Programs Seek Better Returns," *Chicago Tribune* (September 11, 2011): 1.

35 P. C. Verhoef, "Understanding the Effect of Customer Relationship Management Efforts on Customer Retention and Customer Share Development," *Journal of Marketing*, *67*, 4 (October 2003): 30–45.

36 B. J. Pine II, D. Peppers, and M. Rogers, "Do You Want to Keep Your Customers Forever?" *Harvard Business Review*, *73*, 2 (March 1995): 103–113.

10 The CRM Strategy Cycle: Acquisition, Retention, and Win-Back

1 M. Georgiadis, R. Seshadri, and C. Yulinsky, "Tactical CRM: Three Steps to Mining Profits, Not Data," *McKinsey Marketing Solutions* (August 2001).

2 L. Story, "Online Pitches Made Just for You," *New York Times* (March 6, 2008): 7.

3 C. Fishman, "This Is a Marketing Revolution," *Fast Company*, *24* (April 30, 1999): 204–218.

4 R. Kivetz and S. Itamar, "The Idiosyncratic Fit Heuristic: Effort Advantage as a Determinant of Consumer Response to Loyalty Programs," *Journal of Marketing Research*, *40*, 4 (November 2003): 454–467.

5 See note 4.

6 J. L. Heskett, T. O. Jones, G. W. Loveman, W. E. Sasser Jr., and L. A. Schlesinger, "Putting the Service–Profit Chain to Work," *Harvard Business Review*, *72*, 2 (March–April 1994): 164–174.

7 "Conversational Marketing: What's Next in Customer Engagement?" *Neolane, Inc.* (2011): 1–9.

8 K. Kalyanam and M. Zweben, "The Perfect Message at the Perfect Moment," *Harvard Business Review*, *83*, 11 (November 2005): 112–120.

9 V. Knight, "Financial Advisers Tap Tech for Personal Touch," *Wall Street Journal* (August 15, 2006), D2.

10 A. DeFelice, "The Money Tree," *CRM Magazine*, *9*, 8 (August 2005): 44.

11 M. Beaujean, J. Davidson, and S. Madge, "The 'Moment of Truth' in Customer Service," *McKinsey Quarterly* (2006): 62–73.

12 K. Mukerjee and K. Singh, "CRM: A Strategic Approach," *The ICFA Journal of Management Research*, *8*, 2 (2009): 65–82.

13 K. Bankston, "Works in Progress," *Credit Union Management*, *27*, 3 (March 2004): 48–56.

14 See note 4.

15 W. J. Reinartz and V. Kumar, "On the Profitability of Long-Life Customers in a Noncontractual Setting: An Empirical Investigation and Implications for Marketing," *Journal of Marketing*, *64*, 4 (October 2000): 17–36.

16 S. Dull in J. G. Freeland, ed., *The Ultimate CRM Handbook: Strategies and Concepts for Building Enduring Customer Loyalty and Profitability* (New York: McGraw-Hill, 2003).

17 J. S. Thomas, R. C. Blattberg, and E. J. Fox, "Recapturing Lost Customers," *Journal of Marketing Research*, *41*, 1 (February 2004): 31–45.

18 Ibid.

19 B. J. Pine II, D. Peppers, and M. Rogers, "Do You Want to Keep Your Customers Forever?" *Harvard Business Review*, *73*, 2 (March 1995): 103–113.

20 R. S. Kaplan, "Kanthal (A), HBS Case 9–190–002," *HBS Premier Case Collection* (July 27, 1989).
21 A. Gasparro, "Playing Favorites," *Wall Street Journal* (September 20, 2010): R5.
22 R. Verma, Z. Iqbal, and R. Baran, "Understanding Consumer Choices and Preferences in Transaction-Based e-Services," *Journal of Science Research*, 6, 1 (August 2003): 51–65.
23 B. B. Jackson, "Build Customer Relationships That Last," *Harvard Business Review*, 63, 6 (November 1985): 120–128.

11 Privacy and Ethics Considerations

1 Information taken from the Direct Marketing Association Consumer Assistance's page on "The Mail Preference Service." Accessed at http://www.dmaconsumers.org/offmailinglist.html.
2 Information taken from the Direct Marketing Association Consumer Assistance's page on "Getting Off Telephone Call Lists/Telephone Preference Service." Accessed at http://www.dmaconsumers.org/cgi/offtelephone/.
3 Information taken from the Federal Trade Commission's "Q&A for Telemarketers and Sellers About the Do Not Call Provisions of the FTC's Telemarketing Sales Rule." Accessed at http://business.ftc.gov/sites/default/files/alt129-qa-telemarketers-sellers-about-due-provisions-tsr.pdf.
4 Information taken from Wikipedia's page on "PayPal." Accessed at http://en.wikipedia.org/wiki/PayPal.
5 M. Hines, "Protect Privacy or Jeopardize CRM," SearchCRM.com (August 9, 2002). Accessed at http://searchcrm.techtarget.com/news/843537/Protect-privacy-or-jeopardize-CRM.
6 Information taken from the U.S. Small Business Administration's Office of Ombudsman's page on "Complaints or Comments." Accessed at http://www.sba.gov/ombudsman/1816.
7 Information taken from Interactive Marketing Solutions' page on "Wireless—Ported Numbers." Accessed at http://www.ims-dm.com/products/WirelessPortedNumbers.shtml.
8 Information taken from Interactive Marketing Solutions' page on "Telephone Preference Service." Accessed at http://www.ims-dm.com/products/tpssubscription.shtml.
9 Information taken from Interactive Marketing Solutions' page on "State TPS Lookup Program." Accessed at http://www.ims-dm.com/tpslookupprogramfinal.shtml.
10 Information taken from Interactive Marketing Solutions' page on "The DMA's E-Mail Preference Service." Accessed at http://www.ims-dm.com/products/empsubscription.shtml.
11 Information taken from Webopedia's entry on "CAN-SPAM." Accessed at http://www.webopedia.com/TERM/CAN_SPAM.html.
12 Information taken from Interactive Marketing Solutions' page on "Deceased Do Not Contact List." Accessed at http://www.ims-dm.com/products/ddncsubscription.shtml.
13 Information taken from the Consumer Privacy Guide's entry on "TRUSTe" on their "Glossary of Internet Privacy Terms" page. Accessed at http://www.consumerprivacyguide.org/glossary.
14 Information taken from the Consumer Privacy Guide's entry on "Trustmark" on their "Glossary of Internet Privacy Terms" page. Accessed at http://www.consumerprivacyguide.org/glossary.
15 Information taken from the official website of TRUSTe. Accessed at http://www.truste.com.
16 Information taken from the Consumer Privacy Guide's entry on "BBBOnline" on their "Glossary of Internet Privacy Terms" page. Accessed at http://www.consumerprivacyguide.org/glossary.
17 L. Ponemon, "Opinion: After a Privacy Breach, How Should You Break the News?" *Computerworld* (June 5, 2005). Accessed at http://www.computerworld.com/s/article/102964/Opinion_After_a_privacy_breach_how_should_you_break_the_news.
18 Information taken from Export.gov's page on "Safe Harbor." Accessed at http://export.gov/safe-harbor.
19 Information taken from Interactive Marketing Solutions' page on "UK and Belgium Mail Preference Service." Accessed at http://www.ims-dm.com/products/fmpssubscription.shtml.

12 CRM Program Measurement and Tools

1 R. T. Rust and A. J. Zahorik, "Customer Satisfaction, Customer Retention, and Market Share," *Journal of Retailing*, 69, 2 (Summer 1993): 193–215.
2 R. T. Rust, A. J. Zahorik, and T. L. Keningham, "Return on Quality (ROQ): Making Service Quality Financially Accountable," *Journal of Marketing*, 59, 2 (April 1995): 58–70.

3 W. O. Bearden, K. L. Haws, and R. G. Netemeyer, *Handbook of Marketing Scales: Multi-Item Measures for Marketing and Consumer Behavior Research* (Thousand Oaks, CA: SAGE Productions, 2010).

4 A. Parasuraman, V. A. Zeithaml, and L. L. Berry, "SERVQUAL: A Multiple-Item Scale for Measuring Consumer Perceptions of Service Quality," *Journal of Retailing*, *64*, 1 (Spring 1988): 12–40.

5 Ibid.

6 P. Kotler, *Marketing Management* (Upper Saddle River, NJ: Prentice Hall, 1991).

7 R. L. Oliver, "Conceptualization and Measurement of Disconfirmation Perceptions in the Prediction of Consumer Satisfaction," in H. K. Hunt and R. L. Day, eds., *Refining Concepts and Measures of Customer Satisfaction and Complaining Behavior* (Bloomington, IN: Indiana University School of Business, 1980).

8 T. O. Jones and W. E. Sasser Jr., "Why Satisfied Customers Defect," *Harvard Business Review* (November–December 1995): 88–99.

9 U. M. Dholakia, V. G. Morwitz, and R. A. Westbrook, "Firm-Sponsored Satisfaction Surveys: Positivity Effects on Customer Purchase Behavior?" *MSI Reports* (2004).

10 V. Kumar, "CLV: The Databased Approach," *Journal of Relationship Marketing*, *5*, 2/3 (2006): 7–35.

11 F. F. Reichheld and W. E. Sasser Jr., "Zero Defections: Quality Comes to Services," *Harvard Business Review*, *68*, 5 (September–October 1990): 105–111.

12 W. Boulding, R. Staelin, M. Ehret, and W. J. Johnston, "A Customer Relationship Management Roadmap: What Is Known, Potential Pitfalls, and Where to Go," *Journal of Marketing*, *69*, 4 (October 2005): 155–166.

13 F. F. Reichheld, "The Microeconomics of Customer Relationships," *MIT Sloan Management Review*, *47*, 2 (Winter 2006): 73–78.

14 V. Kumar and W. Reinartz, *Customer Relationship Management: A Databased Approach* (Hoboken, NJ: Wiley, 2005).

15 E. Bummesson, *Total Relationship Marketing* (Oxford, UK: Butterworth-Heinemann, 1999).

16 See Note 14.

17 J. S. Thomas, R. C. Blattberg, and E. J. Fox, "Recapturing Lost Customers," *Journal of Marketing Research*, *41*, 1 (February 2004): 31–45.

18 J. L. Heskett, W. E. Sasser Jr., and L. A. Schlesinger, *The Service Profit Chain* (New York: The Free Press, 1997).

19 J. Anton and N. L. Petouhoff, *Customer Relationship Management: The Bottom Line to Optimizing Your ROI* (Upper Saddle River, NJ: Prentice Hall, 2002).

20 R. T. Rust, K. N. Lemon, and D. Narayandas, *Customer Equity Management* (Upper Saddle River, NJ: Prentice Hall, 2005).

21 V. Kumar, "Maximizing Customer Profitability," *MSI Conference Presentation* (2004).

22 R. C. Blattberg and J. Deighton, "Interactive Marketing: Exploiting the Age of Addressability," *MIT Sloan Management Review*, *33*, 1 (Fall 1991): 5–14.

23 See note 26.

24 R. T. Rust, V. A. Zeithaml, and K. N. Lemon, *Driving Customer Equity: How Customer Lifetime Value Is Reshaping Corporate Strategy* (New York: The Free Press, 2000).

25 See note 14.

26 M. Nycamp, *The Customer Differential: The Complete Guide to Implementing Customer Relationship Management* (New York: AMACOM, 2001).

27 K. J. Dunham, "Beyond Satisfaction," *Wall Street Journal* (October 30, 2006): R4.

28 J. G. Harris and T. H. Davenport, "Beyond the Data: Making the Most of Customer Knowledge," in J. G. Freeland, ed., *The Ultimate CRM Handbook: Strategies and Concepts for Building Enduring Customer Loyalty and Profitability* (New York: McGraw-Hill, 2003).

29 See note 17.

30 R. McKenna, "Real-Time Marketing," *Harvard Business Review*, *73*, 4 (July–August 1995): 87–95.

31 M. Neumeier, *The Brand Gap: How to Bridge the Distance Between Business Strategy and Design* (Berkeley, CA: New Riders Publishing, 2006).

32 A. M. Tybout and T. Calkins, *Kellogg on Branding: The Marketing Faculty of The Kellogg School of Management* (Hoboken, NJ: John Wiley & Sons, 2005).

33 Ibid.

34 P. W. Farris, N. T. Bendle, P. E. Pfeifer, and D. J. Reibstein, *Marketing Metrics: The Definitive Guide to Measuring Marketing Performance* (Upper Saddle River, NJ: Pearson Education, 2010).

35 D. Chaffey, "The Five Ways to Measure Online Customer Engagement," *MyCustomer.com* (January 15, 2010). Accessed at http://www.mycustomer.com/topic/customer-experience/how-good-are-you-really-engaging-your-customers-online.

36 S. Ganapathy, C. Ranganathan, and B. Sankaranarayanan, "Visualization Strategies and Tools for Enhancing Customer Relationship Management," *Communications of the ACM*, *47*, 11 (November 2004): 92–99.

37 See note 14.

38 R. S. Kaplan and D. P. Norton, *The Balanced Scorecard: Translating Strategy into Action* (Cambridge, MA: Harvard Business Review Press, 1996).

13 Social Networking and CRM

1 C. Rozwell and N. Drakos, "Apply a Comprehensive Planning Framework as Business Gets Social," Gartner, Inc. (May 23, 2011).

2 Ibid.

3 A. Sachdev, "Cracking Down on Courtroom Networking," *Chicago Tribune* (October 30, 2011): 1.

4 D. Wolk, "Monsters Inc.," *TIME* (May 23, 2011): 58.

5 A. Tergesen, "Sending Out an Elder-Care SOS," *Wall Street Journal* (March 5, 2011): B8.

6 P. Wallsten, "Palin's Book Tour Builds on Effective Web Strategy," *Wall Street Journal* (November 14, 2009): A4.

7 D. C. Edelman, "Branding in the Digital Age: You're Spending Your Money in All the Wrong Places," *Harvard Business Review*, *88* (December 2010): 62–69.

8 Information taken from Caslon Analytics' page on "Social Network Services: Spaces and Traffic." Accessed at http://www.caslon.com.au/socialspacesprofile15.htm.

9 J. Johnsson, "Twitter Forcing a Strategy Switch for Businesses," *Chicago Tribune* (August 16, 2009): 2.

10 D. A. Williamson, "Social Media in the Marketing Mix: Budgeting for 2011," eMarketer Inc. (December 2010).

11 L. Ramos, P. Burris, and Z. Reiss-Davis, "Rethinking the B2B Tech Marketing Mix in the Digital Age," Forrester Research (March 15, 2010).

12 "Center for Marketing Research Find That Inc. 500 Continue to Embrace Social Media in 4th Annual Benchmarking Study," The Campanil-E @ UMass Dartmouth (January 15, 2011). Accessed at http://campanile.blogs.umass.edu/2011/01/25/center-for-marketing-research-find-that-inc-500-continue-to-embrace-social-media-in-4th-annual-benchmarking-study/.

13 E. Thompson, M. Maoz, K. Collins, and M. Dunne, "What's 'Hot' in CRM Applications in 2011," Gartner, Inc. (March 17, 2011).

14 E. Steel, "To Stem Privacy Abuses, Industry Groups Will Track Web Trackers," *Wall Street Journal* (June 24, 2010): B2.

15 S. Vranica, "Social Media Draws a Crowd," *Wall Street Journal* (July 18, 2010): B7.

16 E. Steel and G. A. Fowler, "Big Brands Like Facebook, But They Don't Like to Pay," *Wall Street Journal* (November 2, 2011): A1.

17 J. E. Vascellaro and E. Steel, "Application Companies Join the Ad Chase," *Wall Street Journal* (June 5, 2008): B6.

18 Information taken from Website-Monitoring's page on "Facebook Facts and Figures 2011 (infographic)." Accessed at http://www.website-monitoring.com/blog/2011/10/14/facebook-facts-and-figures-2011-infographic/.

19 "Social Media Will Spread Terror Alerts," *Chicago Tribune* (April 9, 2011): 3.

20 G. A. Fowler and Y. Iwatani, "Gadget Makers Follow Facebook's Lead," *Wall Street Journal* (January 7, 2011): A4.

21 E. Listfield, "Generation Wired," *PARADE* (October 7, 2011): 10.

22 W. Wong, "Digital Life: Ad-Sponsored Social Media Updates May Have Limits," *Chicago Tribune* (April 2, 2009): 1.

23 P. Guenzi and O. Pelloni, "The Impact of Interpersonal Relationships on Customer Satisfaction and Loyalty to the Service Provider," *International Journal of Service Industry Management*, *15*, 4 (2004): 365–384.

24 J. A. Deighton and L. Kornfeld, "Digital Interactivity: Unanticipated Consequences for Markets, Marketing, and Consumers," *Harvard Business School—Working Knowledge* (September 28, 2007). Accessed at http://hbs.edu/research/pdf/08–017.pdf.

25 R. Rothenberg, "Facebook's Flop," *Wall Street Journal* (December 14, 2007): A21.

26 "Social Media and Marketing: Transitioning from Listening to Customer Engagement," Neolane, Inc. (September 23, 2010).

27 D. Johnson, Socialtimes.com (August 30, 2010).

28 J. Bughin and M. Chui, "The Rise of the Networked Enterprise: Web 2.0 Finds Its Payday," *McKinsey Quarterly* (December 2010). Accessed at http://www.mckinseyquarterly.com/The_rise_of_the_networked_enterprise_Web_20_finds_its_payday_2716.

29 C. Figello, *Hosting Web Communities: Building Relationships, Increasing Customer Loyalty, and Maintaining Competitive Edge* (Hoboken, NJ: Wiley, 1998).

30 H. H. Bauer and M. Grether, "Virtual Community: Its Contribution to Customer Relationships by Providing Social Capital," *Journal of Relationship Marketing*, 4, 1/2 (2005): 91–110.

31 "Using Social Networking for Marketing," Yaffe Center for Persuasive Communication—University of Michigan's Ross School of Business (May 27, 2011). Accessed at http://webservices.itcs.umich.edu/mediawiki/YaffeCenter/index.php/Using_Social_Networking_for_Marketing.

32 K. N. Hampton, L. S. Goulet, L. Rainie, and K. Purcell, "Social Networking Sites and Our Lives," Pew Internet & American Life Project (June 16, 2011). Accessed at http://pewinternet.org/Reports/2011/Technology-and-social-networks-aspx.

33 B. Chiang, "Tale of the Falling SNS: 51.com" (June 10, 2011). Accessed at www.Technode.com.

34 M. Colaizzi, "Social Media and China: What You Need to Know," SmartBlog on Social Media (March 31, 2010). Accessed at http://smartblogs.com/socialmedia/2010/03/31/social-media-and-china-what-you-need-to-know/.

35 T. Crampton, "Social Media in China: The Same, but Different," *The China Business Review*, 38, 1 (January–March 2011): 28.

36 L. Lam, "Chinese Social Media Sites No Mere Clones," *South China Morning Post* (February 27, 2011). Accessed at http://topics.scmp.com/news/china-news-watch/article/Chinese-social-media-sites-no-mere-clones.

37 See note 33.

38 "Chinese Consumer Report 2010—Brands and Buzz: Understanding How to Reach Today's Chinese Consumers," Roland Berger Strategy Consultants (July 23, 2010). Accessed at http://www.rolandberger.com/media/pdf/Roland_Berger_tas_Chinese_Consumer_Report_20100723.pdf.

39 See note 31.

40 See note 33.

41 Ibid.

42 Press Release, "Research Says Brands Take Note: Chinese Social Media Users Actually Want to be Your Friend," Ogilvy & Mather (July 15, 2010). Accessed at http://www.ogilvy.com/News/Press-Releases/July-2010-OgilvyOne-Connected-report-released.aspx.

43 See note 38.

44 Ibid.

45 R. J. Baran, "Customer Relationship Management and the Asian Company Experience," *AFBE Journal*, 3, 2 (December 2010): 296–312.

46 "SaaS Provides Nearly Half of Asia-Pacific's CRM," *The Nation* (May 26, 2009). Accessed at http://nationmultimedia.com/2009/05/26/technology/technology_30103521.php.

47 S. A. Mertz, "The Business Impact of Social Computing on the CRM Software Market," Gartner, Inc. (September 3, 2008).

48 "From Social Media to Social Business—Topic One: An Overview of the Evolution of Chinese Social Media," Communication Intelligence Corp. (CIC) (March 2011).

49 Microsoft Dynamics® CRM, "CRM and Social Networking: Engaging the Social Customer," Microsoft Corporation (July 9, 2009). Accessed at http://www.microsoft.com.tr/dynamics/CRM_Social_Networks_Marketing.pdf.

50 B. Solis, "Twitter and Social Networks Usher in a New Era of Social CRM," BrianSolis.com (March 20, 2009). Accessed at http://www.briansolis.com/2009/03/twitter-and-social-networks-usher-in/.

51 R. J. Baran, R. Galka, and D. P. Strunk, *Principles of Customer Relationship Management* (Mason, OH: Cengage Learning, 2007).

52 Ibid.

53 See note 30.

54 Ibid.

55 M. Strutton, "$3.60 Facebook Fan Valuation Is Just the Tip of the Iceberg," Vitrue (April 14, 2010). Accessed at http://www.vitrue.com/360-facebook-fan-valuation-is-just-the-tip-of-the-iceberg/.

56 D. Fost, "Facebook a Friend to Business," *Orlando Sentinel* (October 28, 2009): 25.

57 Ibid.

58 See note 9.

59 A. Meyer, "Facebook, Twitter, Other Social Media Help Drive Business for Small Firms," *Chicago Tribune* (April 27, 2009): 19.

60 S. E. Needleman, "Firms Get a Hand with Twitter, Facebook," *Wall Street Journal* (October 1, 2009), B5.

61 A. Meyer, "Small Businesses Learn to Use Social Media to Connect with Customers," *Chicago Tribune* (July 12, 2010): 19.

62 "The Social Media Dilemma: Is Your Content Being Trashed?" Zmags (September 2010).

63 J. Deighton and L. Kornfeld, "United Breaks Guitars," Harvard Business School [Case No. 510–057] (April 12, 2010).

64 R. Flandez, "Domino's Response Offers Lessons in Crisis Management," *Wall Street Journal*, WSJ Blogs (April 20, 2009).

65 E. Steel, "Nestlé Takes a Beating on Social-Media Sites," *Wall Street Journal* (March 29, 2010), B5.

66 M. Eng, "Arizona Mom Seeking Clean Playgrounds Is Banned from Eight McDonald's," *Chicago Tribune* (October 26, 2011): 21.

67 See note 50.

68 See note 48.

69 C. Gillam, "Farm Groups Tap Social Media," *Chicago Tribune* (October 26, 2011): 18.

70 Z. Karabell, "To Tweet or Not to Tweet," *TIME* (April 11, 2011): 24.

71 R. Briggs, "The Momentum Effect: Creating Brand Value in the Social Networking Space," Marketing Evolution, Inc. (April 2007). Accessed at http://www.marketingevolution.com/downloads/MomentumEffect_RexBriggs.pdf.

72 S. Smith, "Creating Customer Experiences in a Digitally Connected World," smith+co (March 2011). Accessed at http://www.smithcoconsultancy.com/wp-content/uploads/2011/03/social-media-2011.pdf.

73 A. Dizik, "@Foodies: Peek Into My Kitchen," *Wall Street Journal* (October 26, 2011): D1.

74 K. Stock, "A Bakery Gets Sweet Returns from Social-Media Blitz," *Wall Street Journal* (February 14, 2011): R4.

75 K. Pang, "Ditch 10 Facebook Friends, Get a Free Sandwich," *Chicago Tribune* (January 13, 2009), 3.

76 L. Gaines-Ross, *Corporate Reputation: 12 Steps to Safeguarding & Recovering Reputation* (Hoboken, NJ: John Wiley & Sons, 2008).

77 K. Patel, "How AT&T Plans to Lift Its Image Via Social-Media Customer Care," *Advertising Age* (June 21, 2010). Accessed at http://adage.com/article/digital/t-plans-lift-image-social-media/144561/.

78 C. Musico, "You're Not Social (Enough)," *CRM Magazine*, *13*, 6 (June 2009): 39–43.

79 A. Sarner, E. Thompson, M. Dunne, and J. Davies, "Top Use Cases and Benefits for Successful Social CRM," Gartner, Inc. (December 3, 2010).

80 S. Nassauer, "'I Hate My Room,' The Traveler Tweeted. Ka-Boom! An Upgrade!" *Wall Street Journal* (June 24, 2010), D1.

81 S. McCarthy, "Using Twitter to Pressure Airlines: It Works," *Wall Street Journal* (October 28, 2010), D1.

82 V. Zeithaml, M. J. Bitner, and D. Gremler, *Services Marketing: Integrating Customer Focus Across the Firm*, 4th ed. (New York: McGraw-Hill, 2005).

83 M. H. Beers and R. Berkow, *The Merck Manual of Diagnosis and Therapy*, 17th ed. (New York: John Wiley & Sons, 1999).

84 S. S. Tax, M. Colgate, and D. E. Bowen, "How to Prevent Your Customers from Failing," *MIT Sloan Management Review*, *47*, 3 (Spring 2006): 30–38.

85 S. Thurm, "Next Frontier in Credit Scores: Predicting Personal Behavior," *Wall Street Journal* (October 27, 2011): B1.

86 D. Nishi, "How to Sell on YouTube, Without Showing a Video," *Wall Street Journal* (November 15, 2010), R7.

87 G. Alvarez, "How to Profit from Social CRM," Gartner, Inc. (November 17, 2010).

88 E. Steel, "Marketers Take Search Ads Beyond Search Engines," *Wall Street Journal* (January 29, 2009): B4.
89 V. Bauerlein, "Gatorade's 'Mission': Sell More Drinks," *Wall Street Journal* (September 13, 2010), B6.
90 M. Bustillo and A. Zimmerman, "Phone-Wielding Shoppers Strike Fear Into Retailers," *Wall Street Journal* (December 15, 2010): T14.
91 G. A. Fowler, "A High-Tech Edge on Black Friday," *Wall Street Journal* (November 24, 2010): D1.
92 A. Loten, "Crowd-Fund Sites Eye Boom," *Wall Street Journal* (May 12, 2011): B8.
93 See note 9.
94 P. Barwise and S. Meehan, "The One Thing You Must Get Right When Building a Brand," *Harvard Business Review, 88* (December 2010): 80–84.
95 E. Steel, "New Tools for Picking Hits," *Wall Street Journal* (May 23, 2011): B4.
96 G. A. Fowler, "Facebook Friends Used in Ads," WSJ.com, *Wall Street Journal* (January 26, 2011): B9.

14 CRM Trends, Challenges, and Opportunities

1 C. Homburg, J. P. Workman Jr., and O. Jensen, "Fundamental Changes in Marketing Organization: The Movement Toward a Customer-Focused Organizational Structure," *Journal of the Academy of Marketing Science, 28,* 4 (2000): 459–478.
2 S. Li, "Online Community Managers Riding High—and Getting Paid," *Chicago Tribune* (October 4, 2011): 3.
3 S. Christensen, D. Craig, J. Gross, T. Hourigan, R. Israch, M. Krigsman, and R. Mehta, "2011 Trends Report: Enterprise Resource Planning (ERP)," Focus Inc. (December 29, 2010). Accessed at http://media.focus.com/assets/research-briefing/2011-trends-report-enterprise-resource-planning-erp/TR-erp-3.pdf.
4 K. Collins, "Hype Cycle for CRM Marketing Applications, 2011," Gartner, Inc. (July 26, 2011).
5 A. Palmer, "Brands Turn to In-the-Cloud CRM Services for Better Collaboration and Timely Data," *Direct Marketing News* (March 1, 2011). Accessed at http://www.dmnews.com/brands-turn-to-in-the-cloud-crm-services-for-better-collaboration-and-timely-data/article/197191.
6 "GMC Software Technology Joins Cloud Standards Customer Council," Presort.com, http://www.presort.com/2011/08/23/gmc-software-technology-joins-cloud-standards-customer-council/.
7 See note 3.
8 B. Beal, "What You Should Know About RFID and CRM," SearchCRM.com (January 28, 2004). Accessed at http://searchcrm.techtarget.com/news/946415/What-you-should-know-about-RFID-and-CRM.
9 E. W. T. Ngai, K. K. L. Moon, J. N. K. Liu, K. F. Tsang, R. Law, F. F. C. Suk, and I. C. L. Wong, "Extending CRM in the Retail Industry: An RFID-Based Personal Shopping Assistant System," *Communications of the Association for Information Systems, 23,* 1 (2008): 277–294.
10 "Extending CRM in the Retail Industry: An RFID-Based Personal Authors from the Hong Kong Polytechnic University: E. W. T. Ngai, K. K. L. Moon, James N. K. Liu, K. F. Tsang, R. Law, F. F. C. Suk, I. C. L. Wong, Communications of the Association for Information Systems http://aisel.aisnet.org/cais/vol23/iss1/16/
11 M. Woodridge and N. R. Jennings, "Intelligent Agents: Theory and Practice," *The Knowledge Engineering Review, 10,* 2 (1995): 115–152.
12 S. Daskou and E. E. Mangina, "Artificial Intelligence in Managing Market Relationships: The Use of Intelligent Agents," *International Journal of Relationship Marketing, 2,* 2 (September 2003): 85–102.
13 R. Plant, "The Benefits of Data Talking to Data," *Wall Street Journal* (April 2, 2012): R5.
14 S. Li, "New Apps Enhance Consumers' View of the World Around Them," *Chicago Tribune* (October 18, 2011): 4.
15 "Untangling the Social Web," *The Economist* (September 2, 2010): 16–17.
16 See note 13.
17 See note 14.
18 See note 15.
19 S. M. Jones, "Smart Phones Signal New Shopping Trend," *Chicago Tribune* (November 26, 2010): 1.

20 M. Bastillo and A. Zimmerman, "Phone-Wielding Shoppers Strike Fear into Retailers," *Wall Street Journal* (December 15, 2010): 14.

21 S. Thurm and Y. I. Kane, "Your Apps are Watching You," *Wall Street Journal* (December 17, 2010): C14.

22 V. Kumar and W. J. Reinartz, *Customer Relationship Management: A Databased Approach* (Hoboken, NJ: Wiley, 2006).

23 R. L. Hotz, "Songs Stick in Teens' Heads," *Wall Street Journal* (June 13, 2011): A3.

24 A. Park, "The Brain: Marketing to Your Mind," *TIME* (January 29, 2007): 112.

25 See note 23.

26 E. Steel, "Does Shopping Stress You Out Too Much?" *Wall Street Journal* (November 23, 2011): B5.

27 R. E. Hotz, "The Really Smart Phone," *Wall Street Journal* (April 23, 2011): C9.

28 "A Sea of Sensors," *The Economist* (November 4, 2010): 6.

29 See note 12.

30 Ibid.

31 See note 13.

32 Ross Kimbarovsky of Crowdspring.com.

33 P. Sonne, "Mink or Fox? The Trench Gets Complicated," *Wall Street Journal* (November 3, 2011): D1.

34 E. B. York, "Nestle Raises the Bar on Getting Personal," *Chicago Tribune* (October 20, 2011): 1.

Index